SAMS
Teach Yourself

Microsoft®
Windows® 2000
Server

in 24 Hours

Barrie Sosinsky
Jeremy Moskowitz

SAMS   *201 West 103rd St., Indianapolis, Indiana, 46290 USA*

Sams Teach Yourself Microsoft® Windows 2000 Server in 24 Hours

Copyright ©2000 by Sams Publishing

International Standard Book Number: 0-672-31940-3

Library of Congress Catalog Card Number: The Library of Congress has catalogued an earlier edition of this book.

Printed in the United States of America

First Printing: March, 2000

04   03   7   6   5

Trademarks

Warning and Disclaimer

ASSOCIATE PUBLISHER
Bradley L. Jones

EXECUTIVE EDITOR
Chris Denny

ACQUISITIONS EDITOR
Neil Rowe

DEVELOPMENT EDITOR
Tony Amico

MANAGING EDITOR
Lisa Wilson

PROJECT EDITOR
Dawn Pearson

COPY EDITOR
Mike Henry

STYLISTIC EDITOR
Elizabeth Marshall

INDEXER
Angie Bess

PROOFREADER
Jill Mazurczyk

TECHNICAL EDITOR
Chris Crosby

TEAM COORDINATOR
Karen Opal

INTERIOR DESIGNER
Gary Adair

COVER DESIGNER
Aren Howell

COPY WRITER
Eric Borgert

PRODUCTION
Darin Crone

Contents at a Glance

Contents

About the Authors

BARRIE SOSINSKY, PH.D. is the News Editor for *Windows NT Magazine*. He is the author of 24 computer books, and a co-author on a dozen more book projects over the last 15 years. Among his past titles are *The BackOffice Bible* and *Building Visual FoxPro 5 Applications* (IDG Books); *The Windows NT 4 Answer Book* (McGraw-Hill); *Inside Windows NT Server 4 RAS* (New Riders); *The Warp Book* and *Visio 4: Drawing Has Never Been Easier* (Prima Press); and many others.

Over the years, Barrie Sosinsky has published more than 150 articles on computer technology, ranging from operating systems to desktop applications, to database technology and graphics that have appeared in major publications. In his current beat as News Editor, he follows the industry as an analyst covering hardware, software, and services provided by companies on Windows NT and Windows 2000. Among the many different areas he covers are the Internet and broadband, enterprise computing, workgroup software, hardware trends, and networking products.

Barrie Sosinsky is a principal in the company Killer Apps, Inc. (Medfield, MA)—a consulting group that builds database software for workgroups and provides system evaluation, training, and other services for clients.

JEREMY MOSKOWITZ, MCSE, MCT, CNA is an Enterprise Architect for InfoSystems, Inc. in Wilmington, Delaware. After earning a Bachelors degree in Computer Science from the University of Delaware, he went on to become one of the first MCSEs in the world. Since then, he has performed Windows NT, Windows 2000, and SMS planning and implementation for some of the largest organizations on both the east and west coasts of the United States. Jeremy has also taught advanced classes in Windows NT across the country to employees of many Fortune 500 companies. Jeremy has written for *Windows NT Magazine*, *BackOffice Magazine*, *Windows PRO Magazine*, *Inside Technology Training Magazine*, *PC Magazine*, and Ziff-Davis' *Windows Professional Journals*.

Dedication

Barrie Sosinsky writes:

I dedicate this book to my family: Carol, Alexandra, and Joseph.

Jeremy Moskowitz writes:

I dedicate this book to the speedy recovery of Y. Avellan.

Acknowledgments

Barrie Sosinsky writes:

I would like to thank the various people who made this book possible, including the staff of Sams Publishing who were involved in commissioning the title and in its production. First, I would like to thank Chris Denny and Neil Rowe for serving as the acquisition editors on the project and making sure that the book was produced on schedule. Tony Amico was the development editor, and he added his insight to the project and made sure that some very significant features were added to the book during its development. I would like to thank Chris Crosby for being an excellent technical editor, and Dawn Pearson for her work as production editor. To the other people involved in the production of this book at Sams, I also thank you.

My involvement and interest in Windows 2000 was fueled by a desire to learn more about the operating system so that I could write more effectively about it in my "News & Analysis" column in *Windows NT Magazine*, and on the *Windows NT Magazine* site (http://www.winntmag.com) in my role as News Editor for that magazine. Many of the people I have worked with at *Windows NT Magazine* have been a delight, and it is impossible to thank them all. I would specifically like to thank Karen Forster (Editor-in-Chief) and Mark Smith (Group Publisher) for their encouragement over the last year, as well as Amy Eisenberg (my Acquisition Editor), Christy Wolfe (my column's editor), and Warren Pickett (the online magazine editor). Their professionalism is most appreciated.

In writing this book, I was fortunate to have as my co-author an expert in Windows NT technology, and an active practitioner in the field. During the course of the project, Jeremy never failed to go the extra mile to help make this book a reality and to make it the best book it could be.

This author also acknowledges all the hard-working people at Microsoft and their various partners who have toiled long and hard to bring this new operating system to market. Windows 2000 continues to advance network workgroup computing into new areas, bringing us powerful new technologies at much more affordable prices than have been possible before. To build this operating system on top of the personal computer, which is essentially a legacy platform, and to bring this technology to enterprises from small offices to the largest corporations is a Herculean feat that is worthy of praise. This small book, which can only scratch the surface of this major work, is but a glimpse on what the people at Microsoft have achieved.

Jeremy Moskowitz writes:

I would like to thank some of the people who were instrumental in helping me achieve this career milestone.

First, thanks to Jill Knapp for letting me commandeer your only machine for more than four months while abusing (I mean, using) it as a test machine. You can check your email now.

Next, I want to thank Elizabeth Marshall who rose to the challenge to become my Stylistic Editor, clean-up artist, and all around voice of reason. Without you, this book would never have been a reality. Your tireless efforts to meet deadlines, wordsmith with flair, and conjure magic were extraordinary. I am honored to present my work through your filter and to call you my friend.

Additional thanks go to Rebecca Drury for selflessly being the human file-transfer-agent between me and Stylistic Editor Elizabeth Marshall.

I would also like to thank William Boswell for acting as a sounding board for my most difficult Windows 2000 matters and helping me verify my results. Thank you also to Dave Woodside and Mike Teplinsky for their technical input on the TCP/IP sections and Evan Morris for his additional Exchange insights.

My thanks would not be complete without thanking my co-author Barrie Sosinsky. It's been a long road together to get here, but it's been worth it. Thanks for the opportunity and the friendship.

Special thanks to Tom Boutell, M.L. Grant, and Christopher Adams of Boutell.com for allowing me to use their business as a real-world Internet example throughout the book.

I would also like to thank Michael Kearns, Bruce Friedman, Dwayne Robinson, Mark Olazagasti, and Mark Stellini of InfoSystems, Inc. for supporting me in my efforts to finish this book. Additional thanks to the Greater-Pennsylvania Microsoft office for your helpful insights.

Further thanks go to Chris Crosby for tackling a very difficult assignment as technical editor; Tony Amico, Chris Denny, and Mike Henry for your creative input; and to Dawn Pearson for keeping me relaxed and well-informed during the last several weeks.

Lastly, I would like to thank my parents, who in 1986, finally gave in to my relentless kicking and screaming for a computer with some horsepower. When you bought my Apple IIe, it profoundly changed my life. I just want you two to know that this seemingly simple and gracious act was the springboard to launch my life and career into what it is today. Oh, and thanks for sending me to college, too.

Tell Us What You Think!

As the reader of this book, *you* are our most important critic and commentator. We value your opinion and want to know what we're doing right, what we could do better, what areas you'd like to see us publish in, and any other words of wisdom you're willing to pass our way.

I welcome your comments. You can email or write me directly to let me know what you did or didn't like about this book—as well as what we can do to make our books stronger.

Please note that I cannot help you with technical problems related to the topic of this book, and that due to the high volume of mail I receive, I might not be able to reply to every message.

When you write, please be sure to include this book's title and author as well as your name and phone or fax number. I will carefully review your comments and share them with the author and editors who worked on the book.

Email: feedback@samspublishing.com

Mail: Jeff Koch
         Sams Publishing
         201 West 103rd Street
         Indianapolis, IN 46290 USA

PART I
Getting Started

Hour

HOUR 1

Introduction to Windows 2000 Server

by Barrie Sosinsky

Windows 2000 Server is the next version of Microsoft's network operating system, the successor to Windows NT. In the initial phases of its development, it was referred to as Windows NT Server 5.0, but it was subsequently renamed Windows 2000 prior to its release. Nearly every aspect of this operating system has changed, with old features reworked to make them easier to use and understand, and hundreds of new features added.

With Windows 2000 Server at the heart of your network, you can provide a range of services that any modern enterprise needs: file and print, security, Internet access, client support, communication services, and a range of application services and support.

The following topics are covered in this hour:

- What the new features in Windows 2000 Server are
- How Windows 2000 Server has been made easier to manage and use
- Improvements and new features added to file and print services

- The new network services that Windows 2000 offers
- How the domain structure has changed and the benefits Active Directory offers
- What new security features are in Windows 2000 Server
- What additional features Windows 2000 Advanced Server and Datacenter Server offer

What Windows 2000 Server Offers

With the release of the Windows 2000 operating system, Microsoft has taken a major step forward in its quest to have Windows NT (for New Technology) Server become a corporate standard in enterprise computing. The Windows 2000 project was one of the largest software projects ever completed, and although estimates vary at just how large it was, it has been pegged at between 40 and 65 million lines of code. Well over 2,000 programmers worked on this project, and Windows 2000 Server has technology contributions from approximately 24 companies.

We like to compare the magnitude of the differences between Windows NT 4.0 and Windows 2000 Server to that which users experienced in going from Windows 3.1 to Windows 95. Bill Gates has been quoted as saying that "Windows 2000 is the most significant upgrade in the history of Microsoft."

Many of these contributions represent new options in the operating system, such as the incorporation of hierarchical storage where infrequently used files are transferred to tape and retrieved when needed. That work was based on High Ground's product. Some options improve technology that already was offered in some versions of the operating system or in an option pack, such as the bundling of multisession server-based computing in Windows Terminal Services, which is based on the joint work of Microsoft and Citrix.

There's something in Windows 2000 Server to make nearly any system administrator smile, and so Microsoft hopes you folks will absorb the expense and trouble of upgrading your operating system. It is our pleasure in this book to be able to tell you about these new features.

When you ask an audience of Windows NT administrators what their number-one concern is and the number-one feature they would like to see in the next generation of the Windows server operating system, the answer in both cases is stability and reliability. Next on the list is ease of management, and much further down on the list are many of the additional features that have been so highly touted by Microsoft during this operating system's gestation.

In fact, Microsoft has paid close attention to making Windows 2000 more stable, less prone to lockup, and more configurable with many fewer instances of having to reboot the system. Jim Allchin, a VP at Microsoft, was quoted as saying that whereas Windows NT 4.0 had 75 different instances where the operating system required a reboot, Windows 2000 has only five different ones. Anyone who has had the experience of installing and configuring Windows NT 4.0 will appreciate these changes. Just changing the TCP/IP settings of a server required a reboot. Not so with Windows 2000 Server.

1

Although Windows 2000 Server doesn't quite close the gap between itself and Windows 98 in terms of being self-configuring for hardware, Windows 2000 Server is much more compliant to Plug and Play (PnP) standards than previous versions of the operating system. The next time you swap a video or sound board on your Windows 2000 Server, don't be surprised to find that the operating system recognizes the new configuration. However, because powering down a server isn't something that you would normally do, Windows 2000 Server doesn't make great strides in power management capabilities although Microsoft claims support for the Advanced Configuration and Power Interface (ACPI).

Additional improvements for hardware support have been made in the Windows 2000 operating system. Although Windows NT supported exotic disk drives, often there were very few consumer-level color printers or scanners that would work with that operating system. Windows 2000 adopts the Windows Driver Model (WDM), which lets a developer develop one single driver to support both Windows 98 and Windows 2000. That driver must be recompiled for each operating system, but at least now the base code is the same. Thus, peripheral vendors are now encouraged, and will find it easy, to maintain drivers for Windows 2000 Server. The net result is that there should be many more peripheral devices available for Windows 2000 Server than for any other server system on the market today.

Server Management

The second major improvement that Microsoft hoped to make with the Windows 2000 operating system is to make the operating system both easier to manage and easier to understand. To that end, Microsoft rewrote its management tools into a framework called the Microsoft Management Console (MMC). The MMC appeared first in Windows NT 4.0 in the Option Pack with snap-ins for IIS administration. So, although there are something like 28 administrative tools in Windows 2000 Server, most of them are snap-ins to the MMC, and they all at least look similar in operation even if the commands and settings are quite different.

All the administrative tools that Windows NT 4.0 users have become familiar with—User Manager, Server Manager, Disk Administrator, the Event Viewer, and many others—appear as MMC snap-ins. Even named connections, dial-up connections, remote access connections, and other communication pipes appear as MMC snap-ins. All these tools and their important contributions to managing the network infrastructure are described in detail in this book.

Windows 2000 Server is loaded with wizards for your management pleasure. Many, if not most, of the configuration commands you give in an administrative tool open a wizard that walks you through the process. There are hundreds of wizards, as you will see if you scan this book's figures. If you like wizards, you will like the changes that Microsoft has made.

These wizards do a good job of explaining the settings and options as you go along, but they do nothing to help you learn how to install and configure the various components and services that Windows 2000 Server requires an administrator or server operator to know about.

The online help system for Windows 2000 Server is extensive, but contains more information that you will probably want to read and try to understand. Culling this information and putting it in perspective is, hopefully, the added value that this book can provide.

One of the strong marketing messages that Microsoft has advanced for the adoption of the Windows 2000 operating system is that it will lower the Total Cost of Ownership, or TCO, of your network systems. TCO is a measurement concept created by the Gartner Group of Stamford, Connecticut that attempts to determine how much a system costs over its lifetime, considering all factors such as hardware, software, administration, and usage.

Microsoft has rolled up a portfolio of server management tools and techniques into an initiative called the Zero Administration for Windows, or ZAW, initiative. ZAW includes a new automated rollout and update architecture for Windows 2000 Professional workstations, one that will eventually be extended to other desktop clients like Windows 9x.

One of ZAW's most-touted features their IntelliMirror. This technology stores a user's critical documents, their applications, and her desktop settings on a Windows 2000 Server. You can think of IntelliMirror as the Windows 9x Briefcase on steroids. In the past, when a user couldn't log onto the network due to a server being down, a broken network connection, or some other problem, that user couldn't access key network resources and continue their work. With IntelliMirror, the user has access to a local cached copy of the file or program, and changes made are synchronized when the network connection to the server is reestablished. IntelliMirror also copies data from the user's desktop to the server and enables the user to log in at another computer and have his working environment reestablished, including desktop settings, programs, and data files.

File and Print Services

Windows 2000 comes with a new version of the NTFS file system. In many cases, you will want to use the NTFS system because it allows the greatest amount of security, and the most control over the file system and network resources. To provide backward compatibility to Windows NT and 98 servers and clients, Windows 2000 also supports the FAT32 file system. Finally, you can also format volumes in FAT (FAT16), such that Windows 95 (pre-OSR2), Windows 3.1, and MS-DOS clients can access those partitions.

The Disk Administrator enables you to have finer control over the creation and management of partitions and volumes. Disks can be either basic or dynamic, and dynamic disks can have volumes that span multiple disks. Windows 2000 continues its support for various forms of software RAID (Redundant Array of Inexpensive Disks).

One of the new features of the file system, part of ZAW, is the creation of disk quotas. You can now set the maximum limit of disk space that a user is allowed, or set a threshold after which an alert is generated. Disk quotas have been available on NetWare and UNIX, and now they are available on Windows.

1

Among the many new improvements in the Windows 2000 file system is the new Microsoft Distributed File System or Dfs. Dfs enables you to create shares that can be mirrored on different network services. Therefore, when a client needs a file that is in a Dfs share, that read or write request is sent to the nearest server. Dfs, when implemented by administrators, will have several important effects. First, it will lessen network traffic, provided that Dfs shares are established on each geographical location or network segment. Second, it will lessen the load on any single server for this information. Third, it will increase uptime and availability of this information on the network.

Several utilities have also been included with Windows 2000 to provide file and print service support. Veritas's Windows 2000 Backup utility is now integrated into the core distributed services. When you run NTBACKUP on a Domain Controller, Active Directory, File Replication Service, and Certificate Services data is automatically backed up. Executive Software's disk optimizer has also been included in this operating system to enable you to defragment your disk.

Right out of the gate, Windows 2000 ships with drivers for more than 2,500 printers. Any shared printer is integrated into the Active Directory, and published printers can be searched for by a variety of properties. A new feature lets you print to a printer designated by a URL by using the Internet Print Protocol. Printers can be managed by using a browser and their print queue can be viewed. You can also download and install print drivers automatically by using IPP over the Internet or on an intranet.

Network Services

Windows 2000 Server continues to embrace the Internet and its TCP/IP networking protocol throughout. This operating system, in network terms, is a hybrid model straddling the client/server network model of the 1990s and the distributed computing model of the Internet that is most people's best guess at what computing in the first decade of the twenty-first century will look like. Windows 2000 Server supports rich clients such as workstations and PCs, thin clients such as Windows-based terminals, and clients running a variety of other operating systems such as the Macintosh OS and UNIX. In the enterprise, computing will not only be distributed, but heterogeneous as well.

Several of Microsoft's networking services have been improved over previous versions. The improvements of DNS, WINS, and DHCP go beyond simply sporting a new universal MMC interface. The Domain Naming Service now supports the DNS dynamic update protocol, making it easier to manage and track changes in DNS structures. WINS also now provides better redundancy through persistent replication connections. Also, unlike in previous versions of the operating system, when a DHCP server is down clients can still boot and attach to the network successfully. The client will regularly query the network for DHCP until the connection is established.

Microsoft continues to improve the Windows IP stack, adding features such as IPSec (Internet Protocol Security), which is a standard for secure transactions on the Internet; L2PT (Layer 2 Tunneling Protocol) and PPTP (Point-to-Point Tunneling Protocol), which allow for virtual private networking (VPN) services; and IP telephony services for voice over data networks. There is a real attempt here to bring the benefits of low-cost Internet communication to high-cost, high-value transaction systems such as Electronic Document Interchange (EDI). Windows 2000 also continues to expand on the services built into Windows Routing and RAS (Remote Access Services) that enable a Windows 2000 Server to play the role of a sophisticated switching device on your network.

For heterogeneous networking support, Microsoft incorporates the Windows Management Instrumentation (WMI) standard into Windows 2000. WMI allows applications to manage and monitor other operating systems' states by using counters similar in nature to the SNMP standard. In a network of Windows 2000 and UNIX systems, applications may be written using WMI that enable you to open a browser and administer those systems remotely.

Building an operating system that incorporates Internet services is forward-looking, and presupposes that sometime in the near future most people will have broadband access. Although this won't be true on the initial release date of Windows 2000 Server, there is a fair chance that it will be true when Service Pack 3 or 4 comes around, say, in the year 2002. By then, the Windows 2000 operating system will be reaching maturity and well into its adoption curve.

This hybrid networking model offers considerable economic benefit and convenience to distributed organizations, to enterprises engaged in electronic commerce, and to any company using the Internet as a service. However, those benefits do not come without a price. For many of us—most of us, in fact—Windows 2000 Server in its various flavors will require us to radically change our domain structure and migrate our network security model to this new structure. All domains in a native-mode Windows 2000 domain structure (containing only Windows 2000 Server) must be compliant with the DNS architecture of the Internet. Windows 2000 Server also does away with different types of Domain Controllers, creating only one type and, thus, easing the burden on any specific Domain Controller on the network. This new domain model introduces new concepts such as forests, trees, and organizational units, giving a much more granular administrative control to network administrators. Now, for example, an administrator can assign many administrative chores to others in a subordinate position.

In this book, we pay considerable attention to this changeover, and explain how it may be accomplished and what its benefits are. The topology and architecture of domain structures are described, as well as the hands-on procedures you need to know to create your new network structure.

With a network of Windows NT Server (version 4 and earlier) and Windows 2000 Server, you can continue using your current domain structure, operating in what is called the *mixed-mode structure*. However, you lose many of the benefits that the Active Directory gives you. Active Directory is an upgrade of the Windows 2000 security database, and it is a dramatic extension of that security database's capabilities. Ask many analysts what the single most-important feature of the Windows 2000 operating system is, and most will tell you that it is the inclusion of Active Directory.

With Active Directory, you can track a much wider range of user, machine, and peripheral properties. By using policies and profiles stored and managed through the Active Directory, you can configure the access and privileges of users in your organization. Active Directory is replicated and synchronized across your domain controllers. Applications can store data in the Active Directory, and this directory service is extensible by developers. Active Directory is a powerful tool for searching, organizing, and controlling network services. Many of these advanced features are enabled when you go to Native mode. We also pay a lot of attention to the Active Directory, and the description of it occupies several hours in the middle of this book.

One of the biggest changes you will find in the Windows 2000 operating system will be invisible to the user and to many administrators. Windows 2000 improves on the Microsoft Component Object Model (COM) to add message queuing and transaction support. In Windows NT Server 4.0, Microsoft Message Queue Server and Microsoft Transaction Server were additional services that you could add to the Enterprise Edition of that version of the operating system. The technology was referred to as Distributed COM. In Windows 2000 Server, those technologies are all rolled up into the base operating system, and the whole technology is named COM+. Even though COM+ is a Windows 2000 object model, developers on many platforms will write programs that utilize its services, and it is likely to become an industry standard. The major benefits of COM+ are that pieces of applications can be distributed about your network, shared and utilized, managed and updated centrally, and contribute to more fault-tolerant computing—something that transient network connections like the Internet require. The use of COM+ is a boon to electronic commerce applications, and it will help make the Windows 2000 operating system popular in those types of applications.

Windows 2000 Server ships with Internet Information Server 5.0, which has many new features that administrators and ISPs will appreciate. In designing IIS 5.0, Microsoft included features intended to support Internet service providers and others who offer Web hosting services. For example, you can now set up virtual server processor quotas to prevent any one process from dominating a Web server. You can also perform process accounting, a feature that enables you to measure the activity of different Web clients and bill appropriately for that activity. Additionally, Microsoft built HTTP compression for improved throughput, tightened up security, and improved numerous features, such as setting up and working with virtual servers and domains.

It is expected that audio and video data will become widely disseminated on the Internet. That trend already exists with IP telephony, audio and video services, and even things such as Internet radio stations. Formats for streaming media exist and are being improved upon. Windows 2000 embraces several of these standards through the incorporation of Windows Media Services (previously known as NetShow). The new Quality of Services (QoS) standards that have been created to assure the availability of bandwidth for multicasted streaming media presentations are also newly included in this version of the operating system.

Security

One of the goals of Windows 2000 was to improve the network security of both the operating system and applications that run on it. Security services are part of the operating system and have been greatly expanded and beefed up. Whereas Windows NT used a single logon authentication procedure with a challenge and response mechanism, Windows 2000 adopts the Kerberos authentication protocol. When a user logs on to the network successfully, Kerberos creates a ticket for that user's session that is incorporated into each request for a network resource. Thus, many fewer authentication requests are required from domain servers in the Windows 2000 operating system.

Windows 2000 Server also supports the concept of certification servers. You can create a certification server on your own network, register your certification with an authorizing agency, and build secure transactional systems internally. Windows 2000 Servers have this capability as an add-on service as part of the base operating system. What was once expensive additional software is now included with Windows 2000 Server, and it is expected to become a necessary requirement for providing network services on the Internet where the identity of an individual system might not be accurately known.

At the file level, Windows 2000 provides an Encrypted File System (EFS) that you can install as an extension to NTFS. EFS uses a public key encryption scheme to encrypt local data on NTFS drives. A user uses encrypted data transparently when she has appropriate access.

Windows 2000 also supports hardware security devices such as smart cards, although those systems aren't described in this book.

What's in Windows 2000 Advanced Server and Datacenter Server?

Windows 2000 Server is only one of three different versions of the Windows 2000 Server family that you can purchase. You can also purchase Windows 2000 Professional, the workstation version of this operating system.

With Windows 2000 Server, you get many services and tools that once were included with Windows NT Server 4.0, Windows NT Server 4.0 Terminal Server Edition, and Windows NT Server 4.0 Enterprise Edition. For example, Windows 2000 Server ships with Window Terminal Services and with transactional and messaging support. Windows Transaction Server and Message Queue Server were part of the Enterprise Edition, but are now rolled into COM+ and are part of Windows 2000 Server.

Some of the differences between Windows 2000 Server and the other versions of this operating system involve performance, fault tolerance, and scalability. Windows 2000 Server supports systems with up to four microprocessors in a symmetric multiprocessing environment, and up to 4GB of installed RAM. Windows 2000 Advanced Server has support for up to eight processors (an eight way system), and up to 8GB of installed RAM. Windows 2000 Advanced Server's SMP support of up to 8 processors supports the new 8-way Intel Profusion-based servers that came to market in the fall of 1999. The final parameters for Windows 2000 Datacenter Edition were not set when we wrote this first draft, but it is expected to have additional support for up to 16 processors initially, growing to 32 processors soon thereafter, with support for up to 64GB of RAM.

With Windows 2000 Advanced Server, you can load balance applications and components using the Windows Load Balancing Services, up to 32 servers at a time. No special programming is required for load balancing. Requests for TCP/IP services are routed to the server with the least activity. You can also configure the loading of services to provide for custom loading levels. Microsoft had intended to ship an application for load balancing applications using Distributed COM as part of Advanced Server, but late into the beta cycle Microsoft decided to roll the technology up into a product called AppServer that will be released as a separate product when Windows 2000 Datacenter Server ships.

The Advanced version of Windows 2000 Server also enables you to cluster servers together. In a cluster, a shared SCSI or Fiber Channel bus between the servers transmits a heartbeat signal that tells the cluster that a member is alive and kicking. When a cluster member fails to respond, the cluster fails resources and activities over to another member of the cluster. Applications must be written to be not only cluster aware, but also cluster enabled. The good news is that many applications are cluster enabled, such as Exchange and SQL Server, and Windows 2000 also adds cluster support for important network services such as DNS, DHCP, and WINS.

With the initial release of Windows 2000 Advanced Server, the Microsoft Cluster Service will be similar to the version released for Windows NT: a shared nothing, two-node failover cluster. However, by the time the Datacenter version of Windows 2000 Server ships, it is expected that Microsoft Cluster Service will be expanded to a four-node cluster with graceful failover. Datacenter will have load balancing and clustering installed and turned on at installation, whereas Advanced Server will require you to install and configure those services.

In 2000, Microsoft should make great strides in closing the difference between large Windows 2000 Server implementations and large UNIX implementations—and in doing so, provide clustering on a broad range of commodity PC server hardware with an industry standard Application Programming Interface (API) that a large number of applications can utilize. This will make the Datacenter version a unique offering.

Microsoft summarizes the different purposes of the three flavors of Windows 2000 Server as follows:

- Windows 2000 Server is meant for small to medium-sized enterprise application deployments, Web servers, and organizations with numerous workgroups and branch offices.
- Windows 2000 Advanced Server is meant for database-intensive work, and integrates high-availability clustering, network, and component load balancing to provide enhanced system and application availability.
- Windows 2000 Datacenter Server is optimized for data warehouse, econometric analysis, large-scale simulations in science and engineering, online transaction processing, server consolidation projects, and for large-scale ISPs and Web site hosting. It is meant to support more than 10,000 simultaneous users at a strong price/performance advantage over other operating systems.

Table 1.1 lists the differences by features of the three operating systems.

TABLE 1.1   Primary Windows 2000 Operating System Features

Product	Description	Features
Windows 2000 Server	The mainstream business server includes the multipurpose capabilities required for workgroups and departmental deployments of file and print servers, application servers, Web servers, and communication servers.	Active Directory, Windows Management Tools, Kerberos and Public Key Infrastructure (PKI) security, Windows Terminal Services, COM+ component services, Enhanced Internet and Web services, Up to 4GB main memory, Up to 2-way SMP support (existing users will get 4-way SMP).
Windows 2000 Advanced Server	A more powerful midrange server that includes the full feature set of Windows 2000 Server and adds the advanced high-availability and improved scalability required for enterprise and larger departmental solutions.	All Windows 2000 Server features, Enhanced application failover clustering, Network service (DNS, DHCP, and INS) clustering, Print server clustering, High-performance sort, Up to 64GB main memory, Up to 8-way SMP support.

Product	Description	Features
Windows 2000 Datacenter Server	The most powerful and functional server operating system ever offered by Microsoft for large-scale enterprise	All Windows 2000 Advanced Server features, Up to 16-way SMP solutions (32-way through OEMs), More advanced clustering, Component load balancing.

Source: Microsoft Corporation, 1999.

There are really so many new features in Windows 2000 Server that even in this introduction it is hard to tell you about them all. But we hope we whetted your appetite, and that you will now continue reading to learn more. We hope you will enjoy reading this book as much as we have enjoyed writing it for you.

Summary

In this hour, you obtained an overview of the new features contained in Windows 2000 Server. The main design goals of this new operating system are to enhance manageability, make your server easier to use and administer, and lower the total cost of ownership of the product. Internet access and compatibility with Internet services have been greatly enhanced and put directly into operating system services.

Windows 2000 Server adds directory services to the operating system with the inclusion of the Active Directory. Active Directory makes it easier to administer and deploy Windows 2000 in the enterprise. However, this operating system requires major changes to the topology of your domain structure, and offers you new ways of managing users, machines, devices, and applications that you must learn.

Many new services and features have been added to Windows 2000. Many of them are transparent to the user, but are essential to developers, such as the inclusion of COM+ for messaging and transaction support. There is new hardware support, better drivers, access to many more peripherals, and a different security model.

Windows 2000 Server is one of a family of operating system packages from Microsoft. In addition to Windows 2000 Professional, which is the workstation version, Windows 2000 ships as Advanced Server and in the first quarter of 2000 as Datacenter Server. The latter two versions offer additional multiprocessor support, access to more memory, load balancing, and cluster support.

Workshop

As you work through each hour, you will be presented with a short quiz and perhaps an exercise or two. These are designed to help reinforce your learning. Even if you feel comfortable with the material, you will still gain from working these exercises. The answers can be found in Appendix A, "Answers."

Quiz

1. What was the number one concern and desired feature of administrators for Windows 2000?
2. What is the Windows Driver Model?
3. When did the Microsoft Management Console first appear?
4. What is the Zero Administration for Windows initiative?
5. What is the Distributed File System?
6. What is the Windows Management Instrumentation standard?
7. What is mixed-mode domain operation?
8. What major security model does Windows 2000 add?
9. How many processors in an SMP system do Advanced Server and Datacenter Server support?
10. What group of people is Windows 2000 Server meant for?

Exercises

1. Assuming that an enterprise has 100, 1,000, 10,000, and 100,000 users spread out in three different sites, draw up an inventory of the number of Windows 2000 Servers required to support that number of workstations. Assume that the enterprise supports a messaging application where each server can service 1,000 users and a database where each server can support up to 500 users. For argument's sake assume that Windows 2000 Server supports up to 2,000 users.

2. In the exercise described above assume that the servers deployed were fast dual Pentium III Xeon servers. If a Profusion 8-way system using the same processors and disk systems scaled linearly (was 4 times the power) how would that change your deployment plans? Which version of the operating system would you use?

3. Further explore the various advantages of Windows 2000 Server and its various flavors by visiting the Microsoft Web site at http://www.microsoft.com/ntserver.

Hour 2

Architecture and Boot Process

by Barrie Sosinsky

Windows 2000 Server is built on the Windows NT (for New Technology) operating system developed at Microsoft in the early 1990s. The operating system was designed around a small kernel that provides the primary processing capabilities and hardware interactions. The kernel and its hardware abstraction layer (HAL) were written so that the HAL could be easily recompiled for different microprocessors, whereas the kernel remained the same, thus making this operating system portable between platforms. In this regard, Windows NT had much in common with its Digital VMS heritage, which is the operating system that many of the members of the initial design team belonged to. Versions of the Windows NT operating system were built for Intel's X86 architecture, Digital Computer's Alpha processors, Motorola's PPC, and the MIPS processor, although the latter two versions were abandoned.

When you understand the architecture used to create and manage Windows 2000 Server and Windows NT before it, you can understand how the installation process works, how programs run, how devices are installed and work, and a whole host of other things that will make it easier for you to configure, optimize, and troubleshoot your server.

This hour also details the process by which the operating system starts up or boots, and the files, services, and system resources that are used on the Intel platform. Understanding the boot sequence will allow you to troubleshoot a system that has crashed or will not start up correctly.

The following topics are covered in this hour:

- How the operating system is constructed from system modules
- The two different modes of the operating system
- How Windows 2000 processes commands, is able to multitask programs, and can operate on multiple processors concurrently
- The Windows 2000 memory model
- The boot sequence for Intel systems

Modular Construction

Windows 2000 Server's internal architecture was built around a set of modules. This was done so that any module could be updated and improved internally without requiring a major overhaul of the entire operating system. Although the internal source code of the Windows operating system remains undisclosed to the general public, Microsoft makes available a description of the system calls required to many of the various modules in the operating system as a standard set of Application Programming Interfaces or APIs. Figure 2.1 is a schematic that shows the various modules that comprise the Windows 2000 architecture.

By designing a small kernel—the part of the operating system that controls the CPU—surrounded by a set of interacting modules, the NT operating system isolates the most important CPU and hardware I/O processes from those processes that are initiated by applications. Each application also runs in its own protected memory space, which means that Windows 2000 Server has the ability to run multiple applications and can survive many application errors without crashing. For these reasons, Windows 2000 (and NT) is much more reliable than previous versions of Windows, and many other operating systems as well.

FIGURE 2.1

The Windows 2000 architecture is comprised of a set of interacting modules.

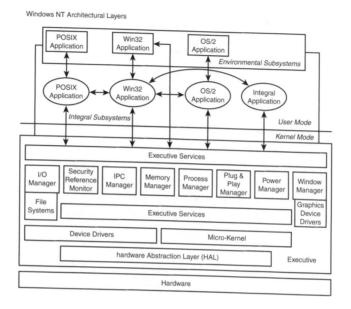

User Mode

The Windows 2000 operating system was designed to isolate applications and other user-specific processes from the core processes required to do I/O to peripheral devices. The part of the operating system that a user interacts with is called the *user mode*. The user mode contains a set of environmental subsystems: the POSIX, Win32, OS/2, and other subsystems that allow programs written for these various operating systems to run on Windows 2000 Server without having to be specially recompiled to do so. The Win32 environmental subsystem provides screen and keyboard I/O, as well as many of the Windows graphics routines and libraries.

Commands that a user specifies inside an application that require access to hardware are handed off through the Executive Services layer of the kernel, and then are translated and executed. In between all devices and programs is the hardware abstraction layer, or HAL, that serves as a gatekeeper. The net effect of this construction is that applications have no direct method of accessing system hardware and must have their commands interpreted. The software that communicates with devices, device drivers, are also controlled by the kernel and are unavailable for direct access by applications running in the user mode.

Processes that run in user mode are assigned a block of memory by the operating system; this block is called their *address space*. When an application requires more memory, it can request that instructions not recently used be swapped out to disk, a process called *paging* or *disk swapping*. Through the use of virtual memory, your system has ready access to a much larger portion of a running program than might be possible using installed RAM alone.

Virtual memory also allows you to load additional programs beyond what your physical installed RAM might allow. The Memory Manager module in the Executive layer manages this process. Virtual memory is slower to access than real memory, and there is also a certain overhead required to manage the process, but the Windows operating system relies heavily on the swap file on your hard drive. See Hour 5, "The Control Panel," for a demonstration of how to configure the swap file.

Applications or processes that run in the user mode compete with those processes required to make your computer work in the kernel mode. Windows 2000 assigns priorities to different processes based on their overall importance, and because kernel mode processes are essential to running your computer system, they operate with a higher priority than processes initiated in the user mode. As a consequence, user mode processes have less access to the CPU than processes that execute in the kernel mode.

Kernel Mode

The *kernel mode* is a set of modules that control hardware and access system data. The kernel mode executes in protected space in the CPU that other programs cannot access.

There are five main parts of the kernel mode:

- The Windows 2000 Executive—This layer of the operating system controls object management and security, and does most of the I/O to peripheral devices.
- Various manager modules—These modules control virtual memory, processes, and objects, manage some I/O operations, and control the interprocess communication (IPC) that makes COM+ operate correctly.
- Device drivers—These are translation routines for communicating with peripheral devices such as printers, network boards, and video cards. Each device requires its own device driver.
- Kernel—The kernel itself is a set of core routines running on the CPU or microprocessor. Because all I/O either passes through the CPU or is managed by the CPU and offloaded to another processor, the kernel acts as a traffic cop coordinating the entire Executive Services system.
- Hardware Abstraction Layer (HAL)—The HAL is the part of the Executive Services system that does the actual communication to various peripheral devices.

Kernel mode provides two distinct sets of services. One set provides system services to the user mode through the Executive Services layer and to other Windows Executive components. The second set of services in kernel mode is the internal processes, which can be accessed only by other components in the kernel mode. Referring to Figure 2.1, you will see that there are several components in kernel mode. They include the following:

- I/O Manager—This module manages input to and output from the file system, device drivers, and the Cache Manager. Requests for file system access and reads and writes from and to devices are routed through the I/O Manager. The network redirector and network server are file system drivers. The I/O Manager communicates through device drivers to hardware. Device drivers are low-level routines that directly communicate with hardware. The I/O Manager also works with the Cache Manager to store disk reads into RAM. The Cache Manager also performs reads and writes to disk as a background process.

- Security Reference Monitor—This module manages the security policies on your server.

- IPC Manager—IPC, or Interprocess Control, is the name for the suite of application services such as OLE and COM that let one application communicate with and command the services of another application. An application running on an environmental subsystem as a client can request services through the Executive Services layer from a component running on the server, and the IPC manages those requests. When the requests are from a client application and a server on the same computer, it is referred to as a Local Procedure Call (LPC). When the client application requests a service from a server application running on another computer across the network, it is referred to as a Remote Procedure Call (RPC). Different facilities exist for both types of calls, and the programming calls are standardized and published so that application vendors can make their products operate with one another and with the Windows 2000 operating system.

- Virtual Memory Manager—The Virtual Memory Manager (VMM) implements a scheme that provides applications with their own private and protected memory address space. When demands on available memory exceed the amount of physical RAM installed on your computer, the VMM controls memory paging to a disk swap file, sending code not in current use to disk and retrieving code required at the moment back.

- Process Manager—The Process Manager is responsible for managing the processes that your system and applications require. These processes are prioritized and broken down into threads of execution that are related commands in a process. The Process Manager can suspend or resume execution of a process or individual threads, as well as provide current information about the state of execution of processes and threads. When a Symmetric Multiprocessor (SMP) system is used, the Process Manager determines which processor gets which thread.

- Plug & Play Manager—The PnP Manager identifies devices that are available to your system and loads the appropriate drivers for those devices. The PnP Manager does an inventory at startup, and determines what configuration your system is in. When a device becomes unavailable during a session, the PnP Manager will post a notification, allowing you to remedy the situation.

2

- Power Manager—This module works with devices to manage power requests by turning off or lowering power to devices for power savings, or by providing power when a device requests it.

- Window Manager—The Window Manager and the related Graphics Device Interface, or GDI, are two of the most visible parts of the Windows operating system because they are responsible for the various elements that users see on their monitors. The Window Manager controls screen output and manages the communication between keyboard, the mouse, and applications. The GDI is a set of graphic routines that process graphics requests, interpret them, and issue the instructions that let the Window Manager draw them to your screen. Both of these components are contained in the WIN2K.SYS device driver.

- Object Manager—This module is a database and registry of all objects currently in use. The Object Manager creates, provides access to, and deletes objects. Objects originate from processes, threads, data that is in use, and from a variety of system resources.

- Micro-Kernel—This module directly communicates with your system's CPU. Among the many central processes that the micro-kernel controls are interrupt timing, thread scheduling, and multiprocessor synchronization. The kernel handles exception errors.

- Hardware Abstraction Layer—The HAL is a software layer that controls various hardware communications. Among the processes that use the services of the HAL are CPU timing requests, interrupt controllers, I/O signals sent to various devices, and other communications. The different versions of Windows 2000 Server for each hardware platform, such as Intel x86 processors and Compaq Alpha systems (for previous versions of Windows), have their own distinct HALs.

Subsystems

The environmental and integral subsystems that are part of the user mode allow Windows 2000 Server to run applications that were designed to run on other operating systems. You can think of these subsystems as emulators for other operating systems such as POSIX (a standardized form of UNIX) and OS/2 (the 16-bit character mode version of IBM's desktop and server operating system). Each environmental subsystem provides an API with the standard system calls that programs running on those other operating systems expect, even if the underlying code in the emulation is quite different from the code that runs those operating systems natively on their own platforms.

The most important environmental subsystem is the Win32 module. This subsystem allows programs written as 32-bit applications to run on Windows 2000, and parts of the system provide backward compatibility for Win16 applications and MS-DOS applications.

As a general rule, programs written as 32-bit Windows applications tend to be more stable and perform more quickly than programs written in 16-bit Windows or for MS-DOS that run on Windows 2000 in emulation.

Windows 2000 also has some integral subsystems that control security and services. The security subsystem provides logon authentication, maintains the security database, monitors rights and permissions, and audits access to system and network resources. There are also two integral networking subsystems: Server Service and Workstation Service. Server Service is the subsystem with an API that allows programs to access a network server, as well as allowing access to network resources. Workstation Service is a system with an API that acts as a redirector to network resources.

2

Processing

Windows 2000 provides services that let two or more applications run at the same time on one or more processors. In order to enable these features, this operating system has the ability to break processes apart and run multiple threads of execution at the same time, a feature called *multithreading*. A multithreaded system enables an application to seemingly perform more than one process at a time. All modern processors and operating systems have this capability. Going hand-in-hand with multithreading is the process by which multiple threads of execution are delivered to your system's microprocessor.

Windows 2000 is a multitasked operating system, where threads are queued, prioritized, and delivered to the CPU based on the number of cycles that the CPU has available. Multitasking allows the CPU to execute threads in a round-robin fashion without letting any single application hog the CPU's time. In some desktop operating systems, such as the Macintosh OS, multiple applications running on the same system rely on the application to release the CPU appropriately. In the Windows 2000 operating system, the CPU traffic cop is built into the operating system itself.

One feature that separates Windows 2000 from some other operating systems, such as the Macintosh OS and early versions of Linux, is its ability to run on two or more processors at the same time, a feature called *Symmetric Multiprocessing* or SMP. Whereas Windows 2000 Server is restricted to a four-processor system, Windows 2000 Advanced Server can run up to eight processors in a single system. Windows 2000 Datacenter Server will run 8, 16, and eventually 32 processors in a single system when the chip sets become available to enable this type of server.

Multithreading

When a program executes a particular command—a print job, communications with another program, calculations on data, I/O with the file system, or any of the many thousands of types of tasks that Windows 2000 is capable of—typically that command requires many steps to execute.

Because any one program is going to have the attention of the microprocessor for only a few cycles at best, that command is broken down into smaller tasks, called *threads of execution*, that allow more timely execution. An executable program starts a process, which then spawns one or more threads. Because Windows 2000 is capable of executing multiple threads at the same time, the CPU is more efficiently utilized.

Any 32-bit program that runs on Windows 2000 contains code and data in its own private memory space. A certain number of system resources are allocated to that program, including files, I/O ports, and other resources. After the program starts to do actual work, threads are generated. A *thread* may be thought of as the part of a process that is executing and doing actual work. Each thread is run in the memory space of the program and utilizes the system resources assigned to that program.

Because Windows 2000 must track many threads executing at the same time, it uses a system to identify which process a thread belongs to. Each thread is assigned a client ID that uniquely identifies that thread. Additionally, part of the thread contains a representation of the current state of the microprocessor so that it knows when to be acted on. Threads maintain two stacks reserved in memory, one for user mode execution and the other for kernel mode execution. A thread also contains memory reserved for information relating to its execution that is derived from the various environmental subsystems, dynamic link libraries (DLLs), and runtime libraries. By storing instructions for the use of the thread in memory with the data and the commands of the thread, the thread has a self-contained set of instructions and data that doesn't require any additional I/O to be acted on by the CPU.

Multitasking

In a multitasked operating system, it appears as if several applications and processes all have the attention of the microprocessor at the same time. This feat of magic is accomplished through a sleight of hand called *time slicing*. Basically, the CPU's cycles are divided up and made available to many threads at the same time through a process called *context switching*. At any one instant, only one thread is executing in a microprocessor, but that instant is so short that for all practical purposes, execution appears to be concurrent and simultaneous. It's a little like watching a motion picture. Each frame goes through the projector one at a time, but your mind isn't capable of discerning each event. To you, it just looks like motion.

In a context-switched system, a thread is executed by the CPU until either the thread completes itself or the operating system interrupts the thread. If the thread doesn't have all the required instructions or data, the execution pauses until they are made available. At some preset amount of time called a *quantum*—some number of CPU cycles that is determined by several factors, including the priority of the process and the CPU's working load—the system stops executing the thread and saves its context in memory. At that point, the next thread in the processor queue has its context loaded and its execution begins.

The kernel is the part of the operating system that acts as the traffic cop. It determines when to interrupt or preempt the execution of one thread and start the execution of the next thread. When the operating system determines that timing, this type of multitasking is referred to as *preemptive multitasking*. In a cooperative multitasked system, applications are responsible for utilization of the CPU and are supposed to release the CPU appropriately. Preemptive multitasked systems are more reliable and less prone to application errors.

Multiprocessing

The Windows 2000 operating system sets a priority level to the different processes that are executed by it. There are thirty-two levels given numbers from 0 to 31. The higher numbers execute with greater access to the multiprocessor, so that user-mode processes are assigned levels from 0–15 and kernel mode processes are given the higher priority levels of 16–31. Each process gets a base priority level that can range up or down a couple of levels. A process with a base priority of 8 might execute between 6 and 10 under normal circumstances.

It is possible to adjust the priority that some processes have from within an application or by using commands at the command lines. When you see an application that has a slider for performance (fast or slow), or sets whether a program executes in the foreground rather than the background, that slider is changing the priority level for the processes involved.

Additionally, the kernel has the capability to dynamically adjust the base level up or down depending upon thread activity, a process called *dynamic priority leveling*. A thread's dynamic priority level might be decreased for a calculation that the kernel identifies as a background process, or raised for important I/O activity such as user input.

Windows 2000 offers the capability to run on two or more processors at the same time, something called *multiprocessing*. In an asymmetric multiprocessing system, a process is sent to a single processor and executes on that processor until it is done. Because processes and the threads they are comprised of often stall waiting for data and instructions, an asymmetric multiprocessor system is relatively inefficient.

Windows 2000 runs on symmetric multiprocessor, or SMP, systems. In an SMP system, processes and the threads that comprise them are sent to any processor with scheduling adjusting the execution queue to balance the load, a form of multitasking across processors. Some processes, such as kernel mode processes, will always be executed on the first available CPU. But user mode processors tend to be distributed across the different microprocessors.

Figure 2.2 shows a schematic of multithreading, multitasking, and multiprocessing.

FIGURE **2.2**

*Windows 2000 is
capable of managing
several running
processes and applica-
tions, and spreading
the work over several
processors.*

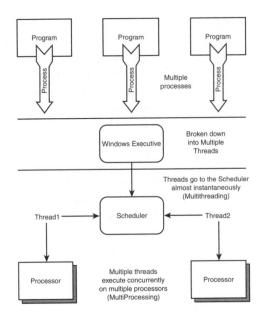

Memory

You might have noticed that Windows 2000 uses a lot of memory for an operating system
compared to your desktop operating systems. Windows 2000 also allows access to very
large amounts of installed physical RAM. Windows 2000 uses a flat, or linear, 32-bit
address space. In 32-bit space, four bytes are executed at the same time. The maximum
amount of RAM that a 32-bit operating system can access is 4GB; that is, the operating
system knows about 4GB of possible addresses or virtual addresses. Future versions of the
Windows operating systems will run as 64-bit systems with even greater (astonishing)
access to memory and virtual address space.

Virtual address space is what an application uses when it references memory. Even though
4GB of addresses are allowed, the first, or upper, 2GB of addresses are reserved for kernel
mode processes, and only kernel threads will execute in it. The lower portion of the upper
2GB is maintained for very fast access to hardware and for I/O. The lower 2GB of memory addresses are used for both user mode and kernel mode processes. The upper portion
of the lower 2GB of virtual address space is divided into a paged and nonpaged pool of
addresses. Code can be earmarked for the nonpaged pool and will always be held in physical memory. The Virtual Memory Manager (VMM) can swap data in the paged pool to
disk, a process that is automatically and dynamically managed by the Windows operating
system. Figure 2.3 shows a schematic of the virtual address scheme.

Windows uses a virtual memory management scheme to extend the amount of physical
RAM by reading and writing data to a file on disk. Instructions that haven't been used in a
while, and aren't earmarked as having to be held in physical memory, can be paged to disk.

This is a first-in, first-out system. When the data is paged to disk, the VMM marks those addresses as free.

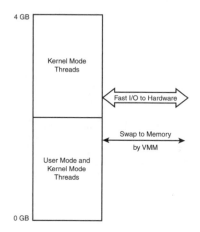

Virtual memory helps prevent one process from requiring the memory space of another process. The VMM manages a swap file on disk and pages data in and out as segments for writes and reads. A *page* is a 4KB chunk of memory transferred to or from the swap file, also called a *page file*. When there isn't enough physical RAM and too much paging is going on, your system slows its execution and you see excessive disk activity—something called *disk thrashing*. Typically, swap files are kept around two or three times the size of installed RAM to minimize disk thrashing.

In a flat or linear memory model, the operating system assigns a range of memory to a system process or to an application, with that memory being protected. Not only does physical RAM have unique addresses assigned, but virtual memory is assigned unique addresses in virtual memory space as well. It is the job of the Virtual Memory Manager to map the location of data on disk or in memory, and to relate that to the virtual address so that when a thread is requested for execution, it is either loaded from RAM or transferred to RAM from disk and loaded—a process called *fetching*. Essentially, the Virtual Memory Manger maintains a table of addresses that point to the locations where processes reside, and the VMM manages the paging process. Figure 2.4 shows how the paging process works.

In virtual address space, pages are marked as either valid pages with a location in physical memory or as invalid pages that do not exist in physical memory. When a thread requires a valid page, it loads from memory. When a thread requires an invalid page, the operating system issues a page fault, traps the error, and loads the required page from disk. In a well-ordered application, the thread will request the page again; when the page becomes valid, it is loaded and the thread is executed.

FIGURE **2.4**

Windows 2000 uses a paging scheme to swap instructions in and out of physical memory, and thereby extend the amount of virtual memory that your system can access.

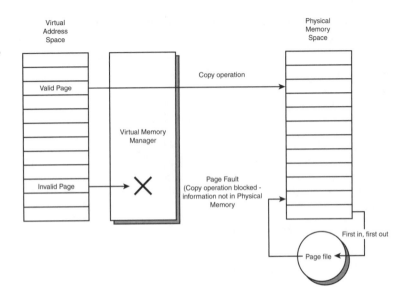

Windows 2000 uses a system called demand paging with clustering to load invalid pages into physical memory. When an invalid page is loaded into memory, the operating system also loads some of the adjacent pages so that the number of page faults is minimized. If there is free physical memory available, the VMM loads the invalid page into the first free page. If physical memory is full, the VMM must first swap out pages from physical memory to RAM before it can load the invalid page. The VMM examines the working set of pages in physical memory for each process and then moves the page that has resided in physical memory the longest without being accessed.

The X86 Boot Process

Having now seen how the Windows 2000 operating system is constructed, it is instructive to consider how the operating system starts and loads. Understanding the boot process can help you diagnose problems that affect your computer, as well as provide some additional useful capabilities. In the event that your system fails, the boot process provides a mechanism for recovery.

On Intel processors, there are five distinct phases associated with booting a computer. They are

1. Preboot—This part of the boot process is where hardware is checked and the boot instructions are loaded.

2. The Boot sequence—The part of the startup sequence called the boot sequence is where hardware is configured in the operating system and where device drivers for hardware are loaded into memory.

3. Kernel loading—The NTLDR file loads the kernel into memory, the Hardware Abstraction Layer is loaded, and a hardware profile is selected.

4. Kernel initialization—The NTOSKRNL.EXE file initializes the kernel, which writes the hardware configuration to the Registry and loads low-level device drivers. At this point, the character-based portion of the boot sequence ends and the graphical portion of startup begins.

5. Logon—At logon, a user session is authenticated, services are loaded, and access to resources are given. The system saves the hardware configuration after a successful logon to the Registry.

As an aid in case your computer's system partition files become corrupted, you should prepare a boot floppy disk after installing Windows 2000. Copy the required system files to a freshly formatted floppy disk. For Intel X86 systems those files are NTLDR, NTDETECT.COM, NTBOOTDD.SYS (for SCSI controllers lacking a SCSI BIOS), and the BOOT.INI file. If the NTOSKRNL.EXE file is corrupted and you can't load it from disk, view the information about Automatic System Recovery (ASR) in the online help system for procedures to use.

The POST and Boot Sequence

During preboot, your system runs the power-on self test (POST) sequence that checks the amount and state of installed memory, handshakes with hardware devices; with Plug and Play, the BIOS configures hardware. The BIOS then finds the boot device and loads the Master Boot Record (MBR) on that device. The MBR examines the partition table to determine the active partition that contains the operating system files. It then loads the boot sector for the active partition into memory and runs the instructions that the boot sector contains. The preboot sequence ends when the NT system loader (filename NTLDR) is loaded into memory.

The first thing that happens in the boot sequence portion is that the NTLDR file switches from real mode to the 32-bit flat memory model. Then NTLDR starts its minifile system drivers that allow Windows 2000 to be loaded from the different types of file systems that the system partition can be formatted in: FAT, FAT32, and NTFS.

Perhaps the most visible part of the boot sequence phase is the appearance of the Boot Loader Operating System Selection menu that appears when the BOOT.INI file is loaded. The BOOT.INI file is a simple text file that lists the different operating systems that are available on your system and the file that initiates the loading of each operating system. One of those listings is the default operating system, so if you don't make a selection from the list, the default operating system loads. If the BOOT.INI isn't present on your disk, NTLDR will try to load Windows 2000 from the \WINNT directory found on the first partition of the first disk.

The BOOT.INI file is found in the root folder of your system partition. It is a hidden system file that won't appear unless you set the View Folder option to allow hidden folders to be viewed (see Hour 5, "The Control Panel," for details on how to view hidden and system files). BOOT.INI also will not show up in a search if you haven't set the view option. The following entries show the BOOT.INI file for a standard Windows 2000–only installation. The [boot loader] section controls what appears in the Boot Loader Operating System Selection menu, and editing this text file can add or remove entries from the menu.

Here's what's in the BOOT.INI file:

```
[boot loader]

timeout=30
default=multi(0)disk(0)rdisk(0)partition(1)\WINNT
[operating systems]
multi(0)disk(0)rdisk(0)partition(1)\WINNT="Microsoft Windows 2000 Server"
/fastdetect
```

The [operating systems] section lists an entry in the form of an Advanced Reduced Set Computing, or ARC, path that points to the boot partition that starts the operating system. ARC paths typically take the form: multi(0)disk(0)rdisk(1)partition(1), where multi (or scsi) identifies the disk controller; disk is the disk number (a number for scsi 0–7, and 0 for multi); rdisk identifies the disk (not used for scsi); and the partition value identifies the partition number.

You will also see a set of switches that appear at the end of the load commands in the BOOT.INI file that modify the action of the loading operating system. Among the most commonly used are the following: /basevideo loads a VGA video driver; /fastdetect= [com x|com x,y,z] disables the detection of a serial mouse; /maxmem:# is the amount of RAM used by the operating system; noguiboot loads the operating system to the command prompt; and /sos displays each device driver as it loads.

To modify the BOOT.INI file and change things such as the timeout or default parameters, you will need to reset the file properties so that you can write changes to it. This involves removing the system and the read only attributes of the file either at the command prompt, or using the file's Properties dialog box. Make your changes in a text editor and save the file to disk. You can, optionally, edit the BOOT.INI file graphically. (See "Startup and Recovery Section" in Hour 5.)

If you press the F8 key when the Boot Loader menu appears, you are taken to a screen that displays a set of Advanced Boot options. Those options are described in the following sidebar.

2

Advanced Boot Options

You can use the F8 keystroke when the Boot Loader Operating System menu appears during startup to go to a set of advanced options that are helpful when you are trying to diagnose or repair a damaged system. The following options are offered to you:

- Safe Mode—In safe mode, Windows 2000 loads only a subset of the devices and device drivers that your system would normally load to enable VGA video, mouse, keyboard, disks, and very standard system services. In safe mode, you can make changes to your system that will allow you to successfully reboot into a standard configuration. You will see the words Safe Mode displayed on your screen when you boot into that mode. If your computer crashed, you might automatically be started up into safe mode even if you don't select it.

- Safe Mode with Networking—This option loads basic network drivers along with standard safe mode features.

- Safe Mode with Command Prompt—In this boot option, you are taken to a command prompt instead of starting in the Windows 2000 Explorer.

- Enable Boot Logging—When you select this function, Windows 2000 logs each driver that is initialized and loaded to the NTBTLOG.TXT file in the \%systemroot%.

- Enable VGA Mode—This option allows you to start up normally, however, it loads the standard VGA driver.

- Last Known Good Configuration—As described in the section "The Logon Sequence" that follows, when a successful login is achieved, Windows 2000 registers the configuration. If your system crashes or fails to start properly, you can use this option to return to that state and perhaps bypass the problem.

- Directory Services Restore Mode—This option enables you to restore the Active Directory on a domain controller.

- Debugging Mode—This option enables debugging.

Each option writes log entries to the NTBTLOG.TXT file in the \%systemroot%. Except for the Last Known Good Configuration option, all these options start up in basic VGA graphics mode (that is, third-party whiz-bang VGA drivers are disabled). When you use an advanced boot option, your environmental variable becomes %SAFEBOOT_OPTION%.

If another operating system, such as Windows 98, was selected in the Boot Loader Operating System Selection menu, NTLDR hands off the boot process to the BOOTSEC.DOS file, which is a copy of the boot sector that existed before Windows 2000 was installed. At that point, the other operating system loads.

At the time the OS Loader menu appears, you have the option of pressing the Spacebar and viewing the Hardware Profile/Configuration Recovery menu. If your computer had startup problems, press the L key to select the Last Known Good Configuration option and you are returned to the configuration saved in the Registry the last time you were able to successfully log in.

The option and how it is implemented is described in more detail in the "Login Sequence" section. Two situations in which you might want to use the Last Known Good Configuration option are when you install a new device driver, and when you disable a device driver, such a SCSI driver that prevents you from starting up.

After a Windows 2000 operating system is selected in the Boot Loader Operating System Selection menu (provided that it was Windows 2000), the boot sequence proceeds to load the NTDETECT.COM and NTOSKRNL.EXE, which then perform various types of hardware detection. NTDETECT.COM will return a list of the components, such as the Computer ID, COM and LPT ports, various bus adapters, coprocessors, video adapters, floppy disks, keyboards, and mice to the NTLDR. In turn, NTLDR writes this information into the Registry in the HKEY_LOCAL_MACHINE\HARDWARE key. When the hardware configuration is known, the OS loader posts a message that tells you that you can press the Spacebar to view the Hardware Profile/Configuration Recovery menu. This menu enables you to select from different hardware profiles or return to the last known good configuration by pressing the L key. Past this menu, you enter the kernel initialization phase of the boot sequence.

The Boot Role of the Kernel

After you have selected the hardware profile you want from the Hardware Profile/ Configuration Recovery menu, the boot sequence loads the NTOSKRNL.EXE file, which controls the loading of the Windows 2000 kernel. If you don't make a selection, the default profile is chosen. You can tell that the kernel is loading because you will see a set of device drivers being loaded, each one appearing as a period at the top of your monitor. You can use the /sos switch (detailed earlier) to expose the periods to actual driver names.

The following things are going on during this phase of startup:

1. NTLDR loads the NTOSKRNL.EXE program.
2. The dynamic link library of the Hardware Abstraction Layer (HLL.DLL) is loaded into memory.
3. The hardware configuration determined at startup from interrogating the various devices and your selection of a hardware profile is written into the HKEY_LOCAL_MACHINE\SYSTEM Registry key from the %SYSTEMROOT%\ SYSTEM32\CONFIG\SYSTEM folder.
4. The control set for the configuration of your system loads, and the kernel copies that control set to a clone control set that serves as a reference for the original configuration of your system before startup begins to modify your configuration. You see the reference to this clone in the Current entry of the HKEY_LOCAL_MACHINE\ SELECT Registry subkey.

5. Low-level hardware device drivers are loaded into memory.

   Device drivers to be loaded are contained in the HKEY_LOCAL_MACHINE\
   SYSTEM\CURRENTCONTROLSET\SERVICES Registry subkey (values 0x1 for
   the Start entry). Drivers load based on their value in the Group entry, and the action to
   be taken for errors when a device driver loads are specified in the ErrorControl entries.

6. The Session Manager (SMSS.EXE) loads the environmental subsystems and services for those subsystems as specified in the BootExecute data item.

   Among the instructions executed by SMSS.EXE are the Memory Management key
   to create the page file; the DOS Devices key, which creates symbolic links between
   components of the file system; and the SubSystems key, where Win32 is first
   loaded followed by the WinLogon process.

After this point, the kernel is loaded into memory and NTLDR ends. Startup passes from
the character-based portion of startup to the graphical phase. A picture appears and the
blue band at the bottom starts to animate.

The Logon Sequence

The last part of the boot sequence is the logon phase, as evidenced by the Logon dialog box.
You see this dialog box when the kernel initialization is almost complete and the Session
Manager has loaded the Win32 environmental subsystem. Win32 starts WINLOGON.EXE,
which in turn starts the Local Security Authority (LSASS.EXE), which is responsible for
displaying the Logon dialog box. Although you can log on when the dialog box appears,
initialization (as evidenced by disk activity) is still ongoing.

The Logon phase has the following components:

1. WINLOGON.EXE initiates

2. The Local Security Authority service starts

3. The Logon dialog box appears

4. The Service Controller starts

5. Services are loaded

The Services Controller (SCREG.EXE) then runs and loads services that are listed in the
HKEY_LOCAL_MACHINE\SYSTEM\CURRENTCONTROLSET\SERVICES Registry
subkey. Two services started up at this point include both the Workstation and Server services. When the logon has been authenticated, the user profile is loaded and access to
server and network services is authorized.

The last part of the logon sequence occurs after a successful logon sequence. Now, the
system copies the clone control set to the LastKnownGood control set, establishing a
potential recovery to this state should the system run into future problems. At this point,
the boot sequence for Windows 2000 on an Intel X86 platform is considered complete.

Table 2.1 summarizes the files that are used in the Intel boot sequence, their location on disk, and the portion of the boot process in which they are loaded.

TABLE 2.1   Files Used in the Intel Boot Sequence

File	Disk Location	Boot Phase
NTLDR	System partition root	Preboot and boot
BOOT.INI	System partition root	Boot
BOOTSECT.DOS (optional)	System partition root	Boot
NTDETECT.COM	System partition root	Boot
NTBOOTDD.SYS	System partition root	Boot
NTOSKRNL.EXE	%SYSTEMROOT%\SYSTEM32	Kernel loading
HAL.DLL	%SYSTEMROOT%\SYSTEM32	Kernel loading
SYSTEM	%SYSTEMROOT%\SYSTEM32\CONFIG	Kernel initialization
Device drivers	%SYSTEMROOT%\SYSTEM32\DRIVERS	Kernel initialization

Summary

In this hour, you learned how the Windows 2000 operating system is constructed around a small microkernel, and how it communicates with hardware through the Hardware Abstraction Layer. Only the HAL needs to be recompiled for a different processor, making Windows 2000 a portable operating system. The operating system further isolates central system processes from application processes to make the operating system robust and hard to crash. You also saw how Windows uses memory, both real and virtual. The basis for multitasking and multiprocessor support was also explored.

The Windows 2000 boot process is a choreographed sequence of both hardware detection and software device control that results in a known and registered configuration being used to support a wide range of devices. Windows 2000 can coexist with other operating systems, and you can select those other operating systems in the boot process. The various stages of the boot sequence were described, as well as which files and systems are responsible for the actions being taken. You learned about various boot options and how to work around and troubleshoot difficult startup problems that might occur.

After reading this hour, you should be prepared now to go on to Hour 3, "Installing Windows 2000 Server," in which you will install the Windows 2000 Server operating system.

Workshop

The workshop is used to provide a quiz and exercises to help reinforce your learning. Even if you feel you know the material, you will still gain from working these exercises.

Quiz

1. What part of the operating system needs to be changed to support different processor types?

2. What is the Windows 2000 Executive?

3. What does SMP mean?

4. What is dynamic process leveling?

5. How much memory can a 32-bit operating system address?

6. What module is responsible for paging?

7. What does POST stand for?

8. What is the last known good configuration and how do you access it?

9. What files do I need on an emergency boot floppy to start up Windows 2000 Server?

10. What operating system has the largest beta program in history?

Exercises

1. Create a boot floppy and test it on your system.

2. Start up into Safe Mode with Networking, and examine your system's capabilities.

3. Open the Registry and examine the HKEY_LOCAL_MACHINE\SYSTEM\ subkey to view the Current, Default, Failed, and LastKnownGood control sets. Use RegEdit to examine the Registry.

HOUR 3

Installing Windows 2000 Server

by Barrie Sosinsky

Microsoft has taken a lot of care to make sure that the Windows 2000 Setup program makes it much easier to install this operating system than previous versions of the operating system. There are fewer reboots during the installation, and Microsoft has worked with a wide range of hardware vendors to ensure that up-to-date drivers exist to support most of the common hardware. Still, there are some things you need to know about what kind of equipment is required for Windows 2000, where to get information about hardware compatibility, various installation options, and where you might run into trouble during an installation. Installing Windows 2000, although straightforward, will take you some time. Reading this hour beforehand will speed up the process.

The following topics are covered in this hour:

- What the hardware requirements are for Windows 2000 Server
- Things you should do prior to an installation
- Performing either a clean install or an upgrade

- How to decide the kind of file system on which you want Windows 2000 Server installed
- What you need to know during the installation at each step of Setup
- Creating a dual boot between Windows 2000 and another operating system
- What the licensing requirements for Windows 2000 Server are
- How to join a workgroup or domain during the installation

What Are the Server Requirements?

Windows 2000 Server has some beefy hardware requirements that make it difficult to run on older systems. Even Pentium-class computers slower than Microsoft's required minimum 166MHz will be sluggish. But, assuming that you meet the hardware requirements for a reasonable configuration of Windows 2000 Server, you will find that Windows 2000 Server is very stable and offers you an enhanced toolset that is easier to learn and use.

Table 3.1 lists the minimum hardware requirements for Windows 2000 Server.

Although Windows 2000 requires more substantial hardware than Windows NT 4.0 and 3.5x, you will be pleasantly surprised to learn that Windows 2000 will install on a wide range of third-party hardware. The third-party hardware includes systems running those older operating systems from major system vendors such as Compaq, Dell, and IBM, as well as "white box" computers that your local system house or brewer has put together for you.

TABLE 3.1   Windows 2000 Server Hardware Requirements

	Microsoft Minimum	Good Performance
Processors(s)	Pentium 133	Pentium II 233
RAM	64MB	128MB
Hard Drive Space	850MB + 100 MB for each 64 MB of memory installed; more temporary space is required if network or CD-less installation	3GB
Hard Drive System	IDE drive(s)	EIDE, Ultra DMA IDE, SCSI, Ultra Wide SCSI, SCSI III
Display	VGA card and capable monitor	SVGA card to 800×600 and capable monitor
Mouse	Optional	Mouse
CD-ROM	2X speed	12X speed
Floppy	Optional if CD supports booting	3.5" inch floppy
Network	Any card on the HCL (see text)	Any card on the HCL (see text)

The range of hardware supported is very extensive. As a general rule, it is safer to install Windows 2000 Server using common components and name brands, but you might find that compatible hardware such as AMD or Cyrix processors and a wide variety of motherboards will work satisfactorily.

Microsoft has published the Windows 2000 Hardware Compatibility List (HCL) on its Web site, as it has for all its operating systems released over the last four years or so. You will find a copy of the HCL in a text file called HCL.TXT in the Support folder of the Windows 2000 installation disk. The most up-to-date version of the HCL is found at http://www.microsoft.com/hwtest/hcl. We also recommend that you visit *Windows NT Magazine*'s Web site. Posted there is another version of a Windows 2000 compatibility list that lists both hardware and software. That site is http://www.winntmag.com.

> If you call for support on a Windows 2000 Server installation, the first question the Microsoft representative will ask you (after he or she asks for your serial number) is whether your equipment is on the HCL. Microsoft supervises the testing of only those devices that manufacturers provide for compatibility. The failure of a device to appear on the HCL doesn't necessarily mean that the device won't work. But it does mean that Microsoft won't support it, and that Microsoft support might not answer your questions. End of story.

3

Best Performance	Maximum Performance
Pentium III, dual Xeons	Up to four processors with Server; up to eight processors with Windows 2000 Server Advanced Server
256MB	4GB (8GB for Advanced Server)
4GB	> 2TB
Hardware RAID controller	As many RAID controllers as can fit in your machine
SVGA card to 1024×786 and capable monitor	As many video cards as can fit in your machine
Mouse with IntelliWheel support	
>12X speed	
3.5" floppy	
Any card on the HCL (see text)	As many cards as can fit in the slots

A word about testing and the HCL is in order. Although a device shows up on the HCL, there is no way that Microsoft and third-party vendors can test every possible solution. Even if all your equipment is on the Windows 2000 Server compatibility list, you might still encounter some problems. However, your odds of a successful and problem-free installation are greatly increased when you consult the HCL first.

Some First Steps

Assuming that your system meets the requirements for Windows 2000 Server, you should take some preliminary steps to ensure a trouble-free installation. A little preparation beforehand will save you both time and aggravation. Here are some things Microsoft recommends that you do:

- Check the Hardware Compatibility List (HCL), as described in the previous section.
- Read the files READ1ST.TXT and RELNOTES.DOC that come with the installation CD-ROM. Late-breaking information that couldn't be included in the manual and some useful technical information are often included in those files. READ1ST.TXT contains installation notes, and RELNOTES.DOC contains information on the use of hardware, devices, software applications, and printers.
- Back up your files for an upgrade. With your files backed up, you can always restore missing or damaged files later should the upgrade go awry.
- Decompress any DriveSpace or DoubleSpace volumes.
- Turn off disk mirroring. Disk mirroring will fail during formatting operations.
- Disconnect UPS devices because those devices and the software that controls them interfere with your server's reboot process.
- Check with your computer manufacturer to see that you have the latest version of your system's BIOS installed. If a later version exists, consider upgrading the BIOS. If your system has a flash BIOS and can be upgraded (most modern systems can), you will often find the upgrade file on either the computer manufacturer's Web site or on the Web site of the motherboard's manufacturer.
- Assemble a list of the devices in your system: video card, network card, sound board, drive system, and so forth, so that you can identify appropriate drivers if required.
- Investigate whether any applications you want to install on Windows 2000 Server are compatible with that operating system.

An operating system upgrade is often an ideal time to upgrade hardware components at the same time. In considering hardware upgrades, consult the HCL.

One of the nice features that Windows 2000 offers is enhanced Plug and Play capability. Users of Windows 95 and Windows 98 have gotten used to computers that recognize missing devices or new devices and configure them. Now, that capability is found in Windows 2000 Server and Windows 2000 Professional. Plug and Play isn't perfect, but it goes a long way toward making it easier to configure your computer.

The Text-Based Installation Process

To install Windows 2000 on a clean system, simply boot from the first provided installation floppy disk. Setup will prompt you for each of the next three disks (for a total of four), and then continue with "Welcome to Setup" message (see the following).

> If, for some reason, you don't have the four installation boot disks, you can create them from the CD-ROM disc on another computer that can mount the disk (Windows 9x, Windows NT, WfW, or Windows 3.1). Open the Run dialog box from the Run command on the Start menu and enter the following command at the prompt: x:makeboot.bat a: (where x: refers to your CD-ROM's drive letter).

3

Getting Started: Upgrade or Clean Install

Before you install Windows 2000 Server, you need to determine the state of your machine. For a computer with no operating system, you will perform a *clean install* (what was called a *full install* in previous operating systems). If you have some version of Windows already on your computer—Windows 3.1 or Windows for Workgroups 3.11 (WfW), Windows 95, Windows 98, Windows NT 3.5, Windows NT 3.51, or Windows NT 4.0—you will perform what's officially called an *upgrade*.

> There is often some confusion due to terminology involved in installation routines vs. packaging. Microsoft describes an upgrade to an operating system as physically replacing only the files that have changed, and upgrading to newer-version things like the file system. A clean or fresh installation overwrites all files, regardless of their status. (For example, you could conceivably have a newer driver than Windows 2000 offers downloaded from the Internet on your system.) When you go to purchase Windows 2000 Server in a box, you are often offered an upgrade package or a full installation package. The upgrade package costs less, but requires a previous version of the operating system on your hard drive before it will install. A full installation package is just that: It installs on your system regardless of what's there.

The two main differences between a clean install and an upgrade is that when Microsoft sells an upgrade package, it is typically cheaper and comes without boot disks because it is meant to overwrite a previous operating system. When you upgrade your system, Setup imports as many of the current settings as possible, to try to create as seamless a change as possible. In an upgrade, you are not given the option of formatting disks as part of Setup, nor are you walked through the process of setting each of the individual groups of settings. You upgrade your installation into the preexisting installation.

A clean install creates a totally new installation in a new directory or new partition. With a clean install you are given the option of creating a new partition on which to install Windows 2000 Server, or installing it on a previously created partition. In the latter case you overwrite all operating system files and delete the contents of the My Documents folder. All settings and security are lost in either case, and you are starting up with a fresh copy of Windows 2000 Server.

Windows 2000 Server will not automatically upgrade Windows 3.1, Windows for Workgroups 3.11, Windows 95, Windows 98, or Windows NT Workstation 4.0 installations. If you're starting from those operating systems you have two choices: upgrade to Windows 2000 Professional or choose to coexist with the previous operating system using a dual boot configuration. Windows 2000 Server will peacefully coexist with any of the aforementioned operating systems if desired (provided the requirements mentioned earlier are met). Windows 2000 Server will simply detect the current operating system in use and give you a chance to place the new installation in its own directory. When you upgrade a Windows NT installation, you are given a choice but told that the upgrade option is recommended over a clean install.

If you choose to coexist with another operating system in a dual boot, put Windows 2000 Server in its own partition. This is because some directories, such as \Program Files, have the same name in different versions of Windows. This arrangement will also require you to install programs twice, once for each operating system for maximum compatibility.

To initiate an installation, do one of the following:

1. Insert the installation disk into your computer.

   - For an upgrade, insert the CD-ROM disc into your drive, and Setup should appear with the AutoPlay feature turned on. For a previous version of Windows that Setup can upgrade and detect, you will see a dialog box asking whether you would like to do so.

- For a clean install, insert the first disk of the four floppy disks into your floppy disk drive and reboot with that floppy in your machine. After Setup begins it will ask you for the additional disks, install a small version of the operating system and then when it reboots it will ask you for the CD-ROM. The option above is more convenient when you can start with a previous operating system.

2. If Setup doesn't AutoPlay or if you are using the floppy disk, open a command prompt or the Run dialog box from the Run command on the Start menu for previous versions of Windows, and enter the command: X:\Setup, where X: is the label of your CD-ROM drive.

   The dialog box shown in Figure 3.1 appears, and Setup runs as a series of dialog boxes in the form of a wizard.

FIGURE 3.1

The initial installation dialog box enables you to choose between a clean install and an upgrade, depending upon the version of Windows 2000 Server you purchased.

3. Click the Next button to view the ever-popular EULA (End User License Agreement). After you agree to Microsoft's terms, you can proceed with your installation by clicking the Agree radio button and clicking the Next button installation proceeds and you will be asked to key in the product serial number in the next screen.

   If your system has an operating system other than Windows NT, the first screen you will see is a dialog box that tells you that Setup cannot upgrade your system. For a Windows NT or Windows 2000 system, you have the option of upgrading the current system or performing a clean installation. The upgrade option will be grayed out if you tried to install over a Windows 98 installation, for example.

4. Click the Next button to view the Select Special Setup Options step, as shown in Figure 3.2, and click on the button for the options you desire.

   - Language Options—Click this button to set the language you want to use. Languages control keyboard layout, sort orders, number and date formats, and other features controlled by the operating system.

- Advanced Options—Click this button and the dialog box shown in Figure 3.3 appears. Here you specify a different installation directory name, and you have the ability to choose which partition you want Windows 2000 Server to be placed in. If you do not select the "I Want to Choose the Installation Partition During Setup" check box, Windows 2000 Server will be installed in the active partition.

FIGURE 3.2

Here you can select language used, location of files, and accessibility options.

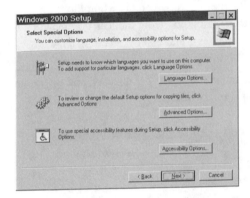

If you are installing Windows 2000 on a computer containing another operating system that you wish to preserve, turn the "I want to choose the installation partition during Setup" option on so that you can choose a different partition than the other operating system during a clean installation.

Also notice the Copy all Setup files from the Setup CD to the Hard Drive check box. When this box is checked, the CD (or network share) need not be available for the duration of the installation. If you have the available time and hard drive space, this option is recommended. It provides a source for files on your hard drive should the CD-ROM disk be unavailable.

- Accessibility Options—This button opens a dialog box that enables you to install special accessories to make your computer more usable by people with disabilities. The accessories include the Magnifier for screen magnification and the Narrator, which reads the contents of the screen for blind users.

5. In the Directory of Applications for Windows 2000 screen that appears next, Microsoft offers you the option of linking to their Web site and obtaining the latest compatibility information for the applications that you might run on Windows 2000. Click the Directory of Applications button to make a connection to the Internet or use your current connection to view this information.

6. Click the Next button and follow the instructions of the Setup program.

   Setup begins by copying over a set of installation files and posts a progress dialog box. At the end of the initial phase of the installation, Setup will ask you to restart your computer. At this point, a minimal bootable copy of the operating system is on your computer.

7. Click the Finish button.

FIGURE 3.3

Use this optional dialog box to specify the location of the installed operating system, and whether all files are copied to disk for future use.

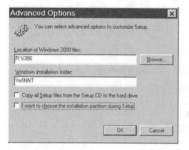

The Text-Based Portion of Setup

WINNT32.EXE, in the i386 directory, is the main Setup program when you run in a 32-bit environment (that is, Windows 9x, Windows NT, and even Windows 2000). WINNT32.EXE guides you through a graphical installation that starts after an initial command-line phase in which you partition your disks and format them, described in the next section.

When the machine reboots, you will see a boot menu in which one of the options listed is Microsoft Windows 2000 Server Setup. Depending on your setup, you might see additional options such as Microsoft Windows and Windows NT Server. When you choose Microsoft Windows 2000 Server Setup, a DOS mode (non-graphical) phase is entered.

From the time you boot into the text phase until you restart your computer and Setup enters the graphical wizard phase, here is the order of the steps you encounter:

1. Setup is loaded into memory.

2. The text portion of Setup begins.

3. Create the installation partition for Windows 2000 (described in the next section).

4. Format your installation partition (also in the next section).

5. Copy the Setup files for devices, networking, and components.

6. Reboot into the graphical phase.

If you are doing an upgrade, you do not see the disk formatting steps described in the next section. Instead, all the necessary device, network, and component files are copied to your disk and configured for you using your previous settings. You reboot one more time into the installed Windows 2000 Server operating system and see the Configure Your Server applet appear, as shown in Figure 3.4. A brief description of this wizard is contained in the section "Configure Your Server" later in this hour.

FIGURE 3.4

At the end of an installation of Windows 2000 Server, the Configure Your Server applet opens up to enable you to perform various tasks. This applet can be opened from the Administrative Tools folder on the Programs menu of the Start menu at a later time.

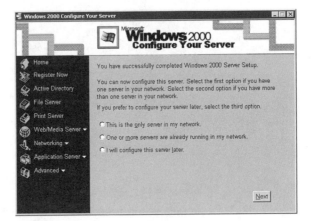

Disk Formatting

For a clean install, when you have finished copying the necessary Setup startup files and after you reboot your computer, you are in a text-based portion of the Setup program. Setup launches this portion of the program automatically after it reboots.

If you are doing a clean install over a previous version of Windows 2000, Setup will offer to repair the installation rather than install a fresh copy. Press R to repair the installation, or ESC to continue with your fresh install. The fresh install enables you to format disks and create new partitions.

Windows 2000 will then try to load your disk drivers and begin to prepare your hard drive or RAID system for installation of the Windows 2000 operating system. If you watch closely, you are prompted to hit the F6 key if you want to load additional RAID controller drivers. For many installations, this is not necessary because Windows 2000 Server comes preconfigured with many popular RAID controller drivers. Additionally, some manufacturers use this F6 option, but some do not. If your hardware manufacturer has a Windows 2000 Server RAID driver that is not included in the Windows 2000 Server distribution files, follow your manufacturer's installation instructions.

The use of the F6 key has become something of an industry tradition. F6 is widely used for custom hardware devices when they are not compatible with the driver supplied by default in Windows 2000. An example of this would be if you had an embedded Adaptec 2940 controller in the mother- board. It very often does not work with the driver supplied with Windows for the Adaptec 2940 and you have to obtain the system manufacturer's spe- cialized driver for that particular type and load it at that point.

First, Setup determines your existing configuration to see what partitions exist, and what free space is available. If you have an existing partition, you can install Windows 2000 into that partition without reformatting it. You can also create a new partition from Setup to install Windows 2000 on, or to use as an additional logical volume. Setup will then run CHKDSK on your drive either for an exhaustive examination or for a sector integrity evaluation before performing any formatting operation.

After a few moments, you'll be greeted with the message "Welcome to Setup." After click- ing the Enter button, you will be presented with a list of available disks and partitions. At this point, you have the following three options for installing Windows 2000 Server:

- To create a new partition on your hard drive from free space of the size into which you specify to install Windows 2000
- To create a new partition from an unpartitioned drive into which you install Windows 2000 Server
- To install Windows 2000 into an existing partition that contains the required amount of disk space

During an installation, Setup will overwrite existing data on the volume, deleting an existing partition to either add it to other free space or using part of the free space to cre- ate a volume into which Windows 2000 Server is installed.

Although Setup gives you the option of creating additional partitions during installation, there is no need to do so. The Disk Management administration tool makes this both easy and convenient to do after installation is complete.

To work with disks and partitions during Setup:

- Highlight a partition and press the Enter key—This will install Windows 2000 Server on the highlighted partition.
- Highlight a partition and press D—This deletes the current partition after you press the L key to confirm that this is what you do. Deleting a partition turns it into free space so that you can use the space to create another partition.

3

Obligatory caution: When you delete a partition, that partition is no longer
available. The information on that partition will be destroyed and you will
not be able to restore it.

- Highlight an area of free space and press the C key. If there is available free space
  on the partition, this will enable you to create a new partition of any size you want.
  When you've done so, rehighlight the partition and click the Enter button to install
  Windows 2000 Server on that partition.

If you are installing Windows 2000 Server over a previous installation of the same operating system, Setup will not allow you to delete an NTFS partition that the system was
installed on. You are given the option to delete the files in the folder \WINNT and to proceed with a clean installation. You can also create another partition and install the clean
version to that new partition.

After you select a partition to install Windows 2000 Server to, you'll be asked what file
system you would like to have on the partition. The options vary depending on what you
have already installed. If you have FAT, FAT32, or NTFS, you are asked whether you
want to format the partition in NTFS (version 5), format the partition in FAT, convert the
partition to NTFS (version 5), or leave the file system intact.

You won't be asked to decide on a partition file system if the partition
already has NTFS 5.

You might want to read Hour 11, "Volumes and Disks," and Hour 13, "Shares and Dfs," to
learn more about the implications of choosing one volume type or file system over another.
To summarize briefly your options, you can create the three following file systems:

- FAT—Use FAT when you want to create a dual boot on a server between Windows
  2000 Server and another operating system, such as Windows 95/98, DOS, UNIX,
  or OS/2. Use FAT when you have downlevel clients, such as DOS, that cannot read
  long filenames. You cannot install FAT on a volume larger than 2GB. FAT does not
  offer file-level security.
- FAT32—Use FAT32 when you want to use downlevel Windows 98 or Windows 95
  OSR-2 clients that can read long filenames, and you want to avail yourself of the
  better block sizes that FAT32 offers. FAT32 supports disks larger than 2GB. FAT32
  does not offer file level-security.

- NTFS—Whenever possible, try to use NTFS as your file system. NTFS offers file- and folder-level security, improved disk compression, file encryption, and disk quotas as part of the Zero Administration for Windows initiative or ZAW (see Hour 20, "Client Services, IntelliMirror, and ZAW"). Disk quotas enable you to control how much disk space is allocated to each user on an NTFS volume.

> If you plan to make your Windows 2000 Server a domain controller, the partition you install the operating system into must be formatted as an NTFS partition.

If you choose to format the partition, Windows 2000 Server does so. Afterward, it does a check on all drives to make sure there are no damaged sectors. Depending on how large your drives are and how many drives you have, this can take quite a bit of time. Windows 2000 then copies the remainder of the files it needs to the new partition. Lastly, your computer is rebooted to start the rest of the installation process in graphical mode, which is Setup in the form of a wizard.

3

The Graphical Installation Process

When you reboot for the second time, you enter the third and last phase of the installation in which the Setup wizard guides you through a number of settings your computer needs to customize your working environment.

Entering General Settings

The first set of screens captures information that is entered into your operating system through various Control Panel applets. You can think of this portion of Setup as akin to the process of opening the Control Panel folder applets one-by-one and entering all of the essential settings, such as your language, keyboard layout, and so forth.

The Windows 2000 Server Setup Wizard leads you through the following settings:

1. Regional Settings—Here you select the system or locale settings and the keyboard layout.

2. Personalize Your Software—In this step, you enter the name and organization to whom the software is registered. These names are used in application installations as the suggested default names during their setup programs.

3. Licensing Mode—Windows 2000 Server requires both server and client licenses, but offers you two different licensing schemes. See the section "What Are the Windows 2000 Licensing Models" later in this hour for more detailed information.

4. Computer Name and Administrator Password—You name your computer with a name by which it is recognized on the network. This name is used in Network Neighborhood to identify the computer, as its NetBIOS name in the domain's browse list, and for the name of the machine account in the Active Directory. Setup will suggest a name, but it is mighty unfriendly. So pick a name that is meaningful to you. A name can be up to 63 characters in length, but only the first 15 letters are used for downlevel (pre–Windows 2000) computers. It is recommended that you use standard Internet names that DNS can recognize.

> To make use of many of the future examples in this book, you will need a total of three machines to load Windows 2000 Server on, a machine on which you can load Windows 2000 Professional to get the Windows 2000 client's perspective, and a Windows 95 machine to see a "downlevel" client's perspective.
>
> The first server you load should be named W2kserver1. If that is the only machine you have access to, you will still be able to perform most of the book's examples.
>
> If you can spare additional hardware for a second server loaded with Windows 2000 server, that machine should be named AZDC1. AZDC1 is referred to many places in the book.
>
> If you can spare even more hardware for a third server, you should name it AZSERV1.

5. Password for Administrative Account—On the same Computer Name and Administrative Password screen, you are prompted to enter an administrator password that enables you to administer the particular server on which you are installing software. A password can be up to 14 characters, and it is recommended that you mix letters, numbers, and symbols to make the password harder to hack.

6. Components—On the Windows 2000 Components screen, you are offered the option of installing a number of different components. The components are described in more detail following this list.

7. Date and Time—The Date and Time Settings screen enables you to enter date, time, and time zone information. You can adjust this later in the Date and Time applet in Control Panel.

8. Display Settings—Here you enter the display settings you choose: screen resolution, number of colors, and the refresh frequency. You can adjust these settings in the Display Control Panel applet.

9. Your Area or Location Properties—If Setup detects a modem attached to your server the wizard will prompt you for these system settings.

10. Terminal Services Setup—If you choose to install Terminal Services this screen offers you two options for Remote Administration mode or Application server mode. The first mode lets a limited number of administrators remotely manage the server and minimizes impact on server performance. The second mode lets users remotely run one or more applications and optimizes program response time. You must set up Terminal Services Licensing within 90 days to use the Application Server mode.

11. You then enter the networking portion of the installation.

> There is some variation in the number of steps and their order in the Windows 2000 Server Setup wizard depending upon the options you chose and the hardware you have installed on your computer.

3

For the optional component step of the wizard (step 6), the total number of components that you can install here requires 80.4MB. They are of the following type, and the dialog box offers these descriptions of the optional components:

- Certificate Services—Installs a certificate authority (CA) to issue certificates for use with public key security applications. This enables you to use X.509 digital certificates for network and internetworking authentication.

- Internet Information Services (IIS – Web server)—IIS services (Web and FTP support), along with support for FrontPage, transactions, ASPs, database connections, and receiving of posts.

- Management and Monitoring Tools—Includes tools for monitoring and improving network performance. Hour 21, "Performance Monitoring and Diagnostics," describes many of the performance and network monitoring tools.

- Message Queue Services—Message Queuing provides loosely coupled and reliable network communication services. MSMQ is a routing server or client that enables you to provide transaction support so that your programs can use Microsoft Transaction Server (MTS) to forward transactions asynchronously (at a later time without client and server being connected).

- Microsoft Indexing Services—Enables fast full-text searches of files.

- Microsoft Script Debugger—Tool for client- and server-side debugging of ActiveX script engines, such as VBScript and JScript. (See Hour 22, "Programming Tools.")

- Networking Services—Contains a variety of specialized, network-related services and protocols. Networking Services is one of the most important sets of components because it enables you to install Dynamic Host Configuration Protocol (DHCP) services, the Domain Naming Service (DNS), the Transmission Control Protocol/Internet Protocol (TCP/IP) (the networking protocol of the Internet),

TCP/IP print services, file services, and other components such as the COM Internet Services Proxy (for enabling DCOM over HTTP), QoS Admission Control Service, Site Server ILS Services, and Internet Authentication Service.

- Other File and Print Services—Shares files and printers on this computer with others on the network. Hour 13 describes some of the optional file and print services that are security enabled. Hour 19, "Printing," describes Windows printing.

- Remote Installation Services—Provides the ability to remotely install Windows 2000 Professional on remote boot enabled client computers. This feature is covered in Hour 20.

- Remote Storage—A set of services and administrative tools that you can use to store data from infrequently used files on magnetic tape. This is also called *hierarchical network storage*. These tape libraries, in essence, become an extension of your NTFS file system.

- Terminal Services—Provides a multisession environment for clients to access Windows-based programs on this computer. Windows Terminal Services are covered in Hour 18, "Windows Terminal Services."

- Terminal Services Licensing—Configures this computer as a Terminal Services license server that provides client licenses.

- Transaction Server—The Microsoft Transaction Server enables you to create a store-and-forward, three-tier architecture. MTS manages transactions so that they are successfully completed from client to server (and vice versa) or rolls back the transaction if it is uncompleted. This option installs the MTS Transaction Manager utility. This option is only available for Advanced Server and Datacenter Server.

> If you intend to follow along with the examples presented in this book, install all the optional Windows 2000 components you can.

If you don't install a particular component or set of components, you can add it later using the Add/Remove Programs applet in the Control Panel folder. The Add/Remove Windows Component option of this applet enables you to specify additional components to install. Unless you chose the option to install all the CD-ROM files to disk, you must provide the installation disk in order to add additional components.

Network Components

After you have specified your desired settings, Setup enters the networking components phase of the installation. This phase has the following steps:

1. Detect your networking card(s) or manually assign a driver to a networking card.

2. Select networking components.

3. Join a workgroup or domain (described in the next section).

4. Install the networking components.

5. Complete the setup, reboot, and display the Configure Your Server applet.

Windows 2000 might have trouble detecting your network card. In our initial installation, the Netgear FA310FX Fast Ethernet card wasn't detected during setup, although that card's driver was included on the installation disk and worked fine in our tests. For a network card that doesn't have a driver, you must supply the driver obtained from the manufacturer.

You will more often run into problems when a system has two or more network cards. There are many instances in which you would want to have two network cards in a server. A simple example is when you use the server as a proxy server; one card communicates with the internal LAN, and the second card communicates with the Internet. This arrangement enables you to configure the system so that you have protocol isolation.

To make a two (or more)–network card installation work, try removing all but one of the cards and adding additional cards after Windows 2000 is fully installed and operational. You might find that having network cards from different vendors creates a conflict as they both try to capture the same IRQ or base I/O memory setting. Then again, you might find that two identical cards from the same vendor gives the same problem. The only way to determine this is to attempt the installation. You can also try to reassign IRQ and I/O addresses before Setup to resolve these conflicts.

Plug and Play is supposed to resolve these situations, but often it gets confused with multiple devices of the same kind (for example, multiple NICs). Plug and Pray.

Setup now copies more files to your hard drive and then shows a screen called Networking Settings. This screen offers you the following two radio button choices with these explanations:

- Typical settings—Creates network connections using the Client for Microsoft Networks, File and Print Sharing for Microsoft Networks, and the TCP/IP transport protocol with automatic addressing.

- Custom settings—This option allows you to manually configure networking components. Choosing this option opens a dialog box that enables you to select networking options.

If you select the Custom settings option, you come to a screen that enables you to deselect Clients for Microsoft Networking, File and Print Sharing for Microsoft Networking, and Internet Protocol (TCP/IP). You can also set the properties for these components. Unless you have a reason to do so, it is best to use the Typical Settings installation and adjust the technical settings or properties of these components later.

3

> If you would like to emulate the examples in the book for training purposes, you can choose to maintain the same IP addresses we use in the book.
>
> If you are installing the first server, W2kserver1, you should set the IP address to 200.100.100.10 and the Subnet Mask should be set to 255.255.0.0. Again, if this is the only machine you are able to use, you will make use of most of the hands-on examples in this book.
>
> If you are installing the second server, AZDC1, you should set the IP address to 200.100.200.10 and the Subnet Mask should be set to 255.255.0.0. If you are able to acquire a second machine to make a server, you will be able to perform about 90% of the book's examples.
>
> If you are installing the third server, AZSERV1, you should set the IP address to 200.100.200.11 and the Subnet Mask should be set to 255.255.0.0. If you are able to acquire a third machine, you will be able to perform all of the server-side examples in the book.

There are many other networking components that you can install, including clients, services, and protocols. These include, but are not limited to, NetBIOS Enhanced User Interface (NetBEUI), AppleTalk, and NWLink IPX/SPX/NetBIOS-compatible transport. They can be installed as part of the Custom settings option, or later through the Add/Remove Program Control Panel applet's Add/Remove Windows Components option. In Hour 15, "Protocols and Networking Fundamentals," we walk through how to install an alternative protocol.

Joining a Workgroup or Domain

Setup proceeds to the step called Workgroup or Computer Domain in which you are prompted to join a workgroup or an existing domain. You can also select the option that this server is not on a network or will be a standalone server not connected to a workgroup or domain.

You can enter the name of an existing workgroup or domain to become a member. In the case of a workgroup, a unique name will create a new workgroup, or the name of an existing workgroup can be entered to join that workgroup. To join a domain, an existing domain must already be established.

Joining a domain requires

- The domain name in Domain Name System (DNS) form—A typical domain name is KILLERAPPS.COM.
- A computer or machine account in the existing domain—You are given the option of automatically creating a machine account during this step of the installation, and you will be prompted to enter a username and password so that the domain can check that you have administrative rights. Or, anyone logged into the network as an administrator can create one for you prior to your installation.

Without a machine account, you will not be able to join the domain.

- An operational domain controller and a DNS server (which can be one and the same) to check your credentials and create the machine account in the security database.

> If you are installing your first server, W2kserver1, or your second server, AZDC1, there will not be a Windows 2000 domain available. For now, you may join the fictitious workgroup called CORPGROUP.
>
> If you are installing your third server, AZSERV1, have it join the fictitious workgroup called AZWORKGRP.

A workgroup differs from a domain in that it is a peer-to-peer arrangement, and the security database is stored locally on each computer. There is no central server in a workgroup, and any desktop, workstation, or server can provide network services, application services, or access to network resources to the workgroup. Windows 3.x, Windows for Workgroups, Windows 9x, Windows NT, and Windows 2000 computers can participate in a workgroup. When a computer providing a service to a workgroup becomes unavailable, that service is no longer accessible.

3

> You are installing your machines in a workgroup because there is currently no Windows 2000 domain available to service your request. When you perform the "Your First Windows 2000 Server Domain Controller" step in Day 6 you will have created your first domain.

In a domain model, the security database is a single database that may be replicated for both fault tolerance and load balancing. The security database is stored on domain controllers, and all the computers in the domain share a common security policy. A login gives you access to all the shared resources of the domain, based on your privileges.

The default workgroup or computer domain name is *Domain*. Remember to change this name to point to an existing domain or workgroup, or use a new name to create a new name or workgroup, if desired. When you click the Next button, Setup posts a dialog box called *Join Computer* to "Name" Domain (or Workgroup). You must enter a username and password for someone with administrative privileges to add your Windows 2000 Server to a domain or workgroup. When you click the OK button, the Windows 2000 Server will browse the network looking for the domain or workgroup, and check to see whether that administrator exists. This process can take some time.

> When you install Windows 2000 Server to a domain that doesn't use DHCP, but uses static IP addressing instead, that new server will *not* find the domain.

DHCP is a feature of domains and not of workgroups. In order to join a domain of that type, you must use the Custom settings option of the Network Settings step, and enter the IP address and subnet address into the TCP/IP protocol.

It gets even hairier: When you install the first Windows 2000 Server on a network and install DHCP, that service is not turned on by default. This is to prevent additional rogue DHCP servers from being installed on the network and providing clients with an unauthorized way of getting a valid network address. You must turn on DHCP services on your Windows 2000 Server in order to enable clients to automatically get a valid network address. This is a common installation gotcha.

To see how to turn on DHCP services, see Day 16, "DNS, WINS, and DHCP."

Completing a Clean Installation

Completing the Workgroup or Domain step in the Setup program essentially completes the operations you must do in order to install Windows 2000 Server. The following steps are then observed:

1. Setup copies various files to your hard drive. This step can take a fair bit of time, depending upon your system.

2. Setup configures your computer.

3. The configuration is saved.

4. Temporary files are deleted from disk.

5. The computer is rebooted for the final time.

6. You log in and the Configure Your Server applet appears.

If you install DHCP Services and Windows Terminal Services, you will get an error message to check the Event Viewer when you first boot the server. These services must be turned on, and the error relates to them being installed but not activated. You should activate those services if desired, or remove them from your server by using the Add/Remove Programs Control Panel applet's Add/Remove Windows Components option.

Additionally, the following services require that you configure them prior to use in the Add/Remove Program applet: Certificate Services, Message Queuing Services, and Remote Installation Services.

The Configure Your Server Wizard

Once you see the Configure Your Server wizard appear (see Figure 3.1) you are in the home stretch of the installation. You are offered three options to help you get started working with Windows 2000 Server. They are

- This is the only server in my network.
- One or more servers are already running on my network.
- I will configure this server later.

You want to choose the first setting for the initial domain controller on your network. When a domain controller already exists, choose the second option to create a standalone server; if a domain controller already exists the first option creates another domain controller (which isn't necessarily a bad thing). You can also skip the basic network configuration steps of the wizard and perform these steps later. Typically, application servers are standalone servers so that performance is not impacted by the authorization tasks that domain controllers perform.

In this book, you will be returning many times to the Configure Your Server wizard as an entry to many of the tasks you need to perform. Although it's covered in later days, it's a good idea to turn on DHCP immediately if your server will perform that function—otherwise clients that rely on this server for IP addresses will fail to see the server or connect properly. You also use the Configure Your Server wizard to set up DNS (Domain Naming Services) so that computers can locate other computers based on their domain name and not their IP address, as well as set up Active Directory.

As an example, clicking the "This is the only server in my network" option leads you to a screen that lets you name your domain and enter the name of the domain as registered on the Internet. This screen is shown in Figure 3.5. When you proceed to the Next step, Windows 2000 Server tells you that it will make these assignments and reboot your server. The process takes a few minutes and returns you to the Configure Your Server wizard after you log in.

The net effect of using the Configure Your Server wizard is to run DCPROMO, Windows 2000's utility for creating domain controllers or standalone servers, or switching between the two. Because the implication of this choice is fundamental in determining your network operating system architecture, this book devotes Day 6 to the topic. You might want to delay using the wizard until you read that chapter. But for now, if you are in a hurry to get Windows 2000 Server up and running, you can use this wizard to perform this procedure.

FIGURE 3.5

Naming your server domain.

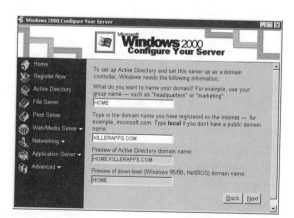

How to Upgrade from Windows NT

You can install Windows 2000 Server on a system from any other operating system that supports your CD-ROM drive. If a system doesn't support your CD-ROM drive, start the installation from the Setup floppies and perform a clean install. For example, you can start the installation on an MS-DOS or Windows 3.1 system by running the WINNT.EXE program either from the command prompt, or in the latter case, from the File Manager. For information about WINNT.EXE or WINNT32.EXE, enter winnt /? at the command prompt. It is recommended that you enable disk caching with Smart Drive for an MS-DOS or Windows 3.1 system for faster execution.

When you talk about upgrading a system, you are really talking about installing Windows 2000 Server over an installation of Windows NT 3.51, Windows 4.0, or Windows 4.0 Terminal Server where some of the settings may be maintained. You have already seen that upgrading a Windows NT Server 4 installation is both easier and faster than the clean install option because Windows 2000 Server Setup will not format your disk and retains most of your previous settings. There are many fewer steps in an upgrade, and the process takes roughly 35% of the time that a full installation does.

Be aware that when you convert Windows NT Server 4.0 to Windows 2000 Server the Setup program will automatically upgrade any NTFS volume from NTFS 4 to NTFS 5 with no questions asked. This upgrade is necessary to install Windows 2000 Server.

 To maintain a dual-boot configuration with NT 4.0, be sure your NT installation has Service Pack 4 or higher on it. This is because the drivers necessary for NTFS 5 are only available in the service pack. See the following dual-boot section for more details.

When you upgrade, you can potentially save the following:

- Users and groups (for a domain controller)
- Rights and permissions
- Various settings
- Applications
- Files

You might find that you need to reinstall some applications or upgrade those applications with new versions, but many applications will work properly with Windows 2000 Server when you upgrade from Windows NT Server 4.0. It is always a good idea to back up your server before you upgrade.

> If you are running Windows NT 4.0 Enterprise Edition, you cannot upgrade
> to Windows 2000 Server; you can only upgrade that operating system to
> Windows 2000 Advanced Server.

One thing you should do prior to an upgrade is run the /CHECKUPGRADEONLY
switch for the WINNT32.EXE program on the Windows 2000 Server Setup disk to see
whether your current system is compatible with the upgrade. This switch checks your
system for compatibility and creates a report named UPGRADE.TXT for Windows 9x
systems; for Windows NT 3.51 and 4.0 systems, the report is saved in the
WINNT32.LOG file in the Windows installation folder.

To run this check, enter the following at a command prompt:

```
winnt32.exe /checkupgradeonly
```

> The WINNT32.EXE program has several switches that control the operation
> of Setup that you might find useful. These switches are detailed in the
> online help topic WINNT32. They include writing temporary files to a drive
> of your choosing, unattended or scripted installations using an answer file,
> automatic recovery options, special driver file folders, and others.

When you perform an upgrade, you copy over the Windows NT Server 4.0 files in the
\WINNT directory and add the Windows 2000 Server files. When you reboot after all the
files are copied to your hard drive, you see the Configure Your Server applet. You do not
see the disk formatting options or settings options of the Setup wizard.

When you upgrade a Windows NT Server that is a domain controller, you are faced with
the decision of having to upgrade your domain. Should you decide to upgrade your
domain controller, you must convert the installation partition to NTFS in order to enforce
the security that the domain controller requires. Use the CONVERT.EXE program to perform this file system conversion.

If you have multiple domain controllers and you decide to upgrade them and implement
Windows 2000 Server, you must first upgrade the Windows NT Server 4.0 primary
domain controller (PDC) before upgrading the backup domain controllers (BDC).
Additionally, you should first upgrade your master account domains before your resource
domains. These topics are discussed in great detail in Hour 7, "Advanced Planning for
Domains, Domain Controllers, and the Active Directory."

Because Windows 2000 domains do not differentiate between PDCs and BDCs, the
following conversions are possible:

- A Windows NT PDC can only become a Windows 2000 domain controller.
- A Windows NT BDC can be converted to a Windows 2000 domain controller or a member server.
- A Windows NT member server can be converted to a Windows 2000 member server or a standalone server.
- A Windows NT standalone sever can be converted to a member server (for a Windows 2000 domain) or a standalone server.

You might want to review Hour 6, "Domains and the Active Directory," Hour 7, and Hour 8, "Server Types, Local Users, and Groups" before you begin to upgrade your domain into the Windows 2000 domain structure.

Installing a Dual Boot Configuration

You might want to use a server so that you have the choice between booting to the Windows 2000 operating system at startup or booting another operating system by using a menu that appears in the boot sequence. This is referred to as a *dual boot arrangement*. Windows 2000 supports this configuration, enabling you switch to Windows NT Server 4.0, Windows 9x, UNIX, or any other operating system compatible with your microprocessor.

In order to protect Windows 2000 Server files, it is recommended that you install this operating system on its own partition. Should you install another operating system or applications on top of a Windows 2000 Server partition, you could potentially overwrite files that Windows 2000 requires.

When you use Windows 95 or MS-DOS as the secondary operating system, you must have a partition formatted as a FAT volume. With Windows 95 OSR2 or Windows 98, you have the choice of using either FAT or FAT32. If you have these volumes compressed with either DriveSpace or DoubleSpace, you are not required to uncompress them for a dual boot, but they will not be available to you when you run the Windows 2000 operating system. The interactions between different file systems can be quite complex. For example, Windows 2000's NTFS file system contains file attributes that make its files unreadable by other operating systems. Consult the topic "Dual Booting and File System Compatibility" in the online help system for more information.

When you want to dual boot between Windows 95 and MS-DOS and Windows 2000, it is recommended that that you install Windows 2000 Server after those other operating systems. You can install Windows 98 and Windows 2000 Server in any order. If you install Windows 95 or Windows 98 after a Windows 2000 installation, you will almost surely overwrite the Windows 2000 boot sector and require a boot sector repair.

You can dual boot between Windows NT and Windows 2000 Server, although you might not want to do so, to save on disk space. It is recommended that you install each operating system into a different partition, and that you not use NTFS as the sole file system. Use Service Pack 4 or greater to upgrade Windows NT prior to creating the dual boot with Windows 2000 Server. Upgrading to Service Pack 4 ensures your NT installation can read the newly converted NTFS version 5 partitions. You should ensure each application is installed on separate partitions under each operating system, NT 4.0 and 2000. For situations in which each server is a member of the same domain, give each operating system a unique machine name during installation.

Many of the same recommendations that apply to dual booting between Windows NT and Windows 2000 Server also apply to dual booting between Windows 2000 Server and other members of the Windows 2000 operating system. You must use a different machine name in this instance; you should consider installing both systems to different partitions; and you should install applications once for each operating system into those different partitions for the best results.

3

How to Install Windows Terminal Services

If you select the option to install Windows Terminal Services (WTS) and its licensing component as part of the Windows 2000 Components step in the Setup program, you have done most of the hard work involved in installing Windows Terminal Services. You can also install this component at a later date by opening the Add/Remove Programs Control Panel applet and exercising the Add/Remove Windows Component option. That applet launches a wizard that leads you through the installation of the server component.

WTS is one of those services, like DHCP, that has to be turned on (registered with the Active Directory) manually to be active. When it is activated, you can configure it to start automatically whenever Windows 2000 Server boots. WTS consumes system resources, so you shouldn't run WTS on a domain server because it will support fewer clients. You shouldn't run WTS on a server unless you intend to support Windows-based terminals (WBTs) or clients running terminal sessions. Hour 18 describes in great detail the installation and configuration of both the server and client components of this service.

What Are the Windows 2000 Licensing Models

Setup asks you to make some decisions about licensing before it proceeds to complete the installation. Although the choices required are actually simple to respond to, the underlying issues of Microsoft's licensing model, what program you use to obtain your licenses, and the licensing scheme for Windows 2000 and Windows NT networks deserve some thought, and you should review your decisions over time. This is particularly true in medium- and large-sized enterprises.

Windows 2000 uses a client/server model for its licensing scheme. When you purchase
the server package, there are often some client access licenses (CALs) included in the
purchase. You can also purchase separate CALs as the need arises. Although Windows
2000 Server doesn't strictly enforce licensing, there is a license server that will assess
your current licenses and tell you whether you meet the requirements.

To view or modify your current licenses

1. Open the Control Panel folder and double-click the Licensing applet icon.

   The Licensing Control Panel applet appears, as shown in Figure 3.6.

FIGURE 3.6

*The Licensing applet is
where you add and
remove licenses and
change your licensing
scheme.*

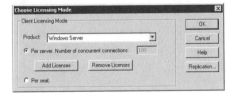

2. To add or remove licenses from your server, click the Add Licenses or Remove
   Licenses button, and enter the new number of connections in the New Client
   Access Licenses dialog box shown in Figure 3.7.

FIGURE 3.7

*The New Client Access
License dialog box is
where you add new
CALs for your server.*

You will be asked to respond to a dialog box that asks you whether you actually
purchased these new licenses before proceeding.

3. To switch from a Per Seat to a Per Server licensing scheme, click the Per Server
   radio button and then click the OK button in the warning dialog box.

   Windows 2000 Server posts a dialog box that tells you that this is a one-way, one-
   time-only conversion.

4. Click the OK button in the Licensing applet to enforce your new licenses.

There are two basic modes for licensing:

- Per Seat License—Here you buy a connection license for a client that lets that
  client connect to any server. This license is best used in large enterprises where
  clients connect to more than one server.

- Per Server License—Each concurrent connection to a particular server requires a CAL. In this model, if you have 100 desktops and only 25 of them require access at a particular time, you could purchase 25 CALs to satisfy the licensing requirements. Per server licensing is best used in a small enterprise where clients typically connect to one Windows 2000 Server.

The Per Server licensing model is also preferred for remote access servers and for access to a server over the Internet. With the Per Server licensing scheme, you are licensed for that number of concurrent connections and logons. Given that it is very hard to predict the number of concurrent access connections to a Web server or anticipate loading, Microsoft will undoubtedly offer a new licensing model for Internet access in the future. This is one area that deserves watching.

During installation, you will be asked to choose between these two models, and to enter the number of CALs. If you are in a medium-sized enterprise and aren't sure which model to adopt, choose the Per Server scheme. Microsoft offers a one-time-only, no-cost conversion from the Per Server to Per Seat licensing model. You cannot convert from the Per Seat to the Per Server model. To change from Per Server to Per Seat, open the Licensing applet in the Control Panel and perform this conversion.

The licenses you buy for Windows 2000 Server access give your clients the right to use file and print services, network services, access printers and shared disks or folders. Some other Windows 2000 Services do not require additional licenses, they include

- Access to Microsoft Internet Information Server any Web server using the Hypertext Transfer Protocol (HTTP)
- File Transfer Protocol (FTP) data transfer

Keep in mind that if you install additional applications to Windows 2000 Server, those applications might require that you purchase server and client licenses of their own. For example, BackOffice components, such as SQL Server and Exchange, require additional client and server licenses. Check with the application vendor to determine their licensing requirements.

Summary

Windows 2000 Server's installation is much easier than previous versions of the Windows NT operating system and requires fewer reboots—although the installation will take you an hour or more to perform depending upon the nature of your server and how familiar you are with all of the options offered. A wizard that makes the process very easy to manage drives the installation. You have a few different options in how you install Windows 2000 Server on your system. You can upgrade a Windows NT or a Windows 2000 partition and retain the settings it contains, or you can upgrade your installation, format a new installation partition, and install Windows 2000 Server using the clean install option. You can use Windows 2000 Server to install Windows 2000 Professional workstations over the network.

Windows 2000 Server enables you to create three different file systems during the installation: FAT, FAT32, and NTFS. NTFS offers you security, encryption, and compression features, whereas FAT and FAT32 offer you the ability to dual boot between Windows 2000 and other operating systems as well as let a broader range of clients access the Windows 2000 volumes.

You need both server and client access licenses to make your network "street legal." Microsoft offers both a Per Server and Per Seat client connection model. The Per Server model is appropriate to larger enterprises, and enables you to buy licenses for concurrent connections. The Per Seat model, appropriate to smaller enterprises, is for a single client connection to a single server. Applications you install over Windows 2000 Server might require their own additional server and client licenses.

Workshop

The workshop provides a quiz and exercises to help reinforce your learning. Even if you feel you know the material, you will still gain from working these exercises.

Quiz

1. What operating systems can Setup perform a full upgrade over instead of a clean install?
2. What is the HCL?
3. What are the floppy disks that come with Windows 2000 Server for?
4. What choices do I have for a file system during Setup?
5. I've installed DHCP during installation, but for some reason it doesn't seem to work. What's wrong?
6. During installation I can't seem to find the domain, although I know it exists and my network connections are good. What could explain that?
7. What is saved during an upgrade?
8. What is the actual program file that I use for Setup?
9. How do I install Windows Terminal Services?
10. What are the licensing requirements for Windows 2000 Server?

Exercises

1. Create a set of installation diskettes.
2. Create a share on one of your network computers and copy all the installation files from the CD-ROM to that share. Connect to that share from a machine to which you want to install Windows 2000 Server, and do a network installation.
3. Use the switches that WINNT32.EXE provides to perform an unattended installation.

HOUR 4

Using the Windows 2000 Interface

By Jeremy Moskowitz

In this lesson, we'll be discussing some Windows 2000 interface basics with an emphasis on the features that server users need to get their job done. Additionally, we'll be talking about the new Microsoft Management Console, or MMC. The MMC also has an Explorer-style interface that we will use as our gateway to many other tools.

In this hour, you will learn how to do the following:

- Use the Start menu and taskbar to launch programs and manage documents
- Recognize elements of the desktop interface
- Work with items on the desktop
- Use the Windows 2000 Explorer to manage files and set options
- Open and work with administrative tools in the Microsoft Management Console

The Windows 2000 Desktop

After Windows 2000 Server is installed, several icons are loaded on the Explorer desktop automatically. The desktop is really a visual display of the files in two specific directories: the All Users Desktop directory and the Desktop directory of the currently logged on user. Both of these directories are found in the Profiles directory in <root drive>\DOCUMENTS AND SETTINGS\%USERNAME%\DESKTOP.

To create a shortcut for the All Users desktop:

1. Right-click on the Start button. This will pop up a context-sensitive menu.
2. Click the Explore command.
3. Click the All Users folder.
4. Click the Desktop folder. Now, you can simply run through the Create Shortcut Wizard.
5. Right-click in the right pane of the Explorer window and click New, Shortcut.
6. Create a new shortcut to \WINNT\SYSTEM32\SOL.EXE.

Every user's desktop should now get Solitaire. You may start the Solitaire program now to continue on with the next exercise.

The Task Manager

An additional useful item can be found on the desktop or, more specifically, the taskbar: the Task Manager. Use the Task Manager if you need to view the current programs and processes. By using the Task Manager, you can end a program, end a process, or bump the priority of a process, among other things.

Sometimes performing these tasks becomes necessary if a program or process is running sluggishly, or not at all. A *program* is something we're all familiar with—a regular application such as Notepad, Solitaire, and so on. A *process*, however, can be part of an application, a service, or a subsystem.

To start the Task Manager:

1. Right-click over some free space in the taskbar.
2. Click Task Manager.

An alternative method of starting the Task Manager:

1. Press Ctrl+Alt+Delete.
2. Click Task Manager.

When you terminate a program, it's usually no big deal to just restart it. You will, however, lose the unsaved data in the application. To terminate a running program:

1. Start the Task Manager by using one of the methods discussed earlier.

2. Click the Applications tab.

3. Select the task you want to terminate. In this case, select Solitaire.

4. Click the End Task button.

5. If prompted, confirm that you want to terminate the task.

More care must be taken when killing a process. Often, it's harder to determine which process name corresponds to what actual process. Microsoft TechNet and Resource Kits are invaluable resources in these cases. Additionally, applications that have gone awry do not always respond right away when requesting termination. Sometimes applications can take several minutes to respond to a termination request. Restart Solitaire by clicking on it's icon on the desktop.

To terminate a running process:

1. Start the Task Manager by using one of the methods discussed earlier.

2. Click the Process tab.

3. Select the process you want to terminate. In this case, sol.exe.

4. Click the End Process button.

5. If prompted, confirm that you want to terminate the process.

You can also boost a process's priority. Suppose you are working on the server and want to give an extra bit of kick to the applications you're currently using. You can change how much processor time that application's process will receive. Restart Solitaire by clicking on it's icon on the desktop.

To boost the priority of a process:

1. Start the Task Manager by using one of the methods discussed earlier.

2. Click the Process tab.

3. Select the process you want to boost. In this case, sol.exe.

4. Right-click over the entry, select the Set Priority menu, and choose the priority you want (see Figure 4.1).

5. Close the Solitaire program now (once you've won the game.)

Setting processes to Realtime significantly decreases the time allocated to all other processes.

FIGURE **4.1**

*Setting the priority to
High boosts a process.*

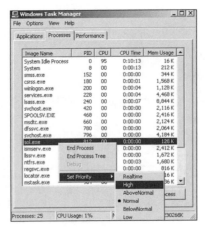

My Documents

The My Documents folder is the default central storage area for all documents that you, as a user of the system, create. Later in the book, I will detail how to leverage this directory so that your users can centralize their data in one place—on your server. For added protection to guide your users to this area, most programs automatically display this directory as the place to save. You can test this tendency by saving a file:

1. Click the Start button, click Run, type `notepad`, and press Enter.

2. When Notepad comes up, type `hello world`.

3. Click on the File menu and click Save As. The file dialog box appears as seen in Figure 4.2. Notice the directory in which you're asked to place the file. Save the file as hello_world.txt.

FIGURE **4.2**

*The new standard file
Save As dialog box
makes it easier to find
commonly or last used
items.*

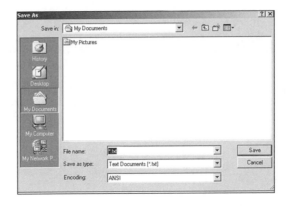

4. Close Notepad.

5. Double-click the My Documents icon on the desktop. Notice the hello_world file you just placed in the folder.

Because we were just investigating the Save As dialog box, let's continue with what we just found there. If you're already familiar with the Windows 95/NT Save As dialog box, you'll notice a welcome change.

The new Save As dialog box has several new goodies to help you navigate around the network and your specific system more quickly:

- My Documents button: You'll notice a My Documents button to move you directly into that directory if you get lost. This is a great tip to give to your users in case they ever forget where to save their files.

- History button: This shows you the last several directories in which you saved documents. If you saved a document in a directory other than My Documents, chances are you'll want to again. The History button is a great improvement to this dialog box.

- Desktop button: Sometimes you need to place or edit a file at the desktop level. Use this quick-access button to take you there directly.

- My Computer button: Just as it does at the desktop level, this button displays all the physically attached hard and floppy drives, CD-ROM drives, and network shared drives. With the My Computer button, you can easily gain access to them.

- My Network Places button: This button has two entries: Computers Near Me and Entire Network. Computers Near Me shows all the machines in your workgroup or domain. Entire Network allows you to surf the network to find the network resource you are looking for.

Showing Hidden and System Files

Some people like to configure this view to show the current path of the folder they're in. Additionally, many people like to display the hidden and system files, as well as show all the files' extensions. By showing the hidden and system files, an administrator can truly see what's going on behind the scenes, without Windows 2000 abstracting any of the nitty-gritty details. Additionally, after they are enabled, hidden and system files are included in search results when used from the Find dialog. And, for the truly brave, you can instruct Windows 2000 Server to let you view the operating system files.

To view hidden and system files:

1. Double-click My Computer.

2. From the Tools menu, select Folder Options, and then select the View tab.

3. To view hidden and system files, click as shown in Figure 4.3. Click OK to save these settings.

FIGURE 4.3

The folder options after allowing hidden and system files to be shown.

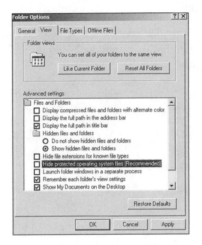

The Microsoft Management Console

Now that you have Windows 2000 Server installed and running, you need to understand the paradigm in which the server is managed.

In the past, Microsoft had a management tool for every manageable item in the environment: one tool for managing users, another for managing servers, another tool for Microsoft Exchange, another for managing DHCP, another for SMS—you get the idea. Not only was there a separate tool for each manageable item, but each user interface was different enough to create a bit of a learning curve.

Instead of continuing to use individual tools to manage individual components, Microsoft has created a new paradigm in which to manage objects and programs of all types. It's called the *Microsoft Management Console,* or the *MMC*.

Alone, the MMC performs no tasks. The MMC is merely a shell, with the capability to add management components as necessary. After you've created your console, you can store it away for quick future reference. You can also create and distribute custom consoles for specialized worker types, such as a help desk support specialist. After you've created your custom consoles, you can send them to your users via email, the Web, or Microsoft Systems Management Server (SMS). Additionally, you can lock down the consoles you create so that no modifications can be made.

As you'll see, you'll be using the MMC and its snap-ins for all sorts of management operations, including disk administration, user and group creation, and Active Directory management.

Snap-ins

Microsoft's latest effort is to make each administrative tool a snap-in component of a unified viewing tool: the Microsoft Management Console, as seen in Figure 4.4.

FIGURE 4.4

This is an MMC console without any snap-ins.

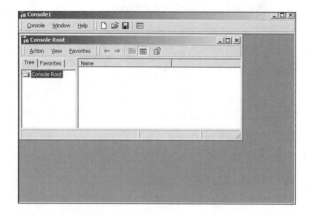

In Figure 4.4, the MMC has no snap-ins loaded.

With the MMC, you can add snap-ins for most Microsoft management tasks. As you'll see a little later, you can customize your view of the MMC for a quick view of the most common tasks. Additionally, MMC views can be saved and distributed to others, such as help-desk personnel, to limit what they can and cannot see.

When you launch most of the administrative tools from the Start menu's Administrative Tools folder, you're really just launching the MMC with a particular snap-in assigned to it.

Snap-ins are created not only by Microsoft, but also by third-party manufacturers, such as those who create backup solutions and disk defragmentation solutions, as you'll see later. That way you can have all the built-in Microsoft snap-ins right beside third-party snap-ins.

Some snap-ins keep a familiar Explorer-style interface, with some entries nested within others. Others have highly customized interfaces, such as the one you'll see in the next section.

Different Types of Snap-ins

Although I already mentioned that most of the administrative tools are really snap-ins assigned to the MMC, let's see how to generate a customized view by hand. In this exercise, we'll be loading the Performance Logs and Alerts snap-in, the Disk Defragmenter snap-in, and the Event Viewer snap-in.

To create a custom MMC console:

1. Click Start, and then click Run, type mmc, and press Enter.

2. After the splash screen, the MMC shell will come up.

3. Click Console, and then click Add/Remove Snap-in.

4. Load the Performance Logs and Alerts snap-in:

   • At the Add/Remove Snap-in page, click the Add button.

   • Locate the Performance Logs and Alerts snap-in, highlight it, and click Add.

5. Load the Disk Defragmenter snap-in by locating the Disk Defragmenter snap-in, highlighting it, and clicking Add.

6. Load the Event Viewer snap-in:

   • Locate the Event Viewer Snap-in, highlight it, and Click Add.

   • Event Viewer will ask you which machine to view events on. Click the setting for Local Computer and click Finish.

   • Click Close to close the Add/Remove Snap-in window.

   • Notice all three snap-ins we chose are loaded.

   • Click OK to return to the MMC.

7. Expand the Console Root window within the MMC.

Your custom MMC should now look like Figure 4.5.

FIGURE 4.5

The MMC has a tree with each snap-in as a root.

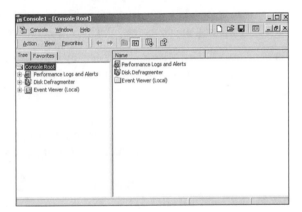

To discover the stuff in the loaded snap-ins:

1. Click on the + symbol to the left of the Performance Logs and Alerts menu item. This is called *expanding* or *drilling down*. Notice that Counter Logs, Trace Logs, and Alerts show up.

2. Click on the + symbol to the left of the Event Viewer (Local) menu item. Notice that Application Log, Security Log, System Log, and others show up.

3. Click on the + symbol to the left of the Disk Defragmenter menu item. Notice that there are no levels under the Disk Defragmenter. Some snap-ins have multiple levels, and some do not. Click on the words Disk Defragmenter, and a window showing your available disk drives and some statistics about them will appear.

> We're not going to defragment the drives in this exercise. We're simply examining different styles of snap-ins.

The MMC has a unique feature: Its help screens are always customized to the snap-ins you have loaded.

To get customized context-sensitive help, press the F1 key to view your help options. Notice that the MMC automatically creates a customized help menu based on the snap-ins you have loaded.

Keep your console as it is and proceed to the next topic.

Working with the Console Tree

In the previous exercise, we loaded some snap-ins and expanded their trees. In this exercise, we're going to examine the most common type of snap-in—one with an Explorer-style interface.

To view events using the MMC:

1. Click on the words Event Viewer (Local) in the left pane. Notice how the right pane contains the same categories as the contents below the Event Viewer (Local). Also notice that there is slightly more information provided in the right pane.

2. From here, either double-click the left-pane Application Log or double-click the right-pane Application-Log, and notice that the output produced is exactly the same. (The contents of your messages onscreen might vary.)

3. Right-click over one of the Application Log entries, and notice the menu provided. Click Properties to see more data about the message.

4. Left-click one of the Application Log entries and then click the Action menu. Notice the menu is the same. You can see that the right-click and the Action menu perform the same function.

5. Right-click over the left pane's Application Log entries, and notice all the entries that affect the items within the Application Log. Feel free to putter around to see all your options.

6. Leave your console up and continue on.

Creating and Saving a Custom Console

With the MMC, you can create saved, customized views that you can send to others electronically—either through email or another distribution method. After the recipients open your designed view, they cannot change it. In the next exercise, you'll customize the layout of a snap-in in your console, save it to your desktop, and check out the results.

Creating your own customized views is a great way to limit what other pseudo-administrators, such as help desk personnel and delegated administrators, can see (as we'll discuss in Hour 10, "Active Directory Entities").

If, for instance, the help desk needs access only to the Active Directory Users and Computers console, you can give them just that.

You'll use the skills you learn in this exercise to create customized MMCs for your delegated administrators.

To save a customized MMC console:

1. In the left pane, right-click Event Viewer and then click on New Window from Here.

2. Click on the Window menu and Tile Horizontally. The results should look like Figure 4.6.

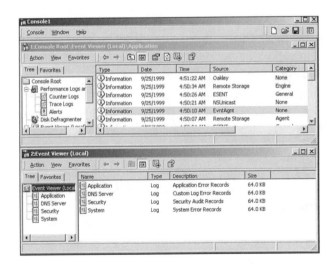

FIGURE **4.6**

*This is a picture of
your finished console.*

3. To save the console, click the Console menu, and then Save As. Navigate to <root drive>\DOCUMENTS AND SETTINGS\ALL USERS\DESKTOP. Call the file my_first_console. The .msc extension is automatically added for you.

4. Quit the open MMC we've been working in. You might be asked if you want to save it again. Click No. Notice the new MMC icon on your desktop.

5. Double-click the new MMC icon to see your results.

Notice the name of the MMC console when it starts.

Restricting Access to a Custom MMC Console

You'll often want a way to create a custom console, but also to make sure that the people who use it don't play with the settings. You can do that easily, using an option available to you within the MMC.

To create a locked-down custom MMC console:

1. Create your MMC with the snap-ins desired, as specified previously, or continue using the current console.

2. From the Console menu, choose Options.

3. From the Options screen, click the Console tab.

4. On the Console tab, find the Console Mode drop-down box, and choose User Mode – Limited Access, Multiple Window, as shown in Figure 4.7.

FIGURE 4.7

You can change the name of the console here, if desired.

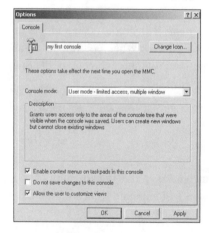

If you had only one snap-in customized, you would only need to specify the Single Window option.

5. Click OK. The Console Tab closes.

6. From the Console menu, choose Save As. In the Save In drop down box, select the drive where Windows 2000 Server is installed. Then select Documents and Settings, Administrator, Desktop. Keep the default name of the console and click Save.

7. Quit the console.

8. Open the console again from the desktop icon you created.

 Some snap-ins have their own settings that can be saved. The Do Not Save Changes to This Console check box prevents these changes from being saved.

The view is not customizable (other than moving the windows around) and the MMC's Console, Window, and Help menus are removed.

Summary

The Windows 2000 interface has some new changes, both to the file dialog box and to the location where user files are stored.

The Microsoft Management Console is not part of Explorer, but it has an Explorer-like interface. Moreover, the MMC is not a management tool, despite its name. It's a tool that enables you to centralize your management tools (snap-ins) in one place to get a unified, customized view of only what you need. When you run the administrative tools from the Administrative Tools folder on the Programs submenu of the Start menu, you're really launching the MMC with a saved view.

After you save views in the .msc format, you can send them to others.

Workshop

The Workshop provides a quiz and exercises to help reinforce your learning. Even if you feel you know the material, you will still gain from working these exercises.

Quiz

1. What is the default location for the storing of documents?

2. How do you kill a process or a program?

3. Where should users store their documents?

4. Who makes MMC snap-ins?

5. Why would you want to create customized MMC consoles?

Exercises

1. Make NOTEPAD.EXE available to both the administrator and All Users on their desktop.

2. Create a custom MMC console with the Computer Management and Device Manager snap-ins.

3. Save the newly created console in user mode.

4

Hour 5

The Control Panel

By Jeremy Moskowitz

In this hour, we'll be going over some of the customizations you can perform on your installation that will make the time you spend in front of the screen more productive, creative, and fun. Here, we'll concentrate on some of the Windows 2000 features that differ from their Windows NT 4.0 and Windows 95/98 counterparts. The skills and tips you learn here will easily transfer over to Windows 2000 Professional.

Additionally, we'll highlight some tips to make your server perform as it should, as well as introduce you to options to get your feet wet with Windows 2000 networking.

We won't be talking about every Control Panel entry or every feature therein—simply the ones we think you'll need to know about to have a smooth-sailing server. Additionally, those entries not discussed in this hour (such as Network and Dial-Up connections folder) are talked about in other hours in the book.

In this hour, you will learn how to

- Configure devices
- Add a local printer
- Tune the virtual memory settings
- Enable Web content on your desktop
- Schedule future tasks

The Control Panel Folder

The Control Panel is the window to your computer's soul. The settings that you change here will affect the appearance of your server, how your server outputs information, and how the server reacts to input.

To get to the Control Panel, click the Start button, click Settings, and then click Control Panel. The window shown in Figure 5.1 will display the Control Panel applets. An *applet* is simply a small program called by a larger one.

FIGURE 5.1

The Control Panel applets.

Control Panel applets can also be spawned individually by hand, if desired. At a command prompt or from the Run line off the Start menu, you can type control <file>.cpl, where <file> is any number of entries, such as control joy.cpl for joystick or control modem.cpl for modem wizard setup. You can see a list of .cpl files by performing a search for *.cpl files in the Search dialog box.

Chances are that you are already familiar with at least some aspects of the Control Panel, so we will only be detailing the applets that affect server performance and client connectivity.

The Display Applet

Before we talk about the entries in the Display applet, let's talk a bit about selecting a video card. It's best not to spend too much money on a super-duper video card. For one thing, the server won't need all that much graphics firepower. Second, the more complex the video card, the more complex the video driver. If the third-party (that is, non-Microsoft) video driver crashes while your server is running, it will probably take the entire server down with it. It is recommended that you use the normal, Microsoft-supplied, tried-and-true VGA or SVGA drivers, if possible. At the very least, make sure your video card is on the Microsoft Windows 2000 Hardware Compatibility List, or HCL. In fact, all your hardware should be on the HCL.

Although the Display applet has many configurable settings, we'll be exploring the two most important tabs: Settings and Screen Saver.

The Settings Tab

You can bump up the resolution of the video card by using the Settings tab. Simply slide the Screen Area slider to the desired resolution and click Apply. You'll be given the opportunity to try your settings for 15 seconds. If the picture blanks out, rolls around, or generally goes south, your screen will automatically restore itself in 15 seconds. If your hardware supports it, you'll want to set the resolution to at least 800×600 or more.

The Colors drop-down box is also related to your screen area. Its overall output characteristics will be determined by how much onboard memory your video card has. When hardware manufacturers describe their maximum settings, they do so in an A×B×C format, where A is the screen's length, B is the screen's width, and C is the number of colors produced. Depending on your card, you might not be able to have both the desired number of colors and the desired screen area. When you increase one, the other might decrease.

The Screen Saver Tab

The Screen Saver tab keeps you from burning in a particular image on your monitor. This section is not to inform you about the virtues and theory behind screen savers, but rather about what *kind* of screen saver you should choose for a Windows 2000 Server.

Because the machine you'll be working will be a server, it's best not to take away from the precious CPU cycles that will be serving so many people. Although it might be aesthetically pleasing to choose one of the keen OpenGL screen savers, those types of programs bog down the CPU, slowing down the entire machine.

5

Instead, choose a non-OpenGL screen saver, such as Mystify or Starfield Simulation. Both of these screen savers will perform the desired screen saving function, without unnecessarily taxing your CPU. And they look pretty decent, too. If you can stand to blank your screen, that is even better.

In addition, password-protect your server console. Because the server houses such sensitive, hands-on information, you'll want to make sure no one but Administrators can get their hands on it.

> If possible, try to physically isolate your server from people traffic: You don't want someone turning off your server.

The Printers Applet

The Printers applet allows you to create a connection to a locally attached printer or a network printer. We'll be going over all the details about printing in Hour 19, "Printing," but for now, note that the function is found here.

In this example, we'll be attaching a fictitious Tektronix Phaser color printer to our server's parallel port.

> You are encouraged to perform this exercise exactly as specified, regardless of whether or not you have a printer (of any type) attached. The results from this exercise are used later in the book.

To create a local printer:

1. To start the Add Printer wizard, click the Start menu, Settings, Control Panel, and then select Printers.

2. Double-click the Add Printer icon, which will start the Add Printer Wizard. At the splash screen, click Next.

3. At the Local or Network Printer screen, make sure the Automatically Detect My Printer check box is unchecked. We are setting up a fictitious color printer.

4. At the Select the Printer Port screen, make sure LPT1: is selected. Click Next.

5. When you can select your printer, be sure to select a Tektronix Phaser PXi (toward the end of the list Tektronix printers.) This is a high-performance color printer. Click Next.

6. At the Name Your Printer screen, clear the default entry and type Tek.

7. At the Printer Sharing screen, keep the defaults, and choose to Share as Tek.

8. At the Location and Comment screen, enter

- Location: Server room

- Comment: For occasional use only!

9. At the Print Test Page screen, choose not to print a test page, and click Next.

10. At the Add Printer Wizard summary screen, click Finish to create and share your printer.

You might or might not be asked for the Windows 2000 Server CD-ROM to load the drivers.

The System Applet

The System applet has a multitude of goodies inside. It's the place where you should go to debug hardware failures and change the performance options. Again, we're only going to touch on the most important highlights to help you customize a smooth-sailing server.

> You can also bring up the System applet by right-clicking over My Computer on the desktop and clicking Properties.

The General Tab

Amazingly, a lot of useful information is in this inconspicuous place. First, you'll be able to find the software revision number currently in use, as well as to whom the software is registered. These items are important when calling Microsoft support.

Perhaps the most important item on this page, however, is an instant display of how much RAM is currently installed. If you ever need a quick way to find out, this is the place.

The Network Identification Tab

With this tab, you can change the computer name as well as join the domain. We'll discuss these options in Hour 9, "Users, Groups, and Machine Accounts on Domain Controllers," so stay tuned.

The Hardware Tab

The Hardware tab has three major sections: the Hardware Wizard, the Device Manager, and the Hardware profiler.

5

The Hardware Wizard

Chances are you won't find yourself using the Hardware Wizard very much. The Hardware Wizard allows you to add or remove hardware that might not have been detected at bootup time. Windows 2000 has a much more robust hardware detection mechanism than its NT 4.0 counterpart. If you do need it, the wizard process that guides you through is very self-explanatory.

The Device Manager

The Device Manager section has two buttons: Driver Signing and Device Manager.

To thwart bogus drivers, use the Code Signing Options dialog, which is opened from the Hardware tab of the System Properties dialog box as seen in Figure 5.2.

FIGURE 5.2

Use the Code Signing options to prevent bogus drivers from being installed.

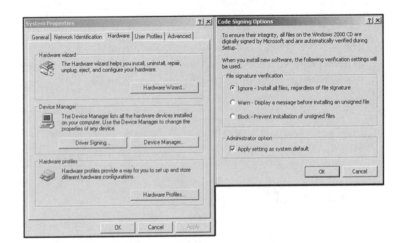

A new Windows 2000 feature called *driver signing* allows the administrator to set the levels of security when new device drivers are loaded on a specific machine. Drivers for devices that pass Microsoft's independent testing process are digitally signed to ensure authenticity. The administrator may choose warnings, no warnings, or a full blockage of all unsigned driver files. When the Apply Setting as System Default box is checked by an administrator, the setting chosen is set for every user on that machine. These settings prevent you and your users from finding a bogus, Trojan horse driver that could harm your machine.

These settings do not apply to users connected to the machine—only those users sitting at the console of the machine.

The Device Manager shows all hardware currently attached to the machine. You can expand the hardware categories to see the hardware revealed underneath. Double-clicking on a specific piece of hardware brings up details about the device (see Figure 5.3). Depending on the device, additional information can be extracted or even changed.

FIGURE 5.3

Double-click a device to get its status.

To view the status of a device:

1. If it's not already open, open the Control Panel by clicking Start, Settings, and then Control Panel.
2. Click the System applet.
3. Click the Hardware tab.
4. Click Device Manager.
5. Expand the category of hardware you want to learn more about.
6. Double-click a specific item to get an expanded view. The General tab will present the current status of the device.
7. In this example for a 3Com Etherlink 3C509b card, we can find out what IRQ and memory addresses the card is currently configured for, as well as get into trouble with some advanced features in the Advanced tab.

5

Not all devices have an Advanced tab. Alternatively, some devices might
have additional and customized tabs.

If a device is conflicted, its IRQ, DMA, or I/O settings are possibly the same as another device. Many conflicts can be resolved by deleting the device from Device Manager, and then restarting Windows 2000.

Windows 2000's new hardware detection features can often work around stubbornly conflicting devices. Depending on the hardware, you might be able to manually set one of the devices by selecting the Resources tab on the property page of the specific device.

To change the resource for a specific device:

1. View the status of a device as detailed earlier.
2. Click the Resources tab, and uncheck the Use Automatic Settings check box.
3. In Resource Settings, select the resource type you want to change (DMA, IRQ, or I/O).
4. Click Change Setting, and enter a nonconflicting value.

If all goes well, both devices will be active by the next reboot.

 If the Use Automatic Settings check box is grayed out, the hardware you
want to modify has unchangeable settings. If this is the case, try making the
changes on the other conflicting device.

Windows 2000 has extra facilities for fixing hardware problems.

First, if you have device conflicts, or a device flat-out isn't working, give the Hardware Troubleshooter a try. It is a Windows help screen that can guide you toward a myriad of resolution solutions.

To start the Hardware Troubleshooter:

1. View the status of a device as detailed earlier.
2. Click the Troubleshooter button.

Next, if your hardware vendor updates a specific device driver, you can use the Upgrade Device Driver Wizard. After you've downloaded the driver from the vendor's Web site, you can use the wizard to ensure a smooth installation.

To start the Upgrade Device Driver Wizard:

1. View the status of a device as detailed earlier.
2. Click the Driver tab.
3. Click the Update Driver button.

A wizard will prompt you for the location of the new driver. Simply provide the location (floppy disk, network drive, and so on), and you're all set.

After a device is selected, there will be three special choices on the Action menu in the Device Manager window: Scan for Hardware Changes, Disable (device), and Uninstall (device). These three items allow easy access to these functions so you don't have to go through the Add/Remove Hardware Wizard.

Hardware Profiles Section

The Hardware Profiles section has only one button: Hardware Profiles.

This section of Windows 2000 is generally reserved for laptops (although you might be putting your Windows 2000 Server installation on a laptop for field testing).

The Hardware Profiles section is meant to disable a particular device should it be incompatible with Windows 2000. One instance might be a sound card built into a docking station. To create a hardware profile that disables the docking station's sound card, copy the current profile and name it accordingly, boot into the new profile, and disable the offending device.

When Windows 2000 starts up, the user is prompted for the hardware profile he would like to use. The user simply selects the name of the correct profile and the incompatible device isn't loaded when Windows 2000 starts up.

The User Profiles Tab

Stay tuned: We'll be discussing more about this tab in Hour 14, "Profiles and Policies."

The Advanced Tab

As seen in Figure 5.4, there are three sections with three buttons in the Advanced tab: Performance Options, Environment Variables, and Startup and Recovery.

Performance Options Section

The Performance section has one button: Performance Options. Clicking Performance Options brings up a box where you can set both the Applications Response and the amount of paged hard disk space to use.

FIGURE 5.4

The Advanced tab allows you to change several useful server options.

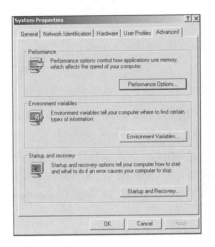

What you use Windows 2000 Server to do will dictate what performance option you'll choose. If this machine will act as a file and print server, you'll want to keep the Background Services option on because this machine will be serving files and performing other tasks in the background.

If, however, this machine will have frequent visits to the console, you might want to choose Applications because it will give preference to applications currently running in the foreground.

Clicking on Change in the Virtual Memory box will allow you to fine-tune your Virtual Memory paging settings, as seen in Figure 5.5. *Virtual memory* is hard drive space that is used when the available RAM is used up. When conditions permit, files in RAM are *paged* to the hard drive in a round-robin fashion. More about paging and performance is in Hour 21, "Performance Monitoring and Diagnostics." You will also find a description of the paging process in Hour 2, "Architecture and Boot Process."

Another rule of thumb is to try to spread the paging file across as many physical disks as possible. That way, each hard drive is working independently to serve up the paging file when necessary.

You might be asking, "Why are there minimum and maximum values at all? Why not just one number?" This is because Windows 2000 server can resize the paging file on the fly. It can, if desired, take up only the space required within the parameters. Although this is advantageous for preserving disk space, it inversely affects the processor and disk performance. The processor and disk must now work at adding that space, if needed. You can offset the workload on the processor and hard drives if you set the minimum and maximum values to the same number; the paging file will never increase or decrease, but the amount of disk space used will always stay the same. This is the preferred method if you have the available free disk space. It's up to you.

FIGURE 5.5

Spread the paging file over multiple physical disks for optimal performance.

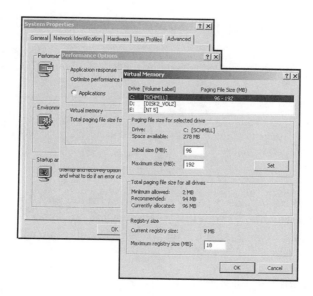

Microsoft's paper and online documentation recommend that a paging file should be at least 12MB more than the amount of physical RAM in the computer. For instance, if you have 64MB of RAM installed, your paging file should be around 76MB minimum. I have found that a good paging file is sized around 1.5 times the amount of RAM you have. So, for 64MB of RAM, an optimum paging file size would be 96MB. In fact, this is the exact number of megabytes that Windows 2000 allocated automatically for this 64MB system.

To modify the paging file:

1. If it is not already open, open the Control Panel by clicking Start, Settings, and then Control Panel.

2. Click the System applet.

3. Click the Advanced Tab.

4. Click Performance Options.

5. Under the Virtual Memory heading, click Change.

6. Click on the drive letter you want to add to the paging pool.

7. Enter a value for Initial Size (MB) and Maximum Size (MB) as described in the preceding text. Click Set.

5

You might or might not be prompted to reboot your machine for the changes to take effect.

Repeat steps 6 and 7 to spread the paging file across additional physical drives.

> Spreading the paging file around multiple *logical* partitions on the same physical disk does not boost performance. It will actually degrade performance.

Last on the Virtual Memory screen is the size of the Registry. The number represented is the total number of megabytes that the Registry can use, either on disk or in memory. As of this writing, Microsoft has not yet published any optimum numbers regarding this setting for standalone servers or domain controllers.

Environment Variables Section

FIGURE 5.6

Set environment variables per your application's documentation.

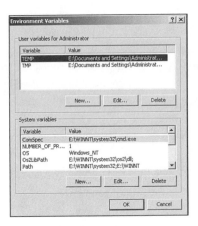

The Environment variables section has only one button, called Environment Variables. The Environment Variables button works the same way for Windows 2000 that it did for Windows NT. If an environment variable is required for a particular program to function, simply decide whether that variable should be available for every user on the system or only for the specific user currently logged on.

To add an environment variable:

1. Decide whether the variable is required for everyone, or just for a specific user who logs on this machine.

2. Click New for a new User environment variable—or click New for a new System variable, as seen in Figure 5.6

3. Type the variable name, type in the value, and click OK.

To change a current environment variable:

1. Double-click the entry. You can select the entry and click Edit for a user variable, or select the entry and click Edit for a system variable.

2. Rename the variable name or change the value.

3. Click OK.

Startup and Recovery Section

FIGURE 5.7

Modify how your system starts up with the Startup and Recovery screen.

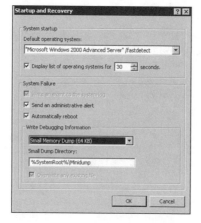

The Startup and Recovery section has only one button, cleverly labeled Startup and Recovery.

As seen in Figure 5.7, the options at the top of this page allow you to specify which operating system will be chosen if none is selected at time of reboot. If you like, you may also change the startup countdown timer to a value less than or greater than 30. Many people choose a value between 5 and 10, which is usually sufficient.

The bottom section displays the recovery options. Most of the values are self-explanatory. Note, however, that the volume you choose to put the dump (.DMP) file in must also have a paging file of at least the same size as the physical memory. Also note the default option for Kernel Memory Dump in the Write Debugging Information section. If the need arises to send your .dmp file to Microsoft for debugging, it's best to have a full .dmp file, not just the small memory dump; however, some would argue that only the small memory dump is most critical.

It is recommended that you leave the options in the Startup and Recovery section at their defaults.

Power Options Applet

Instead of detailing all the many options available in the new Advanced Power Management Interface (APMI), we'll just detail what you shouldn't be doing with the Power Options. In a nutshell, *don't turn any of them on*. Because you're running a server, it would be disastrous if the machine suddenly went into a power-down mode, even for a minute. These options are generally reserved for Windows 2000 Professional worksta-tions, not servers. The only option you should have selected is Always On in the Power Schemes section.

Additionally, although it probably wouldn't affect your system, it's still a good idea to change the default Turn Off Monitor setting from 20 Minutes to Never. You don't want your video card getting any strange ideas about when and when not to show you what's on the screen.

The Power Options Applet is also where you would set up an Uninterruptible Power Supply or UPS. Consult your UPS manual for specific details for compatibility with Windows 2000 Server.

The Scheduled Tasks Applet

The Scheduled Tasks applet lets you do just that: schedule programs and batch files to execute in the future. This Scheduled Tasks applet is an update from the winat.exe executable found in the NT 4.0 Resource Kit. The Scheduled Tasks applet walks you through the basics of selecting a file to run at certain times of the day, week, month, or year. This way, you'll have more free time on your hands to do what you love—to read more Sams books.

In this exercise, you'll be creating a batch file that checks the health of your G: drive. This batch file will

- Run `chkdsk.exe g:\ /F`
- Run once a week, on Saturday nights
- Run only if the machine doesn't have any activity

Perform these steps by creating a batch file, and then instructing the Scheduled Tasks applet to run it on your schedule.

To create a batch file to repair your disks:

1. Open Notepad by clicking Start, selecting Run, and typing notepad. Click OK.

2. When Notepad appears, type chkdsk g:\ /F on the first line. Click the File menu, and select Save As. You will be naming the file checkg.bat. Place the file in the directory where you installed Windows 2000 Server (usually c:\winnt).

To instruct the Scheduled Tasks applet:

1. To use the Scheduled Tasks applet, double-click on it from the Control Panel folder.

2. After it starts, double-click the Add Scheduled Tasks option. A wizard appears to help you through the process. On the splash screen, click Next.

3. On the next screen of the wizard, click Browse. Click on your WINNT directory and select the checkg.bat file we just created.

4. The next screen shows you the name given to the task and allows you to select when you want the program to run. Keep the default for the task name, select Weekly, and click Next.

5. Input the time to run at 11:00 PM, every week on Saturday.

6. Input the user account and password for which you want to run the event. The event will run as if this user started it, so be sure the account you choose has rights to run the program you select. You would probably want the administrator to run the event, so enter in the username Administrator and the password. Click Next.

If you wanted to specify a domain account, you would write it the same way: <domain>\<account in domain>.

7. The next screen informs you that you have successfully created a task. You are also given the option to see more advanced properties for this task when you finish this wizard. You want to make sure the program doesn't start if someone is using the drive, so you need to see some advanced options. Click the Open Advanced Properties for This Task When I Click Finish check box, and click Finish.

8. The Advanced Properties screen now appears (see Figure 5.8). You want to ensure that the batch file starts only when the computer is idle. Click the Settings tab, and

then click the Idle Time check box. The default options will make sure that no activity has occurred for 10 minutes before the batch file starts.

9. Click OK.

FIGURE 5.8

Click the check box to make sure the computer is idle before starting a task.

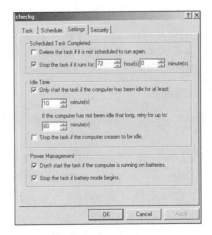

Your task is now ready to run this Saturday!

Summary

Use the Display applet to change the video settings. If possible, use the tried-and-true Microsoft VGA or SVGA drivers. Avoid using OpenGL screen savers because they are CPU-intensive. Use the Device Manager to manage new hardware drivers. Use the performance options to change the virtual memory settings. Try to spread your paging file across multiple physical disks for the best results. Use the Folder Options applet to fine-tune the way Windows Explorer acts. Use the Scheduled Tasks Agent to offload repetitive tasks.

Workshop

The Workshop provides a quiz and exercises to help reinforce your learning. Even if you feel you know the material, you will still gain from working these exercises.

Quiz

1. How can you start a Control Panel entry without entering the Control Panel?

2. How can you be sure your hardware will work with Windows 2000?

3. What is the best video card for Windows 2000 Server?

4. What screen saver should you run on a Windows 2000 server?

5. What additional precautions should be taken to protect your Windows 2000 server?

6. How can you determine how much RAM is installed on a machine?

7. Which feature of Windows 2000 prevents bogus hardware drivers from bringing down your machines?

8. If a device is conflicting, which values should you check?

9. How should you create your server's virtual memory paging file?

10. Which applet helps you run batch files during off-hours?

Exercises

1. Download a copy of the HCL from `http://www.microsoft.com/hwtest/hcl`. Verify your hardware is on it.

2. Open some of the other Control Panel applets that weren't discussed, such as the Folder Options applet. Customize the desktop to your taste.

3. Explore the options available in the Hardware Troubleshooter.

5

PART II

Domains, Users, and Disks

Hour

HOUR 6

Domains and the Active Directory

by Jeremy Moskowitz

At the heart of Windows 2000 Server is its Active Directory. Here, you'll discover new features that should usher in a whole new era to the duties of administration. In order to make the most of the Active Directory, we need to look at how Windows NT has grown up over the years, and look forward to where Active Directory will go. In this lesson, you will learn about the following:

- The history of NT's domains and trusts
- NT and Windows 2000 Server Domain Controller roles
- Why you need a directory
- The features and benefits of the Active Directory
- How to configure trees and forests
- Bringing up your first Windows 2000 Server Domain Controller in a networked environment

The History of NT's Domains and Trusts

For many people domains can be daunting, but the concept is relatively simple. A *domain* is simply a security boundary for groups of users. Its purpose is to separate administrative tasks between groups of administrators, usually geographically or politically. Additionally, administrators of a domain can set up *trusts* between their domains. In ideal circumstances, this allows the trusted domain to hold user accounts, and the trusting domain's administrators can simply choose which users get access to what resources.

Let's look at a quick example. As you can see in Figure 6.1, the SALES domain is a resource domain independent from the CORP domain.

FIGURE 6.1

A resource domain (SALES) trusting an account domain (CORP).

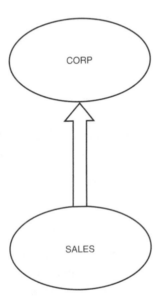

In this example, the SALES domain trusts the CORP domain. Ideally, all user accounts for the enterprise are in the CORP domain. For our example, we'll say there's an account named JOE in the CORP domain. When the SALES administrator wants to grant JOE access to a specific file, printer, or resource, the SALES administrator can simply select JOE from the CORP domain. Why isn't JOE's account in the SALES domain? Because administrative functions are separated between the two domains. The CORP administrator's job is to simply create and delete accounts. The SALES administrator's job is to simply grant JOE access to the resources he knows JOE needs. The SALES administrator is probably close to JOE—the CORP administrator probably isn't.

Let's take another example, where WIDGET is a part of SALES:

FIGURE 6.2

A structure you don't want to encounter with NT domains.

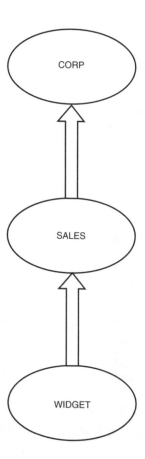

In NT, this is a bizarre and unusual structure. It usually occurs when an unsanctioned rogue domain springs up (WIDGET), and the SALES administrator feels obligated to allow it to participate in the enterprise structure. You might think that if WIDGETS trusts SALES and SALES trusts CORP, it follows that WIDGETS trusts CORP. This is not the case. In NT, trusts do not flow through one domain to another domain; that is, NT trusts are not transitive. Windows 2000 Server trusts, however, are transitive. We'll get into this a bit later.

With a firm grasp of NT trusts, you can shape your enterprise accordingly. NT has several fundamental core models: single domain, master domain, multiple master domain, and complete trust. Chances are that your organization's model doesn't quite match any of the models here. Although we won't go into the details of each model, Figure 6.3 shows a diagram of what each model looks like.

6

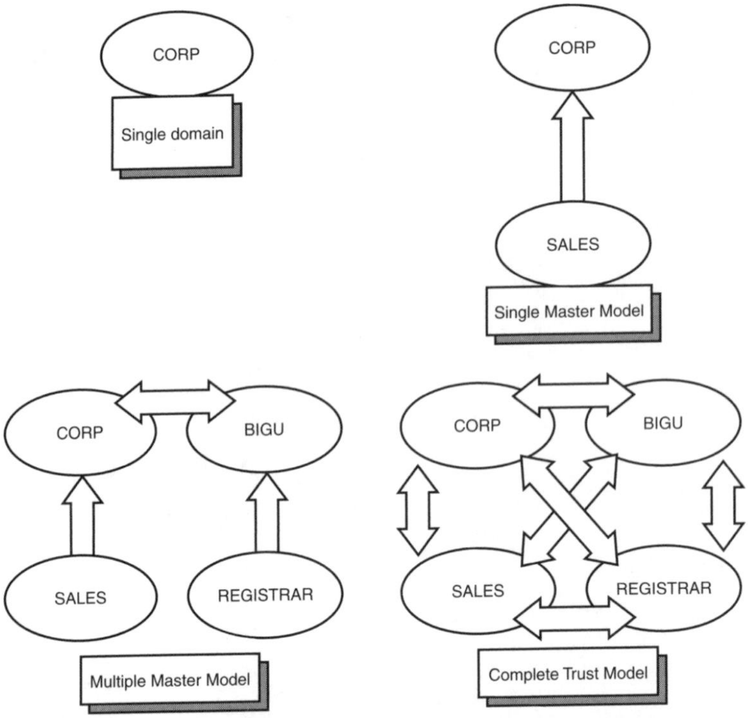

FIGURE **6.3**
*All four regular trust
models.*

The Four Domain Models with NT Server: A Brief Overview

The single domain model is for the smallest of installations. This model is used when the organization does not need to be split up for organizational or administrative purposes. No trusts need to be managed.

The master domain model separates a domain for accounts and a domain (or more) for resources. Users log on to the account domain, but access resources (such as printers) in the resource domain. Administrators may be autonomous: one administrator creates accounts in the account domain, and the other assigns access to resources in another domain. Domains may be (but don't necessarily need to be) geographically isolated.

The multiple master domain model has two-way trusts connecting each of the account domains. After the trusts are established, users can access resources in any properly assigned resource domain. This model can handle many thousands of users.

The complete trust model is really a modified single domain model. Each domain gets to maintain its own security, but allows others certain access rights to resources when necessary.

For both NT 4.0 and Windows 2000 Server, after certain policies are set at the domain level, they are contained at that level for all users. For instance, if the minimum password length for the domain is eight characters, that setting affects only the users who belong in that domain. Users in other domains are not affected. We'll see more about specific domain settings in Hour 14, "Profiles and Policies."

NT and Windows 2000 Server Domain Controller Roles

Every domain must have at least one Windows 2000 Server acting as a Domain Controller (DC) or one Windows NT Primary Domain Controller (PDC). Either of these systems is required to house the database of users and objects for the domain.

Understanding Windows NT Domain Controllers

Windows NT has two types of Domain Controllers: Primary Domain Controllers and Backup Domain Controllers (BDC). Each Domain Controller houses a copy of the user database called the Security Account Manager (SAM).

In NT, a readable copy of the SAM is stored on each Backup Domain Controller; but the only read/writeable copy is stored on the Primary Domain Controller. Whenever a change is made to a domain (that is, a user is added or deleted), the change is written first to the PDC of the domain, and then the PDC updates each BDC at a set interval.

Understanding Windows 2000 Server Domain Controllers

In order to take advantage of the new Active Directory functionality, the design of the Domain Controller was changed. Although NT has PDCs and BDCs, each with a copy of the SAM database, Windows 2000 Server has only one type of Domain Controller—cleverly enough also called a Domain Controller, or DC. The concept of Primary and Backup Domain Controllers was replaced with multiple, equal Windows 2000 Server Domain Controllers.

After a change is made in the Active Directory, it is propagated to other Domain Controllers. This process, called *replication*, occurs at set intervals to each Domain Controller in the domain.

Replicating the information in the Active Directory to other DCs creates benefits for the network. First, fault tolerance can be achieved. If you have multiple Domain Controllers participating in the Active Directory, you are protected should one or more Domain

6

Controllers fail. The added benefit of replication is that users might have a server closer to them that can serve up queried information in the Active Directory. The closer the server, the more quickly users will receive their information.

The downside of replication is that a lot of information must be passed from one DC to another. However, this is mitigated somewhat because only the changes are sent to those Domain Controllers that need it. Additionally, traffic may also be minimized by the utilization of global catalog servers and by creating sites. We'll discuss both of those topics in the next hour.

Why Do I Need a Directory?

The SAM served NT 4.0 very well, but there were some limitations. Administrator-defined attributes cannot be entered into the SAM. For instance, NT 4.0's User Manager for Domains has a place for Name, but there is no place for Social Security Number, License Plate, User Photograph, or Voice Print.

After NT had been out for years and the designers at Microsoft had peeked a bit at the competition, Microsoft decided it needed to meet some of the new challenges of competing directory services. So, Microsoft added features to Windows 2000 Server, granting the following abilities:

- Add additional attributes (such as Social Security Number or user photograph) at any time
- Unify all the information about the enterprise's users, printers, email accounts, and other resources in one easily searchable place
- Grant normal users some administrative tasks, if necessary
- Allow more than one writeable location that could be active at one time
- Have redundancy in validation should one or more servers go down
- Fundamentally tie the structure to the Internet with established Internet protocols

The new database Microsoft developed for Windows 2000 Server is called the Active Directory (AD), its first foray into the realm of directory services.

Directory services as a concept has been around for years with Microsoft's competition. The most popular directory services implementation today is Novell NetWare NDS. Even earlier directory services concepts were found in network operating system products such as Banyan VINES StreetTalk.

Active Directory Versus NDS

In the war of directory services, who will reign as king? If Microsoft has anything to say about it, it will be Active Directory, although there are certainly zealots on both sides.

NDS has been around for more than six years, meaning it already has widespread support, maturity, and reliability behind it.

However, because Microsoft has had the time to investigate what people want from a directory service, NDS will have to look out.

This hour highlights some of Active Directory's biggest advantages, including its claim to fame: its integration with Internet standards. Active Directory is tightly integrated with DNS, whereas NDS is not.

NDS is not without its advantages. Due to the nature of domains and trusts with the AD, if a user requires administrative access, his account must be granted explicit privileges in each domain (or everywhere with the special Enterprise Admins group). In NDS, this is not the case: simply add the user and the rights required at that point in the tree, and rights automatically flow downward to all remaining points. Rights are simply calculated "on the fly."

NDS also has, at this time, better facilities to move users and groups around the directory with minimal penalty. Active Directory isn't quite there yet in its pruning and grafting functions of portions of the tree.

Microsoft knows these limitations exist and is actively trying to close the gap.

These directory services (NDS and StreetTalk) sought to integrate the way users interacted with objects in the system. An application coded to route forms to other users might query the directory service for a list of potential users and groups. You simply clicked on the entry you wanted, and away went the form.

Directory services can be thought of as just that—a directory of services, like a phone book. Simply look up a published entry of a person's name, and out pops a phone number, his email address, his Social Security number, his dog's name, and a picture of his car. Although you can't access that much information with a regular phone book, you *can* with the Microsoft Active Directory.

6

The designation of the entries in the Active Directory is called its *schema*. For instance, the schema enforces that a Social Security Number field must be nine digits long, with a dash after the first three digits, and again after the next two digits.

The Active Directory can be thought of as a searchable, unified repository of all relevant enterprise object information.

Imagine being able to instantly locate all the lawyers on the third floor and the color printers near them. With NT, this simply was not possible.

The fundamental goal of Active Directory is to be all things to all applications. That sounds a bit broad, and it is. Active Directory is not just for our administrative-defined entries, but it also has hooks so other applications can latch on as well. The goal of Active Directory is to have a set of containers that administrators and applications can use to store settings, preferences, and other information that they need to modify their actions.

In fact, Microsoft's next version of Exchange expected in mid-2000 (code name: Platinum) will be 100% reliant on the Active Directory to house the user's information. This makes sense: Why have two user directories with essentially the same information? Earlier versions of the Exchange directory have served as the model for the construction of the Active Directory.

Windows 2000 Server's DNS and Domains

To add functionality, we'll need to stretch our idea of NT's domain models and add some new Windows 2000 Server vocabulary.

When you use a Web browser and type www.boutell.com, you are using the Internet's Domain Name Service (DNS) to convert that easy-to-type name to the IP address of a Web server (in this case, 207.55.56.4).

Because of the convergence of all things toward the Internet, Microsoft wanted its new Active Directory to integrate as seamlessly as possible into standardized Internet practices.

In our previous examples, we've already talked about some domain names, such as CORP, SALES, and WIDGET. Although those names work well under NT, Windows 2000 Server's domains use different names.

Because Windows 2000 Server's domains are made to interact with the Internet, its domain names must be organized around the Internet naming scheme. For instance, our NT CORP domain would become the corp.com domain with Windows 2000 Server. What about the SALES domain? Because SALES trusts the CORP domain, its name becomes sales.corp.com. And WIDGET? It becomes widget.sales.corp.com.

FIGURE 6.4

Some of corp.com's Active Directory structure.

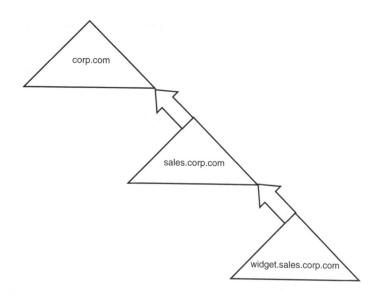

In order for the Active Directory to work as designed, your company must have DNS up and working, or you must be prepared to make your first Windows 2000 Server the first DNS server as well. (We'll talk more about setting up DNS in Hour 16, "DNS, WINS, and DHCP.")

> DNS must be running in your organization for the Active Directory to work properly.

For now, just keep in mind that you need DNS for proper functioning of the Active Directory. The good news is that Microsoft's DNS integrates perfectly into the Active Directory, meaning very little ongoing administration is necessary. Moreover, when you bring up your first Windows 2000 Server DC, you're automatically prompted to set up DNS.

Understanding the Trees and Forests

Everybody knows someone who "just can't see the forests for the trees." In our case, we're going to try to see the *trees* first, and then see the *forests*.

Because domains (under both NT and Windows 2000 Server) are simply giant partitions of groups of users, we need some way to link our domains together. As we discussed,

6

with NT we linked our domains together with trusts. But with Windows 2000 Server, we'll be linking our domains using trees and forests.

Trees

Trees are any hierarchically linked domains that have a *contiguous namespace*. Although that term might not look too friendly, it's easy enough to understand with an example as shown in Figure 6.5.

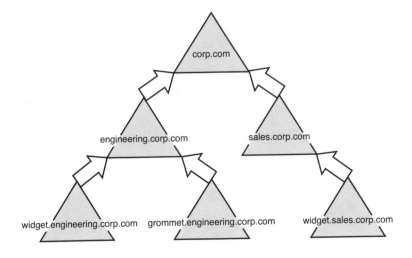

This is a diagram of CORP in the not-so-distant future. In this future, we can see CORP has a sales division whose domain is called sales.corp.com. Even the sales division has a widget-selling division whose domain name is widget.sales.corp.com. Additionally, there's an engineering division, whose domains are widget.engineering.corp.com and grommet.engineering.corp.com.

Notice that each division has the name of its parent? Because they're all fundamentally related to the corp.com domain, they are all considered to be under the same tree.

In our example, corp.com is considered the root of this tree. In this picture, corp.com reports to no other domain.

Consider another organization in Figure 6.6: bigu.edu.

The private two-year college Big U has several divisions under its root of bigu.edu. Big U has english.bigu.edu, compsci.bigu.edu, and registrar.bigu.edu. Additionally, the registrar might have billing.registrar.bigu.edu and records.registrar.bigu.edu. Still, each division has incorporated its parent's name in its own. Once again, all these domains are in the same bigu.edu tree.

FIGURE 6.6

Active Directory of bigu.edu.

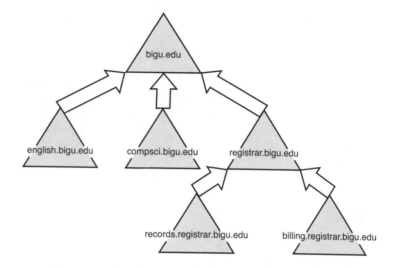

Forests

Forests are a combination of trees in which the roots trust each other. Because we just saw an example of *how* a forest can be created, let us examine *why* a forest might be necessary.

When hard times hit Big U, CORP was ready to buy it out so that CORP could easily train new employees at a very low cost. CORP wanted Big U to keep doing what it did best—running a school. But CORP also wanted a way to integrate the user accounts, equipment, and resources of two institutions, now that it owned both.

In order to join the two structures, administrators at both institutions set their two root servers to trust each other and created a *forest*.

> In the first release of Windows 2000 Server, there are no graphical tools to *join* two trees to create a forest. It is, however, possible to *create* a forest by upgrading existing Windows NT servers and instructing their root domains to join a forest.

6

As you can see in Figure 6.7, the overall structure of corp.com and bigu.edu is a forest. Even though administrators at both CORP and Big U can provide the other with administrative access, their domains don't share the same hierarchical names. For example, widget.sales.corp.com has no relation to records.registrar.bigu.edu.

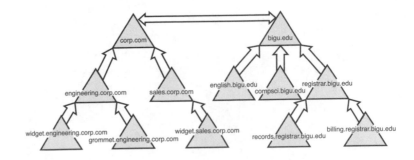

FIGURE 6.7
*Takeover complete by
corp.com of bigu.edu.*

Even a solitary domain is part of a tree, which is part of a forest.
Every domain is part of a tree, and no tree is not part of a forest.

Your First Windows 2000 Server Domain Controller

In Hour 3, "Installing Windows 2000 Server," we installed Windows 2000 Server onto a new partition with NTFS 5. In this exercise, we will promote the basic Windows 2000 Server to a Domain Controller that houses the Active Directory and call it corp.com.

You cannot promote a server to a Domain Controller without NTFS 5 on the machine. If you need to convert the partition, use the command line *convert.exe* utility.

Follow these steps to promote a Windows 2000 Server to a domain controller:

1. Click on Start, select the Run command, type dcpromo, and press the Enter key.

2. At the splash screen, click the Next button. The Domain Controller Type page appears next, as shown in Figure 6.8.

3. Select the first option, Domain Controller for a New Domain, and click the Next button to see Figure 6.9.

4. At the Create Tree or Child Domain screen, choose Create a New Domain Tree and click Next. You are choosing this option because you're not joining someone else's tree.

FIGURE 6.8

The Domain Controller Type screen.

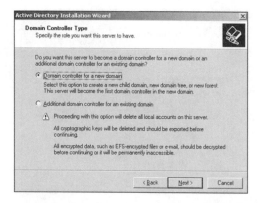

FIGURE 6.9

The Create Tree or Child Domain screen.

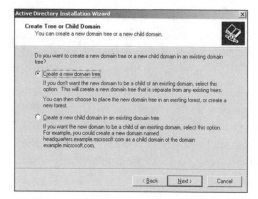

If you were bringing up the sales domain in the already existing corp.com domain, you would choose the other option.

5. At the Create or Join Forest screen (see Figure 6.10), choose the Create a New Forest of Domain Trees option. You are creating a new forest. Remember that even a tree of one domain belongs in a forest.

If you were adding a new root server to an already established forest, you would choose Domain Controller for a New Domain, and then select Create a New Domain Tree. This would occur if corp.com were to buy smallplayer.com.

6

FIGURE **6.10**

The Create or Join Forest screen.

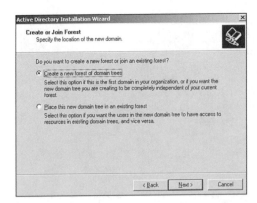

6. At the New Domain Name screen, enter corp.com and click Next.

7. At the NetBIOS Domain Name screen, keep the default of CORP and click Next. This name permits older clients to see your domain. NetBIOS and WINS are covered more thoroughly in Hour 15, "Protocols and Network Fundamentals."

8. At the Database and Log Locations screen, keep the defaults. By default, it installs under the directory where you installed Windows 2000 Server (in my example, it's d:\winnt\). If your systems are not using hardware RAID, it is recommended that the database and log be placed on a different partition for extra safety. For the sake of learning in this example, feel free to leave the location at the default.

9. The next screen, the Shared System Volume screen, asks where you'd like the shared system volume to be kept. As with the database and log locations, it is recommended to assign this location to an alternate partition. For the sake of this example though, just keep the defaults and click Next.

10. If you did not yet load DNS server (for instance, during installation), you should get an error message stating that DNS is not yet loaded. This message is to be expected. Because we've chosen to install a new domain in a new tree in a new forest with a new Active Directory, we must have DNS installed. Click OK to proceed.

11. The Configure DNS screen appears. Because we have no DNS, choose the first option to install DNS and click the Next button. We'll be going over DNS much more in Hour 16.

12. The Permissions screen appears. If you plan to integrate Windows NT application servers or NT RAS servers, you may choose to weaken the permissions; otherwise, choose Windows 2000 compatible only.

13. The Directory Services Restore Mode Administrator Password page appears next. This screen prompts you to provide a new password. This password is entered if

the Active Directory data becomes corrupt, and even the Administrator password cannot be looked up. In that case, you'll enter this password and perform some emergency surgery. Enter a password you'll remember when the chips are down.

13. The Summary page appears next. Review the proposed options on the Summary page shown in Figure 6.11, and if they are satisfactory, click the Next button. If they are not satisfactory, you can go back and modify the information as necessary.

FIGURE 6.11

Verify that all information is correct.

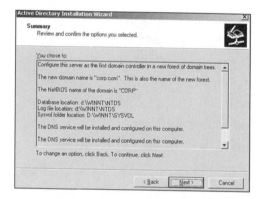

14. This will finish out your hour. Definitely take a coffee break while this is going on because it takes quite a long time, even on powerful machines.

15. After the Active Directory has finished loading, the summary informs you of the results of using the Active Directory Installation Wizard. Close the box by clicking Finish.

16. Click Restart Now to restart the machine.

Summary

The Windows 2000 Server's Active Directory is a replacement for NT's SAM. The Active Directory is a central repository for all sorts of enterprise-wide data, including user accounts, printer accounts, security objects, and more. Additionally, the Active Directory has the ability to let administrators add newly defined objects of practically any type, including photographs and sounds.

Trees are hierarchical Windows 2000 Server domains that form a contiguous namespace. A Windows 2000 Server forest is a grouping of unrelated trees whose root domains trust each other.

Use dcpromo to bring up your first Windows 2000 Server's Active Directory.

6

Workshop

The Workshop provides a quiz and exercises to help reinforce your learning. Even if you feel you know the material, you will still gain from working these exercises.

Quiz

1. What type of machine is required to form a domain?

2. What is the difference between a tree and a forest?

3. Name two non-Microsoft directory services.

4. What are some attributes that may be added to the Active Directory schema?

5. What is a trust? What is a transitive trust?

6. What is a root domain?

7. What is a parent domain? A child domain?

8. How do you promote a standalone server to a domain controller?

9. What Internet service must be running for the Active Directory to function properly?

10. What is the difference between NT domains and Windows 2000 Server domains?

Exercises

1. Analyze your NT structure. Note which domains you would upgrade first.

2. Analyze your NT structure. What DNS names might you assign to your domains?

3. Analyze your NT structure. Note how you would create a tree or a forest.

HOUR **7**

Advanced Planning for Domains, Domain Controllers, and the Active Directory

by Jeremy Moskowitz

In Hour 6, "Domains and the Active Directory," we discussed the history of NT domains and trusts and explored where the new Active Directory will take us. Chances are, however, that your current environment already has some NT 4.0 Server deployed. Perhaps it has only one server; perhaps you have it deployed enterprisewide, or on a department-by-department basis. Before you start rolling out your new Windows 2000 Servers, you'll need to consider strategy for your implementation. In this lesson, we will cover the following topics:

- How to upgrade your existing NT domain structure
- Setting up and working with Windows 2000 Server within a heterogeneous NT4/Windows 2000 Server environment
- Organization units versus domains
- Planning and implementing your sites
- Naming and placement of Domain Controllers

Upgrading Existing NT Domains and Domain Controllers

Instead of starting from scratch, you might already have an NT infrastructure in place. It is important to follow a specific order in your upgrade to guarantee success.

First, map out on paper which domains you'll be upgrading in what order. Start with the domain you'll be using as your root domain and work down the tree. When you upgrade a resource domain, you'll have the option to upgrade its PDC to be either a new domain in a tree, a new tree in a forest, or a standalone forest.

Upgrading Domain Controllers of an Existing NT Domain

As we learned in the previous hour, NT Domain Controllers come in two flavors: PDC and BDC. For each type, you'll need to select a different branch of dcpromo.exe when performing your upgrade.

The first screen DCPROMO will present you with is the Domain Controller Type screen (see Figure 7.1). It is here you will tell DCPROMO if you are upgrading a PDC or BDC.

Upgrading PDCs of an Existing NT Domain

For each domain to be upgraded, you'll want to upgrade the PDC first via winnt32.exe (see Hour 3, "Installing Windows 2000 Server"). When Windows 2000 Server detects that you're upgrading a PDC, it will automatically launch the Active Directory Wizard (dcpromo.exe) at the end of the upgrade and bring you to this point.

At the Domain Controller Type screen, choose Domain Controller for a New Domain.

You'll basically repeat the exercise performed in the previous hour. In both cases, you are bringing up a new Domain Controller for a new domain.

FIGURE 7.1
Domain Controller Type screen.

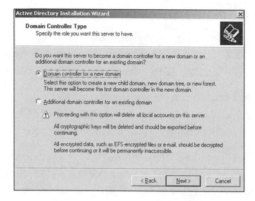

Upgrading BDCs of an Existing NT Domain

After your PDCs are upgraded to Windows 2000 Server, you are then prepared to attack your BDCs. Upgrade each Windows NT BDC of the domain by running winnt32.exe as well. When the upgrade is finished, it will be a *member server*, but not a Domain Controller. When ready, run DCPROMO to bump it up to Domain Controller status.

> See Hour 8, "Server Types, Local Users, and Groups," for more information about the differences between a standalone server, member server, and Domain Controller.

At the Domain Controller Type screen (refer to Figure 7.1), choose Additional Domain Controller for an Existing Domain.

You'll then be prompted for administrative credentials in the domain you want to join.

Forming Your New Active Directory Tree

Instruct the Active Directory to construct your tree at the Create Tree or Child Domain screen (see Figure 7.9).

For the Root Domain

To form your tree, you need to start somewhere, and that somewhere is called the *root domain* (for instance, corp.com). To signify the top of your tree, choose Create a New Domain Tree at the Create Tree or Child Domain screen, and then click Next.

7

For All Other Domains You Want to Keep in the Same Tree

Because all other domains will be within the tree, at the Create Tree or Child Domain screen, choose Create a New Child Domain in an Existing Domain Tree and click Next. This will create a child domain such as sales.corp.com, for example.

The remainder of the exercise can be found in the previous hour, so there's no need to repeat it here. Just remember to upgrade your NT domain's PDCs first, create your Active Directory structure, and then go back and upgrade your BDCs.

When you've finished upgrading all your NT servers to Windows 2000 Servers, you'll change the mode from Mixed to Native. After Windows 2000 Server is changed to Native mode, the Active Directory is fully functional, transitive trusts are activated, and NT servers are no longer allowed to participate in the new Active Directory structure. You'll be upgrading your Active Directory from Mixed mode to Native mode in Hour 9, "Users, Groups, and Machine Accounts on Domain Controllers."

Heterogeneous NT 4/Windows 2000 Server Environments

As we've seen above, it's possible to have any number of NT and Windows 2000 Server combinations. You may have some of your NT servers upgraded to Windows 2000 Server, some freshly created Windows 2000 Servers, and even some systems remaining as NT.

When a mix of NT and Windows 2000 Servers is present in an environment, Windows 2000 Server calls this *Mixed mode*. While in Mixed mode, downlevel clients see the world from the old Windows NT perspective; that is, only explicit trusts between domains are recognized.

When only Windows 2000 Servers are present in an environment, the mode may be changed to *Native mode*.

You might be asking yourself, "If Mixed mode provides the same functionality to my Windows clients, why would I want to change?" It's true that your clients will notice little or no discernable difference. But from an administrative perspective, the new Windows 2000 Server authentication model (Kerberos) is in full force battling hackers. Additionally, Windows 2000 Server doesn't distinguish between Primary and Secondary Domain Controllers—that distinction goes away. Next, you'll be able to nest group types when you create user groups (more about this in Hour 9). Lastly, your transitive trusts start to kick in. Remember our example where widgets.sales.corp.com trusted sales.corp.com, which trusted corp.com? That transitive trust enables widgets.sales.corp.com to trust corp.com. Your Active Directory will be fully operational the moment you enter Native mode.

> Entering Native mode is a one-way operation. After Native Mode is entered, there is no way to retreat to Mixed mode to add an NT 4.0 server. No new NT 4.0 domain controllers will be admitted to the domain.

We'll change to Native mode at the end of Hour 9.

Organization Units

Domains are great if you want to section out entire divisions of users from one another, or have an administrator in a separate domain call the shots for how he runs his turf. Sometimes it's best to create another domain because of language barriers. Other times, it's good to create a new domain to mirror an existing NT domain structure.

But often you'll find you need more finite control over portions of a certain domain. That's where organization units (OUs) come in handy.

Organization units are simply logical containers of objects. An *object* can be almost anything: a user account, a printer, computers, even other organization units! OUs are simply a mechanism for logically keeping together objects that should be together.

After you have set up an organization unit for a group of objects, you may delegate administration for that group of objects. For instance, you can specify that Sally can create new accounts in the Secretaries organization unit. This leaves you more time to do other things that you like to do—like reading Sams books.

Organization units can often substitute for domains, if carefully planned. Striking a balance between numbers of domains and organization units is tricky. You can have too many domains or too many organization units so that your enterprise becomes hard to manage. Planning exactly how you'll break up your users into domains and organization units is key for manageability.

In this section, we'll begin our discussion on the various reasons for creating organization units. Stay tuned—we'll be doing some actual hands-on work with organization units in Hour 10, "Active Directory Entities."

7

When to Create Domains or Organizational Units

Generally, people get bogged down by the number of domains they feel they need to deploy. Often this fear comes from the fact that it takes at least one dedicated Domain Controller to start the structure of a domain. Unfortunately, the hardware manufacturers get the most advantage from this setup because in general, it takes a fairly powerful server to be a Domain Controller. The good news is that you can usually use organizational units to your advantage to minimize the number of domains you need to deploy.

If you're stuck between deciding whether to deploy an organizational unit or a domain, here are some quick guidelines that should help your decision. Almost always create a new domain if

- You need a separate security policy between users. A domain is a discrete security boundary. After a policy for a domain is set (for example, password length), everyone in the domain must follow it.
- You have multiple languages in an organization. Just based on ease of use, it's easier to delegate an administrator who knows the language.
- You want to be 100% certain that a particular administrator has the ability to take absolute control when necessary. A domain administrator will *always* be more powerful than a delegated OU administrator.
- You have around a million or more objects. After you get sufficiently large, only a domain will handle the requirements.

Conversely, almost always create an organization unit if

- You find your users bouncing around from division to division. If you set up one domain and make organization units for the divisions, it's nearly no work to move them from one organization unit to another. (We'll see more about this in Hour 10.)
- You're collapsing a Windows NT resource domain. If you don't have any overriding reason to create a domain (see preceding guidelines), chances are that it can be taken down to the organization unit level.

You can use third-party tools such as Fastlane's DM/Administrator or Mission Critical Software's Enterprise Administrator to help automate the process of collapsing NT resource domains into the account domains. These utilities methodically move users and computer accounts from one domain to another, while preserving permissions.

See Hour 10 for a more focused discussion about some specific strategies for planning and creating your organization units.

Planning and Implementing Sites

When someone says to you, "Hey, I'll be back in 20 minutes—I'll be going over to our other site," what they're really saying to you is, "I'm going to our other physical location."

Windows 2000 Server differentiates between the concepts of domains and sites. As you know, a *domain* is a logical group of computers and accounts. A *site* is a single physical location with high bandwidth connected by TCP/IP. A single domain may span many sites, and a single site may encompass many domains.

> Microsoft's concept of *site* also extends to other products, such as SMS.

The concept of sites is important to the proper functioning of Windows 2000 Server. As we discussed earlier, Active Directory replication happens between all Domain Controllers in a domain. More specifically, replication is automatically set up in a ring structure between all DCs at a specific site.

With this in mind, you may only regulate the bandwidth and replication traffic *between* sites, not *within* a site.

Because the Active Directory lives on all Domain Controllers in a domain, what happens if you have one domain that consists of four Domain Controllers in Delaware and one in Arizona? How can you regulate when changes will be sent to the server in Arizona? Depending on how much money you have allocated to your WAN links and how often you feel you need the most up-to-date Active Directory information, you might not want to send all the Active Directory updates all the time over that very expensive WAN link.

Because a site is defined as single physical location with high bandwidth connected by TCP/IP, we'll first need to detail which TCP/IP subnets define the boundaries of each of our sites. Next, we'll need to set up site links between our sites. A *site link* is merely a representation of how the data flows between the sites. In general, it should resemble your WAN infrastructure. After you set up the sites, you specify which sites are on that link, and voilà! You've connected your sites.

7

When we created our first Domain Controller using the Active Directory Wizard, you might have noticed that there was an entry in the summary page calling our first site Default-First-Site. When new Domain Controllers come up for the first time, they are placed in a site container that might not be appropriate. You'll be using the Active Directory Sites and Services Manager to move the Domain Controllers from one site to another, create and rename sites as appropriate, and create site links between sites.

In our example, we'll rename the Default-First-Site to Delaware, and keep the W2kserver1 server at that site. Then, we'll create a new site called Arizona, and move the AZDC1 to that site. Next, we need to define the subnets that make up each of our sites. We'll then create a site link between the two and regulate the traffic to replicate every 260 minutes (instead of the default 180).

To expedite matters, our example already has a second Domain Controller in the corp.com domain named AZDC1, which was placed in the Default-First-Site by the Active Directory Wizard. If desired, follow the directions outlined in the previous chapter to bring your own AZDC1 online in the corp.com domain. You will make use of the AZDC1 machine throughout the rest of the book.

The first thing we need to do is rename our Default-First-Site-Name to Delaware.

1. Click Start, Programs, Administrative Tools, and then Active Directory Sites and Services. In this example, we have two servers—W2kserver1 and AZDC1—in the corp.com domain. Right now, they're in the same site, as you can see in Figure 7.2.

FIGURE 7.2

W2kserver1 and AZDC1 in the corp.com domain and the "Default-First-Site-Name" site.

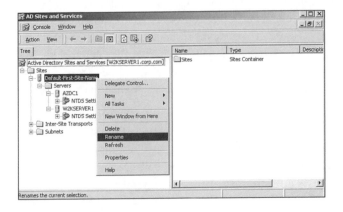

2. Right-click over Default-First-Site-Name, select Rename, and type Delaware as also seen in Figure 7.3.

3. Next, create a new site by right-clicking over the word Sites and selecting New, Site.

4. At the Create a New Object Site screen, enter Arizona. Click the DEFAULTIP-SITELINK then click OK. You now have two sites: Delaware and Arizona. A dialog box appears which provides our roadmap to finishing.

5. To follow the advice of the roadmap, we need to put a domain controller in the Arizona site. To move the AZDC1 server from its current site (Delaware) to Arizona, right-click over AZDC1 and select Move.

6. Select Arizona from the site list and click OK (see Figure 7.3). AZDC1 has now been moved to Arizona.

FIGURE 7.3

AZDC1 has been moved.

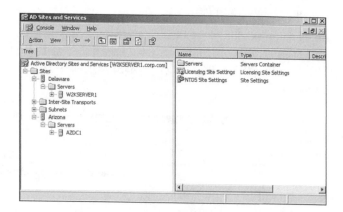

Next, we need to define the subnets that make up each of our sites. We'll pretend for this example that the subnet for Delaware is 200.100.100.0 and the subnet for Arizona is 200.100.200.0 each with a subnet mask of 255.255.255.0.

1. Right-click the Subnets folder (which is in the Sites folder) and select New Subnet.

2. Select Delaware from the sites list, and enter in 200.100.200.0 for the Address field and 255.255.255.0 for the subnet mask. (Note the shorthand name below is completed for you as 200.100.100.0/24. You'll see where this number comes from in Hour 15, "Protocols and Network Fundamentals.") Click OK.

3. Right-click the Subnets folder. Select New Subnet.

4. Select Arizona from the sites list, and enter in 200.100.200.0 for the Address field and 255.255.255.0 for the subnet mask.

5. When done, your subnet list should look like Figure 7.4.

7

FIGURE 7.4

Your subnets are now entered.

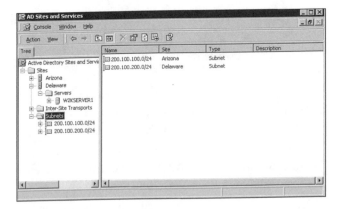

Next we need to join our two sites together and specify the replication schedule. You do this with an inter-site transport.

1. In the left pane, locate the Inter-Site Transports folder. Expand it, and click the IP folder inside it. The right pane should have a DEFAULTIPSITELINK folder, as shown in Figure 7.5. Right-click the DEFAULTIPSITELINK folder, and select Properties.

FIGURE 7.5

Use the Properties selection to modify the link.

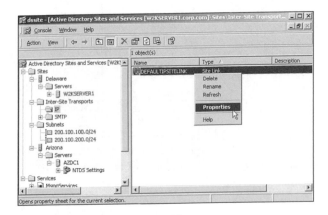

2. By default, the sites are already placed in the site link. But, because we're here, we'll be kind to our slower WAN link and choke the replication schedule. Change the Replicate Every field from 180 to 260 minutes.

As an additional exercise, you can click the Change Schedule button to finitely control which days in the week replication may be active.

If multiple site links are set up, you can raise or lower the Cost setting to force replication traffic to use "cheaper" links.

Naming and Placement Strategy

A good network design using Windows 2000 Servers stems from knowing what your users need from you. You have a lot to think about: DNS naming (for example, corp.com), when to create domains or organization units, how to decide on trees or forests, and numbers and placement of Domain Controllers and global catalog servers. Let's hit each of these in order to see whether we can plan ahead for your implementation.

DNS Naming

First of all, it's important to choose a name that best suits your organization. You must first pick from the top-level domain names, such as .com, .edu, and .org. At some time in the near future, there might be additional top-level names, such as .biz, .firm, and .xxx. After you've chosen your top-level name, say, .com, you'll need decide whether or not you'll ever expose your servers to the Internet.

If you have no plans to be on the Internet, you can feel free to name your domain trees just about anything you like. Again, choose this option only if you're certain you'll never want a public presence of your servers on the Internet. This is because after a name is set in DNS (which forms the structure for your Active Directory), you won't want to have to rename and redeploy everything because someone else is using that name.

To register domain names on the Internet, you'll need to visit www.internic.net and follow its instructions. You need to only register your root name (for instance, corp.com) per tree. In the future, you will be able to register domain names through a variety of providers such as AOL, AT&T, and others, but each of these organizations still creates an entry into the database owned and maintained by InterNIC.

We'll talk more about DNS in Hour 16, "DNS, WINS, and DHCP."

How to Decide on Trees or Forests

This will be the easiest decision you'll never have to make. Your structured namespace will decide this for you. If you have two divisions that must have separate namespace on their root servers (for example, corp.com and bigu.edu), you must have a forest.

7

The only decision you will have to make is if another division comes alive in a current organization. In general, you'd most likely start a new tree branch, except perhaps if there are plans for selling off that new business unit. As of the Windows 2000 Server release date, there is no way via the graphical interface to set free a piece of the tree to be autonomous.

Active Directory Replication and the Global Catalog

Because the Active Directory has a ton of information, it can be a burden on a Domain Controller to search through it all just to pull up one phone number. To alleviate the stress put on the Active Directory servers, a global catalog server can be brought up to be the front line of all user queries.

Moreover, the global catalog eliminates the question of how to share information between domains, trees, and forests. As its name implies, it has global access to information regarding objects (we'll see more about global access in Hour 9).

After it is established, a global catalog server contains a partial replica of the Active Directory for a forest. A *partial* replica simply means that the catalog has a list of all the objects in the forest, but not necessarily all the attributes of the objects. For example, when a query on username Juser is performed for his First Name attribute, the global catalog is sure to have it at its fingertips. If, however, a more esoteric attribute is requested, such as Joe's voiceprint, the global catalog will automatically forward that request to a Domain Controller in the tree and serve back the query as requested.

With the global catalog, you can offload some of the work of the Windows 2000 Server's Domain Controllers. By default, the first Domain Controller in a forest is, itself, a global catalog server as well. It doesn't have to remain that way, however. The role of global catalog may be reassigned to other (or additional) Domain Controllers as you see fit.

Some attributes are predefined by Microsoft to be replicated to the global catalog servers, such as Last Name, First Name, and username. Additionally, you may set the global catalog server to replicate the attributes you feel your users will query the most. Note, however, that sufficient disk space is required on each global catalog server in your enterprise.

Be aware that, although multiple global catalog servers in a forest aren't required, they are certainly recommended. Global catalogs are the last checkpoint for network validation for users. If no global catalogs are available to users, users cannot log on to the Active Directory. This is because Universal group assignments live in the global catalog. (Once again, see more on this topic in Hour 9).

You can change which DCs are global catalog Servers with the Active Directory Sites and Services tool. (We'll see how to do this a bit later on in this hour.)

Numbers and Placement of Domain Controllers and Global Catalog Servers

Let's go back a step and review the definition of site. In the previous hour, we said a site is a single physical location with high bandwidth connected by TCP/IP.

You might think that if you have four buildings, each six feet apart from one another, you must have one site. As soon as you discover that they are connected by a 28.8Kbps modem, you realize you've got four sites. Don't let the proximity of physical buildings fool you. Microsoft's definition of fast connectivity has changed over the years. It used to be 56Kbps, but more recently it has changed to 10Mbps. That's regular Ethernet speeds to you and me.

Therefore, in order to maximize your Windows 2000 Server performance, you'll need to place at least one Domain Controller and one global catalog server at a site. The good news, however, is that a global catalog server may be the same physical box as the first Domain Controller, although it need not be.

A global catalog server is always a Domain Controller, but a Domain Controller need not necessarily be a global catalog server. As we see in the following exercise, the administrator controls which domain controllers become global catalog servers.

When it comes to sizes of Domain Controllers and global catalog servers, remember the following rules:

- Domain Controllers must have enough space to hold every object and every attribute in the directory.
- Global catalog servers must have enough space to hold every object (but not every attribute) from all other directories in the forest.

Now that we've set up our sites, we'll set up AZDC1 to be a global catalog server. Remember, it's best to have at least one global catalog server per site. In the last exercise, you split your servers into two sites: Delaware and Arizona. Because the server in Delaware is already a global catalog server (W2kserver1), you'll need to generate a global catalog server for the Arizona site. This will help speed up searches to the Active Directory and logins to the Active Directory at the Arizona site.

7

To generate a global catalog server for a second site, follow these steps:

1. Click on Start, Programs, Administrative Tools, and then Active Directory Sites and Services.

2. Expand the Site folder (Arizona) and the Server folder (AZDC1) to expose the NTDS Settings entry. Right-click it for the properties.

3. On the General tab, click the Global Catalog check box, as you can see in Figure 7.6. Click OK.

FIGURE 7.6

Click here to tell a domain controller to be a global catalog server.

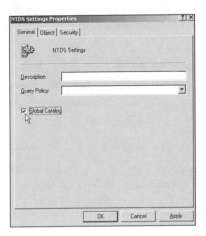

Summary

Don't start bringing up your Windows 2000 Servers or upgrading your existing NT infrastructure until you've planned it out. If you are upgrading NT 4.0 servers, plan which domains you'll tackle first. Start by upgrading the PDC of each NT domain, and then upgrade each BDC of each domain.

Use winnt32.exe to upgrade existing NT 4.0 PDCs and BDCs, and then use DCPROMO.EXE to upgrade your member servers to domain controllers as necessary.

Use organizational units for sectioning users when a domain might be too much.

Use sites to partition physical locations with fast connectivity.

The global catalog is a special type of Domain Controller that houses special indices of the Active Directory for fast query results. You should optimally have at least one global catalog per site, and you are required to have at least one global catalog per forest.

When you've finished upgrading all your NT servers to Windows 2000 Servers, change the mode from Mixed to Native. After Windows 2000 Server is changed to Native mode, the Active Directory is fully functional, transitive trusts are activated, and NT domain controllers are no longer allowed to participate in the domain.

Workshop

The Workshop provides a quiz and exercises to help reinforce your learning. Even if you feel you know the material, you will still gain from working these exercises.

Quiz

1. What happens when the Active Directory is changed from Mixed mode and Native mode?

2. In what order do you upgrade domains?

3. In what order do you upgrade Domain Controllers?

4. What does the global catalog server do? Why would you want to place it close to users?

5. What is a site?

6. What is a site link?

7. How many global catalog servers should you have per site?

8. When should you create domains?

9. When should you create OUs?

10. Whom do you contact to get on the Internet?

Exercises

1. Load a temporary Windows NT 4.0 BDC to experiment with, then take it off-line if it is on your production network. Upgrade this BDC and use dcpromo wizard to make it a Windows 2000 Domain Controller.

2. Load another Windows 2000 Server and make it a global catalog server.

3. Pretend these two servers are destined to be in two sites. Make another site, and move one server to another site.

7

HOUR **8**

Server Types, Local Users, and Groups

by Jeremy Moskowitz

Fundamentally, at the Windows 2000 Server's heart is the capability to serve users. The only thing to keep in mind is how it does that in each of its modes—standalone server, member server, or Domain Controller.

As you'll see, the most efficient way to handle many users at a time is to place them in groups. Groups can help lower the administrative burden by setting permissions on files, folders, or other resources at one time. The changes you make then take effect for everyone in the group immediately.

As we've alluded to several times so far, Windows 2000 Server can lead one of three lives. After the initial setup is complete and your new installation is born, it can arrive either as a standalone server or it can participate in a domain as a member server (you will see how to do this in Hour 9, "Users, Groups, and Machine Accounts on Domain Controllers"). As you also saw in Hour 6, "Domains and the Active Directory," you need to promote a Windows 2000 Server using DCPROMO.EXE to become a full-fledged Domain Controller and participate in the Active Directory.

If you have two machines, one configured to be a standalone server and the other as a Domain Controller, we encourage you to try all the exercises in this hour. Alternatively, you could perform many of the exercises with a Windows 2000 Professional workstation.

If, however, you've already promoted your only Windows 2000 Server to a Domain Controller (and have no Windows 2000 Professional machine available), you will not be able to perform the exercises in this hour. Stay tuned; you'll be back in action in the next hour.

Even if you do not have another machine available, reading the entire discussion is recommended. The next hour will deal with users and groups on Domain Controllers. In those places in which a concept can carry over to more than one hour, we only mention it once, in the first hour.

In this hour, you will learn about

- Standalone servers, member servers, and Domain Controllers
- Account names
- Users on standalone servers
- Groups on standalone servers

Server Types: Standalone Versus Member Versus Domain Controllers

Before a server is promoted to be a Domain Controller, Windows 2000 Servers in standalone mode and Windows 2000 Professional workstations have a lot more in common than just their user interface. In fact, they are nearly identical. They are in a unique position to lead dual lives.

An administrator can choose to have non–Domain Controllers participate or not participate in the domain if desired.

If a Windows 2000 Server does not participate in the domain, it is considered a standalone server because it keeps its own separate, unrelated copy of usernames and passwords, as you'll see later in this hour.

8

If a Windows 2000 Server does participate in the domain, it is considered a member server because it is a "member" of the domain. When access to resources is requested on a member server, the server can query the domain's user database to determine access rights. These member servers (or Windows 2000 Professional workstations) are *not* Domain Controllers—but they have the capability to enforce permissions placed upon objects they do house against the information in the domain.

Why is there a difference? Why would you want to make one machine a standalone server, another a member server, and another a Domain Controller? Microsoft gives you a choice in how you make use of your servers. As an administrator of Windows 2000 Server machines, the way you choose to implement your server should be guided by the following considerations:

- Standalone servers are like islands. If you want to bring up a very powerful machine, but don't want to share it with many people, a standalone server is an excellent choice. Likewise, if a Windows 2000 Professional machine never joins a domain, it is also considered a standalone workstation. Applications run fastest on standalone Windows 2000 Servers because they are free from the administrative load of having to support many accounts. They are not burdened with the extra CPU power or disk space required to house the Active Directory.

- Member servers are like standalone servers in that they also have their own local accounts database. They have the added ability to enforce security to the objects they house against security rights housed in the domain. This enforcement feels exactly the same as with a Windows 2000 Professional workstation. Most organizations force their Windows 2000 Server and Windows 2000 Professional workstations to participate in the domain. That way, user accounts and security permissions can be centralized in the domain. You'll see how to convert a standalone server to a member server in Chapter 9.

- Domain Controllers build the foundation of your network. You rely on them to physically house your Active Directory user accounts, and take care of the business of structuring and supporting your network.

Table 8.1 summarizes the differences between the three servers.

TABLE 8.1 Summary of the Properties of Standalone Servers, Member Servers, and Domain Controllers

	Has Local Accounts Database	May Participate in Domain	Can Assign Security to Objects in Local Accounts Database	Can Assign Security Based on Domain Objects	Physically Houses Domain Accounts
Standalone Server	X		X		
Member Server	X	X	X	X	
Domain Controller		X		X	X

Account Names

User accounts are analogous to a user's first name. It needs to represent the user as he goes along his daily journey. Different organizations choose different naming strategies when doling out user accounts.

Some organizations choose just the first name of the user. This scheme works only in the smallest of organizations. For instance, as soon as two people named Martin are hired, the scheme is already violated.

Other naming schemes include the first initial plus the last name, such as jknapp, emarshall, and jmoskowitz. Others choose the contrapositive: jillk, marshalle, and jeremym. In either of these two naming strategies, a middle initial or incremental numbering scheme may be used to break a tie.

Still others choose schemes that signify a user's designation in the company, be it a temporary employee, a corporate executive, or a four-star general. Such organizations simply append a character to the beginning or end of the name.

Some organizations like to keep an edge on their security procedures. It's not uncommon to see an employee's badge ID become his username. Additionally, it's not uncommon in the highest of security areas for usernames to be random jumbles of numbers and letters. This scheme prevents easily guessable usernames.

Whichever scheme you pick, you should make it extensible for your entire organization and stick with it.

> Usernames can be up to 20 characters long and a mix of numbers and letters. Although Windows 2000 will display the case of the letters in the username, the case is ignored in all other instances (that is, you may log on as jeremym or JeREmyM). You may not use <, >, ", /, \, |, ;, :, +, =, , ",", ?, or * in the name. The last rule is that a name cannot be all "." (periods). With these restrictions, you still have the ability to generate some pretty wacky usernames. f-7 and j.% are two perfectly valid, albeit bizarre, Windows 2000 usernames.

Users on Standalone Servers

Windows 2000 Servers acting as standalone servers and Windows 2000 Professional workstations have only local user accounts. The term *local* describes the place where the user account is created.

For instance, if there is a standalone server called AZSERV1, and a user called joeuser on that server, that account type is called a local account. Furthermore, if you created an account on a Windows 2000 Professional machine and created a user called sallys, that account would also be considered a local account. If you created a user account on a Windows 2000 member server called marcw, that account would also be considered a local account.

These accounts are not stored in the Active Directory; rather, they are housed in a local security database of the standalone server, member server, or Windows 2000 Professional workstation on which they were created. The local security database is a simple database comprised of usernames and passwords.

Directly after installation, standalone Windows 2000 Servers come with several built-in user accounts. In fact, you helped create one during setup in Hour 3, "Installing Windows 2000 Server."

By default, the two accounts that Windows 2000 Server creates for you are Administrator and Guest. You helped create Administrator in Hour 3 during installation of Windows 2000 Server when the installation program asked you for the administrator's password. The Guest account's password was not requested during setup time because it has no password.

Also, depending on the options chosen at time of setup, there may be other local accounts, such as IUSR<*servername*> and IWAM<*servername*>, that SETUP creates automatically to provide access to Internet services. You might also see a TsInternetUser account that is sometimes used in advanced configurations of the Terminal Services features.

To view the local users and groups on a standalone server, follow these steps:

> If you have already promoted your server to a Domain Controller (Hour 6) you will not be able to perform this procedure. If you have a second server in standalone mode, or a Windows 2000 Professional machine, feel free to follow along.

1. Click Start, Programs, Administrative Tools, and then choose Computer Management.
2. Expand the "System Tools" tree, and then expand the Local Users and Groups tree, as shown in Figure 8.1.

FIGURE 8.1

The Local Users and Groups Tree shows you who is in your domain.

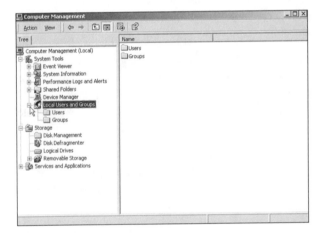

3. Click on Users in the left pane. Notice the user accounts just discussed (see Figure 8.2), including Administrator, Guest, and in this case, IUSER and IWAM accounts, where the server name is automatically appended, as well as a TsInternetUser account for Terminal Server.

Built-in User Accounts

The Administrator account is one you should be somewhat familiar with. In fact, if you weren't using the Administrator account, you couldn't be logged in right now. In the real world, it is recommended that you rename the Administrator account as soon as possible. (Don't do this now.) You should change the account name because it only takes two pieces of information to get into the system: a username and a password. Because hackers, coworkers, and even secretaries know that the most powerful Windows 2000 Server username is Administrator, they need only one additional piece of information to have free run of your server. Sure, that password might be difficult to get, but with a default username of Administrator they already have half of what they need.

FIGURE 8.2

Here are the default local users created at installation time.

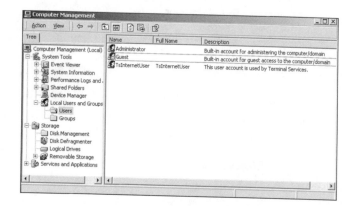

Additionally, you might create copies of the Administrator account to another name of your choice. Do note, however, that a copy of the Administrator account is not the same thing as the original Administrator account. Copying an Administrator account merely copies the account's group membership. (Group membership will be discussed in detail a bit later in this hour.) The actual Administrator account, either in its original name as Administrator or renamed to some other name, has one property that no other account on that system will ever have—the ability to never get locked out of the system. Therefore, although you are encouraged to rename the Administrator account to dissuade people from trying to break into the system, it's equally important to record (either mentally or otherwise safely) the new, renamed Administrator account.

The Guest account is a legacy holdover from LAN Manager (pre-Windows NT) days. As we stated, the Guest account requires no password to allow authentication. The account is disabled by default, so no one can even log in to it. Unless you have a specific application that requires it or another reason to enable the Guest account, it's recommended that you rename the Guest account, and keep its account locked out.

Create Your First Account

In the last exercise, you got a chance to look at the default, built-in usernames. Because you already have the local users on the screen, let's create our first user.

If you have already promoted your server to a Domain Controller (see Hour 6) you will not be able to perform this procedure. If you have a second server in standalone mode, or a Windows 2000 Professional workstation, feel free to follow along.

To create a local user account:

1. Click Start, Programs, Administrative Tools, then choose Computer Management.

2. Expand the "System Tools" tree then expand the Local Users and Groups tree. Click on the Action menu, and select New User.

FIGURE 8.3

A blank user tab awaits your input.

3. When the Create User dialog box appears, enter a new account for a fictitious user (see Figure 8.3): Joe User. For Username, enter Juser. For Full Name, enter Joe User. For Description, enter A regular guy. Enter in number1 for the Password and Confirm password fields. Also uncheck the User Must Change Password at Next Logon check box.

4. Click the Create box, and voilà! You have just created your first user.

5. Click Close to close the Create User dialog box.

Account Options

In your day-to-day administration, you can also choose which options about the account you want to take effect:

- User Must Change Password at Next Logon check box

  When you uncheck that box, the other options become automatically available to you. In this case, you'll be leaving them alone.

8

In normal, day-to-day administration, you would normally leave the User Must Change Password at Next Logon check box on. This is so that when you create a new user account and give that user the initial password, he or she is forced to change it so that even you (the Administrator) don't know what it is.

- User Cannot Change Password check box

  As its name implies, the user cannot change his or her password. Only someone with access to this administrator console can change it for the user. This entry is useful if you have an environment where many people use the same account.

- Password Never Expires check box

  This setting, in conjunction with the User Cannot Change Password box, creates an account that is essentially permanent. This setting is most useful for service accounts, which perform background automated tasks. You want to ensure that the service accounts' password always stays the same.

- Account Disabled check box

  This setting is useful if you need an instant way to shut off people from accessing this account. Many administrators are phoned by the Human Resources division at a company when people are fired. The Human Resources manager will ask the Administrator to disable the account, preventing the fired individual from walking away with sensitive files, or worse, damaging data. This way, after the account is disabled and the user has been escorted from the building, the username and password can be changed and someone else can, if desired, take over the job responsibilities. There is no need to delete the account.

If you delete an account and re-create it with the same name, you have still deleted the original account, as well as all the rights that this account held. This is because underneath the username is a unique SID (Security Identifier) code associated with each username. After a user and his associated SID code have been erased, there is no way to return them. Also, enabling the Account Disabled check box simply prevents new logons. It does not throw a currently working user off the system.

There is another use for the Account Disabled setting. Sometimes accounts can be created in advance, say, for seasonal workers. If desired, those accounts can simply be

disabled when the users leave for the season, and enabled when they return. This prevents the repetition of deleting and re-creating accounts.

User Properties

Besides lockout and password options, users have many more attributes tied to their
accounts. If you double-click a username, you can find out many properties about that
user, as shown in Figure 8.4.

FIGURE 8.4

*The User Properties
dialog box lets you
define user attributes.*

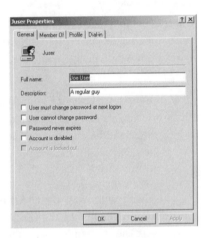

You can see in Figure 8.4 that in the User Properties dialog box are four tabs that can
have values of data. We've already discussed the General tab, but the dialog also contains
the Membership, Profile, and Dial-in tabs. You will learn about the Profile tab in Hour
14, "Profiles and Policies," and the Dial-Up tab in Hour 17, "Network and Dial-Up
Connectivity." The Member Of tab is described later in this hour.

Groups Defined

In our day-to-day lives, when we say that someone is a member of a club, organization,
or group, we're really saying that they have some special status, which usually comes
with some special privileges that outsiders of the group don't get. Joining a group means
gaining credentials. Additionally, there's no reason why one person can't belong to more
than one group and get the privileges bestowed by both groups.

For instance, if you encounter someone snooping around your backyard at 1:00 AM, you
might ask them for some identification. If he showed you a county police badge, you'd
probably let him continue because he is a "member" of the "police" group. If, however,
this person took out a county library card, you'd kick him out of your front yard!

8

In our Windows 2000 Server parlance, the terms *membership* and *group* carry over perfectly from these general descriptions.

When users are members of a group, they get additional privileges and access rights for being a part of that group. As an administrator, you'll be creating users, placing them in groups, and granting the group rights. Perhaps that right is to simply read a directory or print to a printer where others cannot. Other times, you can grant a group the right to shut down the server. You can even, if desired, put groups into other groups.

Groups on Standalone Windows 2000 Servers

When a Windows 2000 Server is in standalone mode, there is only one group type: the Local group. Local groups are pools of users to whom specific rights may be assigned.

Local Groups

Like local user accounts, local groups are only good for the machine on which they're created. Only user accounts defined on that specific machine may be members of a local group. Therefore, local groups cannot contain other users from any other machine. Moreover, you may not nest local groups (that is, put local groups inside other local groups).

Local groups do, however, come in two flavors:

- User-defined groups—These are groups that the Administrator may create to house users as he or she sees fit.

- Built-in groups—These groups, depending on the options at setup time, are automatically created by the system. These built-in groups are special, in that their members are granted some special system privileges. After a user is added to one (or more) of these built-in groups, they instantly get the privileges of that group.

 The user must log off and log back on to a server before a group membership and its privileges take effect.

Built-in Groups on Standalone Servers

A description of each of the built-in groups, and the privileges granted them follows Figure 8.5.

FIGURE 8.5

Built-in local groups.

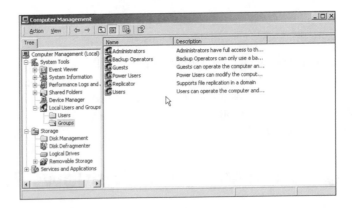

- Administrators—Members of this group have free rein on this server.

- Backup Operators—Members of this group have the ability to bypass normal file security to be able to perform backup. Usually, backup programs put their custom user accounts in here. Not used often in normal life. If a member is in this group, the user also has the ability to log on and shut down the server, if desired.

- Guests—A holdover from LANManager days. Avoid if possible. Use only if specifically instructed to do so by Microsoft Support Services or your application documentation.

- Power Users—Users in this group have the ability to create local user accounts. The only caveat, however, is that they can only delete the accounts they create. Additionally, power users may change the desktop settings.

- Replicator—Used by Windows 2000 to bypass a specific security setting that allows file replication between servers. Windows 2000 automatically puts the required user accounts in here.

- Users—A group for regular users. When new users are created, they are automatically placed in this group. No special functions are granted by being a member of the users group.

Depending on other loaded options, you might have other local groups, which provide additional functionality:

- DHCP Administrators—These users have the ability to change scope options.

- DHCP Users—These users have extra permissions to perform administrative tasks on the DHCP database.

- WINS Users—These users have extra permissions to perform administrative tasks on the WINS database.

Administrator-Defined Local Groups

Now that you understand the difference between different group types on standalone servers, let's create our first group, and put Joe User inside it.

To create a group account:

1. Click Start, Programs, Administrative Tools, and then choose Computer Management.

2. Expand the "System Tools" and "Local Users and Groups" trees. Click the Groups folder to see all the groups.

3. Click the Action menu, and then click New Group.

4. Name the group Paymanagers, give it a description of Payroll Management Group, and click Add to add members, as shown in Figure 8.6.

FIGURE 8.6

Create the Payroll Management Group using the Computer Management tool.

5. Scroll down until you find the Juser account. Select it, and click Add. Juser should now appear in the bottom half of the dialog box that says You Have Selected the Following Objects. Click OK.

FIGURE 8.7

Add Joe User to the group using the Add User dialog box.

6. In the Create Group dialog box, click Create, and then Close.

7. Verify that your group was created by checking in the Local Groups list for Paymanagers.

If desired, you may add or delete members to the group by double-clicking the group, selecting them, and clicking either Add or Delete. Also, if desired, you may delete the entire group by selecting the group, clicking Action, and then Delete. (Don't do this now.)

> For the sake of this book and the exercises therein, don't delete the users you create in this hour or the next. You'll come back to using these user accounts for various reasons throughout the book.

Why Bother with Local Users and Groups?

As we said before, when in standalone mode, Windows 2000 Server acts nearly identically to Windows 2000 Professional (the workstation product), when it comes to users and groups. These machines maintain their user and group membership information in a local database. There is no querying for authentication against the Windows 2000 Server Active Directory or the NT SAM database.

You might be asking yourself how local users and groups are used if there is no tie-in to the authentication provided by the domain, Active Directory, or SAM. They are used in two ways.

First, users can walk up to the console of a standalone Windows 2000 Server, press the Control+Alt+Delete keystroke and log in to the computer. After a valid local username and password are provided, group membership is looked up and permissions are granted or denied, as appropriate. The user can go about his or her business at the console of the Windows 2000 Server or Windows 2000 Professional workstation.

The second way local users and local groups are used is called pass-through authentication. *Pass-through authentication* occurs when logon account information matches the stored account information in an accounts database. If they match, the account is granted access to resources.

Let's peek into the life of Joe User, and see it from his perspective:

- Joe logs into his Windows 95 machine with his username and password (joeuser and number1, respectively).

8

- Joe is *not* validated by the Active Directory nor by an NT domain.

- Joe uses Network Neighborhood, and finds a server named AZSERV1 and a share named payroll.

- Joe tries to access this share by double-clicking it, and he is granted access.

How can this happen? He wasn't authenticated by any server. Or was he?

Let's look at what was set up on the server side to allow Joe this access to see the payroll share:

- Create a local username called joeuser and give it a password of number1 on the AZSERV1 machine.

- Create a local group called paymanagers and put the joeuser account in that local group.

- Create a sharepoint called payroll and assign the paymanagers read and write access to that share.

Let's examine, step by step, what happened on the workstation that enabled Joe to read the payroll share:

- When Joe entered his account information into the Windows 95 machine, his username and password were cached into memory.

- When Joe clicked on AZSERV1, found the share named payroll, and tried to open it, his cached information was automatically checked against the local accounts database on that AZSERV1 machine.

- The username (joeuser) and password (number1) match the local database entries.

- The server did a quick lookup into the local accounts database and confirmed that joeuser is part of the local paymanagers group.

- The paymanagers group has read and write access to that share.

Voilà! Instant access without any Active Directory or domain authentication.

Summary

Windows 2000 Server can lead one of three lives: standalone server, member server, or Domain Controller. Use the mode that suits your need best.

Built-in local groups have some special permissions associated with them. Use administrator-defined local groups to partition like users.

Pass-through authentication allows rights to be assigned without domain assistance.

Workshop

The workshop provides a quiz and exercises to help reinforce your learning. Even if you feel you know the material, you will still gain from working these exercises.

Quiz:

1. What are the three modes Windows 2000 Server can be in?

2. Which type(s) can participate in the domain?

3. Which type(s) has a local accounts database?

4. Which type(s) can assign security to objects in the domain?

5. What are the two built-in user accounts?

6. What are some of the built-in local groups?

7. Which built-in local groups should you avoid placing users in?

8. What can you do to signify an account is a temporary account?

9. What can you do to turn off an account at a moment's notice?

10. A user quits at your organization. Should you delete his account? Why or why not?

Exercises

1. Find a Windows 95 machine that doesn't log on to the domain. Log on locally to the Windows 95 machine as Administrator with the domain administrator password. See if you can use pass-through authentication to get access to the server.

2. Create a new user and place that user in the Power Users group. Can the user shut down and restart the system? Change the time? Backup files? Create additional users?

3. Create a new user, but disable the account. What happens when the new user tries to log on?

HOUR 9

Users, Groups, and Machine Accounts on Domain Controllers

by Jeremy Moskowitz

In the previous hour, you created users and put them in groups to simplify administration. In this hour, we will work with users and groups on Domain Controllers. On the standalone server, there was only one type of group: the local group. When you start working on Domain Controllers, you will find that many new group types and scopes await you.

Back in Hour 7, "Advanced Planning for Domains, Domain Controllers, and the Active Directory," we discussed Windows 2000 Server's ability to function in one of two modes: Mixed or Native. In this hour, we'll take the jump and convert to Native mode.

Finally, you will learn about computer accounts and how, as with users, computers need to authenticate to the domain.

In this hour you will learn about

- Working with users on Domain Controllers
- Working with groups on Domain Controllers
- Changing from Mixed to Native mode
- Computer accounts

Users on Windows 2000 Server Domain Controllers

Previously, you upgraded one of your machines to a Windows 2000 Server Domain Controller. When you did that, you created a machine that participated in a domain security boundary. The accounts created in the domain are shared between all Domain Controllers.

Local Users on Domain Controllers

Local users and groups cannot be created on Domain Controllers. Even if you start the Computer Management console and perform the steps found in the last chapter for creating local accounts, you cannot successfully create a local account, as you can see in Figure 9.1. There *is* no local accounts database on a Domain Controller.

FIGURE 9.1
You are denied the ability to create local accounts on Domain Controllers.

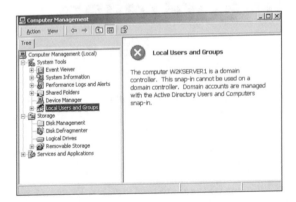

You'll create your first user accounts in the Active Directory of the corp.com domain in this lesson. Theoretically, you could create user accounts on any Domain Controller in the corp.com domain because the Active Directory automatically replicates account changes to the other Domain Controllers on a set schedule.

The default time for sending changes to other Domain Controllers in the domain is five minutes.

Create Your First User Accounts in the Domain

In this example, you're going to be working on W2kServer1, a Domain Controller for the corp.com domain.

To create user accounts in a domain, follow these steps:

1. Click the Start button, select the Programs folder, and select the Active Directory Users and Computers icon from the Administrative Tools folder.

2. Expand corp.com in the left pane of the console window. As shown in Figure 9.2, several folders are displayed under the corp.com domain in the Users folder.

FIGURE 9.2

Click the corp.com entry to expand the folder.

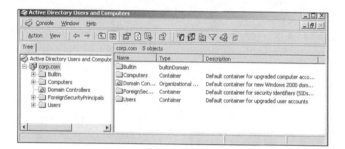

3. Click on the Users folder to select it.

4. Click the Action menu, and select the User command from the New menu; the Create New Object - User dialog box appears.

   This box is different from the Local User dialog box shown in Figure 8.3 in the previous hour. The most striking addition in the Create New Object - User dialog box is the mention of the domain name with an @ sign proceeding it, like an email address. The user will eventually use this "friendly name" to log on to the domain.

Friendly name is a term given to an account that takes the form of user-name@domain.com (or something similar).

5. Enter the user information as shown in Figure 9.3.

6. Click the Next button in the Create New Object - User dialog box (see Figure 9.3).

FIGURE 9.3

Enter the information as shown here.

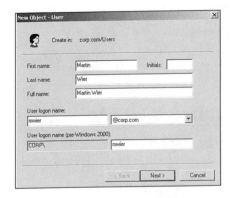

 Sometimes pre-Windows 2000 clients and servers, such as Windows NT and Windows 95 are referred to as Downlevel clients. These clients cannot natively use the `username@corp.com` format to log on.

7. Enter a password of `fastcar6` into the Password and Confirm Password dialog boxes. Leave the other options unchecked (the default). Click Next.

 If both the User Must Change Password at Next Logon box and the Password Never Expires boxes are checked, the user must still change his or her password at next logon.

8. At the Summary screen, click the Finish button.

You've now created a user account named `mwier@corp.com`.

Now that you've created Martin's account, you'll be adding the additional attributes and information into the account shown in Table 9.1.

TABLE 9.1 User Information

General Tab	Martin Wier	John Jones	Beth Martins
First Name	Martin	John	Beth
Last Name	Wier	Jones	Martins
Display Name	Martin Wier	John Jones	Beth Martins

General Tab	Martin Wier	John Jones	Beth Martins
Description			
Office	41	45	22
Telephone	800-555-1212	800-555-2222	800-555-3333
Email	mwier@corp.com	jjones@corp.com	bmartins@corp.com
Home Page	www.corp.com	www.corp.com	www.corp.com

9. Locate Martin's account in the right pane. Double-click his account so that you can add more information. On the General tab, add the information shown in Figure 9.4.

FIGURE 9.4

Basic information may be added on the user Properties page.

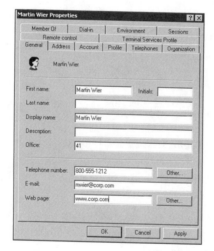

10. Click the Address tab. Enter Martin's information from Table 9.2.

TABLE 9.2 User Address Information

Address Tab	Martin Wier	John Jones	Beth Martins
Street	17 East Main	16 East Main	44 Central Plaza
PO Box			
City	Queens	Queens	Phoenix
State/			
Province	NY	NY	AZ
Zip/			
Postal Code	11375	11375	85283
Country/			
Region	United States	United States	United States

11. Click the Organization Tab. Enter Martin's information from Table 9.3. There is no need to choose a manager for Martin. When finished entering the data for Martin, click OK.

TABLE 9.3 Job Description

Organization Tab	Martin Wier	John Jones	Beth Martins
Title	Director of Customer Relations	Insurance Sales Manager	Claims Processor
Department	Customer Service	Sales	Claims
Company	BIGCORP USA	BIGCORP USA	BIGCORP USA
Manager	Don't enter anything	Click Change, find Martin Wier's account	Click Change, find Martin Wier's account

12. Repeat steps 5–11 until John Jones's and Beth Martins's information is also entered. Create logon of jjones and bmartins, respectively. You will use their accounts later. Although you probably wouldn't do this in the real world, give them the same password of fastcar6.

13. After all the users are loaded, if you double-click Martin's account and click on the Organization tab, you'll see that John and Beth both report to Martin—their names appear in the Direct Reports text box.

Domain Account Attributes

Because you have Martin's account open, let's talk about some of the tabs available in the User Properties dialog box (see Figure 9.5).

- The Telephones tab has additional fields into which you can input personal information.
- The Member Of tab specifies what groups the user belongs to. We'll be talking about groups and Domain Controllers in a bit.
- The Dial-In tab specifies RAS settings. We'll be covering that in Hour 17, "Network and Dial-Up Connectivity."
- The Profile tab lets administrators assign characteristics to the users' desktops. We'll be covering that in Hour 14, "Profiles and Policies."

FIGURE 9.5

The Account tab controls user logon information.

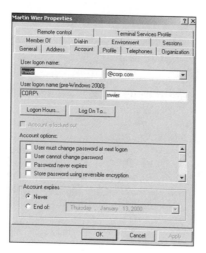

The Terminal Services Profile, Sessions, and Remote Control tabs allow administrators to control Terminal Services features. We'll be covering that in Hour 18, "Windows Terminal Services."

The Account tab has several attributes of note:

- User Logon Name

  To rename the account a user uses to log on, you need only change the entry in the User logon Name text box.

- Pre-Windows 2000

  This is the domain and username that a user on a non–Windows 2000 machine would use to log on. Names take the form of *domain_name\username*, such as `corp\mwier`. This is used only when the client is not a Windows 2000 or Windows 98 machine. It is not recommended that you use a different pre-Windows 2000 username in place of the Windows 2000 username because it could potentially confuse users by forcing them to remember two account names.

- Logon Hours

  Click Logon Hours to restrict when users can and cannot log in to the system. Simply highlight a block of time and select either Logon Permitted or Logon Denied. By default, all users can log on anytime.

Users are not thrown off the system if they are already logged in and the Logon Denied time comes around. After they log off, however, users cannot log back in until the Logon Permitted time arrives.

- Logon To

  After the Logon To button is pressed, an administrator may enter machine names in the Username - Logon Workstations dialog box. This restricts the users to logging in only on the machines specified. This setting is particularly useful for shop-floor or point-of-sale scenarios when you want to restrict specific users to specific machines.

> The Logon To restriction works only when machines have the NetBIOS protocol loaded. If NetBIOS is turned off, Windows 2000 Server has no way of knowing which machine the user is logging in from. See Hour 15, "Protocols and Network Fundamentals," for more information about NetBIOS.

- Account Options

  We have already discussed a number of these options in other sections. Additionally, it is here where some very advanced user settings can be set. Of note, however, is the Account is Sensitive and cannot be delegated. Use this option if you want to disable the account for delegation. You will learn more about delegation in Hour 10, "Active Directory Entities."

- Account Expires

  You can set accounts to be automatically disabled after the set date is hit. This setting is appropriately used for seasonal or temporary employees.

Groups with Domain Controllers

As you saw in the last hour with the standalone server, there are built-in groups and administrator-defined groups. Those elements are present for Domain Controllers, but there are additional options with some more complexity.

Built-in Domain Local Groups

You saw with the standalone server that certain built-in groups gain special "user rights" for that server when users were added to those groups. Take that logic one more step and extend those rights to a domain. When a Windows 2000 Server is elevated to the status of Domain Controller, two types of built-in groups emerge:

Built-in domain local groups: When users are added to groups in this category, they have special privileges to perform maintenance on machines in the domain. Some of the built-in global groups have equivalent local group cousins on the standalone servers. Some highlighted differences follow.

Here are some of the important built-in domain local groups:

- Administrators—Members of this group have free rein on this domain.
- Account Operators—Users in this group have the ability to create, delete, and modify domain user accounts.
- Print Operators—This group can pause print queues and delete print jobs.
- Server Operators—Members of this group can shut down or restart a server, format disks, and change the system time, among other duties.
- Pre-Windows 2000 Compatible Access —Members are placed into this group automatically by some processes or manually by the administrator, if desired. Members of this group can view all users and groups in the domain.

Evaluated Groups

The last type of built-in groups are special. They are special because you, as an administrator, cannot add or remove members from these groups. That is because membership is evaluated on the fly. That is, permissions may be placed upon these groups, and, if the conditions are met, they are applied.

Here are some of the important evaluated groups:

- *Dialup* as its name implies, includes users who are coming in over the dial-up networking services.
- *Interactive* includes all users who log on "locally" to the specific machine in which the permissions are placed (i.e.: users are not coming in over the network).
- *Everyone* includes all users everywhere — those coming in over the network, dial-in, locally, other domains, and guests. Therefore, if the Guest account is enabled by an administrator, any user can log on (usually without a password) and have read access to all files where:
  - *Authenticated Users* anyone with a valid computer account in the domain or local SAM database. Use this instead of the Everyone group to assign most permissions. That way someone in non-trusted domain cannot access files designated for this level of access.
  - *System* is the operating system. Restricting key files from having System access is the fastest way to cause trouble.
  - *Service* is any Windows 2000 or NT service.
  - *Creator Owner* rights are usually assigned to those who create the object in question. For instance, those who create a print job can delete it. Those who create directories can specify who else can read them.

There are more evaluated groups than those listed here, but these are the ones where you will find the most interaction.

Administrator-Defined Group Types: Distribution Versus Security

Distribution: As you learned in Hour 6, "Domains and the Active Directory," the Active Directory is the new "go-to" point for data about the enterprise. The Active Directory isn't just a repository for day-to-day user information. The newest applications will try to leverage the centralized nature of the Active Directory. Distribution groups are simply that: groups of users set up for email distribution lists. The concept of distribution groups was incorporated into Windows 2000 Server to provide a competitive advantage to the upcoming Microsoft Exchange 2000, code named Platinum. In this way, a highly integrated administration can be realized with Windows 2000 Server and Platinum.

Security: Security groups also house groups of users, but instead of using them to send email, you'll place restrictions and grant permissions to the members of the group.

Group Scope: Domain Local and Global Groups

Domain local—As the name implies, groups in this category are visible only from inside the domain in which they are created. Other domains cannot see or act on these groups to place security restrictions on them.

Global groups—When a global group is defined, it is visible anywhere in the forest. The only caveat is that global groups can only contain members from the domain where the group exists. This scheme enables administrators in other domains to grant access to the groups you define.

Why All These Types of Groups?

To get the greatest advantage from the individual characteristics of the group types, administrators are encouraged to use groups in the following ways:

1. Stake out users with the same needs and put them in global groups.
2. Create domain local groups, and assign permissions to objects based on that domain local group.
3. When the time comes, put the global group into a domain local group.

There's an added bonus here: When other domain administrators want to grant permissions to the global groups in your domain, they simply pick the group they want. You needn't even be bothered.

Let's take a look at a scenario: Different people need to print to a very expensive, PostScript-capable, $3-a-page, color laser printer. You want to be sure only specific people are granted this right.

You're told that only people whose job descriptions are either Secretaries or Executives should have the ability to print to the printer.

What's the most efficient way to set up your groups? Apply the 1-2-3 method outlined earlier to this scenario.

1. Find all Secretaries in your domain. Put them in a global group called SECYS. Find all the Executives in your domain. Put them in a global group called EXECS.

2. Create a domain local group called can-print-color. Assign to that group the right to print to the very expensive, PostScript-capable, $3-a-page, color laser printer.

3. Put the two global groups that you want to print color (SECYS and EXECS) in the local can-print-color group.

After you perform those steps, all the SECYS and EXECS can print to that very expensive, $3-a-page, PostScript-capable, color laser printer.

Three months later, you're told to grant the people in the Art Department the ability to print to that very expensive, $3-a-page, PostScript-capable, color laser printer. What do you do? Follow the 1-2-3 method outlined earlier!

1. Find all the folks in the Art Department. Put them in a global group called ARTSY.

2. Step 2 is already done. The can-print-color domain local group is already assigned to that printer.

3. Add the ARTSY global group to the already existent can-print-color group, and voilà! The folks in the ARTSY group can instantly print to the very expensive, PostScript-capable, $3-a-page, color laser printer.

As you can see, you needed to set up access to the printer only one time with a local group to leverage it forever.

At the beginning of this section, we alluded to an added bonus of taking advantage of global groups. When you put your users in global groups, you automatically allow administrators of other domains to assign permissions to your users. This reduces the amount of work you need to do yourself.

For instance, let's imagine every domain in corp.com has an EXECS group. They're all happily printing to their very expensive, PostScript-capable, $3-a-page, color laser printer.

But only one domain houses the user account for the president of the company. The poor administrator in that domain is told to allow every executive from every domain to print to the $10-a-page, laminating printer right outside the president's office. How can this administrator do this without your help?

To add all Executives from every domain to print to the $10-a-page, laminating printer right outside the president's office, the administrator creates a domain local group called can-print-laminated, and assigns rights to the $10-a-page, laminating printer. He then adds all the global EXECS groups from all the other domains. Figure 9.6 shows you this graphical view.

FIGURE 9.6

Graphical Active Directory view of assigning the rights.

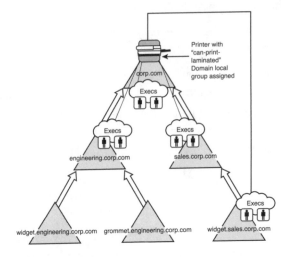

He's just granted all the company executives in every domain access to that $10-a-page, laminating printer. Because *you* already had an EXECS group, you didn't need to do any-thing! With all the time you've saved, this again frees you up to read more Sams books.

Built-in global groups: These groups do not explicitly grant any privileges; rather, they are like groups you create to clump users together. Administrators in other domains can view these groups and grant rights to your users.

Built-in Domain Global Groups

At the beginning of this section, we saw built-in domain local groups that were granted special privileges. Some built-in domain global groups are also automatically generated. The built-in domain global groups are generated merely as a convenience. However, these groups don't inherently grant any special privileges. Rather, as we saw in the 1-2-3 method, global groups round up similar users, and are stuffed into local groups that are granted special access. For example:

- The global Domain Admins, as its name implies, has free rein on this domain. The local domain Administrators group contains this group.
- Domain Users is quite similar. The local domain Users group simply contains this group.
- The global Guests is also the same. The local domain Guests group contains the global Guests group.

Universal Groups

Now that you have your hands firmly around the concepts of domain local and global groups, we're going to look at one additional type of group: the universal group. Think of a universal group as a super-domain local group. In fact, it acts more like a local group than anything else.

Let's revisit our earlier example where our administrator colleague was granting all the EXECS from every domain rights to the local $10-a-page, laminating printer. Here's how he could have accomplished this task using universal groups:

1. Make the can-print-laminated group a universal group.
2. Assign that universal group access to the $10-a-page, laminating printer.
3. Again put the other domain's global EXECS groups in that group.

The universal group is different from a domain local group because it is available for use between every domain, child domain, and domain in other trees in the forest.

In a nutshell, you may assign permissions to objects using the universal group to set up access to global groups located anywhere in your enterprise.

There are two disadvantages to using universal groups:

- The domain mode must be switched to Native mode. Global groups are not available in Mixed mode.
- Universal groups are network resource hogs. This is because universal group membership information is replicated to every global catalog server across your enterprise. (See Hour 7.) Every time you add or remove a user or group from a universal group, you are forcing enterprise-wide replication of the change.

Try to keep universal group membership fairly static. Use global groups to move individual members in and out—those aren't replicated across the global catalog servers.

You'll be changing mode from Mixed mode to Native mode toward the end of this hour. Two new universal groups will appear: Enterprise Admins and Schema Admins. A member of the Enterprise Admins group has full control anywhere in the entire forest, so insert members into this group with care. Members of the Schema Admins group can modify the Active Directory schema, which when performed is an irreversible operation. Again, use caution when placing members in these two very powerful universal groups.

Creating, Using, and Deleting Domain Groups

Let's get a feel for how setting permissions on objects works. You are going to use the phony color printer you created in Hour 5, "The Control Panel," to simulate how group access works. You'll take the accounts you created (Martin Wier, John Jones, and Beth Martins), put them in groups, assign printing rights to those groups, and learn the interaction between them. You'll then use the 1-2-3 method we detailed earlier to make sure it's being performed correctly.

In these examples, we're assuming you have only one computer—a Windows 2000 Server, which you promoted to a Domain Controller in Hour 6, "Domains and the Active Directory" (see "Your First Windows 2000 Server Domain Controller").

Because Windows 2000 Server, by default, doesn't allow regular users like Martin, John, or Beth to log on at the console, you're going to add these users to the Server Operators group. That group has the special Log On Locally right assigned to the group.

Only add these users to the Server Operators group for the sake of this exercise. Normally, you would not place untrained Windows 2000 Server users or operators in the Server Operators group.

To add the users to the Server Operators group for the sake of this exercise:

1. Click the Start button, and select the Programs command. From the Administrative Tools folder, select the Active Directory Users and Computers console. The Active Directory Users and Computers dialog box opens.

2. In the left pane, click on the Built-in folder. Double-click the Server Operators group to open it.

3. Click on the Members tab, and then click the Add button.

4. Select the accounts of Martin Wier, John Jones, and Beth Martins, and click Add to add them to the Server Operators group. Click OK to return to the Server Operators Properties screen.

5. Click the OK button when done. Verify that your Server Operator's Members tab contains the names of Beth Martins, John Jones, and Martin Wier in the Members text box. All their Directory folders should read corp.com\Users.

Now, you are going to use the 1-2-3 method to create a global group with similar users, create a domain local account and assign it rights to a resource, and then put the global group into a domain local group.

You will use the phony color printer you created in Hour 5 to simulate how group access works. You'll put the accounts you created (Martin Wier, John Jones, and Beth Martins) in groups, and assign those groups rights to the printer.

ONE: Create a global group with similar users. Create a global EXECS group with Martin and John.

1. In the left pane, click the Users folder. Click the Action menu, scroll down to New, and then select Group.

2. The Create New Object - Group dialog box appears, as shown in Figure 9.7.

FIGURE 9.7

The Create New Object - Group dialog box.

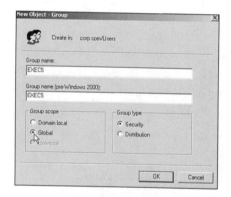

3. Select the Global scope.

4. Select the Security type.

5. Type EXECS into the Name of New Group text box.

6. Click on the OK button. The EXECS group will appear in the Users folder.

7. In the right pane, double-click the new EXECS group.

8. Click the Members tab. Because you want to add Martin and John, click the Members tab. Click Add and select the accounts of Martin and John. Click Add, and then click OK to return to the EXECS properties page.

9. Click OK when done.

TWO: Create a local group for access to the resource. Next, you create a local group to which you assign access to the printer.

1. In the left pane, click the Users folder. Click the Action menu, scroll down to New, and then Group.

2. Select the Domain Local group scope.

3. Check that the Security group type is selected.

4. Type in `can-print-color` as the group name, and click the OK button.

5. Minimize the Active Directory Users and Computers console. We'll come back to it in a minute.

6. Click Start, Settings, and then Printers. Right-click over the printer, and click Properties. Click on the Security tab.

> Although you might normally remove the Everyone group from a printer, it is highly unusual to remove the Server Operators. Please do so only for the sake of this exercise.

7. Remove the Everyone group (and Server Operators group or Power Users group if present) by selecting each of those entries and clicking Remove.

8. Add the can-print-color domain local group you just created. Click Add, select the can-print-color group, click Add, and then click OK.

9. Verify that the Allow/Print check box is checked.

10. Click the OK button when your printer Permissions configuration looks like the one shown in Figure 9.8.

FIGURE 9.8

Remove the Everyone and Server Operators groups, and add the can-print-color group.

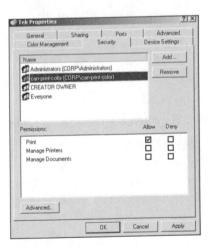

THREE: Add the global group to the domain local group. Finally, you'll add the global EXECS group to the can-print-color domain local group.

1. Maximize the Active Directory Users and Computers console. In the left pane, click the Users folder. In the right pane, double-click the can-print-color domain local group.

2. Click the Members tab. Click the Add button, select the EXECS group, and click Add to add them. Click OK to return to the can-print-color Properties screen.

3. Make sure your can-print-color Members tab contains the name EXECS in the Members text box.

To test your group permissions, you will log off as Administrator and log back in as Beth Martins.

1. Press Ctrl+Alt+Delete and click Log Off. Answer Yes to confirm.

2. The Windows 2000 Login dialog box appears. Press Ctrl+Alt+Delete to get the attention of the server.

3. Enter bmartins in the User Name text box, enter fastcar6 as the password, and click the OK button.

4. Select the Notepad command from the Accessories submenu of the Programs folder on the Start menu.

5. Type in a few lines of text, and then select the Print command. Notice that the Print button is grayed out. Double-click the color printer to see why. You are denied access to the printer based on your group membership rights.

Repeat step 1 and step 2 in the preceding exercise. Use Martin Wier's account, mwier, as your logon name and his password, fastcar6, as your password to log in.

Repeat step 4 to run Notepad, and then perform step 5.

Notice that Martin has access to the printer. This is because he is part of the EXECS group. The EXECS group has rights within the can-print-color group, which has rights to print to that printer.

If desired, log off, and repeat the same steps with the John Jones jjones logon name, and his password of fastcar6. You should encounter the same results as with Beth.

Consequences of Changing from Mixed to Native Mode

You might have noticed that while performing the preceding exercise, the option to create universal groups was unavailable. That is because our Active Directory and Domain Controllers are still in Mixed mode. Mixed mode is when Windows NT Servers and

Domain Controllers live peacefully alongside Windows 2000 Server and Domain Controllers.

In order for our Active Directory to be fully operational, you need to change to Native mode.

Going from Mixed mode to Native mode has the following consequences:

- You can nest global groups inside other global groups, but only if they're in the same domain.
- Universal groups become operational.
- You have the ability to change group scope (see the section "Changing Group Scope").
- All Windows clients can still log on.
- You have the ability to support many levels of nested groups.

Keep in mind that when you've changed your domain from Mixed mode to Native mode, you cannot go back to Mixed mode. Also, no Windows NT domain controllers can participate in the domain. Any additional domain controllers in the domain must be Windows 2000 Servers.

Changing Group Scope

After your Windows 2000 Servers are in Native mode, you have the new ability to "bump up" your global groups and domain local groups to universal groups, if desired.

This is a one-way operation, and comes with one other string attached: If you want to convert a domain local group to a universal group, the group you want to convert *cannot contain* any other domain local groups. If you want to convert a global group to a universal group, the group you want to convert *cannot be contained* in any other global groups.

Changing from Mixed to Native Modes

You need to be logged in as an administrator of the domain. If you are not logged in as an administrator of the domain do so now. To change from Mixed mode to Native mode, follow these steps:

1. Click Start, Programs, Administrative Tools, and then Active Directory Users and Computers. Right-click the domain name (corp.com) and click Properties.

Do not perform this next step if you want to later add Windows NT domain controllers into the domain.

2. Click Change Mode as shown in Figure 9.9.

FIGURE 9.9

*Changing from Mixed
to Native mode.*

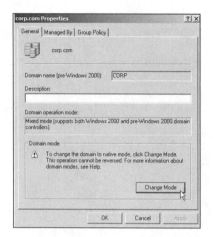

9

3. At the confirmation screen, click Yes, and then click the OK button to close the
   domain properties screen.

You'll get a message informing you that it might take some time for all Domain
Controllers to detect the change.

You should be able to now create groups of any scope—domain local, global, and
universal. Feel free to create your own groups and try to nest them to get the feel of how
nesting works.

Understanding Computer Accounts

In this hour, we described various user account types. User accounts validate a user's
ability to use the resources of the domain. Similarly, in order for machines to be recognized in a domain, they need to be registered and have their own computer or machine
accounts. Standalone servers and standalone Windows 2000 Professional machines have
no such requirement; they are islands unto themselves.

If a Windows 2000 Server or Windows 2000 Professional Machine is to participate in the
domain as a member, it must be registered. When you register, you're creating a computer or machine account in the domain, as you'll see in the next exercise. A registered
machine simply means that it is approved to participate in the domain.

On the System Control Panel's Network Identification tab (see Figure 9.10), you'll find
the computer's name as well as the workgroup or domain to which the machine belongs.

The Properties button on this tab is available only if the machine has not been promoted to a Domain Controller.

FIGURE 9.10

*A system's name and
workgroup or domain
association are found
on the Network
Identification tab
in Control Panel's
System applet.*

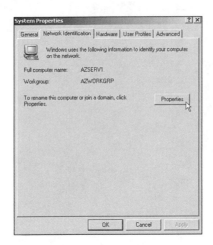

The Properties button affects computer accounts in the domain.

Joining a Domain

The Properties button is available to help guide you through creating a computer account in your domain. If you want to convert the system from standalone to member, but don't want it to be a Domain Controller, you'll need to run through this wizard. This is the same procedure you would perform if you wanted to have a Windows 2000 Professional Workstation join a domain as well.

In the following exercise, we will use the Network Identification Wizard to participate in a domain. To do so, you need two machines: a Windows 2000 Professional workstation and a Windows 2000 Server.

In this example, a computer named AZSERV1 is currently in a workgroup called AZWORKGRP.

To instruct this computer to leave the workgroup and to join the CORP domain, perform the following steps:

1. Click the Start menu, Settings, and then Control Panel. Launch the System applet. Click the Network Identification tab.

2. Click the Properties button.

3. Identification Changes dialog appears. Here, you can choose to rename the machine, join a different workgroup, or join a different domain. In this example

we want to join the corp.com domain. Click the Domain radio button and enter CORP (or corp.com) for the domain name.

4. The Domain User Name and Password dialog box is next, as seen in Figure 9.11. You are prompted for a username and password with rights to create that computer account in the CORP domain. Type in the CORP's administrator account information (in this case, just administrator and the administrator password). Click OK.

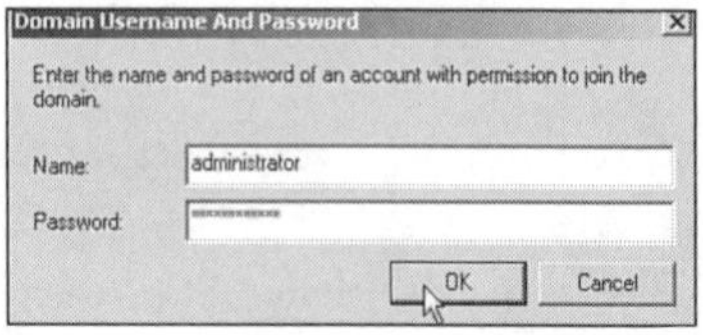

FIGURE 9.11

Provide the administrator account and password for the CORP domain.

5. Once the negotiations are finished, a warm message greets you telling you the computer has joined the domain. Click OK.

6. You'll be prompted to reboot the computer. Close the System Properties tab, and you will again be asked to reboot the computer. Select Yes when prompted.

You just created a recognized computer account for AZSERV1. This is a verified, guaranteed connection between the member server and the Domain Controllers—verified each time the member server (or Windows 2000 Professional workstation) machine starts up. Even if, somehow, another machine called AZSERV1 were brought up on the network, only *this* AZSERV1 would be recognized by the domain. That is because you provided authentication credentials that created the connection. Each computer has an internal SID number (security ID) that is unique.

To see the fruits of your labor, you need to visit a Domain Controller (in this case, the W2kserver1 Domain Controller). To locate a computer account:

1. On the W2kserver1 Domain Controller, click Start, Programs, Administrative Tools, and then Active Directory Users and Computers.

2. Expand the domain name (corp.com).

3. In the left pane, click Computers. You should see the AZSERV1 computer listed in the detail pane on the right, as seen in Figure 9.12.

An Alternative Method of Creating Computer Accounts

You might not want to enter administrative credentials while guiding a member server or Windows 2000 Professional computer into the domain. This scenario comes up when you are rolling out dozens or hundreds of workstations across your environment, but you don't want to give the Administrative "keys to the castle" to the hired help. To prevent this problem, Windows 2000 has introduced an alternative method of precreating computer accounts, while restricting who can join them to the domain.

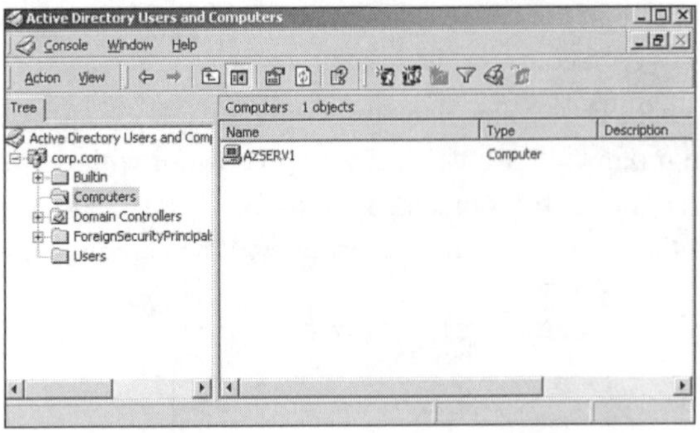

FIGURE 9.12
Your computer account is now registered in the domain.

Let's simulate granting to Martin Wier the ability to add his own workstation to the domain.

To grant the authority to add computer accounts to the domain:

1. On the W2kserver1 Domain Controller, click Start, Programs, Administrative Tools, and then Active Directory Users and Computers.
2. Expand the domain name (corp.com).
3. In the left pane, click the Computers folder. Click the Action menu, and select New, Computer. The New Object - Computer screen appears. Type `martinspc` in the Computer Name box.

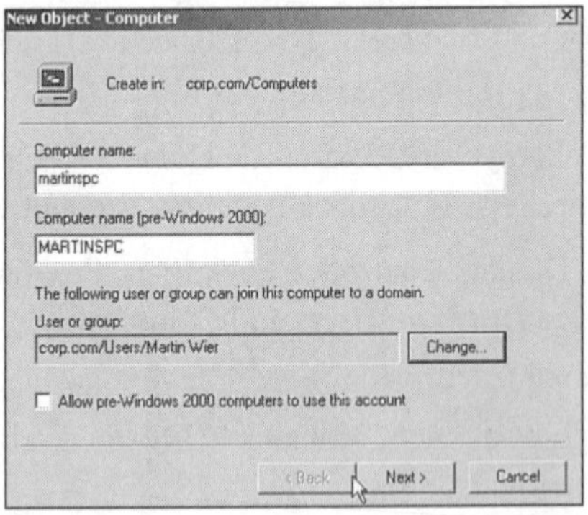

FIGURE 9.13
The New Object-Computer screen.

4. By default, you can see that only members of the Administrators group have the ability to add computers to the domain. In this case, you'll be making an exception, granting Martin the right to add his own machine. Click Change and select Martin Wier's account. Click Add. Click OK to return to the New Object - Computer screen. After selection, your entry should look like Figure 9.13. Click Next.

You can signify that this account is for either Windows 2000 or Windows NT computers by clicking the Allow pre-Windows 2000 computers to use this account checkbox. Otherwise, only Windows 2000 computers can use this account reservation.

5. The Managed screen will appear next and ask whether this machine is a Managed computer. Leave the box unchecked, and click Next. (We'll be talking about managed computers in Hour 20, "Client Services, IntelliMirror, and ZAW.")

6. The summary page appears next, and is one final chance to review the proposed options and change them if you desire. Make sure everything is OK and click finish. If necessary, you may go back and modify the information.

7. The computer named martinspc should appear in the Computers folder.

For Martin to now add his PC into the domain, he can simply run through the Network Identification Wizard as you did earlier, without requiring administrative credentials.

Changing a Computer Name

The Properties button, in the System Properties Network Identification tab (Refer to Figure 9.10) can also, if desired be used to change a computer's name.

Properties button is clicked, the Identification Changes (see Figure 9.14) is again presented.

FIGURE 9.14

The Identification Changes screen is where you can change a computer's name and membership.

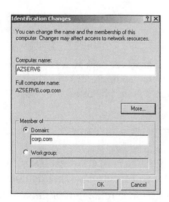

If you are participating in a workgroup, you may change the computer's name at any time. If the machine is a member server, you may change the name of the machine at any time with the appropriate Domain Administrator credentials. This button is grayed out only if the machine is a Domain Controller. The name cannot be changed.

Changing the name of member servers or standalone servers might prevent some users from making network connections to this server. Change the name only when you are sure it will not affect any users.

After changing the name, you are prompted for appropriate administrative credentials in the domain. After the computer name is changed and the server is rebooted, the associated registered computer account in the domain is automatically changed to reflect the new name.

In this example (refer to Figure 9.14), we've changed the name from AZSERV1 to AZSERV6. If desired, you can check the Active Directory Users and Computers console to see that the registered computer name has changed using the procedure outlined earlier.

This procedure was not possible in Windows NT Workstation and member server installations. Changing a computer's name basically ripped that computer out of the domain, creating a state of limbo. This change is a giant step forward in manageability.

The Identification Changes screen also provides the ability to break away from the domain and become a standalone server again. Simply click the Workgroup box and type in the workgroup to join.

Changing from a member server back to a standalone workgroup server leaves a residual associated computer account behind in the domain. It is recommended that you delete it by using the Active Directory Users and Computers console.

Remember, this option is not available to you if the machine is set up as a Domain Controller. If you must rename a Domain Controller, first demote it using DCPROMO.EXE, and then rename it. Once renamed, promote it back again using DCPROMO.EXE.

Summary

You cannot add local users to Domain Controllers. Domain Controllers house the Active Directory, and hence, house the domain user and group accounts.

Use distribution groups for email lists, and use security groups for assigning resources.

Use domain local groups to assign rights to resources. Use domain global groups to group like users together. Use universal groups if you need to export assigned resources to other domains in the forest.

The built-in domain local groups grant special privileges to the users and groups within. The built-in global groups do not.

Changing from Mixed to Native mode is a one-way operation that will prevent Windows NT servers from participating as Domain Controllers in your domain. After you change from Mixed mode to Native mode, universal groups will come alive.

Use the Network Identification tab in the Control Panel's System applet to change the computer name or become a member server.

Workshop

The workshop provides a quiz and exercises to help reinforce your learning. Even if you feel you know the material, you will still gain from working these exercises.

Quiz

1. How do you create local users on Domain Controllers?
2. What is a friendly name?
3. What is a downlevel client?
4. How do you restrict what machine a user can log on from?
5. What are some of the domain local built-in groups?
6. What are some of the domain global built-in local groups?
7. What are the two types of groups?
8. What are the three scopes of groups?
9. When do you use a local group, global group, and universal group?
10. How do you change from Native to Mixed mode?

Exercises

1. Create a new domain account. Enter a different downlevel logon name. Try to log on from a Windows 95 machine with the regular and pre-Windows 2000 logon names.

2. In the new domain account you created in exercise 1, click the Logon To box and restrict the logon to one computer name. Try to log on from that computer name. Try to log on from another computer name.

3. Create a new global group and a new domain local group. Change each group in the group scope to universal. Try nesting group types and then changing the scopes to universal.

Hour **10**

Active Directory Entities

by Jeremy Moskowitz

You have already been exposed to many of the areas of the new Active Directory. You've seen that it's an integrated part of Windows 2000. But there's still more to explore. How can you find objects that are housed in the Active Directory?

We have explored the topic of Organizational Units (OUs) and the power they can bring to your administrative duties. As we learned in Hour 7, "Advanced Planning for Domains, Domain Controllers, and the Active Directory," they can often substitute for NT 4.0 resource domains. But how can we put that power into practice?

In this hour, you will learn to do the following:

- Manually publish entries in the Active Directory
- Search for printers, people, and other resources in the Active Directory
- Create OUs and move user accounts into them
- Create groups from OUs
- Use the Delegation Manager to grant administrative authority

Publishing Objects in the Active Directory

Publishing isn't a term we've used before, but it's one you'll need to know and understand to successfully finish this hour. When an object is published in the Active Directory, it simply means that the object is available for users to view and act upon.

You automatically published quite a few objects in the Active Directory when you created them in the previous hour: users, groups, computers, and domains, to name a few. We saw these items and had the ability to manipulate them when we had the Active Directory Users and Computers console open. In the next section, we'll see just how users would go about locating the published objects.

There are some objects, however, that aren't automatically published in the Active Directory. In general, these are objects that the Active Directory doesn't know about, such as printers or shares on NT servers. Although it's true the Active Directory knows all about the printers we create and share on our Windows 2000 servers, the Active Directory has no ties whatsoever to share-points, such as printer shares and folder shares on Windows 95, Windows 98, Windows NT, or LANManager servers.

The good news is that you may choose to manually select Windows NT (and other down-level clients') printers and shares to publish. You might want to share these items manually, so that your users can have a unified view of your network, even though you might still have some lingering Windows NT Server 4.*x* in your enterprise.

After users locate the newly published shares in the Active Directory, they can double-click on the shares to open them. Newly published shares work like any other share, where users are validated against the security on that share.

To emphasize the point, you'll be performing two exercises. In the first exercise, you'll automatically publish your first printer in the Active Directory. In the next exercise you'll publish a resource that Windows 2000 Server's Active Directory couldn't know about.

Automatically Publishing Resources in the Active Directory

In Hour 5, "The Control Panel," you added your first color printer. That printer was not automatically published in the Active Directory. This is because it wasn't until Hour 6, "Domains and the Active Directory," that you promoted your server to Domain Controller status, and created your Active Directory. Now, you'll create another color printer, which will automatically be published in the Active Directory.

In this example, we'll be attaching a fictitious HP Color Laserjet to our server's second parallel port, LPT2:.

You are encouraged to perform this exercise exactly as specified, regardless of whether or not you have a printer (of any type) attached. The results from this exercise are used later in the chapter.

To automatically publish a printer in the Active Directory:

1. To start the Add Printer wizard, click the Start menu, Settings, Control Panel then select Printers.

2. Double-click the Add Printer icon, which will start the Add Printer Wizard. At the splash screen, click Next.

3. At the Local or Network Printer screen, make sure the Automatically Detect My Printer check box is unchecked. We are setting up another fictitious color printer.

4. At the Select the Printer Port screen, make sure LPT2: is selected. Click Next.

5. When you can select your printer, be sure to select an HP (Hewlett-Packard) Color LaserJet.

6. At the Name Your Printer screen, clear the default entry and type `HPColor` for the name.

7. At the Printer Sharing screen, keep the defaults, and choose to Share as HPColor.

8. At the Location and Comment screen, enter

    - Location: `Server room`
    - Comment: Use only HP Paper!

9. At the Print Test Page screen, choose not to print a test page, and click Next.

10. At the Add Printer Wizard summary screen, click Finish to create and share your printer.

You might or might not be asked for the Windows 2000 Server CD-ROM to load the drivers.

Believe it or not, you've just published your first printer. You'll see how your users will use the Active Directory to locate this printer in just a minute.

Manually Publishing Resources in the Active Directory

One resource that you might want to publish in the Active Directory is the HP IIID double-sided printer named hp3d, shared from John Jones's Windows 95 machine, named Buster. The printer is shared as \\buster\hp3d. You want everyone in your Windows 2000 environment to be able to use this printer. (Why should John Jones get such a great printer for himself?)

> You may perform this exercise by substituting any shared printer on your NT network.

To manually publish a printer to the Active Directory:

1. Click on Start, Programs, Administrative Tools, and then Active Directory Users and Computers. The Active Directory Users and Computers console appears.

2. Expand the domain corp.com.

3. Click to select the Users folder and click the Action menu. Scroll down to New and select Printer.

4. Type in the name of the printer to publish. In this example, we're using \\buster\hp3d. Click OK.

5. A new printer appears in the Users folder.

6. Double-clicking on the new entry shows the properties for this device. Because the printer was not created on a Windows 2000 machine, the characteristics are not automatically provided to the Active Directory. We must manually click the Double-Sided check box because this printer is indeed a duplex (two-sided) printer. Also, enter the fact that this printer is located on John Jones's Desk. For now, you may leave the other information blank. Click OK when you are done.

> For the sake of this exercise, click the Double-Sided check box even if the printer you're setting up is not really capable of this function.

> Publishing shared folder points works exactly the same way. Instead of choosing to publish a printer, simply substitute New, Shared Folder for New, Printer Folder in step 3.

Searching for Entries in the Active Directory

Searches to the Active Directory occur more often than you might realize. They can occur when the Administrator is getting a list of users or groups, or even when getting a list of printers. Because the programmers of Windows 2000 Server strove for Internet standards compliance, even the area of searching in a directory has become a standard.

When searching the directory, the underlying protocol is called Lightweight Directory Access Protocol or LDAP. One way to use LDAP searches is via the searching facility inside the Windows 2000 user interface. Additional means to LDAP searches are available to programmers in the Active Directory Service Interface or ADSI.

> You can read more on the Internet standard LDAP by reading RFC 1777 at
> http://www.andrew2.andrew.cmu.edu/rfc/rfc1777.html.

In this section, you'll pretend to be an average user. As an average user, you know that there are published objects, such as users and printers. But how do you find those objects? In particular, how can you find a color printer on the network? Are there any printers that can print on both sides of the paper? Or how can you find someone's phone number if all you know is his name?

10

Users can do a quick search for objects in the Active Directory by using the Search command on the Start menu. In fact, Windows 2000 machines have two specialized Active Directory search routines: Search Printers and Search People.

Search Printers

In this example, you will search for printers that meet certain criteria. First, you'll need to print to a color printer. Next, you'll need to print to a printer capable of double-sided printing.

To find a specific printer on a network:

1. Click on the Start button, click Search, and then select For Printers. The Find Printers dialog box appears. Notice the In combo box, which shows the scope of our search. You can search the entire AD or portions of the AD by simply pulling down the drop-down box and selecting the scope of the search. Change the scope of the search for just corp.com.

2. Click the Features tab of the Find Printers dialog box.

3. Because we need to print to a color printer, click the Can Print Color check box.

4. Leave all the other options at their default settings, and then click the Find Now button.

Notice that the HP Color LaserJet printer that you created shows up. This is because it is a color printer whose attributes and features were automatically published in the Active Directory.

You might expect the color Tektronix Printer you created in Hour 5 to appear in the returned results as well. By default, printers created before the Active Directory is operational are not automatically published in the Active Directory. You can, however, choose to publish them by clicking the "List in the Directory" option found under the Sharing tab of the printer's properties. Alternatively, you can use this check box to prevent printers that are automatically published from being available in Active Directory searches. Note, however, that preventing them from being published does not prevent users from connecting and printing to them.

To search for double-sided printers:

1. Repeat steps 1–3, deselecting the Can Print Color check box.
2. Click the Can Print Double-Sided check box.
3. Click the Find Now button.

Notice that the printer you manually published earlier shows up! This is because you published this non–Windows 2000 printer and specified that it was duplex capable.

Double-clicking on the printer you want to use will connect you to that printer. (See Figure 10.1.) If the printer is on a Windows 2000 machine, it will even install the printer driver for you automatically. If the printer is not attached to a Windows 2000 system, it will question you as to whether you would like the driver loaded.

FIGURE 10.1

Double-clicking on a "found" printer automatically attaches you to that printer.

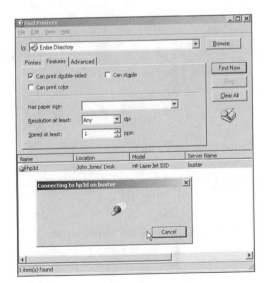

Search People

In this example, you will search for members in your organization. For the sake of this example, pretend you're searching for phone numbers, but all you know are people's names or email addresses. When you locate the person in question, you can add her contact information to your personal contacts manager database, such as Outlook Express.

To search for people in the Active Directory:

1. From the Start menu, click Search, and then For People.
2. The Find People dialog box appears, as shown in Figure 10.2. Be sure Active Directory is the selected entry in the Look in drop-down box.

FIGURE 10.2

The Look in drop-down box has many information services available for searching.

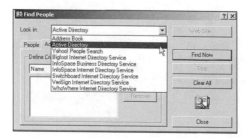

3. Let's first search for John Jones's business phone number. If all you remember is his name, you could simply type it in and see what comes back. Enter John Jones in the Name field, and click Find Now.
4. Clicking Properties brings up all the published information on John Jones. Additionally, selecting the name and clicking Properties enables you to view all the available information about Mr. Jones.

> Clicking Add to Address Book automatically sends the contact to your personal contact manager, such as Outlook or Outlook Express, if appropriately configured. (Windows 2000 comes with Outlook Express, which is automatically configured to accept the entries.)

Now, suppose you want to find the information for someone you met at last year's annual company picnic. You remember that her last name was Mar- something—you can't quite put your finger on it. Was it Martinez? Martoni? Marzipan? We'll use the Active Directory to help us.

To locate a partial text string:

1. Click the Clear All button.

2. In the Name text field, type mar because you know it was Mar- something.

3. Click the Find Now button. Both Beth Martins and Martin Wier will show up in your results (see Figure 10.3) because mar is a partial match for both Beth *Mar*tins and *Mar*tin Wier.

FIGURE 10.3

Typing in a partial string, such as Mar, *brings up all entries that contain that string.*

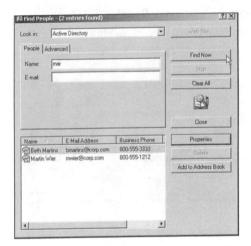

4. Select Beth Martins and click the Properties button to view additional information about that person.

The Advanced tab enables you to use the operators *is*, *starts with*, *ends with*, and *sounds like*.

Planning Your Organizational Units

Before deploying your organizational unit structure, you'll need to formulate a plan. Organizational units are handy. They let you shape your domain to match your unique organization. There is one catch to OUs: The more levels of OU depth you create, the longer the Active Directory takes to return the queried results list.

Microsoft recommends that no more than ten nested levels of OU be implemented in any domain to prevent lengthy queries.

Sometimes users interact with the Active Directory in a "flat" way. We saw this in the earlier example when pretending to be a user searching for resources. No mention of the user's OU was returned with the query results.

There is, however, a way for users to explore the current OU model in a graphical manner. That way, normal users can browse the model you've set up, and see which users, printers, shares, contacts, groups and computers are contained within.

To graphically explore the Active Directory:

1. On the desktop, locate and double-click the My Network Places icon. My Network Places shows various icons.

2. Double-click the Entire Network icon. To show the underlying structure, click the words "entire contents." Various icons appear, including the Directory.

3. Double-click the Directory to open it. Your current directory structure will appear, starting with the root domain, Corp.com. Double-clicking corp.com will open a graphical view of what is currently designed in Active Directory Users and Computers.

Today, you may drill-down to a user's icon and right-click over it. Doing so displays a context menu, which lets you send an email or open the user's home page (provided these properties are defined in their account). If rumors are any indication, this behavior will certainly expand and users will have additional functionality and interaction with the way OUs are laid out when third-party applications are written to integrate into the Active Directory.

For instance, users might be able to route documents based on OU structure: Simply locate other members of your team in your OU and send the document. Again, this functionality isn't quite there today, as there are no applications which support it. But the decisions you make when forming your OU structure could have a lasting impact with future Windows 2000 incarnations.

Microsoft's stance is that you don't need to "get OUs right the first time." This is because creating and deleting OUs and moving users in and out of them is very easy compared to creating and deleting domains. However, once users start to get familiar with the created OU structure and get a feel for the model you create, you will likely want to maintain status quo so your users are not confused by many changes.

Although there are any number of possibilities you could use to leverage organizational units to your advantage, we're going to detail three of the most common here:

- Business division model
- Geographic model
- Administrative model

Business Division Model

In this model, you are leveraging the top-down design most corporations have. Despite the pretty outward appearances a business radiates, most companies' internal business units tend to run nearly or entirely autonomously. Most business units, if possible, would love to have nothing to do with the other business units.

FIGURE 10.4

In the business division model, resources belonging to business units are grouped together.

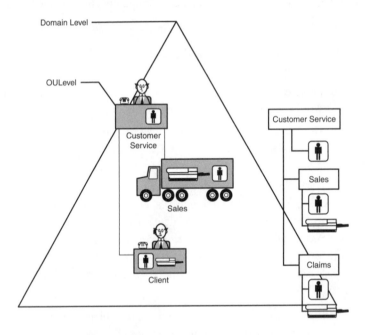

With carefully planned and placed OUs, you can partition the various business units, as seen in the graphical representation in Figure 10.4.

In the earlier example of the corp.com root domain, the Accounting Department's OU has nothing to with the Customer Service Department's OU.

Your users will probably be easily persuaded to use this model because it's something they're already familiar with. Additionally, when a user chooses his division's OU, he knows he's in the clear, and that much closer to finding the resource or object he's seeking.

This model, however, isn't generally the best choice if the business sells off business units frequently or changes fundamental internal structures often.

Geographic Model

In the geographic model, you are separating OUs by physical location. Your first level could have a North American OU and a European OU, with cities as the second level. Figure 10.5 has a graphical representation of what this model looks like.

FIGURE 10.5

In the geographic model, resources are grouped together by physical location.

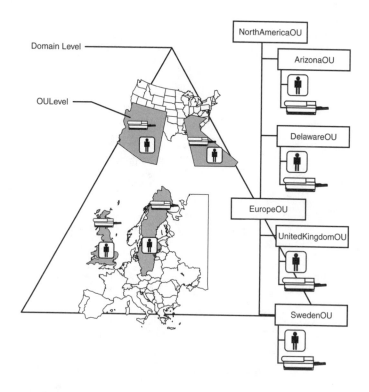

10

If you and your users always want to know where a physical person, printer, or other resource is, the geographic model is the way to go. Additionally, your first level will probably change very little, even if the business unit moves to another city for a larger space.

Some users might not like the fact that additional OUs might be needed to drill down to find the resources.

Administrative Model

In certain companies, each business unit has its own IT division, which must answer to a central governing authority for standards and software. In those cases, the centralized body generally wants some way of keeping tabs on each of the autonomous IT divisions.

With the administrative model, each autonomous IT division can manage its own OUs with the people in its charge, while still remaining subordinate to the centralized authority. A graphical representation can be seen in Figure 10.6.

FIGURE 10.6

In the administrative model, resources are grouped together by where the IT staff is.

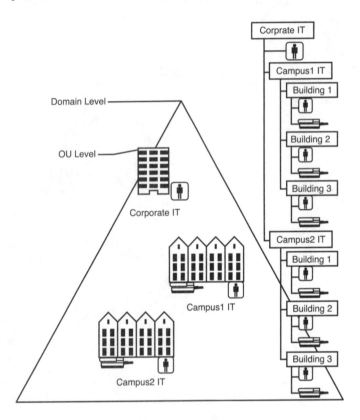

However, users might find this model somewhat confusing because everything will appear to be spawned from the centralized IT authority, not their divisions or geography.

Creating Organizational Units

In Hour 6, we discussed some potential models you could choose when designing your OU structure: geographic, administrative, business model, or whatever you came up with. In this section, you'll fire up the management tool and create your first OUs.

In the fictitious corp.com, you'll be creating OUs using the business division model as seen in Figure 10.5.

The insurance company BIGCORP USA has many divisions, including Accounting, Business Planning, and Customer Service. Customer Service has two divisions: Sales and Claims. We're going to concentrate on Customer Service and its Sales and Claims divisions.

We'll be creating an OU structure that mirrors our business model.

To create a business division model organizational unit structure:

1. Click Start, and point to Programs. Select Administrative Tools, and then select Active Directory Users and Computers.

2. Expand the domain, but keep the domain name selected.

3. Click the Action menu, select New, and then select Organizational Unit. Type in Customer Service for the name, and click OK. Customer Service should now appear in corp.com.

4. Notice that the Customer Service OU icon appears in both panes.

5. Select the Customer Service OU, click the Action menu, and select New Organizational Unit. Type in Sales and click OK. Notice the Sales OU within the Customer Service OU.

6. Select the Customer Service OU again, click the Action menu, and select New Organizational Unit. Type in Claims and click OK. Notice the Claims OU within the Customer Service OU.

7. Expand the Customer Service OU to verify that Sales and Claims are within Customer Service, as shown in Figure 10.7.

10

FIGURE 10.7

Expanding the Customer Service OU reveals the additional OUs underneath.

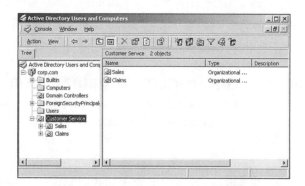

Moving User Accounts into OUs from Their Default Locations

With your business division model OU structure now in place, let's move the existing users we created in the section "Create Your First User Accounts in the Domain" of Hour 9, "Users, Groups, and Machine Accounts on Domain Controllers," into their designated OUs.

Let's review our cast of characters and their roles:

- Martin Wier is a manager of the Customer Service department.
- John Jones is in insurance sales.
- Beth Martins handles incoming insurance claims.

Their roles match up with the OUs you've just created, so let's move them into their new OUs.

To move user accounts into an organizational unit:

1. Click Start, point to Programs, select Administrative Tools, and then select Active Directory Users and Computers.
2. Expand the domain.
3. Click the Users folder in the left pane of the open console.
4. In the right pane, select Martin Wier, click the Action menu, and select the Move command.
5. Drill down until you can locate and select Customer Service. Click OK to move Martin.
6. In the right pane, select John Jones, click the Action menu, and select the Move command.
7. Drill down until you can locate and select Sales. Click OK to move John.
8. In the right pane, select Beth Martins, click the Action menu, and select Move.
9. Drill down until you can locate and select Claims. Click OK to move Beth.

At this point, you should have the structure shown in Figure 10.8.

Creating a Group from an Organizational Unit

When you have your OUs defined and your users moved inside, you can choose to create a group based on the membership of the OUs. Remember—security settings are applied to groups, not OUs.

In order to create a security group from an OU, you'll need to create the global group manually and give it a name. Then you can simply select the OU that constitutes your group, and voilà! Instant group!

FIGURE 10.8

This is a graphical representation of the finished structure for the Customer Service OU.

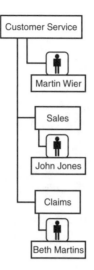

10

Because you have all of your Customer Service employees under the Customer Service OU, it might be convenient to have a global Customer Service group that you can use to apply security rights to objects later down the line (hint, hint).

To turn users in an organizational unit into a group:

1. Select the Users folder. Click Action, and then select New, Group. The Create New Object - Group screen appears. Make sure Global and Security are selected for Group Scope and Group Type, respectively, and then type in Customer Service as the group name. You should see a window similar to that in Figure 10.9. Click OK.

2. Select the Customer Service OU we created earlier. Click the Action menu and select Add Members to a Group.

3. Locate and select the Customer Service global group you created and click OK.

4. A dialog box appears that asks whether you want to add people in all the OUs under Customer Service. If you click Yes, you'll be able to individually select which organizational units' users will be copied into the group. If you click Yes to All, all users in all OUs under Customer Service will join the group. That is what we want, so click Yes to All. You should get a message stating that the operation was successfully completed.

To verify that our Customer Service OU members were successfully added to the Customer Service global group:

1. Click the Users folder.

Figure 10.9

Make sure Global and Security are selected.

2. Locate and double-click the Customer Service global group.

3. Click the Members tab to see whether Beth, John, and Martin were added.

Understanding Delegation

Moving your users into OUs has one additional advantage: you get the ability to delegate control over an OU to a trusted user or group.

For instance, an Administrator might choose to delegate the Change Password right to the Help-Desk group. Or, an Administrator may choose to delegate the ability to create and delete accounts to one trusted secretary or workgroup manager—just for that OU.

Before this feature, you, as the Administrator, had to either do it all yourself or give away the keys to the castle. Sure, there were Account Operators and Server Operators, but there was really no middle ground for things such as simply granting the right to change passwords and the like.

 Some third-party products, such as Enterprise Administrator, can allow this type of control with NT 4.0.

In this example, you'll be delegating some control of the Customer Service OU to the Manager of Customer Service, Martin Wier. We're not going to give him the full set of keys to the castle. Rather, when it comes to the Customer Service OU, we'll let him Reset the Password on a User Account and Read All User Information.

To delegate control of certain privileges in an OU:

1. Click Start, point to Programs, select Administrative Tools, and then select Active Directory Users and Computers.

2. Expand the domain (corp.com). Locate and select the Customer Service organizational unit, click the Action menu, and then click Delegate Control.

3. The Delegation Control Wizard splash screen appears. Click Next.

4. At the Group or User Selection screen, click Add. Find and select Martin Wier, click Add, and click OK. Your Group or User Selection screen should have CORP\Martin Wier added. Click Next.

5. At the Predefined Delegations screen, click the Reset Password on a User Account and the Read All User Information check boxes (see Figure 10.10). Click Next.

10

FIGURE 10.10

Some predefined tasks allow you to delegate the most common functions.

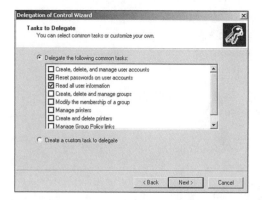

6. Check the summary screen to verify the actions you will be taking. Click Finish.

Before you start doling out widespread delegation duties, it might be a good idea to test out your changes to make sure they work as advertised.

Let's see if the delegation controls you just bestowed upon Martin Wier actually took effect, by logging on as Martin to see if Martin can change Beth's password.

To test the delegation duties:

1. Log off.

2. Log on as Martin Wier with the username mwier and the password fastcar6.

3. Click Start, point to Programs, select Administrative Tools, and then select Active Directory Users and Computers.

4. Expand the domain (corp.com). Locate and expand the Customer Service organizational unit, and click the Claims OU folder.

5. Locate and select Beth Martins's account, click the Action menu, click on the All Tasks entry, and select Reset Password. Type in `fastcar1` for the New Password and Confirm Password fields. Leave the User Must Change Password at Next Logon field unchecked. Click OK. You should get a password change successful message.

Summary

You might need to teach your users how to locate objects, such as printers, shares, and people in the Active Directory. After you do that, you can begin publishing your own information, such as shares and printers from NT 4.0 or Windows 95, which aren't automatically published.

Moving your users into OUs helps you partition users for easy manageability. Some models are the geographic, administrative, and business division models, although there are many possible others. After your users are moved into OUs, you can delegate control to a trusted individual to free yourself from mundane tasks such as changing passwords and creating accounts.

You can create a security group out of your OUs, but you'll need to create the group manually, and then populate it with the OUs or members.

Workshop

The Workshop provides a quiz and exercises to help reinforce your learning. Even if you feel you know the material, you will still gain from working these exercises.

Quiz

1. What are some of the OU models you can use to shape your domain?
2. What types of resources are automatically published in the Active Directory?
3. What types of resources are not automatically published in the Active Directory?
4. How do you create a security group from an OU?
5. What are some of the types of powers that may be delegated?
6. How can you search for a partial string in a name in the Active Directory?
7. How can you drag and drop users to move them from one OU to another?
8. What kind of printer attributes are automatically published?
9. What additional information sources can be searched besides the Active Directory?
10. What is the best OU model?

Exercises

1. Manually publish additional NT or 95 objects such as printers or shares in the Active Directory.

2. Create a new OU and some new users. Move those users into the newly created OU.

3. Assign different delegation tasks to a user of the new OU you just created.

10

Hour 11

Volumes and Disks

by Barrie Sosinsky

This hour introduces the concepts you need to work with disk storage. Windows 2000 Server provides you with the tools needed to manage large volumes of data in a flexible and fault-tolerant manner. It is in the use of these advanced storage tools that the power of the Windows 2000 Server operating system is evident.

In this hour, you will learn how to:

- Format disks and create partitions
- Work with both basic disk and dynamic disk storage
- Convert basic disks to dynamic disks
- Create simple, spanned, and striped volumes
- Use the software RAID Windows 2000 supplies to create fault-tolerant solutions
- Back up your data
- Defragment your disks

Using the Disk Management Windows

In Windows 2000 Server, you perform the various functions necessary to manage disks, create partitions, and work with volumes in the Disk Management section of the Computer Management window, which is accessed from the Administrative Tools sub-folder. The Computer Management tools are a snap-in of the Microsoft Management Console (MMC). You open this section by first double-clicking on the Storage icon in the left tree pane, and then double-clicking on the Disk Management icon. In most of the tasks you specify, you are aided by a wizard that walks you through the procedure.

The Disk Management window can appear as either a graphical view of your system, or in a list view, as shown in Figure 11.1. You alter the view by selecting the Console Tree command on the View menu.

FIGURE 11.1

The Disk Management tool shown in the Graphical view.

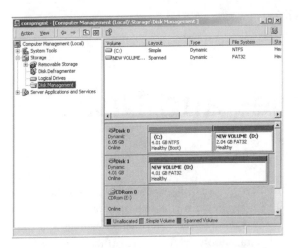

In this window, you can check information about installed disks, their capacities, the amount of free space, and their current status.

About Disks and Volumes

You perform the following three tasks when you set up a hard drive:

1. Initialize the disk as either a basic or dynamic disk.
2. Create partitions or volumes.
3. Format the partitions and volumes with an appropriate file system.

There are two types of hard disk storage that you can configure with Windows 2000 Server:

- Basic storage—Basic storage is a disk that can contain up to four primary partitions, or three primary partitions and an extended partition.

- Dynamic storage—Dynamic storage is a single disk or set of disks that have been combined to create a simple volume, spanned volumes, mirrored volumes, striped volumes, or other types of RAID configurations such as RAID-5.

You create dynamic storage from a basic disk by transforming it. Volumes from dynamic storage can span disks, be resized on the fly, and have other advanced features applied to them. Figure 11.2 shows you some of the different storage types that Windows 2000 Server supports.

FIGURE 11.2

Windows 2000 Server supports basic storage (primary and extended partitions), as well as dynamic storage (volumes and RAID).

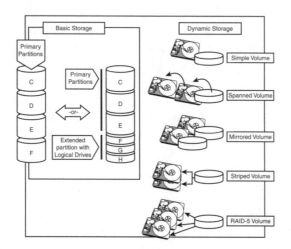

You can't have both basic and dynamic storage on the same physical disk. However, you can combine the basic storage partitions and the dynamic storage volumes you have created into a multi-disk system.

Basic storage and partitions contained therein are supported by all versions of Windows, DOS, and many other operating systems. Dynamic storage is supported by Windows 2000 only.

Converting Between Disk Types

If you want to use a disk for spanned, mirrored, or striped sets, it must be a dynamic disk. You can convert a basic disk to a dynamic disk, but if that disk is your boot disk, doing so will eliminate the option of booting from another version of Windows on that disk. You lose the ability to dual boot your system. Conversion requires that 1MB of unallocated free space be available, and that the data isn't currently in use by any open programs.

Always back up your data on a disk before converting the disk from one storage type to another. Also, save your disk configuration to another location so that you can recall it if you attempt to convert back from a dynamic disk to a basic disk.

You can convert a basic disk to a dynamic disk by doing the following:

1. In the Disk Management window, right-click on the disk label and select the Upgrade to Dynamic Disk command.

2. The disk selected is displayed as is an alert box if the disk contains a boot partition.

3. Click Upgrade to continue.

Windows 2000 forcibly dismounts any other partitions on the disk and reboots your computer before proceeding.

When converting a basic disk to a dynamic disk, existing partitions on the basic disk become simple volumes on the dynamic disk. Mirrored, striped, and spanned volumes created in Windows NT 4.0 become dynamic mirrored, striped, and spanned volumes, respectively. A Windows NT 4.0 stripe set with parity is converted into a Windows 2000 RAID-5 volume. Table 11.1 shows you the mapping of various disk structures. After conversion, the dynamic disk cannot contain partitions and logical drives. Also, only Windows 2000 Server and Windows 2000 Professional computers are able to access dynamic disks.

TABLE 11.1   Conversion of Disk Structures from Basic Disks to Dynamic Disks

Basic Disks	Dynamic Disks
System and boot partitions	Simple volume
Primary partitions	Simple volume
Extended partitions	Simple volume
Logical drives	Simple volume
Volume set[1]	Spanned volume
Stripe set[1]	Striped volume
Mirror set[1,2]	Mirrored volume[2]
Stripe set with parity[1,2]	RAID-5 volume[2]

Key: [1] Windows NT 4.0; [2] Windows 2000 Server

Should you want to restore a dynamic disk to a basic disk, do the following:

1. Click on the disk label in the Disk Management window to select that disk.

2. Select the Restore Basic Disk Configuration command on the Action menu of the Disk Management window.

   An alert box appears to indicate that although no partitions will be created or destroyed, any changes you made during the current session will be lost. Also, volume sets, stripe sets, parity stripes, mirrors, and drive letters might be lost during this operation.

3. Supply the backup configuration data that you have previously saved.

4. Click Yes to restore your basic disk from the dynamic disk.

Adding Disks to a System

If you add an additional disk to Windows 2000, that disk is installed as a basic disk. When you add or remove disks to your server, you must use the Rescan Disks command on the Action menu of the Computer Management window to update the catalog of disks in the Disk Management window. However, you will not generally need to reboot Windows 2000 Server for the disk to be recognized.

 If Windows 2000 Server does not detect your newly added disk, reboot your system and use the Rescan Disks command again.

You can also add disks from another Windows 2000 computer to your server as foreign disks. When you remove a disk from the first computer, make sure that its status in the Disk Management window is healthy. Then add the disk to your server and the disk will appear as a foreign disk in the window. Right-click on the new disk label and select the Import Foreign Disk command. A wizard appears that helps you perform the import operation.

When you move multiple disks from one Windows 2000 system to another, you can continue to use the foreign disks if they are dynamic disks and their status is healthy. If the foreign disks participate in spanned or striped volume sets, you will need to move all the disks at once in order to work with those volumes. If you do not move all the volumes and any part of that volume is missing, you will not see the portion of the disks that participated in a multi-disk volume on the foreign disks.

To move a volume set to another computer:

1. Remove the disks from the source computer and install them in the destination Windows 2000 Server.

2. In the Disk Management window, right-click on any of the new disk labels and select the Add Disk command. All disks in the group will appear.

3. To specify the disks you want to add from the set, click the Select Disk command.

Disk and Volume Properties

You can view the properties of a disk using the Disk Properties window. To view a disk's properties, perform these actions:

11

1. Open the Disk Management windows.

2. Right-click on the disk of interest and select the Properties command from the context menu.

   The Disk Properties dialog box appears.

When you right-click on a volume and select the Properties command in the Disk Management window, you see an entirely different Volume Properties dialog box (see Figure 11.3). The Volume Properties dialog box is described in several places in this book, and is a central location for managing many important system properties. The tabs in this dialog box are discussed in the following list.

- General—This tab lists the capacity of the disk, the file system, and the status of the disk. You can use the Disk Cleanup button to delete files from your system and free up space.

- Hardware—This tab shows a list of drives and devices attached to your system.

- Tools—On this tab, you can check your volume for errors, perform a backup, and defragment your disk.

- Web Sharing—If IIS is installed on your server, this tab enables you to designate whether folders on that volume are shared over the Web.

- Sharing—This tab enables you to share a volume and set permissions and parameters for those shares.

- Security—The security tab is where NTFS access permissions are granted or modified.

- Disk Quotas—A *disk quota* is the amount of space a user is allowed to use on an NTFS 5 volume.

FIGURE 11.3

The General tab of the Volume Properties dialog box.

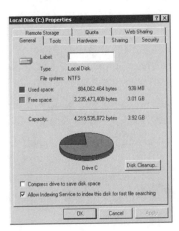

Partitions

Prior to formatting a drive, all the disk space is free space. A *partition* is a formatted and marked area of your physical disk created from free space. The formatting process places a file system on a partition and marks off an area of your disk. The disk is segmented into sectors by boundary lines and a file table is created. Most often you will be formatting your partitions with FAT, FAT32, or NTFS.

Partitions are registered in the boot record and can contain their own operating system. A partition can also simply be a storage area for data used by the file system of an operating system. When Windows 2000 Server boots, it will recognize partitions formatted in compatible file systems, such as FAT32 or NTFS (see Hour 12, "NTFS Permissions").

The primary partition that contains the boot sector and the system boot files is called the *system* partition. Windows 2000 puts its operating system files into the *boot* partition. This naming scheme is counterintuitive, but it's the one that Windows 2000 (and NT) uses.

To create a partition, do the following:

1. Click the Start menu and select the Computer Management command from the Administrative Tools subfolder on the Programs menu.

2. In the left tree pane of the Computer Management window, double-click Storage and then double-click on the Disk Management folder icon to view the Disk Management window.

3. Find the free or unallocated space that you want to modify, and right-click on that area in the graphical display in the lower-right panel. Select the Create Volume command from the context menu.

   The Create Volume Wizard appears.

4. Click the Simple volume radio button, and then click the Next button.

5. Select the disk you want to format as a simple volume and the size of the space you wish to use, and then click the Next button as shown in Figure 11.4.

FIGURE 11.4

The Select Volume Type step in the Create Volume Wizard enables you to select the kind of volume you want to create.

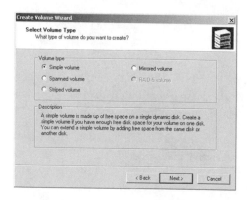

6. In the Assign Drive Letter or Path step that next appears, select a drive letter or leave that letter unassigned, as shown in Figure 11.5.

   You can assign the drive letter after you create the volume. You can also use this step to mount the new volume in a folder that supports drive paths (a share point).

FIGURE **11.5**

The Assign Drive Letter or Path step in the Create Volume Wizard enables you to assign a drive letter to your new volume.

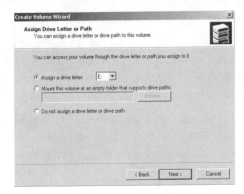

7. In the Format Volume step of the wizard (see Figure 11.6), select the type of file system you want to install. Enter the volume label, and select the other options, such as allocation unit size and the compression that the file system may support. Click the Next button.

FIGURE **11.6**

The Format Volume step enables you to pick file system options for your new volume.

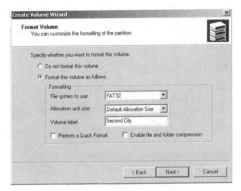

8. In the Completing the Create Volume Wizard step, Windows 2000 shows you the options you have chosen in a scrolling list before it implements them. Click the Finish button to create your volume, as shown in Figure 11.7.

If you want to mark a partition as the active partitions, right-click on that partition and select the Mark Partition Active command.

FIGURE 11.7

As a last check, the Completing the Create Volume Wizard step displays all your selection before formatting.

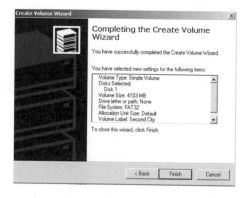

To delete a primary or extended partition, perform these steps:

1. Open the Disk Management window.

2. Right-click Delete Partition command on the partition that you want to delete and select the Delete Partition command.

3. Dismiss the alert dialog box, and Windows 2000 deletes the partition.

You cannot delete the boot partition or any partition with an active paging file. All logical drives and other volumes must first be deleted before you can delete the extended partition.

Extended partitions are known as *logical drives* or *logical volumes*. The advantage of creating an extended partition is that it allows you to exceed the four partition per disk limit. After you create an extended partition on a disk, you will no longer be able to use the free space on that disk.

Dual Boots

You can dual boot between Windows 2000 Server and other operating systems provided that the volume is contained on a basic disk. You lose this ability when you transform a basic disk into a dynamic disk; however, an active partition on a basic disk that becomes a simple volume on a dynamic disk is still the active partition.

Typically, different operating systems are placed on different partitions or volumes, but there is no restriction that prevents the installation of two operating systems on the same partition or volume if that file system is compatible with both. To dual boot between Windows 2000 Server and other operating systems using the same primary partition, you must format the partition with a mutually compatible file system. This means using FAT for dual booting with DOS or Windows 95 (and 95 OSR1), or FAT32 when you want to dual boot between Windows 2000 Server and Windows 95 OSR2 or Windows 98 (release 1 or 2). If you want to dual boot between Windows 2000 Server and Windows 2000 Professional, you have the additional option of formatting your primary partition with the NTFS file system. If you want to dual boot between Windows NT and Windows 2000, it is recommended that you use the NTFS file system.

It is generally recognized as safer to physically partition the files and applications required by two different operating systems.

Additional Partitions

You create extended partitions by marking off free space on your drive. After you create an extended volume, you will not be able to access additional free space, so it's important to use all free space for this purpose. Unlike primary partitions, extended partitions do not have to be formatted prior to their definition, nor do they have a drive letter assigned to them. You segment extended partitions into logical drives, and each of those logical drives is formatted and given a volume label.

Whereas the boot or active partition is typically your C: drive, additional compatible partitions (either primary or extended partitions) will also take a volume label. A physical disk can have up to four primary partitions or three primary partitions and one extended partition, which most often are assigned as C:, D:, E:, and F:. You can reassign, or map, the labels assigned to partitions. Partitions act as if they were independent physical drives because in a multi-disk system of independent simple volumes, your computer would recognize them as volumes with unique labels.

In a two-drive IDE system in which one physical disk is the master and the second physical disk is the slave, as two simple volumes recognized by your computer, one disk would be the C: drive and the second disk would be the D: drive. If you have a CD-ROM drive installed, that removable drive is given a letter D: or E: drive by default, depending upon the order in which the second hard drive and CD-ROM drive were added to the system. If you have an extended partition on one of the drives, that partition may be subdivided into one or more volumes, each of which may take a drive label.

To change the label of a disk or volume:

1. Right-click the disk or volume label in the Disk Management window and select the Change Drive Letter or Path command. (You cannot change the drive letter assignment of your boot disk.)

   The Drive Letter and Paths dialog box appears.

2. Select the drive that you want to modify, and then click the Modify button.

3. In the Modify Drive Letter or Path dialog box, make your selection from the Assign a Drive Letter list box, and then click the OK button.

This dialog box also enables you to enter a path to an empty NTFS folder that can be used as a drive path. That is, a folder with no files or subfolders on a volume formatted using the NTFS system.

If your volume labels are not properly updated, use the Refresh Disks command on the Action menu of the Disk Management window to update them.

Windows 2000 Server supports removable storage devices such as cartridge drives. A removable drive is different than a hard drive in that only primary partitions may be created on them. You cannot create extended partitions, logical drives, or any kind of dynamic volume using a removable storage device. The reason for this is to protect the integrity of a dynamic volume during read and write operations. If a removable disk is taken offline, the entire volume may no longer be accessed. Also, because your active partition is the one your computer uses to boot, you can't mark a primary partition on a removable disk as the active partition.

Volumes

Volumes are logical units with assigned drive letters. You create volumes from free space on your disks, just as you create partitions on basic disks. A volume can be a simple volume, an entire disk, a portion of a disk, or portions of two or more disks. Simple volumes are identical to partitions, but they have the added ability to participate dynamically in storage containers mapped over two or more noncontiguous regions of space. Volumes, being logical units, can be managed in entirely different ways from partitions that always have a physical representation on the disk the partition is on. Volumes in Windows 2000 Server offer you a feature called dynamic storage where data can be written to several locations.

Dynamic volumes offer you the following advantages:

- Enhanced speed due to the use of more drive heads reading and writing data
- Increased and expandable storage capacity by adding additional partitions to a volume as needed
- Fault tolerance due to data redundancy, through either mirroring or data-checking routines
- Fault tolerance due to the ability to hot swap damaged or disabled drives for new ones while the volume still functions on your system, provided that your hardware supports this feature

The ability of Windows 2000 Server to work with disk storage in these different ways is one of the main benefits of buying this operating system.

To extend a dynamic volume:

1. Open the Disk Management window.
2. Right-click on the simple or spanned volume that you want to extend and select the Extend Volume command from the context menu.
3. Indicate in the wizard the additional space you want to add to that volume.

11

A volume can be extended into free space if it is formatted as NTFS, provided the NTFS volume doesn't contain a file system. When you upgrade to a dynamic disk, simple volumes cannot be extended. You can, however, extend a simple or spanned volume that was on a dynamic disk that wasn't converted from a basic disk. You can't extend special partitions or volumes such as boot or system partitions, or striped, mirrored, or RAID-5 volumes. If you extend a volume onto multiple disks, you will no longer be able to mirror or stripe that volume. After a spanned volume is extended, you can't delete the portion that it was extended to without deleting the entire volume. Additionally, note that if any disk in a spanned volume is lost, the entire contents are lost as well.

Simple Volumes

When you format an entire disk and designate it as a volume, you are creating a simple volume. A server with a disk I/O subsystem that contains six disks can be arranged as six separate simple volumes. Simple volumes offer you the use of the maximum storage space that the disk allows under each of the file systems you installed, but you do not get any additional features such as redundancy or data checking. However, you can use simple volumes to create other types of dynamic storage such as mirrored disks or striped disks. Later in this hour, you will see how these conversions are done.

To create a simple or spanned volume set, perform these steps:

1. Click the Start menu and select the Computer Management command from the Administrative Tools subfolder on the Programs menu.

2. In the left tree pane of the Computer Management windows, double-click Storage and then double-click the Disk Management folder icon to view the Disk Management window.

3. Find the free or unallocated space that you want to modify, right-click on that area in the graphical display in the lower-right panel, and then select the Create Volume command from the context menu.

   The Create Volume Wizard appears.

4. Click on the Simple Volume radio button, and then click on the Next button.

5. Select the disk you want to format as a simple volume and the size of the space you wish to use, and then click the Next button.

6. In the Assign Drive Letter or Path step that appears next, select a drive letter or leave that letter unassigned.

   You can assign the drive letter after you create the volume. You can also use this step to mount the new volume in a folder that supports drive paths (a share point).

7. In the Format Volume step of the wizard (see Figure 11.11), select the type of file system you want to install. Enter the volume label, and select other options such as allocation unit size and compression that the file system may support, and then click the Next button.

8. In the Completing the Create Volume Wizard step (see Figure 11.12), Windows 2000 shows you the options you have chosen in a scrolling list before it implements them. Click the Finish button to create your volume.

To extend a simple volume into free unallocated space:

- Right-click on the simple volume you want to extend, and select the Extend Volume command from the context menu.

When the wizard launches, it guides you through the process of enlarging the volume.

To delete a volume:

- Right-click on that volume in the Disk Management window and select the Delete command.

Windows 2000 will post an alert box asking for a confirmation before continuing.

Spanned Volumes

If you combine two or more disks into a single larger logical disk, you can create a spanned volume or what was called a *volume set* in Windows NT 4.0. Spanned volumes behave like a simple volume but spread out over a larger disk space. Windows 2000 Server allows you to combine up to 32 disks into a spanned volume. As you write data to a spanned volume, the space in the first disk added to the volume is filled first, followed by the second, the third, and so forth.

To create a spanned volume, you extend a simple volume onto another disk. Both volumes must be formatted with the same file system, or you must convert the second volume prior to creating the spanned volume. Unlike striped sets where the volume sizes must be the same, there is no restriction on the sizes of the volumes you use to create a spanned set. You cannot use spanned volumes as part of either a mirror set or a striped set.

To create a spanned volume:

1. Right-click on unallocated space on a dynamic disk and select the Create Volume command.
2. Click Next in the Create Volume Wizard and select the Spanned Volume radio button.
3. Select the additional space on other dynamic disks that will participate in the spanned volume, and complete the steps of the wizard.

When you delete any part of a spanned set, the entire volume is deleted or turned into unallocated space. For this reason, Windows 2000 Server does not allow you to use a boot or system volume in a spanned set.

11

You cannot extend a spanned volume that is formatted with either FAT or FAT32. However, you can extend a volume that is formatted with NTFS. After extending a spanned set, deleting any part of the spanned set deletes the entire volume.

It is important to note that a spanned volume is not fault tolerant. If a single disk in a spanned volume set fails, you lose the data contained on all the disks. Put more technically, the volume set's Mean Time Between Failure, or MTBF, is now divided by the number of disks contained in the spanned volume. For this reason, most administrators opt either to mirror a volume or to create striped volume sets.

Understanding RAID

RAID stands for Redundant Array of Inexpensive Disks, a term that has universal industry recognition. RAID may be implemented as a set of hard drives contained in the bays of your server, as a standalone box or enclosure, or as part of a large storage cabinet that is in a Storage Area Network (SAN) attached to your computer network. In any of these instances, Windows 2000 sees RAID devices identically.

As noted previously, there are several different configurations of RAID in common usage. The ones you will most often encounter with Windows 2000 Server are the following:

- RAID-0: striped volumes or striped sets
- RAID-1: mirrored volumes or mirrored sets
- RAID-5: striped sets with parity
- RAID-1+0: mirrored volumes of striped volumes (sometimes referred to as RAID-10)

Windows 2000 Server supports software RAID through the Administration Tools, but various types of hardware RAID exist as well. When you buy a hardware RAID solution, typically you are getting faster performance and more reliable or fault-tolerant configurations. Hardware RAID seeks to eliminate any single point of failure. However, hardware RAID solutions are typically much more expensive than the configurations of software RAID that Microsoft builds into Windows 2000 Server.

The number attached to a level of RAID is not indicative of better performance or enhanced safety, nor is it meant to imply such. Each type of RAID is suitable for a different type of application or purpose.

Mirrored Volumes

Mirroring a volume means writing the same data found on that data to a second volume. Mirroring is RAID-1, and offers a degree of fault tolerance. If a volume fails, you can switch over to the equivalent data on the second volume and continue operating as before.

Mirroring offers only partial protection. If your data is corrupted on the first mirrored volume, it will be corrupted on the second. Also, if your disk adapter fails and you have only one disk adapter, your system will be disabled until a new disk adapter is installed. Mirroring is not a substitute for backing up your data.

> A mirrored volume is slower than a RAID-5 volume in read operations, but faster in write operations.

To create a mirrored volume set (RAID-1), do the following:

1. Right-click on the volume you want to mirror in the Disk Management window and select the Create Volume command.
2. Click Next, and then select the Mirrored Volume radio button.
3. Select an unallocated area on a disk equal to or larger than the volume you want to mirror.
4. Click the Finish button to create the mirror.

   Any additional space on the mirror becomes unallocated free space.

Both volumes must be on dynamic disks to create a mirrored volume.

To add a mirror to an existing volume:

- Right-click on that volume in the Disk Management window and select the Add Mirror command.

If a mirror should fail, it will display the status Failed Redundancy, and one of the disk statuses as Offline. You might see a disk status that reads Missing, and an X icon might appear in the graphical window of the Disk Management console. You might be able to repair a mirror by right-clicking on the remaining disk in the console and selecting the Reactivate Disk command. A healthy mirror should display first Regenerating and then Healthy.

You can force a mirror to be resynchronized by right-clicking on a member of the mirror and selecting the Resynchronize Mirror command. Windows 2000 automatically synchronizes your mirror volume, but in the case when a mirror becomes disconnected, the data might be stale. This forces the issue.

If you need the disk space or need to replace a damaged disk, you can break a mirror volume. The data on the second volume is no longer redundant when you break a mirror.

To break a mirror volume:

- In the Disk Management window, right-click the mirrored volume you want to break and select the Break Mirror command.

11

The two volumes become independent from that point forward. If your intent is to remove a mirror from a mirror volume and turn it into unallocated space, use the Remove Mirror command instead.

Striped Volumes

You can also create striped volumes, or what was called a striped set in Windows NT 4.0, by combining free space on multiple dynamic disks into a single logical volume. Striped volumes will write the data across all the disks based on the proportion of disk space that each disk supplied to the volume. The data is written to disk in 64KB stripes. Windows 2000 can perform I/O to multiple disks at the same time in a striped set, thus enhancing read and write operations. Data is written to all the disks at the same rate.

Because the data for a file on each disk in a striped volume is in nearly the same location, striping greatly improves disk performance for reads and writes by minimizing disk head seek times. Striped volumes require that each component disk contribute about the same amount of disk space to the volume in order to maximize the utilization of each disk. Microsoft designates striped volumes or striped sets as RAID-0.

 A striped volume (just like a spanned set) offers no fault tolerance. If a disk in a striped volume fails, the entire volume is lost. For fault tolerance, create a striped set with parity (RAID-5), as described in the next section.

To create a striped volume, do the following:

1. In the Disk Management window, right-click on unallocated space on a dynamic disk that you want to use in a striped volume and select the Create Volume command.

2. In the Create Volume Wizard, click the Next button, and then select the Striped Volume radio button.

3. Select the disks that will participate in the striped set.

    Windows 2000 requires each volume in a striped set be approximately the same size.

4. Select the file system and other options, and then click the Finish button.

Striped Volume with Parity or RAID-5

You can designate that a striped volume be recorded with parity information, what Windows 2000 Server calls *RAID-5*. When parity is used, information about each stripe is written at the end of a stripe. That parity information allows the volume to recover information in most cases even when a disk in the striped volume fails. Figure 11.8 shows how striped sets with parity are written.

FIGURE 11.8

A striped volume with parity.

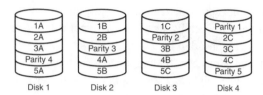

1A	1B	1C	Parity 1
2A	2B	Parity 2	2C
3A	Parity 3	3B	3C
Parity 4	4A	4B	4C
5A	5B	5C	Parity 5
Disk 1	Disk 2	Disk 3	Disk 4

Because striping with parity offers a significant amount of fault tolerance, it is a very popular disk formatting option. Most administrators will gladly accept the loss of disk space associated with maintaining redundant data for the degree of safety that this configuration offers.

RAID-5 requires that you use three dynamic disks or more (up to a maximum of 32) with volumes of approximately equal size. A RAID-5 volume cannot be extended or mirrored.

To create a striped volume with parity (RAID-5):

1. In the Disk Management window, right-click on unallocated space on a dynamic disk that you want to use in a RAID-5 volume and select the Create Volume command.

2. In the Create Volume Wizard, click the Next button, and then select the RAID-5 radio button.

3. Select the three or more disks that will participate in the striped set.

   Windows 2000 requires that each volume in a striped set be approximately the same size.

4. Select the file system and other options, and then click the Finish button.

When a RAID-5 disk fails, the status of the volume changes to Failed Redundancy and the volume status will show Online (Errors). You might see an exclamation point (!) in the graphical section of the console for that disk. Fault tolerance is lost. As soon as you detect this condition, attempt to repair the volume.

To repair a damaged RAID-5 disk:

1. Right-click on the RAID-5 volume in the Disk Management window and select the Reactivate Disk command.

   Regeneration begins. If all the parts of the volume return to healthy, you are done. Otherwise, remove and replace the disk that still indicates an error condition.

2. Right-click the damaged disk and select the Repair Volume command.

3. In the wizard that appears, designate a new disk to take the place of the damaged one.

11

Many servers keep a hot spare in their rack for just this occasion. You might also be able to hot swap a disk into the rack by simply removing the damaged disk and inserting a new disk. The new disk might need to be reformatted. Hot swapping is an option that requires hardware support, and adds about $500 to the cost of a basic server. If your server does not allow hot swaps, you might have to shut down the server first to install the new disk.

A failed member of a RAID-5 group is called an *orphan*. You can regenerate the missing data from the remaining members of the set. If the orphan occurs because of a power failure, the RAID-5 volume will automatically repair itself when the power returns.

How to Back Up Your Disks

Windows 2000 comes with a basic program that allows you to back up your data.

To use Windows 2000 Backup you must:

1. Be logged on as a member of the Backup Operators group, or as an Administrator.
2. Be able to connect to all shared folders that you want to back up.
3. Have a target device for backup that you can connect to and that has adequate space.
4. Run the Remote Storage Manager if you intend to use a media pool.
5. Use the Task Scheduler if you want to schedule a backup.

You can run the Backup Wizard to create an automated backup. The Backup Wizard is one of the options in the Welcome tab.

To open the Windows Backup and Recovery Tools dialog box:

- Select the Backup command from the System Tools subfolder of the Accessories folder on the Programs menu.

The Backup and Recovery Tools dialog box appears, as shown in Figure 11.9.

Click on the Backup Wizard button to launch the wizard and configure your backup. The wizard moves you to the Backup tab of the dialog box shown in Figure 11.10, and then walks you through the backup setup.

 The Schedule a Backup topic in the Help system will walk you through the procedure of scheduling a backup. See the Restore Files with the Restore Wizard topic in the Help system to write your backed-up data to disk.

Windows 2000 offers you the option of a hierarchical storage system. Data that isn't used in a while can be moved off your disks and onto slower and cheaper media such as tape.

FIGURE 11.9

The Windows 2000 Backup and Recovery Tools dialog box offers you three tools for working with disk data.

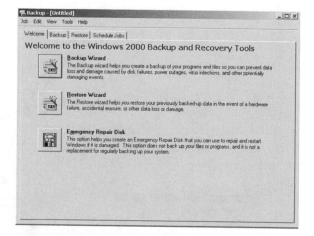

FIGURE 11.10

The Backup tab is where you can manually configure a backup.

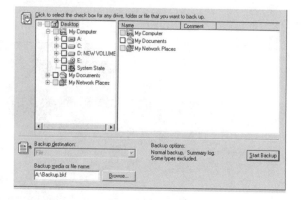

Use the Restore Wizard button to launch the Restore Wizard and use your backup to replace data that has been damaged.

How to Defragment Your Disks

Data on disks and in volumes gets fragmented over time due to use. Although there is some contention about the efficacy of defragmenting a disk or volume in a multiuser environment, studies show some modest improvement in file access speed when a disk is defragmented. Microsoft has chosen to include a disk defragger in Windows 2000. It is easily accessed.

Before defragging a disk, right-click on that disk and select the Analyze command. A dialog box will appear to tell you whether there is enough fragmentation to warrant this operation. You can also open a report to view the analysis.

To defrag a disk:

1. Double-click on My Computer on the Desktop.
2. Right-click on the disk you want to defragment, and then select the Properties command.
3. In the Properties dialog box on the Tools tab, click Defragment Now.

Or, select the Disk Defragmenter command from the System Tools submenu of the Accessories folder on the Program menu of the Start menu to open the Disk Defragmenter dialog box shown in Figure 11.11.

FIGURE **11.11**

The Disk Defragmenter tool lets you defragment disks and volumes.

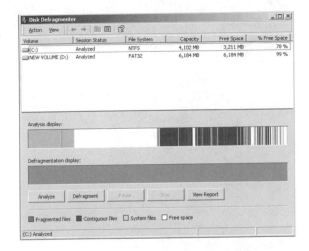

Disk Defragmenter shows volumes on the upper list and a graphic representation of how fragmented the disk is in the lower portion. Red is fragmented files, blue is contiguous files, white is free space, and green is system files on NTFS volume. The Analysis Display band shows the before and the Defragmentation Display shows the after of a defrag operation.

Using Remote Storage

If you are a member of the Administrators or Server Operators built-in groups, you can manage disks on a Windows 2000 computer from any other Windows 2000 computer that is a member of a domain or a trusted domain on the network. Remote management might require that you set up the Microsoft Management Console (MMC) for this purpose.

To manage remote disks, do the following:

1. Select the Run command from the Start menu.
2. Type MMC in the text box, and then click the OK button.

3. Select Add/Remove Snap-in on the Console menu.

4. Click the Add button.

5. Click Disk Management, and then click Add.

6. Click on another computer, enter the name of the computer, and click the Finish button.

Summary

Windows 2000 Server supports various types of hard disk storage, both fixed disks and removable storage. By using the Disk Management console, you can format disks and partition them. You can create both primary and extended partitions on basic disks, and the primary partitions on these disks will support dual booting two or more operating systems. There is support for the FAT, FAT32, and NTFS file systems.

With dynamic disks you can create different kinds of volumes. A basic disk may be converted to a dynamic disk and partitions will be mapped to volumes. Windows 2000 Server supports simple volumes, spanned volumes, striped volumes, and striped volumes with parity or a RAID-5 option. Some of these configurations allow you to make better use of your disk storage space, others provide varying degrees of fault tolerance.

Windows 2000 Server also comes with some tools for working with your hard disk data. The Windows 2000 Backup tool lets you back up to disk, tape, or to a media pool. The Recovery tool lets you restore backed-up data. Windows 2000 also comes with the Disk Defragmenter for defragging your disks and volumes.

11

Workshop

The workshop provides a quiz and exercises to help reinforce your learning. Even if you feel you know the material, you will still gain from working these exercises.

Quiz

1. True or false: A basic disk is incapable of containing more than one partition.

2. True or false: Windows 2000 Server allows up to 32 disks to be managed in a spanned volume.

3. True or false: After you convert a basic disk to a dynamic disk, you cannot got go back.

4. True or false: Mirroring is a fault-tolerant solution.

5. True or false: Spanned volumes is a good solution when you want to create a larger volume from different areas of unallocated or free space.

6. True or false: When a disk in a RAID-5 volume goes bad, the entire volume is lost.

7. True or false: Disks used on one Windows 2000 Server cannot be used on another.

8. True or false: Any volume on Windows 2000 Server can be seen across the network by a Windows 98 client.

9. True or false: A disk defragmenter will dramatically improve your server's performance.

10. True or false: You can use a boot volume in a spanned set, and even extend a boot volume with unallocated space.

Exercises

1. Create a spanned volume over two disks or more, and format it as FAT32. Delete the volume.

2. If you have a one-disk system, change the labels of your volumes and your CD-ROM drive.

3. In a two-disk (or more) system, create a mirrored drive. Break the mirror, and then restore the mirror.

HOUR 12

NTFS Permissions

by Jeremy Moskowitz

NTFS increases your ability to tighten security on your server. When you create security groups and put similar users into those groups, you can assign NTFS permissions to objects based on groups. NTFS volumes also enable you to manage your users' space requirements.

In this hour, you will learn how to:

- Set security on NTFS files and directories
- Compress NTFS files
- Copy and move files across NTFS volumes
- Take permissions off files
- Set up quotas for your users

NTFS Permissions

When you use NTFS as your file system and create security groups to lump like users together, you can set permissions on files so that only those who need access to files actually get access to those files. It sounds pretty simple, but there can be pitfalls, especially when inheritance is involved. *Inheritance* is the general term used when permissions flow downward from parent objects to child objects.

You can assign file permissions only on NTFS volumes. You can assign permissions on NTFS volumes because each file and folder has an Access Control List (ACL) associated with it. Think of the ACL as a list of who has permissions on a file. When a user tries to access a file or folder, the ACL on that file or folder is queried. If the user is not on the list, the user is denied access. If the user is on the list (or is a member of a group that is on the list), a quick lookup is done to see which permissions are available for that user.

File and Folder Permissions

You can assign permissions to folders or to files. For each, there are basic permissions and advanced permissions that may be set. For the sake of this book, we'll only be covering the basic permissions, plus two special permissions—Change Permissions and Take Ownership—that will be discussed later.

Folders have the following basic permissions:

- Full Control—Users may perform all of the following duties, including the two additional advanced properties.
- Modify—Users may write new files, create new subdirectories, and delete files and the directory. Users may also see which other users have permissions on the folder.
- Read & Execute—Users may read and execute files.
- List Folder Contents—Users can view the filenames in the directory.
- Read—Users can view the files in the directory and view who else has rights here.
- Write—Users may write new files and view who else has rights here.

Files have the following basic permissions:

- Full Control—Users may perform all of the following duties, including the two advanced properties.
- Modify—Users can modify, overwrite, or delete an existing file. Users may also view who has permissions here.
- Read & Execute—Users can read files, look to see who has access here, and run executables.
- Read—Users can read files and look to see who has access here.
- Write—Users can overwrite the file and look to see who has access here.

Permissions Inheritance

Think of folders as parents and children. Folders closer to the root directory are parents of their subfolders. In this context, *root* means the top-level folder (exactly the opposite of what you might think of when you think of a tree).

If you assign certain permissions to a parent, the child files and folders underneath it automatically inherit the folder permissions. For example, a new directory created under the \CSERVICE directory would have the same permissions as \CSERVICE.

You can, if desired, change this inheritance behavior.

Looking at the example shown in Figure 12.1, the Orders folder would normally inherit the permissions of \CSERVICE. However, you can block the inheritance so new files and folders will not inherit the parent's permissions. When you block the inheritance, you're effectively creating a new parent, and normal inheritance will apply: Child folders and files created under this new parent will get the permissions assigned to it.

FIGURE 12.1

An example of permissions and inheritance.

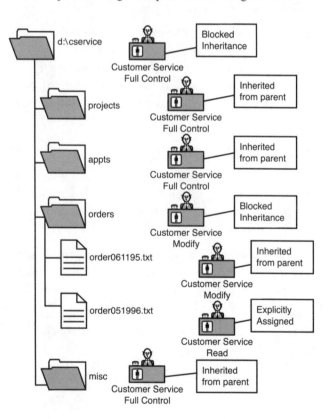

12

In this case, the \ORDERS directory has blocked the inherited permissions from its \CSERVICE parent. \ORDERS has been explicitly assigned different permissions. All new files and folders under \ORDERS will now receive the same permissions as \ORDERS.

Permissions assignments on individual files can *always* be explicitly assigned. Although it's true that new files inherit permissions from the parent folder, they don't have to keep them. In this case, the newly created ORDER051996.TXT file originally inherited the permissions from its \ORDERS parent. Later, it was explicitly assigned different permissions.

Group Permissions

If a user is a member of more than one group that is assigned rights to a file or directory, those rights are added together to make up his *effective permissions*.

Take Martin Wier. Back in Hour 9, "Users, Groups, and Machine Accounts on Domain Controllers," he was put in both the EXECS group and the Customer Service group. Let's examine his permissions in Figure 12.2.

Because Martin is in both the EXECS group and the Customer Service group, he gets both Read *and* Write permissions to the \PROJECTS directory. He can also read and write Proj1.txt. However, Martin cannot read (or write) special.txt because the Deny right overrides all other permissions. Use this rule of thumb: All NTFS permissions are added together, except when a Deny is encountered. Deny wipes out all other occurrences of the permission.

Setting NTFS Permissions

Now that you have a basic handle on NTFS permissions, you need to set up a directory structure that you can use through the rest of the examples in this hour. You'll assign rights to the users and groups you set up in Hour 9 and Hour 10, "Active Directory Entities."

Martin Wier, Manager of Customer Service, has asked for some hard drive space on which to keep projects, appointments, orders, and some miscellaneous files. You tell him that you're pretty busy right now, but will create the first directory of Customer Service, and then he can create all the rest of the subdirectories and files underneath.

You will create the directory structure shown in Figure 12.3 on any NTFS volume—in this case, D:\.

FIGURE 12.2
An example of denied access.

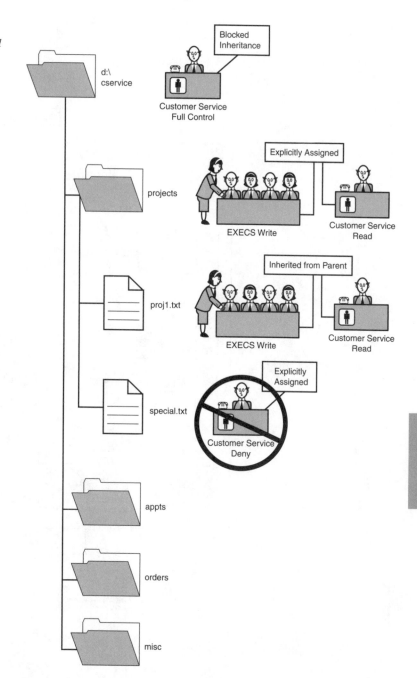

12

FIGURE **12.3**

You will create this directory structure in the following exercises.

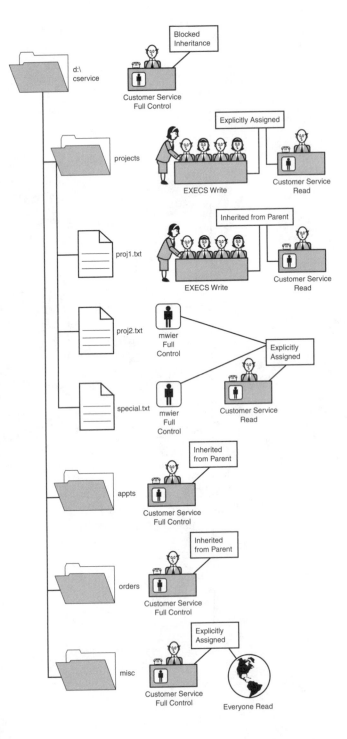

To create the directory structure:

1. Log in as Administrator on the Domain Controller. (In this example W2kserver1.)

2. Choose a volume with NTFS.

3. If you do not have a volume with NTFS, refer to Hour 11, "Volumes and Disks."

4. Use My Computer to get a list of available drives. In this example, use D:\. Double-click the D drive to open it.

5. Right-click in the free space of the folder and select the Folder command from the New menu of the context menu. Type in cservice for the name.

6. Right-click the cservice folder and select the Properties command from the context menu.

7. The cservice Properties screen appears. Click the Security tab.

8. By default, the Everyone group has Full Control here because it is inheriting the default NTFS permissions from the parent of D:\. You want to create a new parent. To create a new parent, you must clear the check box that says Allow Inheritable Permissions from Parent to Propagate to This Object. After you click the check box, a Security dialog box will appear.

9. Click Remove to remove all inherited permissions from the parent, in this case, the Everyone group. Your cservice Properties page should now have no entries inside.

10. By default, you want the Customer Service group to have Full Control everywhere in this cservice directory tree. To ensure this, click Add.

11. The Select Users, Computers, or Groups screen appears. Select Customer Service and Domain Admins and click OK. Back at the cservice Properties page, click the Customer Service group and click the Full Control check box. Click the Domain Admins group and make sure the Read & Execute check box is checked (see Figure 12.4).

12

> If permissions are selected that are a superset of other permissions, the lesser permissions are automatically selected as well. For instance, if you select the Read & Execute check box, the List Folder and Read check boxes are automatically selected.

12. Click the OK button to close the cservice Properties dialog box.

13. Log off as Administrator.

Martin is now ready to start creating files in the new directory structure.

FIGURE 12.4

Administrators should have the Read & Execute check box selected, and the Customer Service group should have the Full Control check box selected.

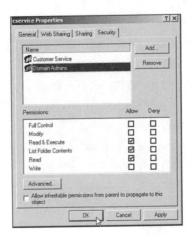

To create the rest of the directory structure:

1. Log on as Martin Wier (username: `mwier`; password: `fastcar6`).
2. Open My Computer, select the D:\ drive, and double-click cservice to enter it.
3. Right-click and select the Folder command from the New menu.
4. Type in `Projects` for the name. Repeat to create subdirectories for Appts, Orders, and Misc.

The cservice folder should now look like Figure 12.5.

Directory Permissions

For the Projects directory, you want all the EXECS to be able to modify the files if the need arises. You'll leverage the fact that Customer Service's inheritance already has Full Control on the Projects directory. You can simply add the EXECS group and give them Modify permissions.

To set permissions on the Projects directory:

1. Right-click Projects and select Properties. The Projects Properties screen appears. Click the Security tab.
2. Click the Add button. The Select Users, Computers, or Groups screen appears.
3. Select the EXECS group and click OK.
4. Back at the Project Properties page, click the EXECS group and click the Modify check box.

The Project Properties dialog should now look like Figure 12.6.

FIGURE 12.5

You should now have these four directories.

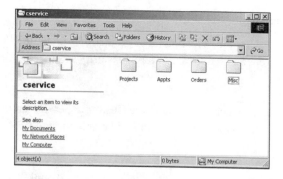

FIGURE 12.6

The EXECS should have Modify selected, and the Customer Service and Administrators selections should be automatically inherited.

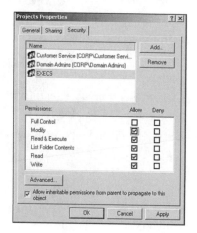

5. Click OK to close the Projects Properties page.

For the Misc directory, Martin wants everyone to be able to read, and he wants the Customer Service group to have full control. To leverage the fact that Customer Service's inheritance already has full control on the Projects directory, simply add the Everyone group and give them Read permissions.

To set permissions on the Misc directory:

1. Right-click Misc and select Properties. The Misc Properties screen appears. Click the Security tab.

2. Click Add. The Select Users, Computers, or Groups screen appears. Select the Everyone group and click OK.

3. Back at the Misc Properties page, click the Everyone group and make sure only the Read check box is selected.

4. Click OK to close the Misc Properties page.

12

File Permissions

In this exercise, you will be creating three project files under the Projects directory. Each one is a bit different and requires a different security setup.

Project 1

Proj1.txt is a file for which everyone in the Customer Service group should be able to have full control, and that the EXECS should be able to modify.

To create project 1:

1. Using Windows Explorer, double-click on cservice, and then Projects to enter the projects folder.
2. Right-click in the free space in the projects folder and select Text Document command from the New menu.
3. Type in Proj1.txt for the name.

    By default, Proj1.txt will inherit rights from its parent. In this case, it will inherit Customer Service: Full Control and EXECS: Modify.

4. Double-click the Proj1.txt file to open it and type THIS IS PROJECT 1.
5. Close Notepad and save the file.

Project 2

Proj2.txt is Martin's top-secret project and he wants to make it unreadable to others. Martin wants to be the only person who can read the file.

To create Project 2:

1. Right-click in the free space in the Projects folder and select the Text Document command from the New menu.
2. Type proj2.txt for the name.
3. Right-click proj2.txt and select Properties.

    The proj2.txt Properties screen appears.

4. Click the Security tab, and then clear the Allow Inheritable Permissions from Parent to Propagate to This Object check box.

    After you click the check box, the Security dialog box will appear.

5. Click Remove to remove all inherited permissions from the parent.
6. Click the Add button.

    The Select Users, Computers, or Groups screen appears.

7. Select Martin Wier (mwier@corp.com) and click OK.

Back at the proj2.txt Properties page, make sure the Full Control check box is selected, as shown in Figure 12.7.

FIGURE 12.7

All entries have been removed except Martin, who has Full Control.

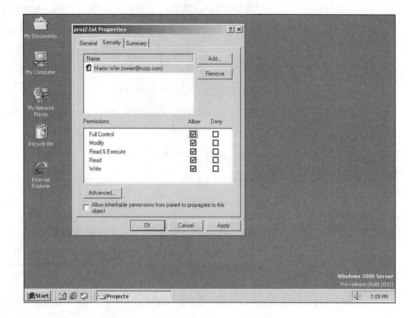

8. Click OK to close the proj2.txt Properties page.
9. Double-click the proj2.txt file to open it and type THIS IS PROJECT 2. Close Notepad and save the file.

Project 3

Proj3.txt is a file for which Martin wants to have Full Control and that everyone in the Customer Service group should be able to Read.

To create Project 3:

1. Right-click in the free space in the projects folder and select Text Document command from the New menu.
2. Type Proj3.txt for the name.
3. Right-click over Proj3.txt and select Properties, and the Proj3.txt Properties screen appears. Click the Security tab.

   By default, the file will inherit the permissions of the parent, and Martin doesn't want that.

4. Clear the Allow Inheritable Permissions from Parent to Propagate to This Object check box. After you click the check box, the Security dialog box will appear.

12

5. Click Remove to remove all inherited permissions from the parent.

6. Click the Add button, and the Select Users, Computers, or Groups screen appears.

7. Select Martin Wier (mwier@corp.com) and Customer Service and click OK.

8. Back at the Proj3.txt Properties page, click Martin Wier and select the Full Control check box.

9. Click Customer Service and then make sure only the Read check box is selected.

10. Click OK to close the Proj3.txt Properties page.

11. Double-click the Proj3.txt file to open it and type THIS IS PROJECT 3. Close Notepad, and save the file.

Martin has now finished creating the files and folders. Log off.

As an optional exercise, you can log on as a member of the Customer Service group, such as Beth Martins (username: bmartins; password: fastcar1), and test which files and directories created by Martin are readable and which are not.

Changing Permissions and Taking Ownership

The person who creates a file is called the *owner*. File owners automatically receive a special right: the ability to assign access permissions to that file. This enables regular, everyday users to set security on the files they feel are important, as Martin just did in the preceding exercise.

Users who have full control on a file or directory also have the ability to take ownership and assign permissions.

But what happens if the owner of a file decides to deny read access to critical company documents and then quits or goes on vacation? How can those files be opened for reading? As the Administrator, you have a special ability called *Take Ownership* that, when used, makes the Administrators group the owner of the file or folder. You can then assign the rights necessary for other people to read the document.

> An Administrator can specify another user as having the permission to take ownership of a file. The user with the new permission can *take* ownership of that file. An Administrator cannot simply assign ownership of a file. Users must take deliberate action to be the owner of a file.

In this example, Martin has gone away on vacation, but a member of the Customer Service group absolutely, positively has to read the secret proj2.txt file. After getting two levels of managerial approval plus signoff from your corporate legal department, you proceed.

To take ownership of a file and assign new permissions:

1. Log on as Administrator to the computer where you placed the directory structure and project files.
2. Open My Computer, select the D:\ drive, and double-click the cservice folder to enter it.
3. Double-click the Projects folder to open it. Try to open proj2.txt by double-clicking it.

   You should get an Access Is Denied message from Notepad.
4. Close the dialog box and Notepad.
5. Right-click proj2.txt and select Properties.

   The proj2.txt Properties screen appears.
6. Click on the Security tab. You will see a message that states you cannot edit or change the permissions, but you can take ownership. Click OK.
7. Click the Advanced button.

   The Access Control Settings for Proj2.txt screen appears.
8. Click on the Owner tab, click on the Administrators group, and then click OK, as shown in Figure 12.8.
9. Back at the Proj2.txt Properties screen, click OK.

Now that you are the owner, you can set permissions on the file. You'll need to re-enter the properties page to make additional changes, so do the following:

1. Right-click over Proj2.txt and select Properties.

   The Proj2.txt Properties screen appears.
2. Click the Security tab, and then click the Add button.

   The Select Users, Computers, or Groups screen appears.

3. Select Customer Service and click OK.

4. Back at the Proj2.txt Properties page, click Customer Service and then make sure only the Read check box is selected.

5. Click OK to close the Proj2.txt Properties page.

FIGURE **12.8**

After adding the Administrators group, click OK.

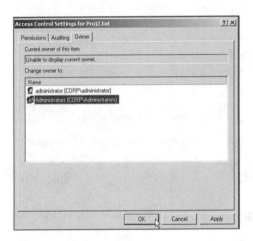

You can now log off and log on as anyone in the Customer Service group, such as Beth Martins (username: bmartins; password: fastcar1) to read the Proj2.txt file.

Compressing Files and Folders on NTFS

NTFS provides the added ability to compress individual files and folders to save disk space. The operation is completely transparent to the end user: the user requests a file, and it is uncompressed for use. When saving, the file is automatically recompressed. Often, the overhead to perform this operation is nearly negligible because compressing the files results in less disk head travel for a disk access.

However, it is best to compress files that are less often accessed for writing because writing is more processor intensive. Additionally, there is little need to compress already compressed files, such as .jpg or .zip files. After a file is already compressed, no benefits are realized from additional compression.

For these exercises, be sure to be logged in as Martin (username: mwier; password:fastcar6).

While using Windows Explorer, you may choose to highlight compressed files and folders by displaying them as a different color.

To select a different color for the compressed files and folders icons:

1. Click Start, Settings, and then Control Panel.

2. Double-click on the Folder Options applet.

3. Click the View tab.

4. Click the Display Compressed Files and Folders with Alternate Color check box.

> This setting is stored in each user's individual profile. Each user on the
> machine will need to perform this operation. See Hour 14, "Profiles and
> Policies," for more information on profiles.

When you compress a folder, you can choose to automatically compress all the folders in
it. Just because a folder is compressed does not mean that the files inside it have to be
compressed. Files and folders can each be individually compressed or uncompressed.
When you put a noncompressed file inside a compressed folder, however, the file will be
automatically compressed. In a sense, the uncompressed file will inherit the compression
attribute from the parent folder.

Martin Wier decides that his proj1.txt file is pretty big, and decides to be a nice guy and
compress it to make room for other files on the server.

To compress a file:

1. On your desktop or in the Windows 2000 Explorer, right-click the file you
   want to compress and select the Properties command from the context menu.

2. Click the Advanced button.

3. Click the Compress Contents to Save Disk Space check box, as seen in
   Figure 12.9.

4. Click OK. Back at the file Properties page, click OK.

5. If you changed the view options as outlined in the previous procedure, the filename
   of proj1.txt file should now be blue. Alternatively, you can single-click the file to
   select it, and see that the Compressed attribute is set.

12

FIGURE **12.9**

*Use the Compress
Contents to Save Disk
Space check box to
compress the file.*

Martin also decides that all future documents in the Misc folder will be compressed.

To compress a folder:

1. On your desktop or in the Windows 2000 Explorer, right-click the folder you want to compress; in this case, Misc.

2. Click the Advanced button.

3. Click the Compress Contents to Save Disk Space check box, as shown in Figure 12.9.

4. Click OK. Back at the file Properties page, click OK.

If you changed the view options as outlined in the previous procedure, the folder Misc should now be blue. Alternatively, you can single-click the file to select it, and see that the Compressed attribute is set.

Copying and Moving Files and Folders

When you copy or move files with NTFS permissions (such as read only) or attributes (such as compression) to other directories or volumes, it is helpful to understand the behavior of those actions. Often, file permissions and attributes are lost unexpectedly when files are moved. By understanding this section, you'll never fall into that trap.

Copying Files and Folders

When you copy files to FAT partitions, all permissions on the copied file are immediately lost. Remember—FAT partitions have no security.

When you copy files or folders into another directory with NTFS permissions, your copied file automatically inherits the permissions of the target directory. It doesn't matter whether the directory is on the same volume or a different machine. The rule is simple: Copied files inherit the folder's permissions.

This is true for uncompressed files as well as compressed files. If you copy a compressed file into an uncompressed folder, the file will become uncompressed. Remember, you inherit the compression attribute from the parent folder.

Martin decides to copy the compressed Projects\proj1.txt file to Orders\proj1.txt. The original proj1.txt file is compressed, but the Orders directory is not. Therefore, the copied proj1.txt will be uncompressed and will inherit the NTFS attributes in the Orders directory.

> You can practice copying compressed and uncompressed files by doing Exercise 1 at the end of this hour.

Moving Files and Folders

When you move a file to a FAT partition, all permissions on the moved file are immediately lost. Remember, FAT partitions have no security. Additionally, if the file was compressed in NTFS, it will not be compressed on the FAT volume.

> Windows 2000 cannot read or write to compressed FAT volumes, such as those created with the Windows 95 DriveSpace utility or third-party tools, such as Stacker.

When files and folders are moved, they get permissions depending on where they are moved to:

- If the file or folder is moved within the same NTFS volume, the file or folder maintains its original permissions.
- If the file or folder is moved to another NTFS volume, the action is treated as a copy, and then a delete. The file or folder loses its original permissions and inherits the permissions of the destination folder.

This behavior is the same for compressed or uncompressed files or folders. Compressed files and folders stay compressed when moved within the same NTFS volume. When moved between volumes, compressed files and folders inherit the compression attributes of the destination folder.

12

Martin decides to move the Projects\proj2.txt file to Misc\proj2.txt. The proj2.txt file is uncompressed, and has NTFS permissions where Martin has Full Control and Customer Service has read permission (as we set in the "Changing Permissions and Taking Ownership" exercise). Misc is a compressed folder (as we set in the "Compressing Files and Folders on NTFS" exercise).

When Martin moves proj2.txt from \Projects to \Misc, the file remains uncompressed and retains the NTFS permissions because it is being moved *to the same volume*. If Martin were to move the proj2.txt file to another volume, proj2.txt would inherit the compression attributes and NTFS permissions of the destination folder.

 You can practice the previous discussion by doing Exercise 2 at the end of this hour.

Disk Quotas

One of the new features of Windows 2000 server is the ability to limit how much disk space a user can use. Novell's NetWare has always had quotas, and several third-party tools have emerged in Windows NT to bridge this omission.

With this latest release, Windows 2000 allows administrators to specify how much disk space a user can use *per volume*. Because of this restriction, additional third-party quota tools should be right around the corner that will limit how much disk space a user can use *per directory, per server,* and perhaps *per domain, per tree,* or *per forest.*

To set quotas on users, quotas must be turned on for the volume. Then each user is assigned a quota warning and a quota limit. When a user has reached the quota warning, a dialog box appears, informing the user that she is approaching her limit. Instead of simply setting a quota warning, you can, if desired, enforce the quota with a quota limit. When the limit is hit, no additional files may be added by that user.

If a user has files located in multiple volumes, quotas must be enabled for each volume, and another quota warning and quota limit must be set for that user on each volume. In other words, quotas are completely separate based on volumes.

An additional feature of setting quotas is how users perceive their free disk space. After a quota limit is set for a user on a volume, Windows 2000 Server will report the quota limit as the new amount of free disk space. Even if there are 9GB of free space on the actual physical volume, the user is presented with only the free space she has until her quota is reached.

When compressed files are placed on volumes with quotas, free-space calculation uses only the uncompressed file size. This is because different types of files compress differently.

There are two quotas for a volume: the default and the specific. Specific quotas override the default quota, whether they are higher or lower than the default. This way, you can set a general quota for everyone on the volume, then tailor the specific quotas for those users who need a little more or, sometimes, a little less.

By default, members of the Administrators group are exempt from all quotas.

In this example, you'll set the default quota warning to 1MB, and enforce the default quota at 2MB. Then you'll specifically set Martin Wier's account to have a whopping 3MB.

Typically, you would not want to limit quotas to such low values. These were chosen only for the sake of the example.

12

To enable quotas for a volume:

1. Log on as Administrator.

2. Open My Computer and select the volume on which you want to enable quotas. In this case, use the D:\ drive. Right-click on the drive letter of the volume and select Properties. The Local Disk (D:) Properties page appears. Click the Quota tab.

3. To enable quota management, click the Enable quota management check box. To enforce the quota, select the Deny Disk Space to Users Exceeding Quota Limit check box.

4. To set the default quota for the volume, make sure the Limit Disk Space radio button is selected. Use the pull-down boxes to select 2MB. Change the Set Warning Level to 1MB. These settings are shown in Figure 12.10.

FIGURE 12.10

You can set a warning and enforceable limit.

5. To enable separate quotas for individual users, select the Quota Entries button. The Quota Entries for Local Disk (D:) screen appears.

6. To grant Martin Wier a different quota, click the Quota menu and select New Quota Entry. The Select Users dialog appears. Select Martin Wier and click OK.

7. The Add New Quota Entry screen appears. Here, you can wipe out the quota for a user or specify a different quota. In this case, you want to give Martin Wier 3MB of space on the volume. Click the Limit Disk Space radio button and set the value to 3MB. Set the warning level to 2MB.

8. The Quota Entries for Local Disk (D:) screen returns with Martin Wier's entry. You can use this screen in the future to monitor the disk usage. Close the Quota Entries for Local Disk (D:) screen.

9. Back at the Local Disk (D:) Properties screen, click OK to enable the quotas. You will be asked to confirm your desire for quotas. Click OK.

Summary

Use NTFS to secure files and folders. Permissions are inherited from one folder to another, unless they are blocked. NTFS permissions are added together, unless a Deny right is encountered. Take ownership of files if no one else can read them and reassign permissions to them.

When copying files, the files always inherit the permissions of the destination directory. When moving files, permissions are maintained when moving *within* a volume. Moving *between* volumes is just like a copy.

Use quotas to set either a space warning or space limit. By default, Administrators are exempt from quotas.

Workshop

The workshop provides a quiz and exercises to help reinforce your learning. Even if you feel you know the material, you will still gain from working these exercises.

Quiz

1. What is inheritance?

2. When would you need to take ownership of a file?

3. What are the basic NTFS permissions for folders?

4. What are the basic NTFS permissions for files?

5. Why would you want to compress folders or files?

6. How are NTFS group permissions figured?

7. You move a file with read-only permissions from one directory to another directory on a different volume. Does it keep its permissions? Why or why not?

8. You copy a file with read-only permissions from one directory to another directory on the same volume. Does it keep its permissions? Why or why not?

9. Which takes precedence: file permissions or folder permissions?

   Explicit file permissions always take precedence.

10. Which takes precedence: file attributes or folder attributes?

Exercises

After setting up the NTFS directory structure and compression attributes as described in earlier exercises, log on as Martin. Perform these exercises:

1. Martin decides to move the Projects\proj2.txt file to Misc\proj2.txt. The proj2.txt file is uncompressed, and it has NTFS permissions where Martin has Full Control and Customer Service has Read (as per the "Changing Permissions and Taking Ownership" exercise). Misc is a compressed folder (as per the "Compressing Files and Folders on NTFS" exercise).

   When Martin moves the proj2.txt from \Projects to \Misc, the file remains uncompressed and retains the NTFS permissions because it is being moved *to the same volume.* If Martin moved the proj2.txt to another volume, proj2.txt would inherit the compression attributes and NTFS permissions of the destination folder.

12

2. After setting up the quota limits in the preceding exercise, log on as Beth Martins. Use the Search, File facility to find all the .bmp files on the system, and copy them individually into the \CSERVICE directory to see when your quota will kick in. Repeat while logged in as Martin Wier.

Hour **13**

Shares and Dfs

by Jeremy Moskowitz

It is highly recommended that you learn the skills in Hour 12, "NTFS Permissions," before proceeding with this hour. This hour builds on the skills and procedures already mastered in Hour 12. It is assumed that you already understand the concepts presented and can perform the tasks required.

In Hour 12, you leaned how NTFS can lock down certain files. Locking down files is great, but you need a way for your users to access those files.

In this hour, you'll learn the finer points of sharing files and folders, as well as how to manage your users' files and folders with Windows 2000's new Distributed File System (Dfs).

In this hour, you will learn how to:

- Create shares for your users
- Understand the relationship between shares and NTFS permissions

- Create hidden shares for your own use
- Create standalone Dfs roots
- Create fault-tolerant Dfs roots

Shares

Shares are portals to files on other computers on your network. Whether or not users have access to the share will determine if they can pass through and see the files inside. Securing individual files is not supported on shares; access is granted or not granted to the entire share. Rather, a combination of shares and NTFS can secure individual files.

Chances are that you are already somewhat familiar with shares. In Hour 5, "The Control Panel," you shared your first printer. In Hour 10, "Active Directory Entities," you learned how to make existing Windows NT shares visible in the Active Directory.

In this section, you'll learn the finer points of sharing and the marriage of sharing and NTFS.

In the good old days, shares were the only source of security. Because the network operating system, not the file system, controls access to shares, rudimentary security can be set up. Therefore, before the advent of NTFS, the only security available was sharing.

Sharing Permissions

For shares, the only permissions available are

- Full Control: Users may perform all duties of the Change and Read permissions (listed in the following items), including taking ownership.
- Change: Users may create, delete, modify, and overwrite files, as well as having the permissions for Read.
- Read: Users can view the contents of the share, read files, and run programs.

As with NTFS permissions, if a user is a member of more than one group that is assigned rights to a shared folder, those rights are added together to give him his effective permissions.

Take Martin Wier: In Hour 9, he was put in both the EXECS group and the Customer Service group. Because Martin is in both the EXECS group and the Customer Service group, he gets both Read *and* Change permissions to the \cservice share. Because Read permissions are included in Change, Martin's effective right is Change (see Figure 13.1).

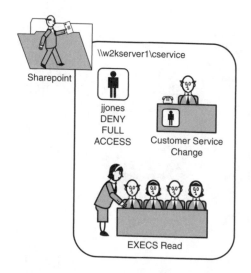

FIGURE 13.1

A graphical representation of the \\w2kserver1\ cservice share.

Individuals can also be denied access to a shared folder. In the preceding example, John Jones is expressly denied access, even though he is a member of the Customer Service group and the EXECS group. This is because the Deny right overrides all other permissions. Therefore, use this rule of thumb: All share permissions are added together, except when a Deny right is encountered. Deny wipes out all other occurrences of the permission.

Sharing and NTFS

When users connect via a share and try to access files on an NTFS volume, the most restrictive permissions apply.

For example, if Beth Martins connected to the cservice share, she would be granted Change rights via her membership in the Customer Service group, as seen in Figure 13.2. When trying to create files in \appts, Beth would have no problem because her level of NTFS access is Full Control. The more restrictive access of shared-level Change and NTFS Full Control is shared-level Change, so she can change files and directories in \appts. However, when Beth tries to modify appt1.txt, she is denied access. The more restrictive access of shared-level Change and NTFS Read is NTFS Read. Therefore, Beth can only read appt1.txt.

13

Figure 13.2

The Customer Service folder can have share and NTFS permissions placed upon it.

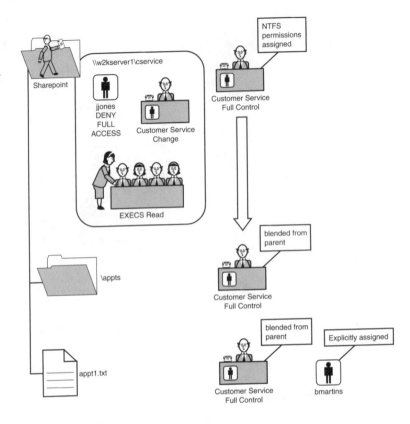

Creating Shares

To create shares on a Windows 2000 Domain Controller, a user needs certain access rights, as summarized in Table 13.1.

TABLE 13.1 Rights Required to Create Shares

Machine Type	Rights Required
Windows 2000 Domain Controller	Administrators or Server Operators group
Windows 2000 member machine (Server or Professional)	Administrators, Server Operators, or Power Users group
Nonmembers (standalone Server and Professional machines)	Administrators or Power Users group

Additionally, if the folder to be shared is on an NTFS volume, the user needs NTFS Read ability.

As the corp.com Administrator, you're going to need a share that permits the Customer Service and EXECS groups to access the directory structure that Beth Martins created in the previous section. To keep it simple, you can share the \cservice folder as the cservice share.

Because you have placed NTFS permissions on all the files and folders in the \cservice folder, you can share it such that the Customer Service and EXECS groups have Full Control.

When files are accessed through the share, the most restrictive permissions between sharing and NTFS will be applied. By default, when folders are shared, the Everyone group receives Full Control rights. We'll change that so only the Customer Service and EXECS are allowed access.

To share a directory:

1. Log on as Administrator.

2. Double-click the My Computer icon to get a list of available drives. In the last example, you placed \cservice on D:\. Double-click the D: drive to open it.

3. Right-click over cservice and select Sharing from the context menu (or select Properties, and then click the Sharing tab). The cservice Properties screen appears.

4. Click the Share This Folder button. Leave the share name as the default, cservice. In the comment line, enter `Customer Service - Delaware`.

5. Leave the user limit at the default of Maximum Allowed.

6. Click the Permissions button. The Permissions for cservice screen appears. Select the Everyone group and click Remove. Click Add. The Select Users, Computers, or Groups screen appears. Select the Customer Service and EXECS groups and click OK.

7. Back at the Permissions for cservice page, click the Customer Service group and click the Full Control check box. Click the EXECS group, and click the Full Control check box. When finished, the screen should look like Figure 13.3. Click OK to close the Permissions for cservice page.

8. Back at the cservice Properties page, click OK to close it.

Hidden Shares

Shares are like huge advertisements for users. When users see the name of the share, they often get curious about what's inside. Sometimes, if permissions are not set correctly, users can get in, root around, and get into trouble. Sometimes you wish you could just keep some shares a secret. Well, you can.

13

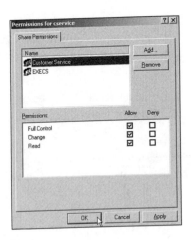

FIGURE 13.3

Remove Everyone and grant Full Control to the Customer Service and EXECS groups.

To make a share hidden, simply share it with a dollar sign ($) at the end of the share name. For instance, you could create a share called GAMES$, which is full of games just for you and your buddies. When users surf the network via My Network Places, the GAMES$ share will not show up.

This means if you and your buddies wanted to connect to the GAMES$ share, you'd need to manually connect to that share. (We'll go over how to connect to shares at the end of the hour.)

Administrative Shares

By default, Windows 2000 automatically shares (and hides) some network resources. This is so you, the administrator, can use them, but your users can't find them to get into trouble or even ask questions as to what they are.

- Drive shares—Every disk's root is shared as *<driveletter>*$; for instance, C$ and D$. This enables you, the administrator, to connect right to the root for maintenance. By default, the only permissions on the share are Administrators: Full Control.

- Admin$—This hidden share equates to where you installed Windows 2000 (sometimes called the *systemroot*). In most cases, this is C:\WINNT. If you have lots of server types across your environment, with lots of administrators installing the software to different places, this is a handy way of zipping right to the installation point.

- Print$—This shares to *systemroot*\system32\Spool\Drivers. Its main purpose is to facilitate the automatic download of print drivers to clients.

Shares and UNC Names

After shares are set up, they can be accessed by their Universal Naming Convention name, or UNC name for short. A UNC name takes the form of
\\SERVERNAME\SHARENAME\DIRECTORY\SUBDIRECTORY\DEEPERSUBDIRECTORY.

In the earlier directory sharing exercise, you manually created a shared resource at \\w2kserver1\cservice. Additionally, automatically shared resources (such as those described earlier) have UNC names, such as \\W2KSERVER1\c$. (There is no period at the end of the UNC name.)

Clients can use multiple methods to map network drives to the UNC shares you set up. You'll be able to explore that ability a bit later in the section "Client Connections to Shares and Dfs Points," at the end of this hour.

Distributed File System

The Distributed File System, or Dfs, is a new feature in Windows 2000 Server.

> Dfs should only be abbreviated Dfs, so as not to be confused with an IBM product that holds the DFS trademark. DFS, coincidentally, provides similar but unrelated functionality on UNIX systems.

Dfs can be thought of as a "share of shares." In fact, Dfs is so powerful in advanced configurations that Dfs can be a "share of Dfs's." For the sake of this book, we'll only set up the most widely used case.

Dfs is useful because it can group together shares that are important to your users. In the past, users needed to individually map a drive letter to each share, and then remember which drive letter was meant for what share. Sometimes, the users would even run out of drive letters!

In Dfs parlance, the topmost point is called the *Dfs root,* or just *root* for short. Each server can house only one Dfs root. Off the root are *child nodes.* A child node can be a regular share (as described earlier) or, in more complex situations, additional Dfs points.

Even better, with some added software, the Dfs child nodes don't even necessarily have to be on Windows 2000 Servers. In fact, there is a strong possibility that NetWare,

13

UNIX, Macintosh, and Banyan VINES Dfs server software is on the way. Dfs can be the one go-to point for users, where they can look at a list, find the one place they know and love, and everything they need will be under one roof.

> Windows 2000, Windows 98, and Windows NT 4.0 include a Dfs client. When you update your Windows 95 clients for Active Directory with the included update, they also receive a Dfs client.

FIGURE 13.4
You can deliver a one-stop-shop of all required shares via Dfs.

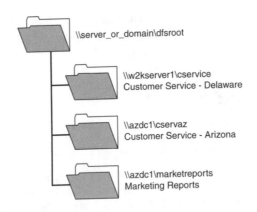

In the example shown in Figure 13.4, both the Customer Service and Marketing clients need to know only one piece of information: what you call your Dfs root. If they can remember that, those clients can simply double-click into their folder and see the shares underneath.

There are no permissions to set on Dfs roots. The underlying real shares will permit or deny access just as they normally would. Dfs also enables you to fashion another name for existing shares. This is helpful if you want to provide a homogeneous view of your shares.

Dfs comes in two flavors: standalone and fault-tolerant configurations.

Standalone Dfs Configuration

A standalone configuration is the simplest way to configure Dfs. In a standalone configuration, you use one server to act as a traffic cop for real shares. In Figure 13.5, the traffic cop is w2kserver1.

FIGURE **13.5**

A graphical representation of a standalone Dfs root.

\\w2kserver1\saroot

\\w2kserver1\cservice
Customer Service - Delaware

\\azdc1\cservaz
Customer Service - Arizona

\\azdc1\marketreports
Marketing Reports

After users enter the Dfs root, they can click the folder they want and get the information you set up for them. That information can reside on any server in the network. The user doesn't even need to know that little secret; Dfs seamlessly translates Dfs child nodes to regular shares in the background.

In this exercise, you will leverage some of the exercises performed in this and previous hours. For instance, you have already created the \\w2kserver1\cservice share. For the sake of this book, presume that the \\azdc1\cservaz and \\azdc1\marketreports shares have already been created on the azdc1 server. In this example, we'll create the standalone root on the w2kserver1 machine. \\w2kserver1.corp.com\saroot will be the name of the resulting Dfs root.

To create a standalone Dfs root:

1. Log on as Administrator to W2KSERVER1.

2. Start the Distributed File System administrator by clicking Start, Programs, Administrative Tools, and then Distributed File System. A notice comes up telling you that currently there is no Dfs root.

3. The Distributed File System administrator appears. Because there is no root, you must create one. Click the Action menu and select New Dfs Root Volume.

4. The Create New Dfs Root Wizard appears; click the Next button to continue.

5. The Select Dfs Root Type screen appears. For this exercise, you should choose Create a Standalone Dfs Root and click Next.

6. The Specify Server to Host Dfs screen appears. By default, it will enter the server you are currently working on. Leave the defaults as W2KSERVER1.corp.com and click Next.

7. The Specify the Dfs Root Share screen appears. This screen allows you to use an existing share or new share as the name people will remember. For this example, click the Create a New share entry and type in d:\saroot in the Path to share box

13

and saroot in the Share Name box. The entire pathname to your standalone Dfs share will therefore be \\W2KSERVER1.corp.com\saroot (no ending period). Click Next. A dialog box appears asking if you would like to create the new share. Click Yes.

8. The Name the Dfs root screen appears. This screen allows you to enter a comment if desired. Type in Customer Service Standalone Root and click Next.

9. The Summary screen appears, as shown in Figure 13.6. Click Finish. Click OK if a success message appears.

FIGURE 13.6

The Create New Dfs Root Wizard summary screen.

Now that you have your root, you can add child nodes to it. You want to generate the Customer Service tree, as shown previously in Figure 13.5. You have already created the \\W2KSERVER1\CSERVICE share. For the sake of this book, the \\AZDC1\CSERVAZ and \\AZDC1\MARKETREPORTS shares have already been created. You can use either Windows NT or Windows 2000 shares, if desired.

To create child nodes:

1. Start the Distributed File System Manager, if it isn't already started, by clicking Start, Programs, Administrative Tools, and then Distributed File System.

2. Select the root; in this case, \\W2KSERVER1\saroot. Next, click the Action menu and select New Dfs Link. The Create a New Dfs link screen appears. In the Link Name field, enter Customer Service - Delaware. In the Send the User to This Shared Path field, enter \\w2kserver1\cservice. You can leave the Comment field blank for now, as shown in Figure 13.7. Leave the caching default at 1800 seconds. Click OK.

If the number of seconds the client uses for caching is high, your network will be less congested. The lower the number of seconds, the more accurate the cached information will be.

FIGURE **13.7**

Create a child note off the Dfs root.

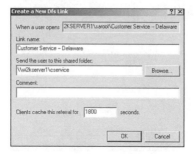

3. Repeat the previous steps for the additional child nodes as shown in Figure 13.5. When you have finished, the Dfs Manager should look like Figure 13.8.

FIGURE **13.8**

The Dfs Manager is now configured like the graphical representation in Figure 13.5.

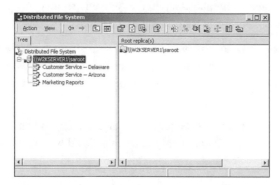

When clients connect to \\w2kserver1\saroot, they will see the Dfs root and shares as shown in Figure 13.9.

See the later section titled "Client Connections to Shares and Dfs Points" to see how clients can actually connect.

Creating a Domain (Fault-Tolerant) Dfs Root

A fault-tolerant Dfs root enables multiple Domain Controllers to maintain their own copies of all the information in all the shares off the Dfs root. A graphical representation can be seen in Figure 13.10. Each copy of the information is called a *replica*. This enables clients to choose the replica that will respond the fastest. Clients automatically choose the fastest replica based on the site information, like the kind you set up in Hour 7, "Advanced Planning for Domains, Domain Controllers, and the Active Directory."

FIGURE 13.9

This is what clients will see when they connect to \\w2kserver1\saroot.

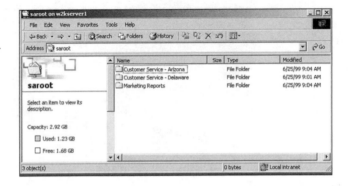

Additionally, if the closest Dfs replica isn't available (due to a power failure or a server crash, for example), Dfs will automatically choose another replica in the domain using information automatically published in the Active Directory. All this magic works behind the scenes and is completely transparent to the end user.

It takes a lot of disk space to house a copy of your shares multiple times—one time for the real share, and one more time for each replica of the share. With this in mind, you need to carefully plan your fault-tolerant Dfs so that only the most critical information is replicated.

Dfs will automatically update the replicas as needed, depending on the files that have changed, but there are two cautionary notes associated with this behavior.

- Entire files are copied—When any changes to a file are detected, the entire file is recopied back to all replicas. If the file is 20MB, but only 1 byte is changed, the entire file is sent to all replicas, which could severely impact your network.

- Two users can open the same file—Because replicas are automatically chosen for users, two users might open the same file, say, with one replica in Arizona and one replica in Delaware. There is no synchronization strategy in Dfs. Users should be aware that the rule for updates is "The last writer wins."

With these facts about Dfs in mind, you should use Domain (fault-tolerant) Dfs roots only for the most critical information that can never be unavailable to your users for an extended length of time.

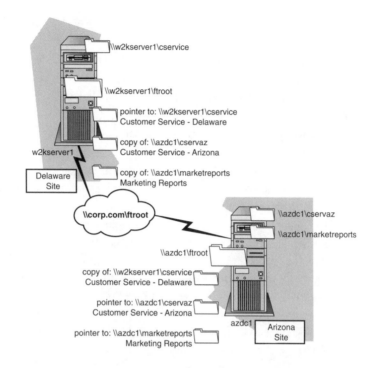

FIGURE 13.10

A graphical representation of a fault-tolerant Dfs root.

In this exercise, you will leverage some of the things you have already done in this hour. For instance, you have already created the \\W2KSERVER1\CSERVICE share. To expedite matters, we have already created the \\AZDC1\CSERVAZ and \\AZDC1\MARKETREPORTS shares on the AZDC1 server. In this example, we'll create the fault-tolerant root in the corp.com domain named \\corp.com\ftroot.

You can, if desired, have more than one root for a server. To minimize confusion, it is recommended that you delete the root you created in the last exercise. You can delete the Dfs root you created in the last section (\\w2kserver1\ saroot) by selecting the Dfs root, clicking the Action menu, and selecting Delete Dfs Root. Answer Yes when asked if you really want to do this.

13

To create a Domain (fault-tolerant) Dfs root:

1. Log in as Administrator to W2KSERVER1.

2. Start the Distributed File System administrator by clicking Start, Programs, Administrative Tools, and then Distributed File System. A notice might come up to tell you that currently there is no Dfs root.

3. The Distributed File System administrator appears. Because there is no root, you must create one. Click the Action menu and select New Dfs Root Volume.

4. The Create New Dfs Root Volume Wizard appears. Click Next to continue.

5. The Select Dfs Root Type screen appears. For this exercise, we want to choose the first option, Create a domain Dfs Root, and click Next.

6. The Select Domain to Host Domain for the Dfs root screen appears. By default, the wizard will enter the domain you are currently working in. Leave the default as corp.com and click Next.

7. The Specify the Host Server for the Dfs root screen appears. By default, the wizard will enter the server you are currently working on. Leave the default as W2KSERVER1.corp.com and click Next.

8. The Specify the Dfs Root Share screen appears. This screen allows you to use an existing share or new share as the name people will remember. For this example, click the Create a New share entry and type in d:\ftroot in the Path to share box and ftroot in the Share Name box. The entire pathname to your standalone Dfs share will therefore be \\ corp.com\ftroot (no ending period). Click Next. A dialog box appears asking if you would like to create the new share. Click Yes.

9. The Name the Dfs root screen appears. This screen allows you to enter a comment if desired. Type in CORP Domain Root and click Next.

10. The Summary screen appears, as shown in Figure 13.11. Notice that the Domain field is now set to CORP.COM and Dfs root name is now set to ftroot. Click Finish. Click OK if a success message appears.

Now that you have your fault-tolerant root, you need to add another server that will participate in this fault-tolerant scheme. That way, if one server goes down, the other server will automatically pick up. Because you have a Domain Controller in Arizona called AZDC1, you can use it to replicate your data.

To add additional replica servers:

1. Click the Dfs root you've created in the left pane then click the Action menu, and select New Root Replica.

2. The Specify Server to Host Dfs Root screen appears. Enter the name of the replica server, in this case, AZDC1.CORP.COM. Click Next.

3. Follow steps 8–10 from the previous exercise to finish setting up your replica server. When you have finished, your Dfs manager should look like Figure 13.12.

FIGURE 13.11

The Create New Dfs Root Wizard Summary screen now has the domain as well as the Dfs root name information filled in.

FIGURE 13.12

A fault-tolerant Dfs root is replicated across Domain Controllers.

You might have to hit F5 to refresh the display.

You can repeat this procedure as desired for additional Domain Controllers in corp.com that you want to participate in the fault-tolerant Dfs root.

Now that you have the servers assigned for your Dfs replication, you must perform a one-time procedure to turn on the replication and inform Dfs which server is the master for initial replication.

To start Dfs replication:

1. Select the Dfs root, click the Action menu, and select Replication Policy.
2. The Policy screen appears. Click the \\W2KSERVER1.CORP.COM\ftroot selection and click the Set Master button.

You will never see the Set Primary button again after this screen is closed.

13

3. Click the \\AZDC1.CORP.COM\ftroot selection, and then click Enable.

4. Click OK to close the Replication Policy screen.

Now that you have replication set up, use the procedure to create child nodes previously described in the "Standalone Dfs Configuration" section. The child nodes will be automatically replicated to the replicas.

When you have finished, the Dfs Manager should look like Figure 13.13.

FIGURE 13.13

Your Dfs root now has the shares hanging off of it.

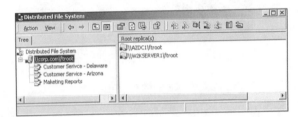

Client Connections to Shares and Dfs Points

You'll want to teach your clients to connect to shares and Dfs points. When clients connect to a share, a single drive letter is used to represent the share. For instance, G: could represent \\W2KSERVER1\CSERVICE.

In addition, because Dfs is really a "share of shares," a single drive letter can now be used to represent many share points that live under a Dfs root.

Clients can map connections to share and Dfs points in four ways:

- The Map Network Drive Wizard—Clients can right-click over My Network Places on the desktop and click Map Network Drive. A wizard can help them select a free drive letter and map to the UNC name.

- The Run command—Clients can open UNC paths by entering their name in the dialog of the Run command. Simply click Start, Run, and then enter the UNC name. Additionally, drive letters can be mapped using the Run command in conjunction with the Net Use command. Type net use <driveletter>: \\server\sharename. For instance, net use s: \\W2KSERVER1\CSERVICE.

- The Windows Explorer—Clients can open UNC paths by entering their name in the Address dialog of the Windows Explorer.

- My Network Places—Users can surf the machines located in My Network Places and double-click the folder representing a share or Dfs root.

Two views can be seen in Figure 13.14. The top window is focused on \\w2kserver1\cservice and the bottom window is focused on \\corp\ftroot.

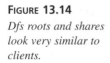

FIGURE **13.14**

Dfs roots and shares look very similar to clients.

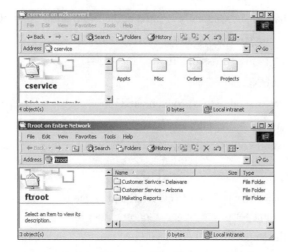

When viewing the desired UNC path, clients can click the folder desired. Share permissions and NTFS permissions will either allow or deny access to the folders.

After clients get the hang of using UNC shares, it will be smooth server sailing.

Summary

Use shares to enable clients to access files. Permissions on files are always the most restrictive between sharing and NTFS. Hidden and administrative shares are hidden with a $ as the last character in the share name.

Use Dfs to create a "share of shares." Dfs roots can be standalone or fault tolerant. Standalone Dfs roots are hosted by one server. Fault-tolerant roots are replicated to multiple Domain Controllers.

Workshop

13

The workshop provides a quiz and exercises to help reinforce your learning. Even if you feel you know the material, you will still gain from working these exercises.

Quiz

1. What types of users can create shares on a Windows 2000 Domain Controller?

2. How do you create a hidden share?

3. What share is automatically created at the root of a drive?

4. What share is automatically created at the installation point of Windows 2000?

5. What are the possible permissions for shares?

6. How are group permissions figured on shares?

7. What is a UNC name?

8. Where are standalone Dfs roots hosted?

9. Where are fault-tolerant roots stored?

10. When would you use a standalone Dfs root rather than a fault-tolerant root?

Exercises

1. Bring up another Domain Controller, and create two folders and share them. Then use Dfs Manager to create a standalone Dfs root.

2. Delete the standalone Dfs root you just created. On W2kServer1, add the new Domain Controller as an additional replica server.

3. Get familiar with the command Net Use to connect to shares and Dfs roots. Use net /? and net use /? to get a command structure overview, as well as the built-in Windows help facility to get more information.

HOUR 14

Profiles and Policies

by Jeremy Moskowitz

Often when users log on to a machine for the first time, they immediately start making changes to how the desktop is set up. Those changes are saved in their *profiles*. In this hour, you'll explore profiles and learn how to maintain them on servers.

You'll also want to make sure your users can't get into too much trouble on the new servers. You'll make sure that doesn't happen by implementing group policies, which restrict some of the actions users can perform.

In this hour, you will learn to do the following:

- Create and assign local, roaming, and mandatory profiles
- Migrate local profiles to roaming profiles
- Assign local, roaming, and mandatory profiles to your users
- Create and assign policies based on domain, OU, and group membership
- Block or force inheritance of policy objects

What Is a Profile?

A *profile* is a collection of user settings, including desktop attributes, such as fonts and color schemes, as well as printer and network connections.

There are three types of user profiles:

- Local user profiles
- Roaming user profiles
- Mandatory user profiles

Local User Profiles

A local user profile is the repository of settings and documents that a user maintains on his workstation. You can see local user profiles on the System Properties Control Panel applet's User Profiles tab, shown in Figure 14.1.

FIGURE 14.1

The User Profiles tab of the System Properties applet is in the Control Panel.

Local user profiles are created when a new user physically sits down at a Windows 2000 (or Windows NT) machine and logs on for the very first time.

If you work at a machine and use the Display applet to change the display scheme to, say, Rose, that scheme will still be in effect the next time you use that machine.

These settings are stored in the Documents and Settings\\<*USERID*> folder of the root drive that Windows 2000 was installed on, as shown in Figure 14.2. For instance, if you installed Windows 2000 to d:\winnt and logged in as the username bmartins, your profile would be located under D:\Documents and Settings\bmartins.

FIGURE 14.2

Every user who has logged on the Windows 2000 machine has a profile.

The profile consists of several directories and one special file. The directories include several desktop settings: the Start menu, the Desktop, and the My Documents folder. (For a detailed discussion of each, see Hour 4, "Using the Windows 2000 Interface.") The profile also includes Internet settings: Cookies, Favorites, and a directory for Microsoft's FrontPage editor. Finally, there are some hidden folders and a special hidden file called NTUSER.DAT, which holds settings such as the display scheme.

Local profiles are in effect if the user is not logging in to the domain or if roaming profiles are not yet set up (see the next section). Local profiles don't do you much good in a networked environment, so you'll want to migrate away from them as soon as possible. Sometimes, however, users configure their workstations just-so before getting a network account with a roaming profile.

In this example, you'll make a quick and easy change to a user's local profile to simulate any of the thousands of changes a user can make. You'll use this procedure in later examples in this hour.

To log on as Martin Wier and change the display scheme:

1. If you are currently logged in as Administrator, log off now by pressing Ctrl+Alt+Delete and clicking Logout.
2. Press Ctrl+Alt+Delete to get the attention of the server.
3. Log on as Martin Wier, and use the username mwier and password fastcar6.
4. Open the Display applet in the Control Panel by clicking Start, Settings, and Control Panel, and then double-clicking the Display icon.
5. Click the Appearance tab. In the Scheme drop-down box, select Rose.
6. Click OK and log off.

Martin's display is now changed in his NTUSER.DAT file.

14

Roaming Profiles

Local profiles are great if your users don't attach to the network. But to get real power to your users, you'll want to give them the freedom to have their profiles follow them when they roam from machine to machine.

When roaming profiles are used, a user's settings are still written locally as described in the previous section. When the user logs off, the changes are automatically saved to the server location specified (you'll see how later). The next time the user logs on to another machine, the settings are simply copied from the server and used locally until the user logs off. This can be done for any number of machines.

Roaming profiles haven't changed much from Windows NT Server 4.0. If you've never set up roaming profiles before, however, this section will show you how.

To do this, you'll need to have a shared directory on the server that can house your users' profiles. Then you will modify the user accounts to point toward this newly shared directory. Optionally, you can choose one of the local profiles you already set up to be used as the template for one or more of your users' roaming profiles.

To create and share a directory to store roaming profiles:

1. Log on as Administrator.

2. From the desktop, double-click My Computer.

3. Find a place to create a Users directory. In this example, we'll use D:\Users. Double-click on D: to open the drive. Right click in the free area and select the Folder command from the New menu; then type in Users as the name.

 Some administrators prefer the directory and share name to be Profiles, although any name will work.

4. Right-click over the newly created Users directory, and select the Sharing command from the context menu.

5. Click Share This Folder, keep the rest of the defaults, and click OK.

Now you need to specify which network user account can use roaming profiles. In this example, you'll specify Martin Wier.

To. modify accounts to use roaming profiles:

1. Click Start, Programs, Administrative Tools, and then Active Directory Users and Computers.

2. Expand corp.com in the tree pane, open the Customer Service OU, and double-click on Martin Wier's account; click his Profile tab.

3. In the Profile Path text box, specify the server, sharename, and directory you want to use.

4. Type in \\w2kserver1\users\mwier (as shown in Figure 14.3). Leave all other fields blank.

FIGURE **14.3**

Type in the
\\SERVERNAME\
SHARENAME\
DIRECTORYNAME
you want to give to the
user.

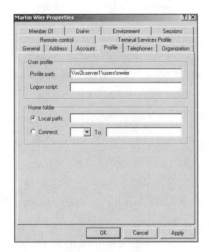

5. Click OK.

Home Directories

Figure 14.3 shows a field designated for home directory. Home directories may substitute for the function of the My Documents folder, if desired.

Whereas the My Documents section of the profile is designed for Windows 2000 machines, the home directory entry is designed for downlevel clients, such as Windows 95 or Windows NT.

With Windows 2000 Professional, home directories become no longer necessary. Because data files are stored in the My Documents section of the profile, the files stored there are automatically copied to the client and back to the server when the user logs off.

Even if you use Windows 2000 Professional machines, you might want to maintain home directories. If you have many users with large files who often roam from machine to machine, particularly across sites (WAN links), you might want to consider home directories. Because the My Documents folder in the profile is copied down to the Windows 2000 client every time a user first logs on to that machine, significant strain on your network could occur. If you choose to assign home directories, those files are not copied at logon, and a shorter logon time is realized.

14

> The downside to using home directories, however, is that users must be trained to use a specific drive letter to store their documents. If Windows 2000 Professional is used, this is not required. You simply tell your users to store their documents in the My Documents folder and forget about it.
>
> You'll see a third way of housing user data files—a hybrid of the My Documents and home directory strategies—in Hour 20, "Client Services, IntelliMirror, and ZAW."

If you want to win the Administrator of the Year award, you can preserve Martin's existing local profile and copy it up to his newly created roaming profile directory. This will save Martin the time and effort of trying to re-create his local settings on his new roaming profile.

To preserve a local profile and make it a roaming profile:

1. Log on as Administrator to the machine Martin has been using.
2. Open the System applet in the Control Panel by clicking Start, Settings, and Control Panel, and then double-clicking the System icon.
3. Click the User Profiles tab and select the profile of Martin Wier (mwier).
4. Click the Copy To button. The Copy To dialog appears.
5. Enter the server, share name, and directory name of the profile storage path, just as you did in the last exercise. Enter \\W2KSERVER1\USERS\MWIER and click OK.

Martin can now log on as mwier to any Windows 2000 Server or Professional machine, and his profile will follow him.

Mandatory Profiles

Mandatory profiles are like roaming profiles, except that none of the changes users make to their settings are saved back to the server. Some environments are ideal for mandatory profiles, such as a shop-floor. Usually, these users in these environments have a group of applications they need to use, and nothing more. There is no need to change the settings—indeed, setting changes could spell a support call at 2 a.m. for you-know-who.

Making mandatory profiles is easy: simply follow the instructions for roaming profiles, but add one more step.

> To perform this exercise using the graphical user interface, you must have turned on the Show Hidden Files and Folders option in Hour 4.

To create a mandatory profile:

1. Locate the user's profile on the server share.

2. Rename the file NTUSER.DAT to NTUSER.MAN.

After the name is changed, no settings will be saved back to the server when the user logs off.

Group Policy

So far, you've spent a lot of time forming your enterprise into a hierarchy. Let's review what you've done thus far.

In Hour 6, "Domains and the Active Directory," you created your first Domain Controller. In Hour 7, "Advanced Planning for Domains, Domain Controllers, and the Active Directory," you created two sites, Delaware and Arizona, as shown in Figure 14.4.

FIGURE 14.4

The corp.com root domain is spread over Arizona and Delaware.

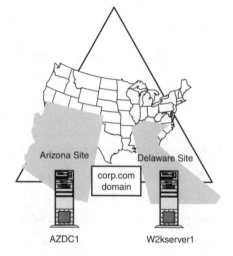

You also learned how and when to create domains rather than OUs. In Hour 10, "Active Directory Entities," you implemented your OU structure. If you zoom in on the root of corp.com, you can see the Customer Service OU as well as the other OUs and users you have placed inside it (see Figure 14.5).

Examine all that you've created so far: Two sites, a corp.com domain, a Customer Service OU within it, and additional OUs. You've got a genuine hierarchy!

14

FIGURE **14.5**

A zoom-in on the root of corp.com and the OUs inside.

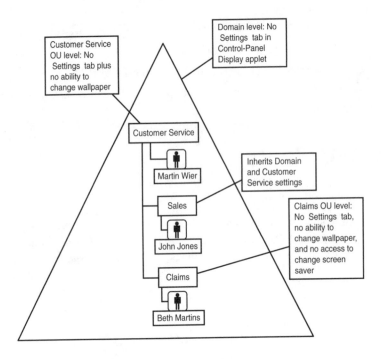

As noted in the introduction, sometimes you want to make sure that your users don't get into too much trouble. The Group Policy Editor lets you tweak specific *user* and *computer* settings, and then apply them in a hierarchical fashion. Group policies are inherited down the hierarchy. The order of the hierarchy is as follows:

1. First, group policy settings focused for the site are applied.
2. Next, the group policies are applied for the domain.
3. Finally, each OU group policy is applied from parent OU to child OU.

Some examples of user settings include restricting desktop settings, such as restricting users' ability to open the Display applet in Control Panel, hiding all icons on the desktop, or if necessary, even preventing users from logging off!

Some examples of computer settings include modifying the behavior of the Task Scheduler (as seen in Hour 5, "The Control Panel") and preventing printers from being automatically published in the Active Directory. Additionally, some major security settings such as account policies can be modified. Examples of account policies include password, lockout, and audit policies.

Group policy configuration also adds the feature of scripts that can fire off when users log on or off, or when a computer starts up or shuts down.

You will be able to explore the myriad of options available in user settings and computer settings in just a bit.

In this section, you'll be going through some of the examples highlighted earlier.

Creating Group Policies

In our examples, we'll be forgoing setting up group policies for sites and focusing on creating group policies for our domain and OUs. Just remember that if site settings are created, they are the first to be applied, then, inherited.

Although there are many possibilities to what can be set via Group Policies, we will be concentrating on an area you are already familiar with: the Control Panel settings. Or, more specifically, the Display applet in the Control Panel folder.

Dozens of calls per month are being logged to the corp.com helpdesk because users are playing with their display settings and then don't know how to change them back. Display settings are a dangerous area: a user can inadvertently change the video driver, for instance.

To prevent this, you have decided to create a group policy based on your environment. At the domain level, you decide to disable the Settings tab. No one in the domain will be able to access the Settings tab.

The Manager of Customer Service, Martin Wier, tells you that his people are constantly changing the desktop background—causing a severe decrease in office productivity. He wants to know if you can make that behavior stop. You decide to enable the Disable Changing Wallpaper setting for the Customer Service OU.

The Manager of Customer Service also tells you that the people in the Claims OU are obsessed with changing the screen saver. You tell him you can arrange to disable that.

You will implement each of these changes via the Group Policy editor, which can be started within the Active Directory Users and Computers MMC snap-in.

To change the default domain-wide group policy:

1. Log in as the Administrator of the domain.
2. Start the Active Directory Users and Computers MMC snap-in by clicking Start, Programs, and Administrative Tools, and then selecting Active Directory Users and Computers. The Active Directory Users and Computers MMC appears.

14

3. Right-click the domain (corp.com) and select the Properties command.

   The domain Properties box appears as shown in Figure 14.6. Click the Group Policy tab.

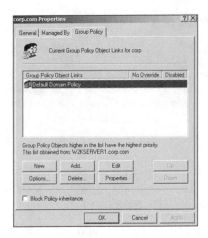

4. A default domain policy exists for the domain. Select it, and click Edit.

   The Group Policy editor appears. In this lesson, do not concern yourself with the Computer Configuration section. Rather, you want to concentrate on the users' Control Panel settings.

5. Open the settings by expanding User Configuration, Administrative Templates, Control Panel, and then Display. Your screen should look like the one shown in Figure 14.7.

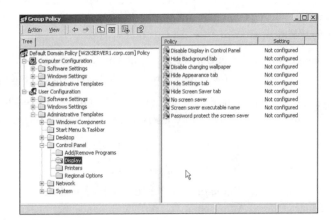

6. At the domain level, you want to use the Hide the Settings Tab. Double-click the item to view it's status. Notice how the setting is currently set to Not Configured.

7. Click the Enabled setting.

8. Click OK; back at the Group Policy screen, the setting should change from Not Configured to Enabled.

9. Close the Group Policy editor. Click OK at the domain Properties screen. You should now be back at the Active Directory Users and Computers console.

Now that you've disabled the Settings tab for the entire domain, you need to disable the ability to change the wallpaper for the Customer Service OU.

To create an OU-wide group policy:

1. If you don't already have the Active Directory Users and Computers console open, open it now using the instructions in step 2 in the last exercise.

2. Right-click the OU (Customer Service) and select Properties. The domain Properties box appears. Click the Group Policy tab.

3. There is no default policy for OUs you create. You'll need to create one now. Click New. Type in Cust_Svc_GP and press Enter. Select the new policy and click Edit.

4. The Group Policy editor appears.

5. In this lesson, do not concern yourself with the Computer Configuration section. Instead, you want to concentrate on users' Control Panel settings. Get to the settings by expanding User Configuration, Administrative Templates, Control Panel, and then Display.

6. Your screen should look like Figure 14.7 (as seen in the last exercise). At the Customer Service OU level, you want to disable changing wallpaper. Notice that the setting is currently set to Not Configured. Double-click that entry.

7. Click the Enable radio button.

8. Click OK. Back at the Group Policy screen, the setting should change from Not Configured to Enabled.

9. Close the Group Policy editor. Click OK at the OU Properties screen. You should now be back at the Active Directory Users and Computers console.

Now that you've disabled the wallpaper settings ability for the entire Customer Service OU, you must disable the ability for the Claims OU to change the screen saver.

To create an OU-wide group policy:

1. If you don't already have the Active Directory Users and Computers console open, open it now using the instructions in step 2 of the domain-wide group policy exercise.

14

2. Right-click the OU (Claims) and select Properties. The domain Properties box appears. Click the Group Policy tab.

3. There is no default policy for OUs you create. You'll need to create one now. Click New. Type in `Claims_GP` and press Enter. Select the new policy and click Edit.

   The Group Policy editor appears. In this lesson, do not worry about the Computer Configuration section. Instead, you want to concentrate on users' Control Panel settings.

4. Get to the settings by expanding User Configuration, Administrative Templates, Control Panel, and Display. Your screen should look like Figure 14.7.

5. At the Claims OU level, you want to hide the screen saver tab. Notice that the setting is currently set to Not Configured. Double-click the Hide Screen Saver tab entry, and then click the Enable radio button.

6. Click OK. Back at the Group Policy screen, the setting should change from Not Configured to Enabled.

7. Close the Group Policy editor. Click OK at the OU Properties screen. You should now be back at the Active Directory Users and Computers console.

Testing Group Policies

In the previous section, you set policies that affected users in your domain. You have just set up policies that affected

- All users in the domain
- The domain and the Customer Service OU
- The domain, the Customer Service OU, and the Claims OU

A graphical representation can be seen in Figure 14.8.

Group policy settings usually take effect within 90 minutes of their inception. To accelerate the process, you can manually refresh the policies if you want quicker results.

To manually refresh policies:

1. Click Start, Run.

2. In the Run line, type `secedit /refreshpolicy USER_POLICY` or `secedit /refreshpolicy MACHINE_POLICY`, as desired.

In the first exercise, you turned off the Settings tab in the Display applet for everyone in the domain. We can easily see whether the changes you made were successful because they affect everyone in the domain.

FIGURE 14.8

A graphical representation of what you performed in the last section.

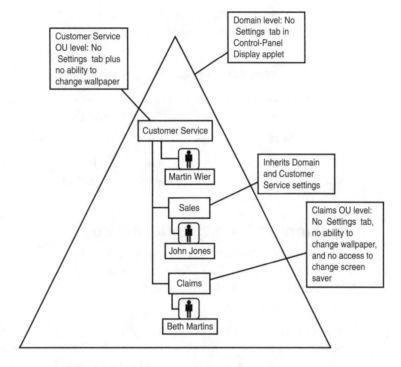

To test group policy settings made to the domain:

1. If you're not already logged on as Administrator, do so now.
2. Click Start, Settings, and then Control Panel. Double-click the Display applet.

Even logged in as Administrator, your Display Properties screen should have the Settings tab missing. The Administrator is not immune from domain-wide policies. (Note that the Background and Screen Saver tabs are both still fully functional.)

In the second exercise, you turned off the ability to change the wallpaper for everyone in the Customer Service OU. Martin Wier, the manager of the Customer Service department will try to see whether your settings took effect.

To test group policy settings made to the Customer Service OU:

1. Log on as Martin Wier. Use username mwier and password fastcar6.
2. Click Start, Settings, and then Control Panel. Double-click the Display applet.

Martin's display properties should also have the Settings tab missing. This is because this setting is inherited from the domain Group Policy. Additionally, the Background tab will not let him change the current background. (Note that the Screen Saver tab is still fully functional.)

14

In the third exercise you turned off the ability to change the screensaver for everyone in the Claims OU. Beth Martins, a member of the claims OU will try to see if your settings took effect.

To test Group Policy settings made to the Customer Service OU:

1. Log on as Beth Martins. Use username bmartins and password fastcar1. (Martin changed Beth's password in Hour 10, "Active Directory Entities.")
2. Click Start, then Settings, then Control Panel. Double-click the Display applet.

In the Display Properties screen, the Settings and the Screen Saver tab should be missing. All of the previous settings were inherited from the Domain and Customer Service OU.

Blocking or Forcing Inheritance

At first, nobody really complained about the new policies in the domain and at the OU levels. Sure, people grumbled a bit when they lost the ability to change their background and screen savers, but, in their hearts they knew they should have been performing their job-related duties anyway.

But about a month after the policies were put into place, John Jones in the Sales OU called his boss, Martin Wier, and wanted to know if he could get back the permission to change his background. He wanted a snazzy background for when clients were in his office. Martin agreed, and he called you to tell you to allow people in the Sales OU to change their backgrounds.

If you've already applied a Group Policy setting that denies this ability to the Customer Service OU, how can you "un-deny" it to the child Sales OU? The answer is *inheritance blocking*.

Blocking inheritance at an OU level is analogous to wiping the slate clean and ignoring the settings added at previous levels. You may block inheritance at an OU level provided that the No Override check box is not selected at a higher level. Take a look at Figure 14.9.

If you had optionally specified No Override at the Customer Service OU level, you would not be able to block inheritance at the Sales OU level for the entries specifically set. For instance, in the example shown in Figure 14.9, we know that the Cust_Service_GP prevents people from changing their background. If the No Override check box were selected at the Customer Service OU level, none of the child OUs (such as Sales) could ever change their backgrounds. This check-and-balance system is available for times when you delegate control of your OUs to OU Administrators. Sometimes you'll want to force certain policies on your OUs that they cannot override.

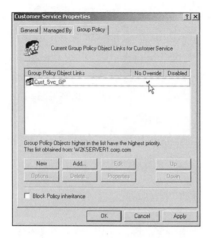

FIGURE 14.9

An example of how to force a policy from a higher level. Don't do this now; it is only an example.

However, because you did not select the No Override check box in the previous section, you can still wipe the slate clean and block inheritance.

In this example, you'll block the inheritance from the above levels for the Sales OU. You'll still want to restrict the Sales OU from gaining access to the Settings tab, however, so you'll need to create a new group policy just for the Sales OU.

To create a policy that blocks inheritance:

1. Log in as the Administrator of the domain.

2. Start the Active Directory Users and Computers MMC snap-in by clicking Start, and then Programs. Find Administrative Tools and select Active Directory Users and Computers. The Active Directory Users and Computers MMC appears.

3. Open the Customer Service OU and select the Sales OU. Right-click the Sales OU and select Properties. The Sales Properties box appears. Click the Group Policy tab.

4. Click the Block Policy Inheritance check box. This will prevent the effects of the domain and Customer Service OU's policies from affecting the Sales OU.

5. There is no default policy for OUs you create. You'll need to create one now. Click New. Type in Sales_GP and press Enter. Select the new policy and click Edit. The Group Policy editor appears.

   In this lesson, do not concern yourself with the Computer Configuration section. Rather, you want to concentrate on the users' Control Panel settings. Get to the settings by expanding User Configuration, Administrative Templates, Control Panel, and then Display. Your screen should look like Figure 14.7.

14

6. At the Sales OU level, you still want to enable the Hide the Settings Tab entry. Double-click the entry. Click the Enabled entry.

7. Click OK. Back at the Group Policy screen, the setting should change from Not Configured to Enabled.

8. Close the Group Policy editor, and then click the OK button at the OU Properties screen.

You should now be back at the Active Directory Users and Computers console.

Now that you've blocked the inheritance from the Customer Service OU to the Sales OU, you'll want to test it to make sure it worked.

To test blocked inheritance:

1. Log off as Administrator. Log on as user jjones with password fastcar6.

2. Click Start, Settings, and then Control Panel. Double-click the Display applet.

John's display properties should have the Settings tab missing, but should have access to change the background picture. None of the previous settings were inherited from the domain and Customer Service OU.

Computer Settings

In the previous examples using the Group Policy editor, you used the User Configuration settings to change things such as the behavior of the Control Panel. There is also an entire tree dedicated to the computer configuration. These settings affect every user who logs on to that machine.

 A special group of rights, called user rights, can also found in the Computer Settings tree. These settings determine who has special rights to log on or manage the computer. These can be found under Windows Settings, Security Settings, Local Policies, User Rights Assignments.

A machine must be a member of the domain (usually a Windows 2000 Professional workstation), and that machine's account must be inside the OU on which the group policy is to take effect.

After a Computer Configuration GPO setting is applied to an Active Directory object (such as a site, domain, or OU), this setting takes effect only when the computer that the configuration affects is restarted.

Once again, Martin Wier has called us up asking for help on the following two issues:

- Issue number 1: When some of the Customer Service co-workers go to lunch, the others sneak over to their machines and use the Scheduled Task applet in Control Panel to fire off obnoxious .wav files at random times during the day. This has to stop. Martin asks whether there is any way to disable the creation of new tasks. He still wants predefined tasks to run as scheduled (such as the task you created in Hour 5).

- Issue number 2: By default, when logon times expire users are still able to work. Martin wants to control his overtime expenses. Martin wants these users to be forcibly logged off when logon hours expire.

For the sake of this example, Martin Wier's PC (named martinspc) has been added as a member of the domain, and his computer account has been moved from the default Computers group to the Customer Service OU (see Figure 14.10).

FIGURE 14.10

martinspc is in the Customer Service OU.

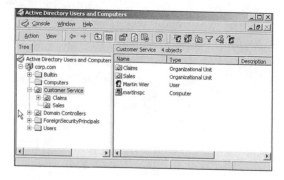

For an explanation of how to make a Windows 2000 machine a member of a domain, be sure to see Hour 9, "Users, Groups, and Machine Accounts on Domain Controllers." For an explanation of how to move Active Directory objects into OUs, see Hour 10.

14

To create a computer configuration policy:

1. Log on as the Administrator of the domain.
2. Start the Active Directory Users and Computers MMC snap-in by clicking Start, and then Programs. Find Administrative Tools and select Active Directory Users and Computers. The Active Directory Users and Computers MMC appears.

3. Right-click the Customer Service OU and select Properties.

   The domain Properties box appears.

4. Click the Group Policy tab.

5. Because you already created an OU policy for this OU, you can simply select it (Cust_Svc_GP) and click Edit.

To solve Martin's first problem, you'll want to turn off the ability to add tasks with the Scheduled Tasks applet. It is here that you use the Computer Configuration section.

To deny the ability to add tasks in the Task applet, do the following:

1. Get to the settings by expanding Computer Configuration, Administrative Templates, Windows Components, and then Task Scheduler.

2. Double-click the Disable New Task Creation line item. The Disable New Task Creation Properties screen appears.

3. Click the Enable setting.

4. Click OK. Back at the Group Policy screen, the setting should change from Not Configured to Enabled, as shown in Figure 14.11.

FIGURE 14.11

Although the wording is roundabout, you are "Enabling" the "Disable Task Creation" setting.

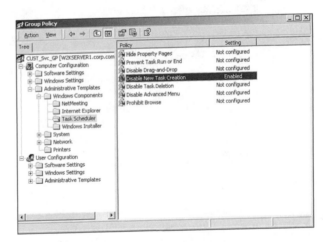

To solve Martin's second problem, force Customer Service users to log off when logon hours expire.

To force a log off when logon hours expire:

1. Get to the settings by expanding Computer Configuration, Windows Settings, Security Settings, Local Policies, and then Security Options.

2. Double-click The Automatically log users off when logon time expires entry.

3. Check the Define this policy setting check box and click Enabled as seen in Figure 14.12. Click OK.

FIGURE 14.12

This setting will auto-matically log the Customer Service users off when logon hours expire.

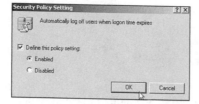

4. Close the Group Policy editor. Click OK at the OU Properties screen. You should now be back at the Active Directory Users and Computers console.

You won't be able to immediately verify the automatic logging off unless you specify logon hours. (See hour 9, "Users, Groups, and Machine Accounts on Domain Controllers.") But you can immediately verify the change you made regarding the Scheduled Tasks.

To test a group policy computer configuration change:

1. Reboot the machine named martinspc. Remember, computer configuration changes are read only when the computer starts.

2. On martinspc, log on to the domain as any Customer Service OU member, includ-ing Martin, John, or Beth.

3. Click Start, Settings, and then Control Panel. Double-click the Scheduled Tasks applet. Notice that there is no way to add a task.

Summary

Profiles house user settings. Local profiles are stored under the \Documents and Settings\<*username*> folder. Profiles can be made to be roaming by sharing a directory and pointing a user account to use the Profile entry to point to the share. The Profile consists of several directories and one special file: NTUSER.DAT. To make a roaming profile a mandatory profile, rename NTUSER.DAT to NTUSER.MAN.

Policies change user and computer settings. Use the Group Policy editor to create changes on a site, domain, and OU level. Group Policy User settings take effect almost right away, but can be forced to be refreshed manually. Computer settings take effect after the machine that will be affected is rebooted. Use the Block Policy Inheritance check box to stop inheritance from affecting the current objects.

14

Workshop

The workshop provides a quiz and exercises to help reinforce your learning. Even if you feel you know the material, you will still gain from working these exercises.

Quiz

1. What are profiles?
2. Where are local directories stored?
3. Where are roaming profiles stored?
4. How do you convert a roaming profile to a mandatory one?
5. In what order are policies applied?
6. What are the two major groupings of policies?
7. How do you set up policies that don't affect a nested OU?
8. How do you manually refresh the policies?
9. What are some computer configuration policy settings?
10. What are some user configuration policy settings?

Exercises

1. Configure the Sales GPO such that the Sales OU has no Run command from the Start menu. Hint: It's in User Configuration, Administrative Templates, Start Menu & Taskbar.
2. Configure the Claims GPO such that members of the Claims OU have no Internet Explorer icon on their desktop. Hint: It's in User Configuration, Administrative Templates, Desktop.
3. Configure the Sales GPO such that members of the Sales OU cannot save any files they download from the Internet. Hint: It's in User Configuration, Administrative Templates, Windows Components, Internet Explorer, Browser menu.

PART III
Networking

Hour

HOUR 15

Protocols and Networking Fundamentals

by Jeremy Moskowitz

Before we can run headlong into deploying Windows 2000 Server's networking services, it helps to have a solid foundation of the avenues of communication from one computer to another. There's a lot of history to be discovered in the way computers have evolved to communicate over the years, and this hour could be an entire book unto itself.

In this hour, you'll get a crash course in the following topics:

- The Windows 2000 Network Protocol Stack
- Alternative protocols (NetBEUI, IPX/SPX, DLC, and AppleTalk)
- Implementing an alternative protocol
- TCP/IP client options and command-line utilities

The Windows 2000 Network Protocol Stack

When two foreign dignitaries meet for the first time, each is usually prepared in advance by his advisors on what to expect from the other dignitary. For instance, if an American dignitary were to meet with a Japanese dignitary, the American would look his best if he knew to bow during his greeting. The Japanese dignitary would look his best if he knew to outstretch his arm for a handshake. These behaviors are part of a protocol. Each of these men needs to know the correct way to start and stop a session and work together with common rules.

Sometimes, neither man knows what to do, and each might do what is native for him. In the case of a protocol mismatch, the conversation might never get started. If the two men cannot agree on a protocol to start their conversation, they are at an impasse, and no further communication can take place.

In the world of computers, protocols have the same function. *Protocols* are the collections of rules that start, stop, and regulate a conversation over the network.

In this hour, we'll be going over various protocols: TCP/IP, IPX/SPX, NetBEUI, and DLC.

Compare the way we hear sound to how a computer receives information from a network. For us to hear a sound, the following events must occur, in order:

1. A sound is generated.
2. Vibrations are created from that sound.
3. The vibrations travel in waves through air or water.
4. The vibrations in the medium in turn vibrate our tympanic membranes at the same frequency.
5. Our tympanic nerves send the vibrations as electrical signals to our brains.
6. Our brains understand the sound.

This is a *stack* of events. One of the steps cannot happen without the previous step. If any of these events does not happen, the sound is not heard.

But, in the same way that sound vibrations in the air carry our conversations, we also need a way for our computers to understand the "vibrations" on the network wire. That method is called a *protocol stack*. After a computer creates a message for another computer, it must encapsulate the message around various layers in the stack. When the message is received on the other end, the layers are peeled off and the message is understood. These messages are sent in chunks called packets. A *packet* is simply a unit of routable data that can be sent from source to destination in a switched environment, such as TCP/IP or IPX/SPX. It takes many packets to make a single message.

We'll be discussing each layer in the protocol stack (see Figure 15.1), understanding what each does to get the message from one computer to the next. In particular, we'll be analyzing the TCP/IP stack because that is Windows 2000 Server's protocol of choice.

Note, however, that each protocol (IPX/SPX, NetBEUI, AppleTalk) has its own layers with slightly different functions and, sometimes, different names. For the most general theoretical case, there is the 7-layer *OSI model* that describes these layers for almost any protocol.

Physical Layer

Like air or water for sound, the network packets need a physical medium in which to travel. This is called the *physical layer* or *network interface layer*. When you plug a cable into your network card, you've created the first layer of connectivity. There are lots of media to transport data, including Ethernet, Token Ring, ATM, Frame Relay, Satellite, wireless—you name it.

Internet Layer

This is where the *IP* in TCP/IP is housed. IP stands for Internet Protocol. Packets are sent with sequence numbers. This enables the receiving end to look at the numbers and reorder the packets, if necessary. This sequence number is important because IP does not guarantee that the packets will be sent or received in order. The Internet is a scary and unregulated place, where the quality of the connection is dubious at best. Packets of the same message may take completely different paths to their destination. IP is the speedy half of TCP/IP.

Transport Layer

This is where the *TCP* in TCP/IP is housed. TCP stands for Transmission Control Protocol. TCP ensures that the packets will be resequenced in the proper order for the next layer. In addition, TCP verifies that the data packets are valid. TCP is generally used for network applications that dump large amounts of data at one time. TCP is the robust half of TCP/IP.

Application Layer

This is the layer that we, the users, interact with. Web browsers and email clients are two examples of application-layer programs. We'll see some command-line utilities in this layer that also let us perform network functions, such as `ping` and `ftp`.

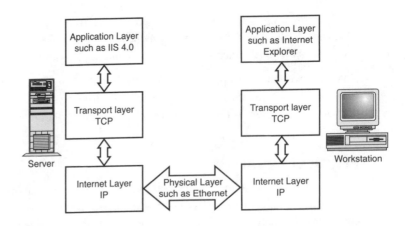

FIGURE 15.1
Packets travel down one stack and up another to get to their destination.

Alternative Protocols (NetBEUI, IPX/SPX, DLC, and AppleTalk)

Not all networks use TCP/IP as their preferred transport protocol. In this section, we'll be going over alternative network protocols and when and why you should or should not use them.

NetBEUI

NetBEUI (or NetBIOS Extended User Interface) is a protocol that grew up from the days of LAN yore. The granddaddy of them all, NetBEUI is still around, and it still has a bit of life left in it.

Before we talk about NetBEUI, we first need to talk about NetBIOS. NetBIOS is a protocol that we still use to call computers by a unique name.

NetBIOS isn't a protocol that can live on its own. It must be encapsulated or wrapped inside another, more robust protocol, such as NetBEUI, NWLink, or TCP/IP. Windows 2000 Server is trying to eliminate the need to use NetBIOS names for choosing specific computers. DNS is the new preferred way for making named connections to remote computers.

NetBEUI is a nonroutable protocol, meaning that when it encounters a physical router, its packet of data cannot be passed through. This is because there is no information within a NetBEUI packet that specifies the path to its destination. Thus, NetBEUI can travel only as far as it can broadcast its signal. NetBEUI is good for only the smallest of installations, such as a workgroup on a floor, and is provided only for backward compatibility. However, NetBEUI, for all its limitations, does have some advantages over other protocols.

NetBEUI's advantages are

- Speed—Depending on the type of communication, NetBEUI can often beat the pants off TCP/IP for speed. Its packet size is much smaller.
- Self-tuning—After NetBEUI starts detecting errors or retries on the wire, it uses a windowing technique to slide the packet size according to how quickly the sender and receiver can send the data.

IPX/SPX and NWLink

NetWare 5 (the current competitor for Windows 2000 Server) uses TCP/IP as its native protocol, but it didn't always do so. In fact, Novell designed a widely used proprietary protocol that it hoped could connect the entire world together (as TCP/IP is doing today). That protocol is called IPX/SPX.

When Novell was creating the first stable LAN systems, the Internet was barely in diapers, so choosing TCP/IP as the default protocol would have been overkill by anyone's standards. Because Novell wanted a fast, routable protocol (unlike NetBEUI), it created IPX/SPX. NetWare used IPX/SPX as the default protocol from the original conception of NetWare on through to NetWare 4, so there's still quite a bit of IPX/SPX in production computer systems worldwide. Because of this, Windows 2000 comes with an IPX/SPX-compatible protocol called NWLink. Microsoft's NWLink is very useful.

The advantages to IPX/SPX protocol using NWLink are

- NWLink is excellent for small to medium-sized environments whose administrators don't want to hassle with the myriad of TCP/IP protocol settings. Although some of the tools we will talk about later make that endeavor a bit easier, there's almost nothing to the job of configuring NWLink.
- NWLink enables your clients to connect to existing NetWare servers, as well as NT and Windows 2000 Servers that use the NWLink protocol. Additionally, an add-on product called File and Print Services for NetWare can enable an NT server to emulate a NetWare 3 server. After the protocol is on the client and the server, the clients will think they are talking directly to a NetWare server.
- NWLink is routable, meaning that it can pass through routed subnets. This means, theoretically, that your enterprise could run on this fast, easy-to-configure protocol. In fact, many organizations do.

NWLink comes in four flavors, called frame types. These frame types are Ethernet 802.2, Ethernet 802.3, Ethernet II, and Ethernet SNAP. Although we're not going to go into the details of each flavor here, just keep in mind that the same NWLink frame type must be running on any two machines that have to communicate. Also note that 802.2 is the most common flavor, with 802.3 a close second.

DLC

DLC (Data Link Control) is a protocol whose roots go way back to the mainframe days. DLC's claim to fame was that after a session was established, it took very little overhead to keep that session established. From those roots came the ability for a server to remotely connect to printers. It was nice to have a low-overhead protocol that excelled in maintaining a connection to a device. Hence, DLC became the protocol of choice for network printer servers, such as the HP JetDirect series. DLC doesn't work well for normal (nonprinting) LAN traffic, so Windows 2000 Server doesn't support it in this fashion. You will see where DLC can be loaded in Hour 19, "Printing."

AppleTalk

AppleTalk, as its name implies, was designed at Apple Computer, Inc. Apple's goal was simple: plug machines together, and have the connection work. And Apple succeeded. AppleTalk is still very popular today with Macintoshes. It's been updated to run over Ethernet, from its original conception over a somewhat proprietary cable. AppleTalk is included in Windows 2000 Server to allow Macintoshes to connect to Windows 2000 Server. We'll see more about AppleTalk in Hour 20, "Client Services, IntelliMirror, and ZAW." Although AppleTalk is almost universally used when Macintoshes are deployed, Apple's long-term plans seem to be to move to TCP/IP and to make AppleTalk a legacy protocol.

Implementing Alternative Protocols

To implement an alternative protocol, we'll be visiting some entries in the Control Panel, as we did in Hour 5, "The Control Panel." It is in the Network and Dial-up Connections applet that you find and modify network protocols.

To add the NWLink protocol:

1. Click Start, select Settings, and then open Control Panel. Double-click Network and Dial-up Connections. Right-click Local Area Connection and click Properties.

Another way to get to this information is to right-click Network Properties on the desktop and select Properties. After you are there, double-click Local Area Connection and click Properties.

2. At the Local Area Connection Properties screen, click the Install button, double-click Protocol, and then Add. Select NWLink IPX/SPX/NetBIOS Compatible Transport Protocol (see Figure 15.2). Click OK.

FIGURE 15.2

Choose the alternative protocol desired and click OK.

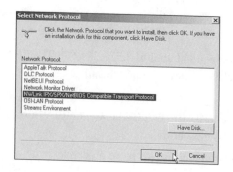

3. At the Local Area Connection Properties screen, select NWLink IPX/SPX/NetBIOS Compatible Transport Protocol and click Properties.

4. If you happen to have two network cards in your machine, you'll need to have a unique internal network number set. You can also rely on Windows 2000 Server's auto frame type detection, or set it to the type or types you will require your clients to use.

5. Click OK in the NWLink properties dialog, and Click Close in the Local Area Connection Properties dialog. You won't even have to reboot your server.

TCP/IP Addressing and Subnetting

TCP/IP addresses and subnets are complex subjects, but you will probably want to master them should you need to design or understand a complex and modern networking system. In the sections that follow, you will learn about different address, network classes, and how to compartmentalize them with subnets.

Addressing

TCP/IP addresses are made up of four 8-bit fields, called *octets* (that's base 8). When we convert the four groups of eight into decimal notation for us, we call it *dotted-decimal*. When we refer to an IP address as 24.0.64.18, we're saying 24 is the first octet, 0 is the second octet, 64 is the third octet, and 18 is the fourth octet.

Each octet can have a maximum value of 255. This is because octet means 2 to the 8th power, or 256. (One digit is the zero.)

A TCP/IP address is 32 bits in total length. Some of those bits comprise the network ID (that is, "What road am I on?"), and the remaining bits represent the host ID (that is, "What's my mile marker on the road?").

To make the most out of the grand total of 3,720,314,628 TCP/IP hosts, the address space is split into three classes, cleverly enough called Class A, Class B, and Class C.

- Class A—Class A addresses are given out only to the largest of organizations. In the Class A address space, 16,777,214 hosts can each fit on 126 separate networks. That's 2,113,928,964 total hosts.
- Class B—Class B addresses are for more moderate-sized universities, corporations, and organizations. In the Class B address space, 65,534 hosts can each fit on 16,384 separate networks. That's 1,073,709,056 total hosts.
- Class C—Class C addresses are for small groups of computers, usually for LANs. Often, a company will request several Class C addresses after the first is outgrown. In the Class C address space, 254 hosts can each fit on 2,097,152 separate networks. That's 532,676,608 total hosts.

If we know there are 126 networks in Class A, that must mean that the first octet is in the range of 1–126. Class B's range for the first octet is 128–191, and class C's range is 192–223.

You might have noticed 127 is missing from the range of valid first octets. That is because 127 is a special reserved address for *loopback*. We'll use the 127 address space a bit later.

Private Addressing

When we use the term *private addresses*, we mean special groups of TCP/IP addresses that are not passed through the public Internet. These private addresses are fully legitimate, non–Internet-routable addresses for internal use within your organization. If you use private addresses, you need have no fear that you will ever conflict with anyone outside your organization because private addresses are not routable over the Internet.

The scope of these addresses is as follows:

- Class A—Range: 10.0.0.0–10.255.255.255; subnet mask 255.0.0.0 yields 16 million addresses

- Class B—Range: 172.16.0.0–172.31.255.255; subnet mask 255.255.0.0 yields 65,000 addresses

- Class C—Range: 192.168.0.0–192.168.255.255; subnet mask 255.255.255.0 yields 255 addresses

If possible, use private addressing in your internal network, especially if the machines getting IP addresses have no chance of ever servicing people's requests on the Internet (Beth, John, and Martin's PCs, for instance).

Subnetting

A *subnet mask* is another 4-octet, 32-bit address that "masks" the associated IP address assigned with it. The mask reveals the bits used for the network ID and the host ID.

Default Subnet Masks

The class of addresses your network has will determine its default subnet mask. For Class A, this is 255.0.0.0; for Class B, this is 255.255.0.0; and for Class C, this is 255.255.255.0.

Imagine that the subnet mask is a stained-glass window. The darker the staining on the glass, the less light shines through. The subnet mask allows you to fine-tune how dark or light you want to get. Imagine the number 0 to be a totally clear, nonstained window. This lets all the light shine through. Also imagine 255 to be a completely blackened stained-glass window, through which no light can pass. Between 0 and 255 is an entire array of possibilities, where varying percentages of the light can shine through the glass.

Let's briefly look at how the classes match with the subnet masks by examining the Class C address space and the Class C subnet mask. We said in the previous section that a single Class C network can consist of 254 hosts on that network. How do we get that seemingly random number? Begin with the default subnet mask of 255.255.255.0.

Because you have four octets, and three of the four are being completely blocked by the mask, that only leaves us another octet (the fourth) through which "light" can shine. In fact, it's a completely clear window. This leaves you one full octet (2 to the 8th power) or $255 - 1 = 254$ hosts on the subnet.

Custom Subnet Masks

Just because there are default subnet masks for each of the classes doesn't mean there aren't custom subnet masks as well. Custom subnet masks simply allow you to fine-tune your situation. Depending on how "dark" you tint the glass, you can allow fewer hosts to "shine through" for a given subnet.

This sounds like you are limiting yourself, and you are. But after you do this, you create a tradeoff: the fewer hosts you put on a single subnet, the more subnets you can have. This is advantageous if, say, you are assigned a Class C address, but only have three buildings with 10 people in them. Why should you have to lump them all into the same subnet? If you tint the glass to create a custom subnet mask, you can create 16 subnets of 14 host addresses on each of them. We'll choose this combination to give you a little breathing room to add hosts to each of your subnets at a later date. The subnet mask generated from this is 255.255.255.240.

How was *that* seemingly random number calculated?

Although there are about a dozen ways to get to this number, we will detail the most expedient. You know that there are 255 total addresses available using the default subnet. If you explode 255 using the power of 2, you get 128, 64, 32, 16, 8, 4, 2, and 1 because those numbers are in binary (2^7, 2^6, 2^5, 2^4, 2^3, 2^2, 2^1, 2^0). Each one of those numbers represents one bit.

Note that when you add 128, 64, 32, 16, 8, 4, 2, and 1 together, you get 255. Just what we expected.

If you know how many bits you need in a subnet, the math is simple: $2^{(\text{number of bits you need})}$ − 2. You must subtract 2 from the result because the first (0) and last (255) bits are reserved in host addresses.

First, let's reexamine the problem: You want blocks of addresses in groups of 10 (or slightly higher to grow in to). You have three buildings, so that's three subnets of 10 or more hosts each.

To figure out how many bits you'll need for your hosts, start adding from right to left until at least the number of hosts you want is achieved (1 + 2 + 4 + 8 = 15). That's 4 bits. Next, take the number of bits and raise 2 to that power (2^4). Then subtract 2, and you get $2^4 - 2 = 14$.

Armed with the fact that your subnets can contain 14 hosts, how many subnets can you get? Remember, in a Class C address, there are a total of 8 bits available for the subnets and the hosts. If you've already used 4 bits for the host addresses, that leaves you with the remaining 4 bits for the subnets. Use a similar formula to find the number of subnets, once you know the number of remaining bits. $2^{(\text{number of remaining bits})}$. That's 2^4 or 16 subnets.

This is exactly the answer we got earlier: 16 subnets of 14 addresses on each subnet. 16 subnets is *way* more subnets than you need right now. Maybe you'll grow into them.

Now, how do you formulate the subnet mask? If you used the *last* 4 bits for the number of hosts, that means you need to use the *first* 4 bits for the mask.

Add 128 + 64 + 32 + 16 = 240. Your subnet mask is 255.255.255.240.

If all this math gives you a headache, an excellent subnet calculator can be downloaded for free at http://www.net3group.com/ipcalc.asp, which simplifies the mental processing.

Microsoft Subnet Mask Shorthand

In some instances, Microsoft Windows 2000 requires the inputting of the subnet mask in shorthand. Instead of inputting 255.255.255.240, you might have to enter the subnet shorthand number of 28.

How did we get 28?

28 is the number of masking bits in 255.255.255.240. To calculate the number of masking bits, there's the hard way and the easy way. We'll present the easy way.

To calculate subnet mask shorthand:

1. Open up Microsoft's calculator by clicking Start, Run, and typing in calc.
2. Switch to scientific mode by clicking View, Scientific Mode.
3. For each of the numbers in the octet, click the DEC radio button, type in the number, say 255, and then click BIN.
4. Write down the binary representation of the number.
5. In the preceding example, you get:

    255 = 11111111
    255 = 11111111
    255 = 11111111
    240 = 11110000

Count the number of 0s from right to left until you hit your first 1; in this case, 4. Subtract $32 - 4 = 28$.

Therefore, the subnet mask shorthand for 255.255.255.240 is 28.

TCP/IP Client Options

Because you already installed TCP/IP as the default protocol of Windows 2000 Server back in Hour 3, "Installing Windows 2000 Server," we won't need to do that here. We will, however, detail some of the possible configurable options when installing Windows 2000 Server.

TCP/IP Settings

To view the Client Network Properties, right-click My Network Places on the desktop and select Properties. After you are there, double-click Local Area Connection and click Properties.

Select Internet Protocol (TCP/IP) and click Properties.

FIGURE 15.3

The Internet Protocol (TCP/IP) Properties page is where you enter TCP/IP addresses for a computer.

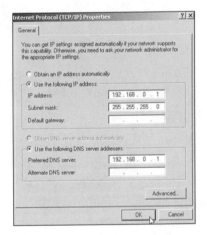

In the General tab shown in Figure 15.3, you see the following options:

- Obtain an IP address Automatically radio button—As you'll see in the next hour, running the DHCP server service can be an amazing timesaver. You'll be setting it up to allow clients to utilize this very setting. When it's set up, clients that have this setting enabled will automatically receive an available TCP/IP address and other administrator-set attributes. Clients that can use DHCP include Windows 95, Windows 98, Windows NT—even the LANManager 2.2c for DOS client!

- Use the Following IP Address radio button—This button has three text boxes: IP Address, Subnet Mask, and Default Gateway.

- IP Address—This is a dotted-decimal number that is unique to the network in which it is run. Contrary to popular belief, this number does *not* need to be unique in the world. Theoretically, any valid IP address may be used. Note, however, that this is not recommended if this machine is ever to join the Internet. All IP numbers are registered through Arin, and the numbers must be unique on the network in which they are run—including the Internet.

> If you require your own unique TCP/IP addresses, ask your ISP or visit http://www.arin.net.

- Subnet Mask—This is another dotted-decimal number that masks part of the IP address so the protocol stack can determine whether certain packets are destined for the local network segment or need to be routed via the default gateway.

- Default Gateway—As its name implies, this is a gateway to other machines that are not on the local segment. Generally, this number corresponds to the IP address of a router. When packets have to go outside the local segment, they are passed on to the default gateway, which determines the next gateway for the packets to go through until the destination is reached. This is another dotted-decimal value that represents the IP address of the gateway.

- Obtain DNS Server Address Automatically—Just as with a TCP/IP address, you can receive the DNS server information automatically via DHCP. You'll see how to configure that setting in Hour 16, "DNS, WINS, and DHCP."

- Use the Following DNS Server Addresses—This button's two text boxes, Obtain DNS Server Address Automatically and Preferred DNS Server and Alternate DNS Server, are the entries for the manual setting of the addresses of the DNS server computers. Without these, the computer cannot fully communicate to all machines on the local network or Internet. We'll be detailing DNS in Hour 16.

Click Cancel to close the Internet Protocol (TCP/IP) Properties screen, Cancel to close the Local Area Connection Properties screen, and Close to close the Local Area Connection Status screen.

TCP/IP Command-Line Tools

Now that you've explored the setup of TCP/IP, you will also want to learn about the built-in debugging tools available to you, should something go wrong.

In this section, you will experiment a bit with some of the built-in command-line utilities that can help you debug failing TCP/IP installations.

When you click the Start menu, click the Run command, and type cmd into the Run dialog box, you enter a whole different world of the command-line interface. Although the graphical user interface can enable you to perform most of the day-to-day tasks of running a server, there are still some commands that can only be found in their command-line form.

Most of these commands grew up from their UNIX counterparts—so much so that while normal command-line switches for PC programs take the form of /option (for example, net /? for help on the net command), many of these ports of UNIX programs take either / or – for the option switch (such as ping -? for help). Some of them, such as tracert (see the later discussion) only take the – character for options.

Command-line utilities fall into two major categories: debugging and application.

Debugging Tools

In your travels with TCP/IP, some things are bound to go wrong. The good news is that built in to Windows 2000 are debugging tools to help you track down pesky connectivity problems. In this section, we'll review the most useful command-line and graphical tools to help you on your journey.

ipconfig

Although this command didn't originate on UNIX, it's still a very powerful information tool. ipconfig is very useful for quickly determining the TCP/IP address and other standard variables to make sure they are not out of whack.

The command line of ipconfig can simply be

```
>ipconfig
```

but that will only tell you the information you entered at the time of installation. To get a much more thorough picture of your current network configuration, type:

```
>ipconfig /all | more
```

where the | more will keep the information from scrolling off the screen if you have lots of information on multiple network adapters. We'll be discussing many of the entries exposed by ipconfig /all (see Figure 15.4) in the place where they are affected.

Windows 95 and Windows 98 have the graphical winipcfg, which we'll use a bit later. It shows the same information and has the same options as ipconfig, but it is graphical.

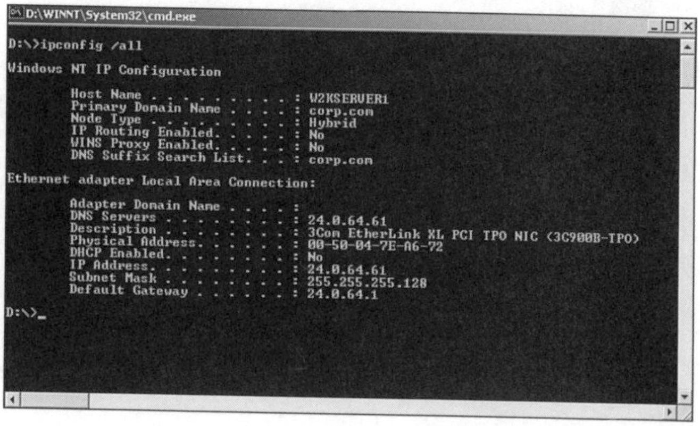

FIGURE 15.4

`ipconfig /all` *shows advanced characteristics about your IP setup.*

```
D:\WINNT\System32\cmd.exe                                          _ □ ×

D:\>ipconfig /all

Windows NT IP Configuration

        Host Name . . . . . . . . . . . : V2KSERVER1
        Primary Domain Name . . . . . : corp.com
        Node Type . . . . . . . . . . : Hybrid
        IP Routing Enabled. . . . . . : No
        WINS Proxy Enabled. . . . . . : No
        DNS Suffix Search List. . . . : corp.com

Ethernet adapter Local Area Connection:

        Adapter Domain Name . . . . . :
        DNS Servers . . . . . . . . . : 24.0.64.61
        Description . . . . . . . . . : 3Com EtherLink XL PCI TPO NIC (3C900B-TPO)
        Physical Address. . . . . . . : 00-50-04-7E-A6-72
        DHCP Enabled. . . . . . . . . : No
        IP Address. . . . . . . . . . : 24.0.64.61
        Subnet Mask . . . . . . . . . : 255.255.255.128
        Default Gateway . . . . . . . : 24.0.64.1

D:\>_
```

ping

`ping` is perhaps the simplest of all TCP/IP debugging tools, yet quite possibly is the most powerful. If a TCP/IP computer is pinged, an appropriate response is generated, acknowledging connectivity.

> Officially, *PING* stands for *Packet InterNet Groper*, but unofficially, `ping` gets its name from its similarity to the SONAR term. In order to communicate from one submarine to another, you send out a ping sound. If the submarine is actually out there, the sound will bounce back. For a movie with an example of this, be sure to see *The Hunt for Red October*.

The command line of `ping` is simple:

```
>ping ip_address
```

or

```
>ping ip_name
```

such as

```
>ping 207.55.56.4
```

```
>ping www.boutell.com
```

If connectivity is working, and the server is indeed up and running, you will receive a response like the one shown in Figure 15.5.

`ping` is very useful because it can help you determine whether you are having a connectivity problem. For instance, you open a Web browser, type `http://www.boutell.com` and receive no response. There are several items to ping if you suspect a connectivity problem.

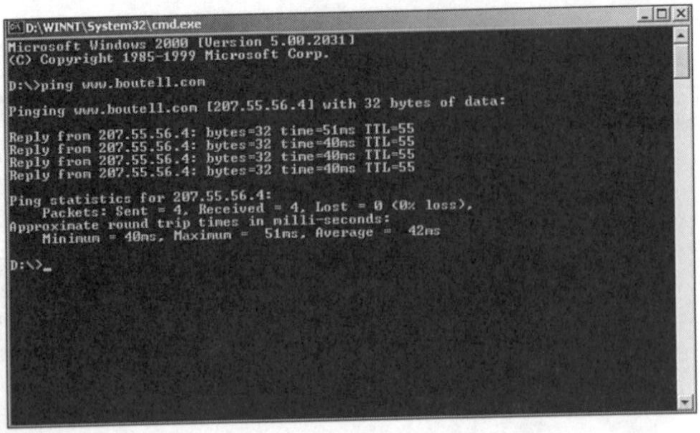

FIGURE 15.5

*You can see whether a
machine is alive or not
via the* ping *command.*

- First, try pinging the addresses of your primary and secondary DNS servers. If DNS is down, you won't be able to translate www.boutell.com to 207.55.56.4. It is probably rare that both servers (if there are two) would be offline at the same time (that's why there are two). If you get no response from either, perhaps you have a more serious configuration error. Do note, however, that it is possible for the DNS servers to be pinged, yet not respond to resolving addresses.

- See if you can ping yourself. There are two ways to do this. One way is called the *loopback address.* It's a special TCP/IP address that always means "this computer." That address is 127.0.0.1. Try pinging 127.0.0.1 at the first sign of a connectivity problem. If you get no response, it means TCP/IP itself is either not loaded properly or is perhaps damaged. Unloading, reloading, and reconfiguring the TCP/IP protocol will generally clear up this issue.

- Ping yourself by IP address. If you get a response, you're in good shape because it means that you're the only one on the network with that IP number.

- Ping your default gateway. If you get a response from the gateway, it means your packets are at least trying to make it past your local segment.

- Ping the address of the computer in question. If you're not getting a response from DNS, and don't know www.boutell.com's address, you're out of luck. If you get a response from pinging just the TCP/IP address of the remote computer, you *must* have a DNS resolution problem.

tracert

Use tracert to determine *why* connectivity is slow from a client to a server.

The command line of tracert is simple:

```
>tracert ip_address
```

or

```
>tracert ip_name
```

tracert will inform you how many router hops a packet took to reach its destination. This is useful information should you suspect that a router is down.

NetStat

Without any command-line arguments, NetStat will display the current status of all listening TCP/IP ports. A *port* is simply a hook into TCP/IP where applications may connect. When you type http://www.boutell.com, you're implying the default port of http: port 80. On servers running IIS (see Hour 24, "Internet Information Server"), you might want to use NetStat to see if your port 80 is ready to accept incoming connections. Use NetStat -a to display all the connections.

Nbtstat

This command displays statistics about your current NetBIOS statistics in conjunction with TCP/IP.

Internetworking Applications

After TCP/IP is up and running, you will usually need to communicate between connected computers. These utilities will help you get connected from one TCP/IP stack to another.

ftp

FTP stands for File Transfer Protocol. The ftp command-line tool enables you to perform file transfers with FTP servers. Although most organizations use file shares to share internal information, you'll generally find FTP servers used over the Internet.

Windows 2000 Server's IIS can be configured as an FTP server. See Hour 24 for more information.

telnet

telnet allows you to run a terminal emulation on a telnet server machine. Usually only command-line utilities with minimal screen output can be run when in telnet mode.

Windows 2000 Server has it's own version of a telnet server. To start the Windows 2000 telnet server, start the Computer Management console, drill down to Services and Applications, click services, and start the telnet server. Once started, you can manage the telnet server via the command line tool called tlntadmn.exe.

finger

`finger` responds to requests from finger daemon servers. Most UNIX machines run the finger daemon, which will serve up information about a user if requested.

The command line of `finger` is simple:

```
>finger name@host.com
```

Some servers are configured to reply with detailed information about a user. This is sometimes considered a security risk because, once again, a hacker needs only two pieces of information to break in: a valid username and a password.

In this example, the server is configured only to reply with a standard greeting of the critical users' email addresses.

Summary

TCP/IP is the default protocol of Windows 2000, but there are additional, alternate protocols available as well. Use NWLink to integrate with NetWare environments, DLC to integrate with older HP-JetDirect print servers, AppleTalk to integrate with Macintoshes, and NetBEUI to integrate with older Microsoft LANs.

Use private addressing to minimize your exposure to the Internet. Contact Arin if you need your own legitimate IP addresses.

Use the TCP/IP command-line tools and applications to help you debug your TCP/IP environment and enable connectivity.

Workshop

The workshop provides a quiz and exercises to help reinforce your learning. Even if you feel you know the material, you will still gain from working these exercises.

Quiz

1. What must be common between two computers before communication happens?
2. What are the four major protocol layers?
3. Which protocols may be used in a routed environment?
4. When would you use DLC?
5. What is the loopback address?
6. How can you determine if your TCP/IP protocol stack is alive?

7. How can you figure out the subnet shorthand?

8. Which command will easily show your IP address?

9. Which utility moves files from one machine to another?

10. Which utility enables you to test for connectivity?

11. Why would you make a custom subnet mask?

Exercises

1. Ping the loopback address 127.0.0.1. What happens?

2. Look up the 7-layer OSI model on the Internet. What are the major differences between the Microsoft view and the OSI model?

3. Talk with your ISP to learn how to register your DNS name and get IP addresses or visit the InterNIC (`http://www.internic.net`) and Arin (`http://www.arin.net`) for DNS registration and IP addresses, respectively.

HOUR 16

DNS, WINS, and DHCP

by Jeremy Moskowitz

Windows 2000 Server has some very powerful networking features and utilities. These services will allow you to connect with a variety of clients and servers in the easiest manner possible, to identify computers on the network, and to automatically assign networking addresses—thus eliminating a lot of tedious manual administration work.

In this hour, you will learn to:

- Configure DNS servers and clients
- Configure WINS servers and clients
- Configure DHCP servers and clients

DNS

Before we jump into the nitty-gritty details about the *how* of DNS, let's take a quick refresher about *what* it does and *why* it does it. DNS, quite simply, resolves easy-to-use host names to TCP/IP addresses (and back again, if desired). Host names aren't the same as NetBIOS names, as discussed in Hour 15, "Protocols and Network Fundamentals." (Refer to the section "Alternative Protocols [NetBEUI, IPX/SPX, DLC, and AppleTalk].") To resolve NetBIOS names to TCP/IP addresses on your network, you must use WINS.

As you might know, DNS stands for Domain Name Service. The word *Domain* in DNS has absolutely nothing whatsoever to do with the Windows 2000 Server domains. Rather, these domains constitute *partitions* in the namespace.

> DNS is a very commonly used acronym at Microsoft these days. The component-based architecture used for distributed applications is described as an architecture called the *Distributed Nervous System* or (also) DNS. Although the world in general uses DNS to mean internetworking, you should be aware of this secondary usage as well.

DNS has multiple levels of domains. In our examples of bigu.edu and corp.com, we can infer things about them just by their names alone. Both .edu and .com are considered *top-level domains* because working from right to left, they are the first to be read.

> Some valid top-level domains include .com, .edu, .org, .gov, and .mil, as well as country codes such as .au (Australia), .uk (United Kingdom), and .fi (Finland). You should assume that domains without country codes are registered in the United States.

Even before the top-level domains is the implied "." domain, called the *root domain*. Every top-level domain is subordinate to the root domain.

Next, reading an address such as corp.com or bigu.edu from right to left, you come across corp or bigu, which constitute part of the second-level domain.

When, back in Hour 6, "Domains and the Active Directory," corp.com and bigu.edu grew to include widget.sales.corp.com and records.registrar.bigu.edu, respectively, sales and registrar were the third-level domains, and widget and records would be considered fourth-level. Every level down you go is considered a *subdomain*. Therefore, we would say that records is a subdomain of registrar.

> When you register your company name on the Internet with the InterNIC, you need to register only the second-level domain names, such as bigu.edu. Subdomains don't need to be registered via the InterNIC because you control the DNS servers for that level (see the following discussion).

The last piece of terminology you'll need to know is FQDN or Fully Qualified Domain Name. That's just the fancy term given to a specific computer's host name, such as azdc6.registrar.bigu.edu. (including the ending dot, as it represents the root domain). In this example, the FQDN of server azdc6 in the registrar.bigu.edu domain is fully stated. When DNS resolves a specific host name to a TCP/IP address, it resolves it using the FQDN of the machine in question.

DNS Installation

In Hour 6, when you promoted your corp.com root server (W2kserver1) to a Domain Controller, you were either prompted to install DNS or you pointed your server toward an existing DNS server. But if you have another Windows 2000 Server and would like to install DNS to try some of these exercises, here is how to install DNS:

1. Select the Add/Remove Programs command from the Control Panel folder on the Settings menu of the Start menu.

2. Click on Add/Remove Programs, and then on Add/Remove Windows Components.

   The Windows Components Wizard starts.

3. Click the Next button, and then use the slider to scroll down and select Networking Services.

4. Click Details, click the Domain Name Service (DNS) check box, and then click OK.

5. Back at the Windows Components screen, click the Next button.

   You might or might not be asked to provide the Windows 2000 Server CD-ROM.

6. Once it has finished loading, click the Finish button.

   When Windows 2000 Server is finished loading DNS server, a reboot is not required.

7. Start the DNS manager by clicking Start, Programs, Administrative Tools, and then DNS.

For the following examples, assume DNS server has been loaded on the AZDC1 server (which, like W2kserver1, is a DC in the corp.com domain). Additionally, for the sake of this example, AZDC1 has been assigned both a second IP address and gateway address enabling it to see the Internet.

To test your new DNS server:

1. Right-click the server name (that is, AZDC1), and select the Properties command on the context menu.

2. Click the Monitoring tab, check the Simple Query and Recursive Query check boxes, and click Test Now.

Ideally, your server will respond as in Figure 16.2. If not, skip to the end of this section to learn how to debug your DNS server, and come back here again to test.

FIGURE **16.2**

After connecting to the Internet, try the simple and recursive queries to test your DNS.

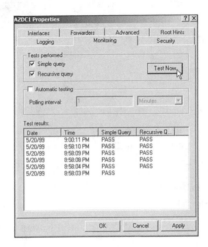

If your simple query fails, it means that the server itself cannot look up DNS entries. Make sure the server's own network card's IP settings have the DNS IP address inputted correctly. The recursive test sends a query to another DNS server, higher in the tree. If the recursive query fails, make sure your root server list is up-to-date, and you can ping some of the higher-level servers.

Don't make any other changes now; we'll be going over some options you can choose later.

Integrating with a Preexisting DNS Structure

Microsoft's DNS is fully compatible with all approved Internet standards for a DNS server. Unfortunately, not all DNS servers are fully compatible with Microsoft's DNS server. This is because some older DNS servers do not support the most up-to-date DNS services that Microsoft's DNS does.

In order for your existing structure to work with the Active Directory, you'll need to check with your DNS manufacturer to see whether your current DNS can handle incremental zone transfers. If it can, you can choose either to use or not to use Microsoft's DNS implementation at all.

If your current DNS servers are running BIND version 4.xx (very common), they will not support this feature. If you want to leverage an existing DNS implementation, be sure the BIND level is 8.1.2 or higher.

Additionally, although it is not strictly enforced, it is recommended that your existing DNS be able to perform dynamic update and secure update as well.

DNS Zones

16

Before we get headlong into configuring our DNS server, a quick lesson in terminology should occur.

A DNS zone is simply a section of the DNS space. Although it doesn't necessarily have to be this way, it's typical to have a zone for each of the larger Windows 2000 Server domains. That way the same administrator who has autonomous control in his Windows 2000 Server domain also has autonomous control for his DNS zone.

A zone database file houses the table for the names and addresses on the server where it is created. As you'll see in a minute, zones come in two flavors: forward and reverse.

Additionally, zones come in three styles:

- Standard Primary—This zone type creates a new lookup database. It is stored in a flat text file of host names and IP addresses.

- Standard Secondary—This is a read-only copy of a standard primary database. Use it to lessen the burden on heavily loaded standard primary servers. DNS uses zone transfers to send records from a primary to a secondary DNS server.

- Active Directory Integrated—Just like the Standard Primary style, except that all information is stored in the Active Directory among the Domain Controllers in the domain. This is the preferred method of creating a new zone.

Forward Lookup Queries

Now that you understand the structure of DNS, let's examine what happens when a user at widget.corp.com tries to look up a Web page at `www.boutell.com`.

First, widget.corp.com's TCP/IP stack looks to see what DNS server will be handling the request. It will be a server in the widget DNS domain. The widget DNS server takes the request and checks whether it has looked for `www.boutell.com` lately. If it has, the name was cached and the DNS server can simply return the address. The computer can quickly pull up the Web page of `www.boutell.com` from the address in cached memory.

If the DNS server does not have the address of `www.boutell.com`, it takes only a second to realize that it itself is not part of the boutell.com DNS domain, which means that some other server must have that information. The DNS server passes the request up the tree, in this case to the corp.com DNS server. Once again, if `www.boutell.com` has been cached, the address is sent back down the tree to the user's widget DNS server, and that information is passed back on to her computer.

If the corp.com DNS server does not have the address of `www.boutell.com`, it also takes only a second to realize that it itself is not part of boutell.com's DNS domain. This again means that some other server must have that information. The corp.com's DNS server passes the request up the tree, in this case to the root name server. The root server gives it the address of one of the master servers for the .com domain. The .com domain then gives an address for one of boutell.com's DNS servers, located either on the network or on the Internet.

There are only a handful of master servers for each top-level domain (.edu, .com, and so on). They are ultimately controlled by the InterNIC, and access InterNIC's proprietary domain database. These machines receive quite a pounding, daily.

boutell.com's DNS server then does a quick lookup, finds out the address of the www machine, and sends it to the corp.com DNS server. The corp.com DNS server sends it down to the widget.corp.com DNS server, which sends it on to our user's machine. The user's machine now knows the address, and it views the Web page.

This process is called a *recursive process* because each step higher in the hierarchy did the same job (that is, it checked to see whether it knew the address, and then looked up the tree to get the answer) until the root was met. As previously noted, if a server up the chain of command has already recently done a search for `www.boutell.com`, the response is sent considerably more quickly back to the querying machine. Requests are cached for one hour before they are thrown out of the cache. Although this parameter may be tuned, it is good to keep it set at a low value. If the requested computer's IP address changes while the value is in the cache, incorrect data will be returned.

Resolving Internet Requests

To get your enterprise on the Internet, you'll need to contract with an Internet Service Provider (ISP) who can physically drag the line from its office to your office. After that is done, the ISP can usually assist you in filling out the paperwork to get valid IP addresses as well as registering your domain name with the InterNIC.

You will probably also want some kind of firewall protecting your internal resources from outside attacking forces.

By default, your DNS servers are configured as DNS root servers. But this configuration doesn't help your DNS servers resolve names to addresses on the Internet. As we saw earlier, requests are passed "up" the hierarchy until a DNS server could resolve the request or until a root server was encountered. A root server is just that—the final level of a request. If your DNS server is configured as a root server, your DNS server will act as the final level of a request.

Having your DNS configured as a root server is generally fine for your intranet (internal) namespace. If, however, you want to set up DNS such that it forwards requests to the Internet, it should not be a root server, as it would theoretically be the "topmost" point in the hierarchy.

A Windows 2000 DNS server is configured as a "root" server when it contains a "." (dot) lookup zone. If you choose to delete the "." (dot) lookup zone, you are instructing the DNS server to no longer act as a root server for your DNS namespace. When you do this, you enable the forwarders tab and root hints tab, so it can look "up" the hierarchy through either of these paths. Thankfully, the root hints tab is automatically populated with the InterNIC's root servers.

> Remember that the InterNIC root servers have pointers to all the rest of the DNS servers in the world. However, those servers take quite a bit of abuse, and they're only getting slower over time. So, although you could use the root servers for all your name resolutions, it's not recommended because it will ultimately be slower.

A better option than solely relying on the InterNIC servers in the root-hints tab is to use the Forwarders tab to have your ISP's DNS servers to resolve your requests. Because ISPs are so busy handling Internet traffic all day, chances are good that the requests you want are already in their cache files. This speeds up your user's perceived connection to the Internet. Additionally, this takes the burden off the root servers, which is good for everyone. If the ISP's DNS cannot resolve your request, then, the root-hints tab kicks into gear and tries to resolve the request.

> Every once in a while, the Internic's root servers' IP addresses change. For the most up-to-date copy, you can modify by hand the `cache.dns` file that stores the entries you see on the root hints tab. The `cache.dns` file can be located by default at %systemroot%\system32\dns\cache.dns. Obtain it from `ftp://rs.internic.net/domain/named.root`.

To look up addresses on the public Internet via an ISP:

1. Start the DNS manager by clicking Start, Programs, and Administrative Tools, and then clicking DNS.

2. Right-click the machine name where the DNS server is running (in this case AZDC1), and select the Properties command.

3. Select the Forwarders tab.

4. Click Add and enter in your ISP's DNS TCP/IP number.

   In this example, BIGISP.NET's DNS server is 24.1.240.33.

FIGURE 16.3

Click the Enable Forwarder(s) check box to get DNS requests forwarded to another DNS server.

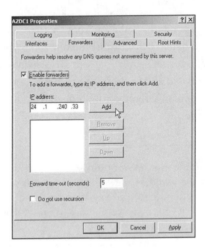

Reverse Lookup Queries

In some cases, an application must go the *other* way; that is, it must map an IP address to a name. You will find this occasionally with a program requiring extra security to be sure it's running from a certain machine.

For this feat of magic, there is in-addr.arpa—a specially named domain that maps numbers to names. Think of the in-addr.arpa as the Bizarro world in the *Superman* comic books. Everything there is backward:

- Instead of resolving names to numbers, it resolves numbers to names.
- Instead of reading the IP address from left to right, you're going to feed it back right to left.
- If your Class C address space was 192.247.233.0, your reverse lookup zone will be 233.247.192.in-addr.arpa.

You can create a reverse lookup zone now. If you promoted your server using DCPROMO in Hour 6 (see "Bringing Up Your First Windows 2000 Server Domain Controller in a Networked Environment"), you can follow along for future reference because this was already done for you. In this example, you'll be creating a reverse lookup zone on AZDC1 and using the Class C address space of 192.247.233.0.

To create a reverse lookup zone:

1. Start the DNS manager by clicking Start, Programs, Administrative Tools, and DNS.
   In this example, DNS server was just loaded on the AZDC1 server.

2. In the left pane, expand your DNS server, then highlight the Reverse Lookup Zones, click the Action menu, and click Create a New Zone.
   The Create New Zone Wizard appears.

3. Click the Next button. When the Select a Zone Type screen asks what kind of zone you want to create, select the Active Directory Integrated radio button, and click Next.

4. On the Network ID screen, because you're creating a reverse lookup zone, click the bottom radio button and type 233.247.192.in-addr.arpa, as shown in Figure 16.4.

FIGURE 16.4

Enter reverse zones by reading from right to left.

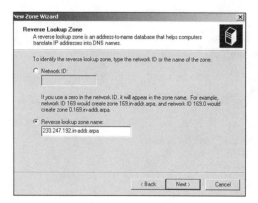

5. Click Next, and then click Finish at the review screen.

Your DNS server should look like the one shown in Figure 16.5.

Troubleshooting DNS

If you suspect a problem with your DNS setup, first try the simple and recursive tests from the previous two sections.

Next, try using the command-line utility nslookup. nslookup can take any FQDN as an argument; for example, nslookup www.boutell.com.

Figure 16.5

The reverse zone appears in the DNS manager.

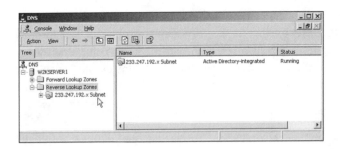

To use `nslookup` to debug your DNS server:

- Click Start, Run, and type `cmd`. Click OK. The command shell opens. Type `nslookup www.boutell.com`.
- Alternatively, you may simply type `nslookup` on a line by itself and enter the `nslookup` shell. Type `?` for a full array of debugging options.

Additionally, you can start debugging logging options by selecting the Logging tab in the DNS server's properties.

To enable debugging of your DNS server:

1. Start the DNS manager by clicking Start, Programs, and Administrative Tools, and then clicking DNS.

2. Right-click the DNS server name, and click Properties.

3. Select the Logging tab, and then click the conditions you want to test for.

After the conditions are selected, the results go to the `dns.log` file found in the %systemroot%\system32\dns\ directory.

WINS

If the preferred method of name resolution with Windows 2000 is via DNS, for clients such as Windows 95 and Windows NT Workstations, the preferred resolution is via WINS.

> As you'll remember, non–Windows 2000 and non–Windows 98 machines are called *downlevel clients*.

WINS stands for Windows Internet Name Service. It was Microsoft's answer to DNS, and it never did quite catch on. It's provided in Windows 2000 Server for backward compatibility with your downlevel clients.

Imagine the first day of school in second grade: no one knew anyone else. The only one who knew who everybody was the teacher, who had a seating chart with everyone's name.

If you heard a rumor that a boy named Joseph had a pencil, and you needed one, what could you do? You didn't know where he sat because you really didn't know who he was.

You could walk up to the teacher's desk and ask the teacher where Joseph sat. The teacher would look on her seating chart, find Joseph, and tell you, "Second row, third seat." You could then go to the second row, third seat, and politely say, "Joseph, may I have a pencil?"

In this case, the teacher resolved the name of the student from whom you wanted a resource.

The WINS server is like the teacher. Everybody has registered their (NetBIOS) name and location (TCP/IP address) with the teacher, and only the teacher knows everyone's name and where everyone sits.

What if the teacher were not there? You would have had only a couple of other options to get what you wanted. If you had a copy of the seating chart, you could have simply looked at it yourself. Alternatively, you could have just crawled on top of your desk and shouted, "I'm looking for a boy named Joseph!" That's called *broadcasting*, something that both Windows 2000 and a second-grade teacher are hoping to avoid. In the former case, it substantially increases network traffic, and in the latter case it might get you after-school detention.

Without WINS, these are your only two choices:

- Maintain your own lookup table in a flat file called lmhosts.
- Broadcast your request to the local subnet, and hope the resource you want is there. Broadcast requests can not pass across routed subnets. WINS requests, however, *can* pass across routed subnets.

This last reason is why WINS is so appealing, and so often used.

> Your routers must have port 137 (UDP Datagram) support enabled for WINS requests to be passed.

WINS works because every NetBIOS client is registered with the WINS server. When a client's TCP/IP stack is initialized, it sends the WINS server a message to this effect. Additionally, when a computer is properly shut down, another message is sent telling the WINS database to release its name for future use. That way, the WINS database is always up-to-date.

16

When a client needs to query a NetBIOS computer name and get back an IP address, the client simply queries the WINS server, a lookup is performed, and an answer is returned.

WINS has some degree of fault tolerance built into it. Two or more WINS servers may be set up to share the list of registered clients through a replication process. This way, if one WINS server goes belly up, the other will have the duplicate information.

Simply set up the WINS servers as replication partners and inform the client of the two WINS servers' IP addresses.

Do note, however, that WINS is only necessary because of the legacy NetBIOS protocol. If you are using a pure Windows 2000 environment, you should strive to ban WINS out of your environment. WINS is supplied simply as a way to maintain compatibility with your downlevel clients which still need NetBIOS support.

WINS Installation

You haven't had a need for WINS until now. You may choose to install it on the AZDC1 server, although you might want to install it on two servers for redundancy.

To install WINS:

1. Double-click on the Add/Remove Programs applet in the Control Panel folder.
2. Click Add/Remove Windows Components and when the Windows Components Wizard starts, click the Next button.
3. Use the slider to scroll down and select Networking Services, and then click Details.
4. Click the Windows Internet Name Service (WINS) check box, and then click OK.
5. Back at the Windows Components screen, click the Next button.

   You might or might not be asked to provide the Windows 2000 Server CD-ROM.
6. When the CD-ROM has finished loading, click Finish.

When AZDC1 is finished loading WINS server, a reboot is not required.

You'll need to configure a client to register with the new WINS server. You can configure it manually, as seen in Figure 16.6. In this example, John Jones's Windows 98 machine, named Buster, has been configured to register with the AZDC1 WINS server.

WINS requires little configuration. In order to monitor the activity on the WINS server, however, you'll need to start the console.

To start the WINS console, start the WINS manager by clicking Start, Programs, Administrative Tools, and then WINS. In this example, the WINS server was loaded on the AZDC1 server (which, like W2kserver1, is a DC in the corp.com domain).

FIGURE 16.6

Use the TCP/IP Properties dialog to manually enter WINS information on a client machine.

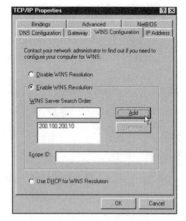

16

You'll come back to the console a bit later.

Now that you've loaded the service and opened the console, you need to configure your clients to register with the WINS server.

To test a WINS server:

When the client machine (Buster) reboots, you can click Active Registrations, go to the Action menu, and choose View Records. Click Show Records from Selected Owner, and click OK. You should have entries like Figure 16.7.

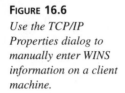

The *owner* is simply the WINS server that the client registers with.

FIGURE 16.7

A view of your clients, computers, users, and domains registered in WINS.

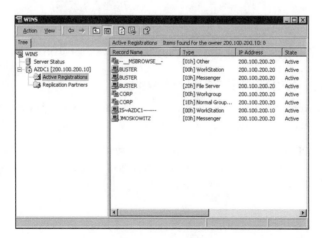

> You might have to exit and re-enter the console, and then perform the View Records command for the records to initially appear.

You might have noticed that there are several different entries for each client, domain, and server registered. Each one must be registered with WINS to be fully operational. You can choose to display which entries are displayed in the results.

To change which WINS record types are displayed in the results:

1. Start the WINS manager by clicking Start, Programs, Administrative Tools, and then WINS.

2. Expand the WINS server name, and right-click the Active Registrations folder in the left pane and select the Find by Owner command off the View menu, then select the Record Types tab.

3. Click the Record Types tab shown in Figure 16.8.

FIGURE 16.8
WINS has many different record types that need to be registered for proper functionality.

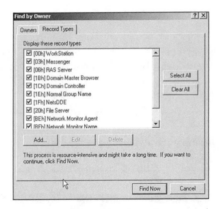

4. Check or uncheck the record types you want to display.

WINS Replication Partners

As stated before, you may set up more than one WINS server for redundancy. After it is online, each server has the ability to push or pull the database from the other partner.

By default, partners are each push/pull partners of one another. This means that on a set interval, each requests the other to send over its list of registered clients. When a push/pull has occurred, both partners know all there is to know.

> The relationship is called push/pull because WINS partnerships can be configured in either a push, pull, or push/pull configuration.

To set up redundancy, you will set up AZDC1 to replicate with W2kserver1. (W2kserver1 already has the WINS server running.)

To set up WINS replication:

1. Start the WINS manager by clicking Start, Programs, Administrative Tools, and then WINS.

2. Right-click the Replication Partners folder, and select New Replication Partner from context menu.

3. Enter the name of the partner.

In this case, enter W2kserver1. Your replication partner's folder should resemble the Figure 16.9.

FIGURE 16.9

Use the Replication Partners folder to view the servers participating in the replication.

DHCP

In the good old days, network administrators used a low-tech way of keeping track of available TCP/IP addresses: a spreadsheet. In those days, you simply wrote down the number, the computer it was assigned to, and maybe the person's name. If that computer was moved to another subnet without the administrator finding out about it, another IP address was irrevocably lost. Additionally, users themselves typed in random IP addresses if theirs were lost for whatever reason, causing conflicts throughout the enterprise.

DHCP (Dynamic Host Configuration Protocol) dishes out TCP/IP addresses to client computers that request addresses. Its main goal is to reduce the amount of administration needed to manually assign and keep track of an address assigned to a client.

DHCP servers are populated with scopes of valid IP addresses. When a client needs an address, it sends out a DHCP request broadcast (like a distress call). After the request finds its way to a DHCP server, the client is granted a little relief care package in the form of a new IP address.

Additionally, DHCP is the gelatin that jells WINS and DNS together. This is because the DHCP care package can contain not only the client's new IP address, but also the client's default gateway, preferred WINS Server address, and preferred DNS server address! This makes configuring a client a breeze.

Clients don't just get a TCP/IP address and hold it forever. Actually, they "lease" an address for a set period of time, and then "renew" their lease on that address. This renewal happens at 50% of the lease time. If the server is unavailable to handle the update (for example, if it's down), another renewal attempt is made at 87.5% of the lease time. If, at 100% of the lease time, the DHCP server is still not available to service the lease renewal, the client must forfeit the IP address.

Even though this situation sounds grim, there is a ray of hope for Windows 2000 and Windows 98 clients (but not downlevel clients such as Windows 95 or Windows NT). If a Windows 2000 client's DHCP lease expires, it is automatically assigned a private IP address in the range of 169.254.0.0–169.254.255.255 with a subnet mask of 255.255.0.0. Although this doesn't mean the client will be able to connect to resources across the router, it will be able to communicate with other systems in its subnet that have also lost their leases.

DHCP Installation

When you loaded all options in Hour 3, "Installing Windows 2000 Server," you automatically loaded the DHCP server component on W2KSERVER1. In this example, you'll manually install DHCP on the AZDC1 server.

To install DHCP:

1. Double-click Add/Remove Programs in the Control Panel folder.
2. Click Add/Remove Windows Components, and when the Windows Components Wizard starts, click the Next button.
3. Use the slider to scroll down and select Networking Services, and click Details.
4. Click the Dynamic Host Configuration Protocol Service (DHCP) check box then click the OK button.
5. Back at the Windows Components screen, click the Next button.

    You might or might not be asked to provide the Windows 2000 Server CD-ROM.
6. When the CD-ROM has finished loading, click the Finish button.

    When Windows 2000 Server is finished loading DHCP server, a reboot is not required.
7. Start the DHCP manager by clicking Start, Programs, Administrative Tools, and then DHCP.

In this example, the DHCP server has been loaded on the AZDC1 server (which, like W2kserver1, is a DC in the corp.com domain).

Configuring the Server

To run a DHCP server while participating in the Active Directory, you must first register the server. This is so unauthorized servers cannot dish out bogus IP addresses without the Administrator's knowledge.

Note that nothing prevents someone from bringing up an entire Windows 2000 Server in a separate forest, installing DHCP server, and authorizing it.

To start the DHCP console and authorize the server:

1. Start the DHCP Manager by clicking Start, Programs, Administrative Tools, and then DHCP.

   The DHCP console starts.

2. Right-click over the server name and click Authorize. This may take several minutes to finish. Hit F5 occasionally until the downward red arrow turns to an upward green arrow.

3. Click Add and type AZDC1, the name of the DHCP server, and click OK, as seen in Figure 16.10. (This has already been done for W2kserver1.)

FIGURE 16.10

Once a server is authorized to participate in Active Directory DHCP, scopes can be created.

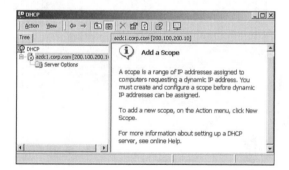

Creating a Scope

Next, you'll use the Create Scope Wizard to guide you through your scope creation. In this example, you'll be serving addresses of 200.100.200.20 to 200.100.200.30, with a subnet mask of 255.255.0.0.

You'll automatically inform your clients of the following:

- The gateway is 200.100.200.1
- The primary DNS server is 200.100.200.10 (which is server AZDZ1)

16

- The primary WINS server is 200.100.200.10 (which is server AZDC1)
- The secondary WINS server is 200.100.100.10 (which is server W2kserver1)

To create a scope:

1. Make sure DHCP manager is open. If it isn't, click Start, Programs, Administrative Tools, and then DHCP to start the DHCP console.

2. Select the server name (azdc1.corp.com), and then select the Scope command from the New submenu of the Action menu.

3. At the Create Scope Wizard splash screen, click the Next button.

4. Enter a name for the scope as well as an optional comment, and then click the Next button.

5. At the Address Range screen, enter the range of addresses as seen in Figure 16.11, and then click the Next button.

   In this case, you're entering 200.100.200.20 to 200.100.200.30. You want your subnet mask to be 255.255.0.0, which is a length of 16 of your 32 total bits (refer to Hour 15). Change the length to 16, and the subnet mask changes accordingly. Or, alternatively, just type in the subnet mask.

FIGURE 16.11

Enter the range of addresses this server can assign.

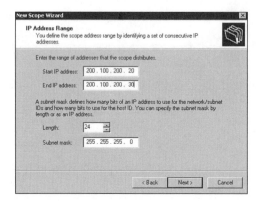

6. At the Add Exclusions screen, enter addresses that you wish to exclude from the scope, and then click the Next button.

   You would enter an exclusion if a certain computer in this range had a hard-coded TCP/IP address and could not participate in the scope (such as servers or print servers). You don't want that number being dealt to a client and inadvertently colliding with the fixed address. There are no exclusions for this example.

7. At the Lease Duration screen, enter the lease desired and click the Next button. The default is 8 days. You can have any number of days, hours, or minutes—or unlimited.

> It is highly recommended that you do *not* give a scope an unlimited lease (by selecting the Unlimited Scope radio button). Clients never release their leases after obtaining them in this mode. The leases are very difficult to manually reclaim if it becomes necessary. To reclaim the leases, you would need to modify the scope properties for a set (not unlimited lease time), and run the command `ipconfig /release` on each client.

8. The next screen asks whether you want to configure your scope options, such as default gateway, DNS server, and WINS server. Click the Yes button, and then click Next.

9. Your first scope option is the gateway. Add 200.100.200.1 and click Add. This is your only gateway, so click Next.

> As you'll remember from Hour 15, your gateway is the first address to the outside world in a switched environment.

10. Your next scope option is on the Domain Name and DNS Server screen. Again, this is the DNS domain, so you'll be entering `corp.com` in the Parent Domain text box. For your DNS server address, enter either `200.100.200.10` for AZDC1 or AZDC1 in the Server Name box and click Resolve. Click Add to add the entry and then click Next.

11. Next is your WINS server address. Enter `200.100.200.10` (AZDC1) and 200.100.100.10 (W2kserver1), in that order, for primary and secondary WINS servers. Click Next.

12. The next screen asks whether you would like to activate the scope now. Make sure Yes is selected and then the Next button.

13. At the summary screen, click the Finish button.

Your scope is ready to go. Your DHCP configuration should look like the one shown in Figure 16.12.

16

FIGURE 16.12

Your scope is now activated.

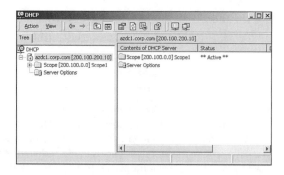

To test your new DHCP server, you'll need to configure client machines to automatically get TCP/IP addresses from the new DHCP server. The good news is that Windows 95, Windows 98, Windows NT Workstation, and Windows 2000 Professional clients are automatically configured to receive DHCP requests by default.

If, however, you have already configured your clients with static TCP/IP address, you will have to modify them to use a dynamically defined address (as in the following example).

In Figure 16.13, John Jones's Windows 98 machine, named Buster, has now been configured to automatically request a DHCP address.

FIGURE 16.13

Click Obtain Address Automatically to enable DHCP.

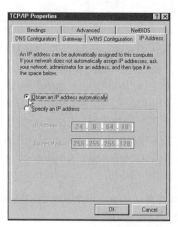

It's helpful to erase the information on the other tabs, such as Default Gateway, DNS Configuration, and WINS Configuration.

To verify the leased address on the server and client:

1. Make sure DHCP manager is open. If it isn't, click Start, Programs, Administrative Tools, and then DHCP. The DHCP console starts.

2. After the client reboots, you can expand the scope, double-click Address Leases, and see the address the client received, as seen in Figure 16.14. In this case, it received the first address in the pool (200.100.200.20).

FIGURE 16.14

Use DHCP manager to see which clients are assigned what addresses.

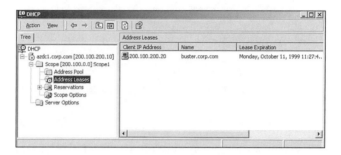

3. Additionally, you can run `ipconfig` on Windows NT or Windows 2000 clients (or `winipcfg` on Windows 95 and Windows 98 clients) to verify what has been configured.

On a Windows NT or Windows 2000 client:

- Click Start, click Run, type in `cmd`, and click OK. The command console appears.
- Type `ipconfig /all`.

On a Windows 95 or Windows 98 client:

- Click Start, click Run, type in `winipcfg`, and click OK. The command console appears. See Figure 16.15.

4. Make sure the address of the client matches what the server leased out.

You can see that all the options you specified in the scope have been drop-shipped to the client. If, for any reason, you feel a client should get a new address, you might need to renew it.

To renew an address for a Windows 95 or Windows 98 client:

1. Click Start, click Run, type in `winipcfg`, and click OK.

   The command console appears. Refer to Figure 16.15.

2. Click Release.

3. Click Renew. You should have another address.

FIGURE 16.15

Use winipcfg *on*
Windows 95 or
Windows 98 to see
what IP address is
currently in use.

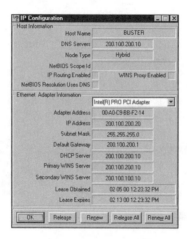

To renew an address for a Windows NT or Windows 2000 client:

1. Click Start, click Run, type in cmd, and click OK. The command console appears.

2. Type ipconfig /release.

3. Type ipconfig /renew.

You should have a new address for your client. However, that new address will often be the same number you just released, if no other client requested an address between your release and renew commands.

DHCP, DNS, and WINS Interoperability

At the beginning of this section, DHCP was called the gelatin that jelled the other services together. As we've already seen, DHCP care-packets not only contain valid IP addresses for the client, but also addresses for the WINS and DNS servers. There is one added bonus to using Windows 2000 DHCP: automatic updates to the Windows 2000 DNS servers.

As you saw, WINS automatically and dynamically keeps itself updated. After a WINS client appears on the network, it registers itself with the WINS server. Then all other servers and clients can simply ask the WINS server for the latest information to communicate with that computer.

DNS server does not work the same way that WINS does. There is a 1-to-1 fixed relationship between host name and address.

There is good news. When you use Microsoft Windows 2000 Server DHCP server and DNS server with Windows 2000 clients, you get the added benefit of DHCP interacting with the DNS server to inform it when clients change their IP addresses. That means you will always have up-to-date information in your DNS server. This is called *dynamic DNS*, or DDNS.

There is also some bad news. By default this behavior only works with Windows 2000 clients — not downlevel clients. You might expect to turn this behavior on with the DNS manager, but you'd be barking up the wrong tree. This setting is enabled with the DHCP manager.

16

To enable dynamic DNS for downlevel clients:

1. Start the DHCP manager by clicking Start, Programs, Administrative Tools, and then DHCP.

2. Right-click over the authorized DHCP server and select Properties from the context menu.

3. On the DNS tab, click the Enable DNS updates for clients that do not support dynamic update.

As stated, nothing needs to be changed in order for Windows 2000 clients to automatically use dynamic update. If you need to turn it off, however, you may.

To disable dynamic DNS (DDNS) updates:

1. Start the DNS manager by clicking Start, Programs, Administrative Tools, and then DNS.

   In this example, the DNS server was loaded on the AZDC1 server (which, like W2kserver1, is a DC in the corp.com domain).

2. Expand the forward or reverse zone you wish to manage, then right-click over it, and click Properties.

3. On the General tab in the corp.com Properties dialog box shown in Figure 16.16, click the Dynamic Update pull-down box.

4. Selecting No turns off the dynamic DNS feature. Yes is the default, which will send DHCP records to the DNS server. Only Secure Updates is a feature that can use a secure method of verifying the authenticity of the sent records.

FIGURE **16.16**

*Use the pull-down box
to choose how dynamic
updates are handled.*

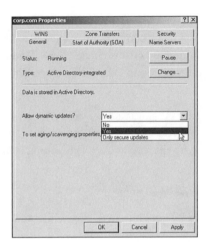

Summary

Windows 2000 Server has some powerful networking components to help you manage
your clients. Use the DNS manager to create forward and reverse lookup zones to assist
in translating host names to TCP/IP addresses (or vice versa). You can use the WINS
manager to create a database of all NetBIOS names on your network. WINS uses a system of push/pull replication partners for fault tolerance between multiple WINS server.
Use DHCP to automatically assign TCP/IP addresses, and to automatically configure
clients with the list of DNS and WINS server addresses. These utilities will help clients
find other computers on the network and lower the amount of manual configuration that
an administrator must do.

Workshop

The workshop provides a quiz and exercises to help reinforce your learning. Even if you
feel you know the material, you will still gain from working these exercises.

Quiz

1. In DNS, what are some top-level DNS domains?

2. What is the root domain?

3. What version of BIND must be used to integrate with Microsoft DNS server?

4. What does a forward lookup query do?

5. What does a reverse lookup query do?

6. What does WINS resolve?

7. How can you make WINS fault-tolerant?

8. What networking component can you use to assign TCP/IP addresses, DNS server addresses, and WINS addresses?

9. Why would you want to exclude IP addresses in a DHCP scope?

10. What feature allows automatic updates of DHCP information into the DNS database?

Exercises

16

1. Verify your WINS replication is working by ascertaining that replicated entries are showing up on the partner.

2. Use Windows 95's `winipcfg` to see what address your client has received.

3. Turn on DNS logging and explore the log.

HOUR 17

Network and Dial-Up Connectivity

by Jeff Bankston

The evolutionary growth of Microsoft Windows NT Server has brought forth quite a few changes to its functionality. Aside from native network connections and Remote Access Server dial-up connectivity, NT Server was previously enhanced with tools such as Routing and Remote Access Server (RRAS), which is now integrated into the Windows 2000 platform. Previously, RRAS was an add-on product to NT Server v4 systems.

RRAS allows you to use the server as a software-based routing platform by using standard network adapters as the routing interface. By using Routing Information Protocol versions 1 and 2 along with the Bay Networks implementation of Open Shortest Path First (OSPF) protocol, you can turn your Windows 2000 server into an efficient router for small networks. This can be done without the cost of more expensive hardware routers when there isn't a large volume of routing needs.

Dial-up connectivity has traditionally been a strong point for NT Server v4, and it remains so with Windows 2000. More modems are recognized, more connection possibilities are used, and Wide Area Networking (WAN) cards are supported, such as frame relay and ISDN devices directly plugged into the server.

In this hour, you will learn how to

- Create dial-up connections
- Establish RAS and RRAS connections
- Create and manage virtual private networks
- Recognize some of the features of Windows telephony

Dial-up Connections

The old way to create dial-up connections in Windows NT Server v4 was to go to the Dial-up Networking group and answer a few questions. Microsoft Windows 2000 makes things a bit easier with the use of wizards and cascading information screens. If you didn't install a modem first, Microsoft Windows 2000 will take care of that for you with more wizards. It is now much easier than before to add, remove, or edit existing modems or connections.

Different Connectivity Devices

Let's talk about the forms of connections available in Microsoft Windows 2000. There are at present five forms of connections available with Microsoft Windows 2000. Some of these were around with Windows NT Server 4, but in Windows 2000 they are enhanced tools:

1. Dial to a private network, such as to a business partner or some other server that is not publicly accessible over the Internet. This is usually done when the calling network does not have Internet access, but some other network provides this access. Also, the two networks could be entirely private, yet carry on some form of commerce between them.

2. Dial to the public Internet, such as with a Point-to-Point Protocol (PPP) connection—much as you do to surf the Web. This could be done when a proxy server is using fake TCP/IP addresses internally, but the clients still need to get to the public Internet.

3. Create a Virtual Private Network (VPN) connection. VPNs are used to "tunnel" through the Internet by encapsulating the data stream with some form of protection, which prevents prying eyes from seeing the data. VPNs, if properly used, are nearly as secure as option 1.

4. Accept incoming calls. This is the same as the old RAS tools from Windows NT Server v4 of the past. It is enhanced with clearer screens and choices, as well as more modem selections. The auto-detect function within Microsoft Windows 2000 is significantly improved from Windows NT Server v4 RAS.

5. Direct to another computer. This form of connection worked in Windows NT Server v4, but was crude and obnoxious to set up and configure. Microsoft Windows 2000 makes it so much easier to use that some might even consider it useful! You can use serial ports, parallel ports, or the newer (but slower) infrared port found on most new motherboards.

How to Make and Configure a Dial-up Connection

To create a new dial-up connection, click on START, SETTINGS, Network and Dial-up Connectons, which will bring you to the main dialog box for this connection. You'll be presented with a clean screen showing the Make New Connection icon, unless you've already added more network adapters to the server. Let's go through this process presuming you've already installed the modem. If you've not previously installed a modem, the modem wizard will take you through this process.

You should double-click this icon to begin the connection process. You'll be presented with a welcome screen in which you'll just click NEXT to get through it. You'll now reach the main screen where you'll decide on the type of connection, such as the one shown in Figure 17.1. For this example, we've chosen the Accept Incoming Connections option; the option we would use to support incoming connections from our clients using a modem.

FIGURE 17.1

Choose the type of connection you would like to create.

In choosing the incoming connection type, Microsoft Windows 2000 now has you use the RRAS configuration to define and configure modem connections. This is because any incoming modem connection requires routing of the packets. When used in Windows NT Server v4, IP Forwarding had to be enabled to allow for routing of packets to all parts of the network. Otherwise, the caller could see or use resources only on the local machine that received the call. If you forgot how to do this, Microsoft Windows 2000 now reminds you (or rather forces you) to use RRAS to complete this connection type, as shown in Figure 17.2.

FIGURE 17.2

RRAS won't let you make a mistake on this connection type.

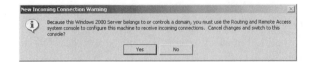

In order to do this, you'll need to answer YES to the question and switch to the RRAS configuration program, which the server will do for you. Once there, highlight the current RRAS server. Click on the ACTION tab, then on CONFIGURE AND ENABLE ROUTING AND REMOTE ACCESS. Add the appropriate protocols and interfaces needed to suit the need.

After this is done, you'll come to a screen option to choose the type of routing that you want RRAS to perform (see Figure 17.3). Be careful here—enable the routing you need and nothing else. If you don't have a WAN card, don't enable WAN and LAN routing. By enabling remote access, you're actually enabling routing between the modem and the network adapter installed within the server.

FIGURE 17.3

Enabling routing between services cements the communications paths together.

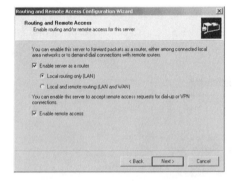

You then choose to configure the devices individually so that you can see the different devices Microsoft Windows 2000 knows it installed. These devices can be routed between each other using different protocols. Click the device that you want to configure, and then click the Next button. Figure 17.4 shows the devices that our server has installed at the moment.

Figure 17.5 shows all the possible forms of authentication and encryption for RRAS. Note that you can select levels of security specific to your needs. Advanced encryption is available with the Layer 2 Tunneling Protocol (L2TP) that offers extended protection for data streams, and that is above and beyond the Point-to-Point Tunneling Protocol (PPTP) used between PPTP devices. Most commonly, you'll find PPTP running between Microsoft devices such as a pair of Microsoft Windows 2000 servers.

Finishing up the RRAS configuration is little more than making the next selections for the protocol to use, deciding whether you want to use static IP addressing or Dynamic Host Configuration Protocol (DHCP) for the clients, and then completing the binding for the service.

After it is completed, RRAS is then ready to serve your clients with dial-up services, either inbound or outbound.

FIGURE 17.4

These are the devices installed in this server, but we could add a T-1 circuit card if we chose to do so.

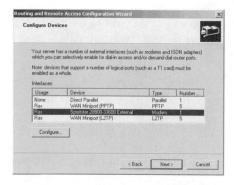

FIGURE 17.5

Select the desired security method from this screen.

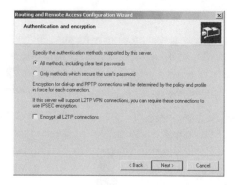

Remote Access Services

Let's take a walk through the routing services that are now integrated with Microsoft Windows 2000. These services are a combined effort of past Windows NT Server v4 projects, new development, and a merger of both. In doing so, Microsoft Windows 2000 tightens the noose on other network operating systems such as Linux in terms of client/server operations.

However, this merger of server functions benefits the network in several respects. One benefit is the smoother operation of these specialized tasks while maintaining the same simple design that was used to gain interest in the products in the first place. Think of it this way—Microsoft used all of those previously separate functions as test beds and extensions of Windows NT Server v4, but now has melded the original products with bug fixes and enhancements to form this cohesive product.

Before pressing onward with the rest of the RRAS system, a fundamental understanding of routing is required.

Understanding Routing

Routing is the process of making intelligent decisions of where to forward packets based upon the address of the source and destination packets. The most common protocol used in networks is the TCP/IP protocol, so that will be used here. The other protocol in network routing is Novell NetWare's IPX/SPX, but it will not be discussed here because TCP/IP is the de facto standard.

As you learned in Hour 15, "Protocols and Network Fundamentals," TCP/IP itself consists of an address made up of four octets, or sections. The address 192.168.0.1 is an example of an address. There are multiple levels of classes of addresses, but the ones most often used are

- Class A—Enterprise-scale operations into the tens of thousands of devices.
- Class B—Medium-size business operations between 254 and 65,536 devices.
- Class C—Smallest whole subnet, supporting 254 or fewer devices.

Routing is based upon addresses, as was previously mentioned, and the concept of a subnet. Think of a subnet as a *sub*ordinate *net*work, or a smaller network. A cool example is city streets: Cities typically have dozens, if not hundreds, of streets and intersections. Each street has people and business using the same street name, just different numbers of that street.

TCP/IP addressing is based upon two parts: the network address and the host address. Another important part of this equation is called the *subnet mask*. The subnet mask defines which part of the IP address is to be considered the network address, and which is the host address. Typical subnet masks are 255.255.255.0, which means that the TCP/IP address of 192.168.0.1 is a Class C address. A mask of 255.255.0.0 is a Class B address, whereas 255.0.0.0 is a Class A address.

This means that a Class A network supports fewer subnets, but more hosts on each subnet. A Class C supports more subnets, but fewer hosts on each subnet. Class B falls between these two. How is this possible? Using the Class C address of 192.168.0.1 with the mask of 255.255.255.0 means that this is one subnet of 254 maximum devices. The zero in the mask is ANDed with the .1 in the address to determine how many hosts are available on the network.

However, if the address 192.168.0.1 used a mask of 255.255.0.0, this Class B network could also have neighbors of 192.168.1.1, 192.168.2.1, and 192.168.3.1 ... Do you see the pattern? The second octet from the right denotes the network's possible hosts with the mask used (255.255.0.0); so by using the Class B designator, 254 networks are possible, each with 65,536 hosts.

We're not trying to make a routing expert of you, but to let you know that the use of RRAS requires that you know something of the IP structure and how to use it effectively. Therefore, for the purpose of this discussion, we'll presume that all Class C networks are being used.

If you need to learn more about the IP structure, there's a ton of material on the Web about it. One such link was found at www.3com.com/nsc/501302.html if you're interested in pursuing the discussion to deeper levels.

Before pressing on, consider the network in Figure 17.6.

FIGURE 17.6

This is a typical inter-network using routers with all Class C subnets.

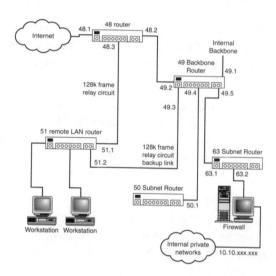

Now, when you drive this street (a subnet) and come to an intersection (the router), which way do you go? The policeman (routing tables) at the intersection is the traffic cop who makes the decision. You wanted to go to the right? Sure, the traffic cop sees your turn signal on, makes the decision for you, and tells you to go that way.

The routing of TCP/IP packets occurs in much that same way. Let's say that this one intersection has four streets that come together. So there are four subnets to this router, with each street's junction with the router itself being the port interface. So, there are four streets—four ports on the router. Keep Figure 17.6 in mind when reading this, and pay particular attention to the 49 subnet router with its five ports.

How does the router know what is routed out of which port? Keeping in mind the 49 subnet router, let's say that a user on the 63 subnet needs to get to the public Internet. The request goes from the client to the 63 subnet router's .2 interface, through the router, out of the .1 interface, and enters the .5 interface of the 49 subnet router. The 63 subnet router then adds this connection information into its own routing tables so that it knows how to move data to the 49 subnet when future requests comes up.

Next, the 49 subnet router looks at the packet and determines that it must find a way for the data to make it to the Internet. After a series of requests and searches, the 49 router determines that it can go out of its .2 interface and go into the .2 interface of the 48 subnet router.

In being successful, the 49 router adds this connection information to its own routing tables just as the 63 router did earlier.

Lastly, the 48 router examines the packet just received. Because this router already knows how to get to the Internet by way of its .1 interface, the data is then sent out to the Internet via the .1 interface of the 48 router.

When the routing process completes, the 48, 49, and 63 routers now have internal routing tables created, so they know for the future how to make these routing decisions faster. Those routes can be distributed between other routers, if necessary, so that they, too, know where and how to move data around the network.

The mechanism just described is the creation of a path from one point within the internal network out to the Internet. This path is, therefore, the shortest path possible for this user on the network. In routing terminology, this is called the Open Shortest Path First protocol method (OSPF). The RRAS function uses OSPF and Routing Information Protocol v1/2 (RIP) as the two methods for performing this learning of routes between networks.

OSPF is used primarily where there are discrete areas of routers, such as businesses, overlapping networks, and redundant networks, so that the quickest route can be learned and routing loops can be prevented. RIP is noisy as the devil because it sends out updates every 30 seconds to other routers. Neither protocol is used for small networks because this overhead is unnecessary.

But, if only one or two routers are involved, static routes are sometimes used to even further expedite movement of data. Because the 50 subnet connects to the 49 router, the 50 router could be told that it connects to the .4 interface on the 49 router via its own .1 interface. A command such as

```
Iproute 192.55.49.0 255.255.255.0 192.55.50.1 permanent
```

issued at the 50 subnet router is the same as saying verbally, "For any user on the 50 subnet needing to get to anywhere else, use the 50.1 interface, which is directly connected to the 49 router," such that you don't have to specify the fact that it would use the 49.4 interface. This route is, therefore, static in nature, meaning that it will never change even if the router is powered off. Should that ever occur, the routing tables are dumped and have to be rebuilt again. That would place a lot of stress on the router because the router has to rebuild the routing table as well as process data itself during the routing function.

This is the essence of routing, whether it be server-based routing or hardware-based traditional routing. If server routing is used, the server absolutely must be a machine of high quality, stable in operations, and capable of sustaining heavy loads should it be used as a router. If Microsoft Windows 2000 were to hang up, the router is detrimentally affected as will be the users on each connected subnet.

However, using the proper server, someone who knows Microsoft Windows 2000 can have quite an effective router without knowing all those arcane routing commands or becoming a routing expert. In the next sections, various scenarios will be examined to show how this routing technology within RRAS can be put to efficient use.

Different Routing Scenarios

In a none-too-frequent situation, a perfect deployment of RRAS is in small businesses. As a past consultant specializing in small business operations, I've seen that most of these networks start out at fewer than 10 users. Growth normally sneaks up on them to the point that the network reaches saturation, and a death knell is sounded. See Figure 17.7 for the typical small network.

FIGURE 17.7

A typical small network, small and large businesses alike.

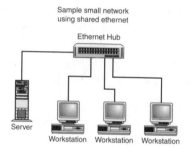

Sample small network using shared ethernet

Ethernet Hub

Server

Workstation   Workstation   Workstation

This network uses shared Ethernet technology, meaning that all computers vie for the 10Mbps bandwidth of the hub. Some shared hubs exist that are 100Mbps Fast Ethernet, but the same principle exists in that everyone shares the same communications path.

To break this up, routers create what is called a *collision domain*. This is nothing more than separate communications paths that separate the computers and data. Think about the traffic lanes on a highway—each lane is where vehicles travel, and each lane can support a limited number of vehicles. To increase the volume capacity of the highway, lanes are added. This is the same principle with collision domains.

Refer to Figure 17.8 below to see how a router creates new collision domains, called *segments*, where data can flow in different lanes of traffic.

Note from the figure that there are five segments, but actually only four exist where the users or servers are connected. The fifth segment is the Internet connection from the back of the router out to the wide area network circuit. The four segments can be any speed that the router supports, including 155Mbps Asynchronous Transfer Mode running on fiber optics cables. In fact, many servers use fiber optics cards to get this scale of performance.

17

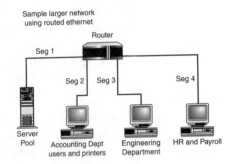

FIGURE 17.8

Routers create new collision domains by the use of segmentation.

However, using Microsoft Windows 2000 RRAS as a router means that you need to use network adapters compatible with your hubs, switches, and/or routers in terms of the speed and type of connection. In some testing we did on the test network, Microsoft Windows 2000 worked really well using 3Com network adapters for 10Mbps Ethernet, but no drivers existed for our 3Com Fast Ethernet 100Mbps adapters. Just like any major operating system upgrade, Microsoft Windows 2000 will limit what you can use for the time being until new drivers are released.

We were not able to immediately put RRAS through its paces in a full-fledged product review, but it should be able to handle 25 concurrent users on four segments routed via one server. A caution still is warranted: No matter what else the server is planned for, we recommend that this RRAS machine perform only this RRAS function, and no other functions such as printing. It is acceptable to run functions such as DNS or DHCP on this server as well—those functions are expected.

Internet Connectivity

Yet another good use for RRAS is to connect your network to the Internet. You can install one network adapter within the server, and then install a T-1 or frame relay circuit card in this server to promote routing between the local network and the Internet, as shown in Figure 17.9.

FIGURE 17.9

Turning your Microsoft Windows 2000 server into a router for the Web.

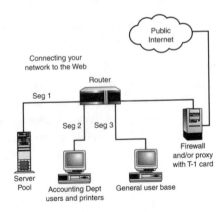

This situation reveals that you could be using two Microsoft Windows 2000 servers, one as an RRAS router for the main network, and a second one for the Internet access point. Not a bad idea if you have servers available, or no one who understands how to maintain traditional hardware routers.

Creating and Managing Virtual Private Networks Using Secure Tunneling (PPTP)

Nearly every major corporation uses the public Internet in some shape, form, or fashion to communicate business to and from clients, or other departments of their business. In doing so, they open themselves to a host of security and cost issues that are sure to make a Chief Financial Officer weak in the knees. Among the solutions presented in the past were several encryption mechanisms. Among those are some of the more common ones used by Microsoft Windows 2000 as a delivery mechanism for secured data.

Please note that this section does not attempt to dissect the level of security, nor certify any of the Microsoft Windows 2000 options as neither valid nor truly secure.

These options for communications are presented to show the evolutionary process that Microsoft Windows 2000 has gone through in order to bring new functionality to networks all around the world. It is up to each owner of Microsoft Windows 2000 to make that determination of security. So, here are the options that we'll review:

- Overview of Virtual Private Networking (VPN)
- Point-to-Point Tunneling Protocol (PPTP)
- Layer 2 Tunneling Protocol (L2TP)
- Internet Security Protocol (IP-Sec)
- Methods of encryption

Let's take each in order and see what they have to offer in remote access to and from different networks.

Virtual Private Networking, VPN for short, is a method used to connect two networks or devices using a commonly available medium. This medium is more likely than not in reference to the public Internet. A VPN uses the Internet to create a virtual tunnel, or connection, between two devices geographically separated so that they operate just as if they were on the same physical network. The only obvious difference in using a VPN is the speed at which the flow of information actually occurs.

Figure 17.10 shows you a simple VPN connecting a main office to a branch office. Because the branch office doesn't have the capability of a full dedicated leased line Internet connection, dial-up technology, such as v.90 modems or ISDN, must be deployed. Long distance charges would be a terrible blow to the company's bottom line, so the branch office will connect to a local Internet point of presence (often called a POP) and create a VPN back to the main office.

FIGURE 17.10

The basics of a VPN.

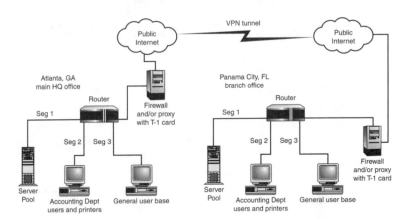

To do this, let's examine the next technology called PPTP, which Microsoft has been using for several years. First used in early editions of Windows NT Server v4, PPTP works on the basics of the Point-to-Point Protocol, or PPP for short. Let's take a few minutes to review the basics of PPP before pressing onward to deeper discussions of PPTP.

PPP was first developed some seven years ago in response to the weaknesses of the Serial Line Interface Protocol (SLIP), which has its roots in early UNIX RAS deployments. SLIP was a good start, but it lacked some basic functions, such as enhanced error detection and correction for the data stream, and other functions such as encryption.

PPP works to create a connection using four basic phases of operation:

1. Using Link Control Protocol (LCP), the physical connection is created between two devices. Speed negotiations, error controls, and similar characteristics of the actual link are negotiated. Also, the two devices decide whether any form of encryption is implemented during the fourth phase of this process.

2. Two basic forms of authentication can take place in phase two: Password Authentication Protocol (PAP) and Challenge Handshake Authentication Protocol (CHAP). These two forms have been established forms of authentication for quite sometime now. A third more stringent form is called Microsoft CHAP, or MS-CHAP, and it works exclusively with Microsoft client and server products because the Microsoft Point-to-Point Encryption mechanism is used. After the client and the server agree on the method of authentication, the session proceeds to phase three.

3. In this phase, the need for callback processing is determined. This means that phases one and two informed the server that a caller has requested to be called back at a specific telephone number as an additional form of authentication and protection. If callback is requested, the session terminates and the RAS calls the client to complete the connection.

4. This phase of the process actually assigns the IP address to the caller, establishes any requested forms of compression and encryption of the data, and then opens the communications channel between the two devices.

At the completion of phase four, the session is active and data begins passing between the two devices. This session continues until the server terminates the session, the caller requests termination, or a line error kills it completely when the Link Control Protocol determines that the link is unreliable.

With the session running, encryption ensures the data is relatively safe for transmission. In Microsoft Windows 2000 implementations, PPTP and L2TP are the two main choices, with IPSec following up closely.

PPTP has been around with Microsoft since the original release of Windows NT Server v4. It performs VPN actions using a method developed by Microsoft using a proprietary set of actions to encrypt data, and then encapsulate it within a TCP/IP header. Then the encrypted and encapsulated data is transmitted across an IP-only network, such as across the public Internet.

L2TP takes this a bit further by performing similar actions to protect the data, but it extends the process to include IPX and NetBEUI traffic for transmission over frame relay, point-to-point, or ATM circuits. This works great given the fact that more protocols are supported than PPTP, and that support extends across more types of network topologies. Whereas PPTP is an IP-only system, L2TP requires only that the connection be a form of point-to-point system, typically using the User Datagram Protocol (UDP) method of transmission. Also, L2TP supports multiple tunnels between endpoints, whereas PPTP is a single-tunnel system.

IPSec takes the process of PPTP and makes it more secure, or rather, more common to industry standard protocols. IPSec, which has been around for quite some time, has garnered an increasing support base with other industry heavyweights such as Cisco Systems and security companies. It has advanced security support using various key encryption mechanisms, including private and public keys using the MD4 hash form.

By using one of these forms, tunneling is established in a somewhat similar process to how PPP works. Tunneling can occur only when each endpoint in the tunnel agrees upon the type of connection, encryption, and so forth. This action is controlled under the name *Layer 2 Tunneling*, which controls the tunnel itself.

17

Layer 3 Tunneling presumes that all the previously mentioned controls are already in effect, have taken place, or are performed unrelated to the transmission of secured data. Regardless of the layer action, the control sessions occur in a PPP-like manner to establish the tunnel. Additionally, cryptographic certificates are used to ensure that the desired ends of the tunnel are actually reached.

Using Windows 2000 Telephony Services

In creating the many options for secure communications, Microsoft had a very interesting opportunity in mind: IP telephony. By using standard telephone lines, IP telephony, such as video conferencing, whiteboarding, and electronic meetings of all shapes and forms, become possible. These functions can use broadband, satellites, plain telephone lines, ADSL, ISDN, and any other form of communications that is capable of carrying IP-based traffic.

By leveraging the Component Object Model present in previous versions of TAPI, the third generation of the Telephony API has the advantage of being ready for the future via programmatic tools such as Visual Basic and C/C++. Active Directory already plays an important role in Microsoft Windows 2000, but even more so makes IP telephony a reality with its advanced directory schema.

There's definitely much work to be done to get ready for IP telephony, but Microsoft Windows 2000 is well on the way to accomplishing this task.

There are four major components to TAPI 3.0:

1. TAPI 3.0 COM API
2. TAPI Server
3. Telephony service providers
4. Media stream providers

It is interesting to note that the new TAPI 3.0 standard is now presented as COM objects within Microsoft Windows 2000. This offers the advantage of easier extensibility than in previous TAPI versions, and with a wider range of supported delivery mechanisms. TAPI provides the complete end-to-end solution for existing modems, H.323 video standards, media streaming between conferencing devices, and much more.

To accomplish this task, Microsoft Windows 2000 uses five objects in the TAPI 3.0 API:

1. The Telephony API
2. Address of the devices
3. Terminal services
4. Units at each end of the call
5. The CallHub used to connect the two

The TAPI object is the application's entry point to TAPI 3.0. This object represents all telephony resources to which the local computer has access, allowing an application to enumerate all local and remote addresses.

An *Address* object represents the origination or destination point for a call. Address capabilities, such as media and terminal support, can be retrieved from this object. An application can wait for a call on an Address object or can create an outgoing Call object from an Address object.

A *Terminal* object represents the sink, or renderer, at the termination or origination point of a connection. The Terminal object can map to hardware used for human interaction, such as a telephone or microphone, but it can also be a file or any other device capable of receiving input or creating output.

The *Call* object represents an address's connection between the local address and one or more other addresses. (This connection can be made directly or through a CallHub.) The Call object can be imagined as a first-party view of a telephone call. All call control is done through the Call object. There is a Call object for each member of a CallHub.

The *CallHub* object represents a set of related calls. A CallHub object cannot be created directly by an application; it is created indirectly when an incoming call is received through TAPI 3.0. By using a CallHub object, a user can enumerate the other participants in a call or conference, and possibly (because of the location-independent nature of COM) perform call control on the remote Call objects associated with those users, subject to sufficient permissions.

TAPI represents the next major evolution in this process, and Microsoft Windows 2000 elevates it to a new level. The API itself requires a moderate level of development and the experience to fully deploy the solutions. In developing these solutions, a certain level of Quality of Service is possible by offering different levels of communications across different channels.

This evolution is even further extended with streaming video media and multicast call conferencing. This allows a wider set of options for users to get together effectively using standard POTS lines or the dedicated access of a network. We did not yet have enough of a system deployed here to test Microsoft Windows 2000's TAPI support over our frame relay network, but we look forward to testing it soon. Our initial findings indicate that calls over the Internet using NetMeeting run quite well.

Summary

Microsoft Windows 2000 brings forth many new features with exciting potential. Getting together with people has always been a problem, especially on short notice, but TAPI and RRAS help bring together important aspects of a network. We can even envision a time when video conferencing to the desktop will be as easy as printing a document, and doing so by using cheap network connectivity or phone lines.

17

We've found that the improvements from previous product versions of Routing and Remote Access Server are significant enough to warrant a revisit of the operating system. Sure, Microsoft Windows 2000 RRAS can't hold a candle to hardware-based routing in the middle- to upper-tier products, but it does a superb job with smaller networks with a respectable server in use.

Even though this was Microsoft Windows 2000 Beta 3, the products were amazingly solid performers. We did notice that the server requirements are much higher than Windows NT Server v4 ever was, or was ever intended to be. If you do use Microsoft Windows 2000 as an RRAS machine, just make sure it has plenty of horsepower. We recommend a Pentium-II 400MHz and 192MB of memory to start.

Workshop

The workshop provides a quiz and exercises to help reinforce your learning. Even if you feel you know the material, you will still gain from working these exercises.

Quiz

1. What is Dial-up Networking?
2. What are some reasons I would want to use DUN?
3. When DUN is used to connect different office networks, can I make the communications path a secure link?
4. Are these means of security absolute, or are there other security issues to be aware of?
5. What is Routing and Remote Access Server?
6. Can I use RRAS as an enterprise router?
7. Can I use multiple Microsoft Windows 2000 Servers as additional routers?
8. How can I use Dial-up Networking and RRAS in combination to join disparate networks?
9. What is Microsoft Windows 2000 telephony?
10. Do I need specialized equipment or devices to use TAPI?

Exercises

1. Create your first RRAS machine and test it both for dial-in and for dial-in and dial-out.
2. Set up a VPN connection.

HOUR 18

Windows Terminal Services

by Barrie Sosinsky

Windows Terminal Services (WTS) takes the notion of the personal computer and client/server network computing and turns it on its head. With WTS installed and active, Windows 2000 Server can service Windows-based terminals (WBT) and Windows clients, performing the bulk of the processing for applications on the server. Using a wire protocol to transmit display data from the server to the client, it appears to the client as if they were working on a fully functional personal computer.

The benefits WTS offers to the enterprise are numerous: less administration overhead due to a centralized computing model, better security, the ability to lower total costs of ownership, the use of outdated or lower cost computers or workstations as clients, and the ability to create geographically dispersed network configurations. Windows Terminal Services and the related and interlocking product from Citrix called MetaFrame offer real value, and give substance to the thin client/server computing model.

The following topics are covered:

- What terminal services are, and how they operate
- How to install and configure Windows Terminal Services on a Windows 2000 Server
- How to install clients, and how to connect to the service
- How to create profiles and manage them
- How to install software and manage application sessions
- Understanding factors that influence WTS performance
- What licensing scheme is used by Microsoft for WTS
- The features and benefits offered by Citrix MetaFrame

What Is Windows Terminal Services?

Windows Terminal Services, or WTS, is an add-in component of Windows 2000 Server. WTS logs clients in to the server and runs their desktops and applications on the server each in their own session. What's displayed on the client screen looks like a standard desktop or the application that they would normally run on a personal computer, but the application processing is taking place on the server. The graphical display on the remote client is transmitted over the wire to the client, and any subsequent changes to the display are updated as required. As the client uses the keyboard and mouse to interact with his computer, only those keystrokes and mouse movements are sent back over the wire to the server to command the session in progress. Depending on the power of the server and on the processing load placed on it, running a session on a Windows terminal feels as if the application is local and as if the user is working on a PC. The response is typically that good for all applications other than ones requiring large amounts of graphics transfer (video, images, and so forth).

In many ways, WTS is a Windows version of the X Window standard created at MIT for running graphical user interface sessions on clients using the UNIX operating system. In X Window, the terms *client* and *server* are reversed from the way Microsoft uses the terms, but the concept of processing on the server and transmission of graphics display data are the same.

A Windows 2000 Server with WTS installed and running manages all aspects of client's sessions. When a user logs on to WTS, she is authenticated and her session begins. WTS controls her access to both network resources and applications. Each user's profile is stored on the WTS server, and an administrator can control various aspects of a user's environment.

For example, you can set a user's home directory. WTS manages one or more simultaneous sessions originating from connected clients. Each session runs in protected memory separate from other users' sessions, but with sharing of application code used by two or more sessions concurrently.

Windows 2000 Server supports—with minor modification and setup—most programs that run on the Win16 or Win32 platform. This includes various versions of Microsoft Office, custom databases, accounting programs, and thousands of other applications. Not only can clients run these applications on the server, but also sessions can be shadowed (followed on another person's screen) so that a teacher or administrator can provide support or instruction directly on the client's screen.

Right Sizing Your Server

Typically, WTS is installed on a member server (see Hour 8, "Server Types, Local Users, and Groups"), and not on a domain controller. This relieves the server of the additional activities that authentication requires. In a production environment, WTS servers are often the most powerful servers that a company can afford. The more powerful the servers used, the greater the number of sessions that the server can support. More sessions means more connected clients, requiring fewer servers and fewer administrators to support them. The real savings measured in Total Cost of Ownership (TCO) models for WTS is in reducing administrative overhead.

To aid administrators planning WTS deployments, Microsoft breaks down computer user sessions into three categories:

- Task-based users—This kind of user does a single task with little processing. An example is a data entry operator.

- Typical users—The typical user has one or possibly two programs running in a session. Most current activity is relegated to the foreground application, with little or no background activity. As an example, a typical user might be doing word processing and have a browser open.

- Advanced or power users—These users run three or more applications, and task the server with significant processor demands. An example of this type of usage is a database administrator running a query against the database during a session. Graphics, video, or multimedia applications move a client's session into this category.

Based on the number and type of users using WTS running on Windows NT 4.0, vendors published studies that enable their customers to right size their system purchases. Similar studies will likely be appearing that can help you determine the hardware required for a particular client load. System planning requires an understanding not only of application performance, but also of the types of peripheral devices used.

18

As a rule of thumb, Windows 2000 with WTS requires 64MB of RAM for base operation, and 4MB to 8MB for each additional typical user. Advanced users will require a larger amount of installed RAM. Client load also increases in direct proportion to the computational power of your server. Going from a single processor 350MHz server to a 500MHz server, one could expect to increase the number of clients by roughly 43%. Going from a single 500MHz processor to a dual 500MHz processor system might double your overall capacity. With Windows NT 4.0, Microsoft quoted the following figures for a quad-processor with 200MHz CPUs and 512MB of RAM: 100 task-based users, 60 typical users, and 30 advanced users.

Other factors play a role in limiting performance for WTS. The system bus of an ISA or AT system is considered too slow for adequate WTS performance, and Microsoft recommends that you use either an EISA, MCI, or PCI bus to a WTS server. Additionally, those systems tend to be I/O limited. Systems with SCSI-2 or FAST SCSI will often significantly outperform those with IDE, ESDI, or ST-506 adapters communicating with local disks.

In communications with network clients, WTS uses the Remote Desktop Protocol or RDP. This protocol is optimized to lower network traffic, and to support dial-in connections over phone lines with as little as 28.8Kbps transmission speed—a speed typical of remote access services. It is recommended that you use a high-performance network interface card, regardless. Large numbers of users connected through phone lines will benefit by the use of a multiport asynchronous communications adapter that provides greater throughput and lower processing interrupt requests. WTS is a great solution for supporting remote users because of the modest demands it makes on the size of the communications pipe between client and server.

Installing and Configuring Windows Terminal Services

Windows Terminal Services is offered to you as an install option during the standard Windows 2000 Server installation. Installing WTS doesn't make it active. You must turn the service on, and you can also turn the service off. If you think you are going to use WTS, install the files. The wizard will ask you during the installation whether you want to install WTS in the application mode (to add applications running on the server); or in remote mode, where the server may be remotely managed.

If you decide to install WTS at a later time, do so using the Add/Remove Programs applet in the Control Panel folder. During the installation, you will need to supply the Windows 2000 Server installation disks. This applet opens the Windows Component Wizard, and Terminal Services and Terminal Services Licensing are toward the bottom of the component list. They require 14.3MB and 0.4MB, respectively. The Wizard will ask you during the installation whether you want to install WTS in the application mode (to add applications running on the server), or in remote mode, where the server may be remotely managed.

The Terminal Services Configuration applet is where you specify whether temporary folders are deleted or retained upon exit, whether each session uses its own temporary folder, the default connection security, and whether the Internet Connector License is enabled.

> Before installing WTS, you might want to read Chapter 16, "Integrating Terminal Services" in the *Windows 2000 Deployment Guide* that is part of the Windows 2000 online help system.

How to Configure Windows-Based Terminals and Other Clients

Windows-based terminals have an auto-boot feature that lets them discover WTS on a network. In most instances, the WBT installation is automatic.

To use Terminal Server on Windows clients, you must install client software. One way to do this is to create an installation disk and then run that install program locally at the client. You can also create a connection file on the server from the installation disks and run the installation over the network from that file.

To create an installation disk, do the following:

1. Select the Terminal Services Client Creator applet from the Start menu and choose the Terminal Services Client Creator command from the Administrative Tools folder on the Program submenu.

    The Create Installation Disks dialog box appears.

2. Select the type of client from the Network Client or Services list box.

3. In the Destination Drive list, select the disk drive you want to use, click the Format disks check box if desired, and then click the OK button to create the disk set.

For 16-bit Windows clients, you will need three floppy disks; 32-bit setups need one disk.

You can also create a connection file using the Client Connection Manager by doing the following:

1. Use the installation disk set to install the Terminal Services client on your WTS server through the Add/Remove Programs control panel. The Server requires you use the User Change command prior to installation should you wish to install the client on the server directly from the disk set.

2. Open the Client Connection Manager from the Terminal Services Client applet on the Programs folder of the Start menu, then click the Client Connection Manager.

18

3. Select the New Connection command from the File menu.

   A wizard opens that enables you to define the new connection. Enter the name of the connection, the IP of the Terminal Server, the name of the user to log in as if wanted, and then to accept the defaults for the remaining screens and click Finish.

4. Create the connection, highlight the connection icon, and then select the Export command from the File menu.

5. Specify the location in which the connection file will reside on your network and the name of the .CNS file. This then exports the connections you created to the .CNS file.

To install client software from your installation disks, use the Setup program on Disk 1. Or connect to the server, find the location of the connection file you created, and run a network installation from there. After you have installed the client software, you can run the Terminal Server Client program from the Program submenu on the Start menu.

For Windows-based terminals, turn the terminal on (or restart) to see the logon screen, and start from Step 2 in the next exercise.

For Win16 clients (Windows for Workgroups or Windows 3.1) or for Win32 clients (Windows 95/98, Windows NT Server or Workstation, and Windows 2000 systems), use the following procedure to log on to WTS and start a session.

To connect to WTS from a client and start a session:

1. Select the Terminal Services Client command in the Terminal Services Client folder of the Programs subfolder on the Start menu to open the Terminal Services Client dialog box.

2. In the Terminal Services Client dialog box shown in Figure 18.1, select the server from the Server list box, or use the browse list in the Available Servers list box to select a WTS server.

   If you are logging in from a Win32 client, you can also specify a TCP/IP address.

FIGURE 18.1

The Terminal Services Client dialog box makes your connection to a specific WTS server.

3. Select the resolution in the Screen Area list box. (Don't forget this option, or you might get unexpected results when you try to run a session.)

4. For an RAS connection, click the Low-Speed Connection check box.

5. The Cache Bitmaps to Disk option will speed up your performance somewhat by using a local disk, and you should select this option if you have local disk space.

6. Click the Connect button.

> There are many more connection properties that you can set using the Client Connection Manager.

7. A standard Windows authentication dialog box or Logon Information dialog box appears if you have set the logon property for using the default Windows authentication, and if you required login to WTS.

8. Enter your logon information and click the OK button.

The Terminal Server desktop appears, either in a window or full screen, as shown in Figure 18.2.

18

FIGURE 18.2

A terminal session running in a maximized window. Note the two taskbars, one for the Win32 client (Windows 2000 Professional) and the other for the session running on the server.

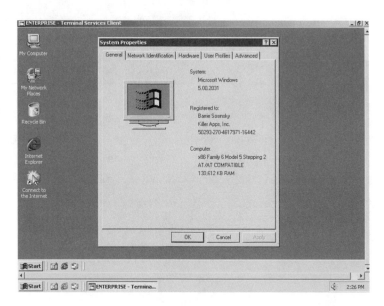

At this point, you are running a session and can start an application, open files or work in the file system, and access disks and printers. In short, you can do everything that your profile and privileges allow you to. Just for grins, Figure 18.2 shows you a terminal session on a Windows 2000 Professional client, a desktop within a desktop. The central window and taskbar are the terminal session; the outer and bottom taskbar and window are the Windows 2000 desktop itself. On a Windows-based terminal, you would see only a single desktop appear.

Table 18.1 shows you some useful shortcuts for Terminal Server sessions.

TABLE 18.1   Terminal Server Shortcut Keys

Shortcut Keystroke	Action
Alt+PgUp	Switch programs left to right, similar to Alt+Tab ("cool switch")
Alt+PgDn	Switch programs left to right, similar to Alt+Shift+Tab
Alt+Ins	Cycle through running programs in their session initiation order
Alt+Home	Open the Start menu
Ctrl+Alt+Break	Toggle between windowed and full-screen sessions
Ctrl+Alt+End	Open the Windows 2000 Security dialog box
Alt+Delete	Open the Windows pop-up menu
Ctrl+Alt+- (minus)	Take a screen shot of the active window and place it on the Terminal Server clipboard (like PrintScn)
Ctrl+Alt++ (plus)	Take a screen shot of the client desktop and put it on the Clipboard (like Alt+PrintScn)

To disconnect a session and leave it active:

- Select the Disconnect command from the pull-down selector of the Shutdown command off the Start menu of the client.
- Click OK in the Disconnect Windows 2000 Session dialog box.

To log off and terminate the session on the server:

- Select the Shut Down command from the Start menu of the client.
- Click Log Off in the Shut Down Windows dialog box.

How to Manage Connections

WTS has the capability to communicate with clients using one of two wire protocols: the Remote Desktop Protocol (RDP) and the Citrix ICA wire protocols, which are embedded with other transfer protocol packets, such as TCP/IP. When you install WTS, the TCP/IP connection is automatically established and assigned a default set of access permissions that only an administrator can change. To use the other connection protocols, you install those connections. Each RDP connection requires its own dedicated network adapter, through which multiple clients can connect. You would typically use the following procedure to install the ICA protocol. In most instances, the default installation of RDP will suffice.

 Studies of ICA versus RDP wire protocols show that they perform similarly in many instances, although some significant differences are noted. A year ago, the most significant difference between the two was that there were many more terminals with ICA support than RDP support. That has changed with many new models being offered running the Windows CE operating system and RDP support. It is possible to buy terminals to support both protocols, although not in the same session. A session requires its own protocol. However, you can log off a session and start a second session using a terminal if your terminal has both protocols and you want to test them with your application.

18

Creating WTS Connections

To create a new connection

1. Select the Administrative Tools command on the Programs submenu of the Start menu and double-click the Terminal Services Configuration applet.

2. Select the Create New Connection command from the Action menu.

   The Terminal Services Connection Wizard appears.

3. Click the Next button, and then select the type of connection you want to create in the Connection Type list box.

4. Click the Next button to view the Data Encryption page.

5. Select the desired encryption level from the Encryption Level list box, and click the Use Standard Windows Authentication check box if you desire that feature; click the Next button.

   Encryption is described in more detail later.

6. On the Remote Control screen shown in Figure 18.3, select the kind of remote control you want to enable the administrator to have in a session using this protocol, and then click the Next button.

7. On the Transport Type page, specify the name of the new connection, select the transport type from the list box, enter an optional comment, and click the Next button.

8. On the Network Adapter page, specify which of the server's NIC cards can use this protocol and the number of connections clients can make to the server, and then click the Next button.

9. Complete the remaining steps of the wizard.

FIGURE 18.3

On the Remote Control page, you can set properties that enable an administrator to monitor client sessions.

Server Connection Properties

Connections have properties that enable you to control client sessions. Among the settings that you can manage are maximum connection times, maximum idle times, data encryption levels, and the access provided users and groups. If you use the Terminal Services extension to Users and Groups, you can set access permissions for individual users. By using the Terminal Services Configuration applet, you can control access permissions at the server on a connection basis for temporary folders, connection security, and for the Internet Connector licensing.

To modify the properties of a connection, do the following:

1. Open the Terminal Services Configuration applet.

2. In the details pane on the right side, right-click the connection and select the Properties command from the context menu.

   The Connection Properties dialog box appears.

3. To specify a maximum number of sessions that can connect to the server click the Network Adapter tab; click Maximum Connections and enter a number for the concurrently connected sessions allowed.

4. To specify the encryption level of your sessions, click the General tab; in the Encryption Level section, select the level of encryption desired.

Low-level encryption uses a 56-bit (Win32) or 40-bit key (Win16) for data sent from the client to the server, and provides maximum performance. The medium level provides the same security, but encrypts data in both directions. For American and Canadian users, a high-level encryption option of 128-bit keys and bidirectional encryption will be enforced. You will observe lower performance with high encryption. Check the Use Standard Windows Authentication if you want to have your clients default to this method.

5. To specify a program that automatically starts during log on, click the Environment tab shown in Figure 18.4. In the Initial Program section, click the Override Settings from User Profile and Client Connection Manager Wizard. In the Program Path and File Name text box, enter the application's executable file. Enter the working directory in the Start in text box.

FIGURE 18.4

The Environment tab of the Connection Properties dialog box is where you specify a program that starts automatically at log on for a session.

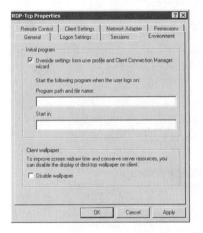

18

6. To let a user log on to the server automatically: Click on the Logon Settings tab (see Figure 18.5), and then click the Always Use the Following Logon Information radio button. Enter the User Name, Domain, and Passwords into those text boxes. If you want the client to be authenticated every time the user tries to log on to WTS, click the Always Prompt for Password check box.

   Terminals are unlikely to be logged on to the domain prior to starting a session. However, if you have the client software loaded on a personal computer or workstation, the Always Prompt option might be useful to you.

7. Use the Remote Control tab to configure shadowing options. This tab shows the same options that were displayed on the Terminal Services Connection Wizard in Figure 18.3.

8. On the Sessions tab shown in Figure 18.6, select the time required to end a disconnected session, a maximum limit for a session's duration or for any idle period, and
the actions that occur when those limits are reached.

9. To connect to client drives and printers at logon (or prevent that behavior): Click the
Client Settings tab and select Connect Client Drives and Connect Client Printers at
Logon check boxes on the Client Settings tab of the Connection Properties dialog box.

   Only Citrix ICA clients support the drive connection option.

FIGURE 18.5

*The Logon Settings tab
is where you let a
client log on without
being authenticated, or
require authentication
for every connection
to WTS.*

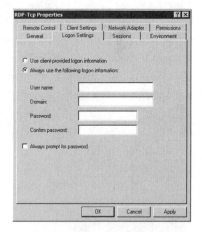

FIGURE 18.6

*The Sessions tab of the
Connection is where
you set session limits so
that timeouts and
reconnections are con-
trolled for idle sessions.*

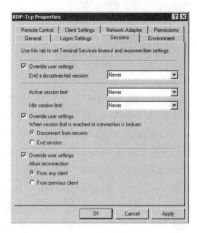

10. To set permissions for the connection, click the Permissions tab, and then add users
and groups and set their access rights. In general, you should try to manage your
permissions on a group basis.

Connections clients make to drives and printers exist only for their session, unless you enable this option of connection at logon. You can map or disable drives, Windows printers, LPT ports, COM ports, the Clipboard, and audio devices. These settings apply to all clients to WTS. To specify each client setting, use the Terminal Server extensions to Users and Groups in the Active Directory Users and Computers.

11. Click the OK button to close the Connection Properties dialog box.

Client Connection Properties

In addition to the server-based connection properties that have been the subject of this section, you can also create a connection and set properties for a connection on the client side using the Client Connection Manager. This applet is installed on your client machine for Win16 or Win32 and is automatically installed for WBT systems. Because many of the properties in this dialog box are similar to ones you've already seen, only the more important client settings you would want to control are described here. When you launch the Client Connection Manager and create a new connection, you see a wizard like the one in the previous connection. Use client connections to create connections to specific applications and for specific purposes.

To create a new connection from your client

1. Select the Client Connection Manager command from the Terminal Services Client folder on your Programs folder of the Start menu.

2. Double-click the Client Connection Manager and select the New Connection command from the File menu.

3. Follow the instructions of the wizard as discussed earlier.

You can export a connection and its properties to disk to use elsewhere, importing it from another Connection Manager.

When the connection exists, right-click it and select the Properties command from the context menu, or highlight the connection and select the Properties command from the File menu.

Important client-side connection properties you should know about include

- Change the server you connect to on the General tab in the Server Name or IP Address text box.

- Change the logon information on the Logon Information tab.

- Change the client window size in the Screen Area section of the Connection Options tab.

18

- Open the connection as a full screen by setting the Full Screen check box in the Connection Startup section of the Connection Options tab.

- Start up with a low-speed connection by default by setting the Low-Speed Connection check box in the Connection Options tab.

- Speed up screen display by using the Cache Bit Maps to Disk option on the Connection Options tab.

Session Limits

When a client logs on to WTS, his session continues until he logs off. This behavior is interesting because it means that your server can be doing processing while your client is not active. There are interesting implications in using WTS as a parallel processing engine. You can disconnect users while leaving their sessions active on the server. To reconnect to his session on the server, the client simply logs back on to the system. As a safeguard, you can set an option that limits your clients to logging back on to their sessions from the terminal that the session originated from—provided that the clients provide serial numbers for their connections. Citrix's ICA clients provide such a serial number.

In most instances, administrators want to conserve system resources while maximizing the number of clients that can connect to the system. You can do this by setting a maximum session limit, or by disconnecting users after an idle period that you set in the Terminals Services Configuration applet.

Use the Connection Properties dialog box's Sessions tab to control numbers of connected users, duration of sessions, and idle time, as well as how users are disconnected. This dialog box was shown in the previous section.

Shadowed Sessions

WTS allows a feature called *shadowing* that permits an administrator or teacher to observe and control a user's session. This feature is similar to several packages available in the marketplace that provide these functions for help desks and educational markets. You use the Terminal Services Configuration Control Panel applet to configure the shadowing feature, and the Terminal Services Manager to start a shadowing session. When taking remote control over a user's session, you can post a message first either informing him of your intention or asking him for permission. Shadowing can be done on a per-user and per-group basis.

When shadowing a client session, your computer must display the same resolution as the screen you are shadowing. WTS is unable to display areas of different resolution on your screen and will abort the connection. When you want to end the shadow session, press the Ctrl+* (asterisk) keystroke.

Managing Accounts and Profiles on WTS

To use WTS as a client, your users must have established accounts on that server or on the domain that the server participates in. Account information is used to control sessions, environment characteristics (paths and folders), remote control, and the Terminal Services profile for a user or group. You can create specific groups and profiles for WTS users. It is recommended that you use mandatory profiles and do not use roaming profiles so that a user cannot access the WTS server twice without closing her session.

User accounts are managed in Local Users and Groups, or, for a domain, Active Directory Users and Computers. Figure 18.7 shows you the Terminal Services Profile tab of the Properties dialog box from the Active Directory. This tab contains some important settings. You can allow or disallow access using the Allow Logon to Terminal Server check box, set the path to the folder where a user's files are stored, and specify that a home directory is on a specific drive using the Connect radio button, the drive list, and the To text box. The syntax for the path is *servername**users**username*. At a minimum, you should set this profile characteristic.

FIGURE 18.7

The Terminal Services Profile tab of the Active Directory Users and Groups dialog box for a user.

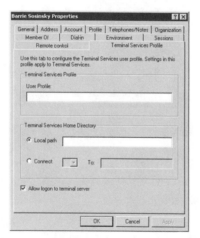

18

It is also a good idea to create a starting program for users on the Environment tab of the User or Group Properties dialog box. Also, you might want to set a profile-based session limit on the Sessions tab. You might also want to set properties based on a profile for remote control.

Managing Users, Sessions, and Processes

You can manage users, sessions, and processes from the Terminal Services Manager dialog box shown in Figure 18.8. Information is available about all WTS servers in your domain and in trusted domains. You can see connected users on the Users tab, their sessions on the Sessions tab, and all the processes that are running on the particular server that you are examining on the Processes tab. You see a console session whenever you connect to WTS. If you see the word *listener* displayed in the tree pane, it indicates that the session is in the listen state and can take a client connection. A disconnected session goes into the listen state. When WTS is started, it creates sessions in the idle state that await client connection; two are created by default.

FIGURE 18.8

The Terminal Services Manager lets you control sessions and users while WTS is running.

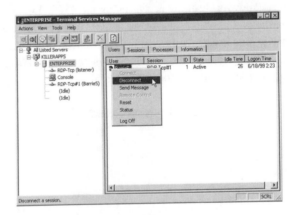

With the Terminal Services Manager you can

- Disconnect a session
- Connect to another session on another server
- Log a user off from a session
- Reset a session
- View session information
- Remotely control a session
- End a particular process

WTS supports a command-line interface. If you go to the command prompt and type in the various commands, you can alter the behavior of WTS. Consult online help (see the "Terminal Server Command Reference" section) for the syntax of WTS commands and the additional options that those commands offer.

How to Install and Manage Application Software on WTS

The recommended method for installing a program on WTS is to use the Add/Remove Programs applet in the Control Panel folder. When you install WTS, the Terminal Service option in the Add/Remove Programs applet is enabled by default. Programs installed in this way are prepared for multisession use on WTS and installed on the server in the \Win2000 directory. No clients should be connected when applications are installed on WTS.

To install an application on WTS, do the following:

1. Log on to WTS as an administrator and close any open applications.
2. Double-click on the Add/Remove Programs applet in the Control Panel folder, and then click the Add New Programs button.
3. In the Add Program wizard, select the installation method and the wizard will then go look for the Setup program of your application on a CD-ROM or floppy disk.
4. Install the application to an NTFS volume.
5. In the After Administration dialog box, click the Next button.
6. When the Finish Admin Install dialog box appears, click the Finish button.
7. When a program installation script is available, open a command prompt and run that script as described later in this section.

After you enable WTS and install a program using the Add/Remove Programs applet, it is prepared for multisession use. If you turn WTS off, programs might not work properly when you turn Terminal Services back on. If you are removing WTS from the system, you should uninstall the applications you want to run, and then reinstall those applications to have them function properly.

After you have installed an application, there might be minor changes required in the program installation to make it compatible with WTS. A number of application-compatibility scripts have been developed to assist you with this task. These scripts are found in the following location: %systemroot%\Application Compatibility Scripts\Install. Each script comes with notes, and each is a text file that is run as a batch file from the command prompt. You will find scripts for the following applications: Corel Perfect Office 7.0 and 8.0 32-bit versions; Lotus SmartSuite 97 32-bit; Microsoft Office 4.3, 95, and 97 SR-1; Microsoft Project 95 and 98; Netscape Communicator 4.0, and Netscape Navigator 3.0. You can edit these scripts to customize your installation, or develop your own install scripts.

As an alternative to the Add/Remove Programs installation, you can choose to use the Change User command from the command prompt to install a program to the \WTSRV directory rather than the user's home directory. This makes the application available for multisession access.

Use the Change User command, as follows:

1. Log on to WTS as an administrator and close any open applications.
2. Select the Command Prompt command from the Programs submenu on the Start menu.
3. Enter **change user /install** at the prompt and press the Enter key. This command puts WTS into install mode and turns off .INI mapping.
4. Locate the installation program and install the application to an NTFS drive.
5. When the installation is complete, enter **change user /execute** at the prompt, and then press the Enter key. This command puts WTS in execute mode, restores .INI mapping, and records the method used by the setup programs to install the program.
6. Run any program installation script at the command prompt.

In a multisession mode, a user running an application would open the program and any user-specific Registry entries would be spawned into the user's home directory. When using the Change User method, you should test the installation to make sure that the application can be accessed and can read and write to the required directories.

It is likely that older applications were not specifically designed to be compatible with Terminal Services, and you should use caution when trying to install and run those programs. WTS runs in a 32-bit architecture, and programs written to the Win32 interface are more likely to be compatible than Win16 programs that run on the Windows 3.1 platform. Although Windows 2000 Server might run 16-bit programs using Windows on Windows (WOW), typically the overhead in translation of a 16-bit program in enhanced mode requires more system resources than the same kind of program running in its native 32 bits. It is estimated that the performance hit when using 16-bit Windows applications might be on the order of a 40% reduction in connected users and a 50% increase in memory requirements.

Programs compiled for the X86 Intel platform run in emulation on Windows 2000 Server on a Compaq Alpha computer will require more resources than an application compiled specifically to run on an Alpha.

For Microsoft Office products where toolbars have buttons that launch other programs, it is recommended that you delete the toolbar.dll file. Additionally, Microsoft recommends that you secure the Microsoft System Information program (MSINFO.EXE) to allow administrator access only through file permissions to prevent users from gaining system information.

Performance Analysis of WTS Servers

You can use the Performance Monitor and the Network Monitor to analyze the performance of WTS and to detect various kinds of bottlenecks. When you add WTS to your server, the service adds User and Session objects and counters that you can observe.

The significant counters that can be observed are the following:

- Processor utilization
- Memory utilization
- Hard disk I/O rates
- Pagefile (swapfile) activity

Keep in mind that you have to manually turn hard disk counters on and off to view them.

One observation that has been made is that you can linearly extrapolate the performance of a system with two to five users based on the results that you observe and determine the maximum number of users that a system will support.

How to Comply with WTS Licensing Issues

Terminal Services uses its own licensing scheme that is above and beyond that required for Windows 2000 Server. WTS requires a Windows 2000 Server license, Client Access Licenses (CALs), and WTS Client Access Licenses. The WTS CALs allows per-seat licenses, with the exception of the WTS Internet Connector, which allows a server up to 200 concurrently connected users. The Windows 2000 Professional license allows access to a WTS server without a client CAL.

WTS licensing scheme makes use of a licensing server, a WTS server, and installed client licenses. Some of these components must be installed separately after WTS is installed on your server. WTS can be installed as part of a Windows 2000 Server original installation, or at a later point using the Add/Remove Programs Control Panel applet.

18

Consult the Windows 2000 help system topic "Understanding Terminal Services Licensing" for further details on licensing options.

The WTS License Server maintains a database of licenses for one or more WTS servers. This database may be on the WTS server or elsewhere, but WTS must connect to the License Server in order to provide client licenses to clients that want to connect to the Windows Terminal Services server.

Citrix MetaFrame

No discussion of WTS would be complete without at least a mention of Citrix MetaFrame. WTS is based on the work that Citrix did on a multisession Windows server in the Win16 architecture of Windows NT 3.5x. The WinFrame product was written using a Microsoft license of Windows NT codes. When Microsoft upgraded to Win32, it did not want to license that code and wanted this functionality inside the base operating system. So Citrix and Microsoft cut a deal in which Citrix licensed back its multisession code, and Microsoft incorporated that functionality only for Windows clients and Windows-based terminals.

MetaFrame supplies heterogeneous client support for MS-DOS, 16-bit Windows (Windows 3.1 and Windows for Workgroups), Macintosh, Java, OS/2 Warp, and UNIX clients. Additionally, MetaFrame 1.8 supports a broad range of client hardware, including legacy PCs, Pentium PCs, Windows-based terminals, network computers, wireless devices, and information appliances.

MetaFrame uses Citrix's ICA protocol to connect to users over phone lines, WAN links (T1, T3, 56kb, X.2), broadband connections (ISDN, frame relay, and ATM), as well as wireless connections, and intranet and Internet connections over TCP/IP. Other protocols you can use include IPX, SPX, NetBIOS, and direct asynchronous connections. Secure connections can be made with SecureICA Services, an RSA RC5 encryption of the ICA traffic. MetaFrame is optimized to provide additional port options to full 16-bit stereo audio, local drives, COM ports, and local printers.

Significantly, MetaFrame adds load balancing to WTS for the creation of server farms, Internet connectivity, and specialized application support. MetaFrame is very feature rich, and deserves your consideration. What Citrix has done is create an application server platform, and a rich one at that. Citrix Load Balancing can load balance across both MetaFrame and WinFrame servers.

Citrix has created a middleware platform for WTS. Its Application Publishing utilities enable you to deploy applications from a central location. Application Launching & Embedding (ALE) enables you to put links into Web pages that launch applications and documents running on MetaFrame/WTS. The ReadyConnect Client allows you to add users and their applications and environments quickly. Another feature, called Automatic Client Update, enables you to update client software automatically from a server.

When you use WTS, you are getting only a small part of this great environment. MetaFrame, which runs on top of WTS, requires its own purchase and additional licenses.

SCO Tarantella

Another application that can provide application server support to clients using Windows Terminal Services is SCO's Tarantella. Tarantella displays multi-user NT applications on thin clients. Tarantella runs on a UNIX server or server farm, and provides access to clients to applications that run on an NT or Win2K Windows 2000 application server. Future versions of Taranatella will run on Windows NT/2000, four versions of Linux, and eventually AIX, True64, and Solaris.

Tarantella can send the screen display to IBM 3270 green-screen terminals and Wyse Technology's terminals, and send X applications to any browser that contains a Java Virtual Machine. Tarantella uses its AIP (Adaptive Internet Protocol) optimized protocol to send X.11 over a dial-up IP connection. Tarantella Enterprise II runs NT applications on UNIX and displays the results courtesy of a translation of the RDP protocol from WTS to AIP, which is transmitted as a wire protocol to thin clients.

SCO has a product that directly competes with Citrix MetaFrame, provides access to many more types of applications running on a variety of operating systems, and runs on UNIX. You can use your existing NT/Win2K Windows 2000 application servers running Windows Terminal Services, and use Tarantella to provide the terminal support to heterogeneous clients (beyond the Win32 clients that WTS supports). SCO claims that it offers more centralized management, better security, and better scalability than MetaFrame, in addition to broader system support.

Tarantella, supports a three-tier architecture (vs.compared to MetaFrame's 2two-tiered onearchitecture) and lets enables administrators to hook servers in a 50-server, load load-balanced array that can serve as many as 15,000 users. In Tarantella, the first tier houses the application servers, the second tier houses the Tarantella middleware servers, and the third tier houses the clients. Application servers can be Windows 2000 Server Terminal Services, IBM 3270, and many types of UNIX (but not Linux). SCO suggests that its software is better suited for data center applications than is MetaFrame is because its

18

SCO's software will run more types of applications than any other thin client/server solution and because its software is fully Web-enabled. Tarantella also saves the state information of a session, so a client can log back on to the system and resume his or her work, as with WTS and MetaFrame does. Clients in the third tier can connect using RDP, X11, TN3270, Wyse 60, and VT52-420. Tarantella doesn't support ISA.

SCO is busy segmenting the thin client/server market. They It now offers Tarantella Express, a low low-priced offering meant for the small business market. SCO has wrapped up the product up with things like such as automated setup and configuration wizards to make this product much easier to deploy, than Citrix MetaFrame. Tarantella Express for the SCO OpenServer operating system began shipping during February, 2000 and for the UnixWare 7 operating system during April, 2000. Additional versions are planned for other popular server operating systems.

SCO also announced an initiative to apply Tarantella to the rapidly developing Application Service Provider (ASP) market.

Summary

Windows Terminal Services creates server-based sessions that Windows users can run from a Windows-based terminal or Windows. Connections are made over a network or through a remote access connection. Because only graphics displayed on the client screen and keystrokes and mouse movements are transmitted over the wire, WTS supports a wide range of clients (even legacy clients such as x486 Windows 3.1 clients), and a geographically distributed enterprise.

This hour described how you install and configure WTS on both the server and the client, how you manage users and sessions, how you install applications, and many of the factors that affect performance on WTS.

Workshop

The following quiz tests for some of the concepts presented in the hour. Even if you feel comfortable with your learning you should try to work these exercises. The answers can be found in Appendix A, "Answers."

Quiz

1. How do I install WTS?

2. What do I need to do to install a Windows-based terminal?

3. How many users can a WTS server support?

4. Where do I go to see who is connected to a WTS?

5. What kinds of licenses do I need?

6. Can I use a Macintosh to connect to WTS?

7. Why aren't roaming profiles recommended?

8. What is the minimum wire speed WTS supports?

9. Why does WTS work with modem speed dial-up connections?

10. What is shadowing?

Exercises

1. Log in for a session and start a Word processor document. Then disconnect, but don't log off. Leave the session. Try to log on from another computer. What happens?

2. Create a specific group of users for WTS. Assign connection privileges to that group.

3. Create an Internet connection to WTS and try to log in to the server using your browser and the Internet.

18

HOUR 19

Printing

by Barrie Sosinsky

Printers on a network can be a shared resource. Windows 2000 Server, as well as previous versions of this operating system, can provide print services to other servers and clients. In fact, Windows NT is often brought into an enterprise specifically for its print and file server capabilities. In this regard, Windows 2000 and Windows NT before it have competed rather successfully with the role that Novell NetWare has played over the last decade.

Right out of the box, Windows 2000 supports many hundreds of printers, providing up-to-date drivers from the manufacturer. This hour covers the installation and setup of printers using Windows 2000 Server. The following topics are covered:

- How Windows 2000 Server processes a print job
- Connecting a printer to the network and appropriating the required resources
- Using the Printer Wizard or a Web browser to set up a printer
- Creating printer shares
- Setting up clients to print to a network printer

- Creating printer pools and setting print priorities
- Resolving printer problems

Understanding the Printing Process

Windows 2000 can print to a local printer or a network printer. It can also make printers available for use over the network as a printer server. Windows 2000 differentiates between a printer and a print device. A *printer* is the software routines that handle a print job. A *print device* is the actual hardware that outputs the print job to whatever medium you want to print to. The distinction is an important one and one that is often very confusing to people just learning Windows server technology.

When you "print" to a printer from a Windows application, the print server processes the action of your application and sends details of the print job to the printer. The printer abstracts the print job, including data transfer, data interpretation, destination port, output type, print scheduling, and print job queuing. The print server then takes the output of the printer and sends the print job to the print device. A *print server* is a computer that processes print jobs and communicates with the print device. The printer is often referred to as a *logical printer* to differentiate it from the physical printer.

The routines that interpret communication between a printer and a print device are called *printer drivers*. When you use the Add Printer Wizard, you are installing a print driver and associating a printer with that print driver. One really nice feature of Windows 2000 is that when a client computer connects to a printer through a Windows 2000 print server, the print driver is automatically downloaded to that client.

There are some generic printer drivers for things such as simple ASCII text, but it is almost always true that each printer requires its own special print driver. Printers with common print engines sometimes can use the same printer driver, but it is always a good idea to have installed the most up-to-date printer driver from the manufacturer. Getting a set of current drivers is one of the benefits of upgrading an operating system.

Sophisticated network printers often contain their own internal computer or CPU for processing print jobs, as well as additional processors for special graphics interpretation, such as PostScript page description language (PDL) interpretation. Support for print command interpretation is also built into the printer driver files.

A printer can be assigned a name and have an identity to a user. For example, say you have an HP laser printer called Flash. Flash is a multitray printer; one tray is set up to print hard copy, and the other tray is set up to print transparencies. As an administrator, you could create two "printers," one called Hard Flash and the other called Clear Flash, and connected computers could print to both of these printers outputting to the same print device. Any factor you want to control can be embedded into the printer definition. You could define one printer for daytime (Day Clear Flash) and another for after hours (Night Clear Flash).

Printers can connect to Windows 2000 Server or other Windows-based computers directly through a physical port on the print server. Typically this is through an LPT port or, less commonly, through a SCSI or COMM port. As USB ports become more popular, connecting printers through USB will eventually begin to replace LPT parallel port connection. USB is preferable because it requires only a single IRQ setting for the port, supplies a higher communication speed, and allows daisy chaining up to 127 devices. Windows 2000 also supports infrared printers. However you directly connect a printer to a Windows 2000 Server, you can create a printer share using that device that is available to connected computers on the network.

If your printer is a plug-and-play device, Windows 2000 will automatically recognize it. If your printer isn't recognized or is a serial device, open the Add Printer Wizard and configure the printer manually.

Network printers come with their own network interface card, most typically Ethernet, and connect to the network through a network hub. They take their own network address and behave just as if they were independent computers. With a network computer, your clients can print to it not only across the network, but across the Internet as well.

Windows 2000 offers you the following new print features:

- A new setup tool
- Improved printer page properties
- Remote administration and printer management through your browser (any browser)
- Internet printing from Internet Explorer 4.0 or higher
- Integration of printers as objects into the Active Directory
- A new standard port monitor and print queue monitor
- Better printing from applications
- The ability for users to change personal preferences

Print Architecture

The print process for network printing is as follows:

1. A print job is specified within an application and a particular printer is chosen.

2. The document is specified, and the application calls for the graphics device interface (GDI) to translate it into a form that the printer driver can communicate to the specified printer in a page description language that the print device understands. The GDI was described in detail in Hour 2, "Architecture and Boot Process".

   If the printer is a non-Windows computer, another set of graphics routines replaces the GDI.

3. The print job is sent to the client spooler and then to the print server's spooler. A *spooler* is a print job queue.

19

The client spooler users a remote procedure call (RPC) to the server spooler to initiate communication. A router on the client side polls the print server for its availability before sending the print job to the server. The print job is transferred as an enhanced metafile data type for Windows or as a RAW (ready to print) file for non-Windows computers.

4. The server then passes the print job to the logical printer and spools the print job by writing it to disk.

5. The logical printer polls the print device's print processor and, after some handshaking is done to determine that the data is recognized, the print job is sent to the print device. In some instances, the print data type may be translated by the logical printer to enable the data transfer.

6. The print job is despooled and appears in the print monitor as a job in progress.

   When a bidirectional printer is involved, a language monitor acts as an interpreter that then passes the print job to a port monitor. Print jobs to a unidirectional printer go directly to the port monitor.

7. The print job passes from the port monitor to the printer, where print codes are created and sent to the physical printer along with a data stream. It is the job of the print processor to convert the data stream into a bitmap that the print engine can image to the output medium. In some cases, the print processor is a set of routines running on the server; in other cases, the print processor is embedded in the physical printer (as in PostScript printers).

Figure 19.1 shows a schematic of the Windows printing architecture.

FIGURE 19.1

The overall Windows printing architecture shown as a block diagram.

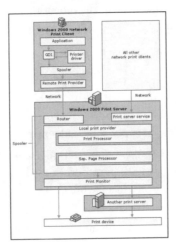

Internet Printing

You can now print to printers across the Internet. The printer is installed on the Windows 2000 system with the printer's URL (Uniform Resource Locator) address used in place of the printer's name. You can enter this address into the Add Printer Wizard when the naming step appears. When printing to Windows 2000 Server, the client print spooler passes the print job to Microsoft Internet Information Services (IIS); whereas when Windows 2000 Professional is used, the print job goes from the client spooler to the Microsoft Peer Web Services (PWS) on that workstation.

Internet printing uses the Internet Printing Protocol (IPP) to communicate. This protocol is embedded into the HTTP data screen. When you print from a browser, that browser makes an RPC call to the printer prior to sending the data. Security for printed documents is part of IIS and PWS, and can be basic authentication (all browsers), Microsoft challenge/response, or Kerberos authentication.

Working with Print Servers

Adding ports and protocols is a function of your print server. You can either add a port during the installation of a printer, or after a printer is installed.

Windows 2000 enables you to access the Print Server Properties dialog box by selecting the Server Properties command on the File menu of the Printer folder window. The four tabs on this dialog box enable you to do the following things:

- Forms—You can set forms and paper sizes.

- Ports—You can add, delete, and configure ports (see Figure 19.2). Local and TCP/IP ports are installed by default; you have to specify other ports in the available port types list.

  For example, you would add an LPR (or line printer) port to connect UNIX or VAX computers to your system, although typically you would want to configure most clients to connect using TCP/IP. Use AppleTalk for Macintosh printers, and use the Hewlett-Packard Network Port to print to older HP-JetDirect cards that support only the DLC protocol. DLC was discussed in Hour 15, "Protocols and Networking Fundamentals."

- Drivers—This tab shows you all the installed drivers and enables you to add, remove, update, and change the properties of printer drivers.

  If, over time, a new printer driver appears for your printer, you can install the new printer driver by clicking the Advanced tab on the printer's Properties dialog box. Click New Driver and supply the printer driver files you obtained from your printer's manufacturer.

19

- Advanced—On this tab (shown in Figure 19.3), you can control the location of the spool folder, other spooler properties, and the behavior of the spooler while printing.

FIGURE 19.2

The Ports tab of the Print Server Properties dialog box enables you to install and modify ports that your printers can use to communicate with print devices.

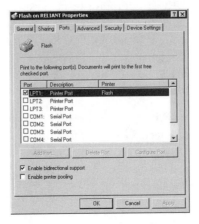

FIGURE 19.3

The Advanced tab of the Print Server Properties dialog box enables you to modify the behavior of the print spooler.

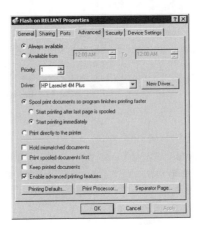

Some printers require the use of soft fonts; that is, fonts installed on your print server. This is common for PCL printers, such as Hewlett-Packard LaserJets, DeskJets, and other PCL printers. You install this type of font by clicking the Device Settings tab of the Properties dialog box (see Figure 19.4). On that tab, click External Fonts and add the new fonts to your system. Soft fonts can be downloaded (downloadable fonts) to the printer's memory as required, if they are not already available on the computer in ROM or in a cartridge.

Hard fonts are those found on cartridges installed on the printer itself. If your printer uses hard fonts, you can enable this on the Device Settings tab using the Installed Font Cartridges option. Your printer will come with instructions on how to configure hard fonts.

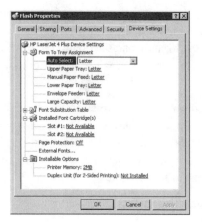

FIGURE 19.4

The Device Settings tab of the Properties dialog box lets you control many options associated with your print devices.

How to Set Up and Share a Printer via LPR

In Hour 5, "The Control Panel," you used the Add Printer Wizard to add and share a local printer. Using local printers attached to the server is great if you have really long parallel cables, but, more often, you'll want to get your printers as close to your users as possible. To do that, you can take advantage of either UNIX LPD (Line Printer Daemon) or JetDirect print servers with TCP/IP.

Before you connect to other print servers, you first need to determine your needs. To support Windows-based printing, you need to designate one computer as the print server. In a production enterprise environment where there is heavy print demand, you might find that the print server must be a dedicated print server. In workgroups with lighter demands, you might find that print servers to a particular printer are only a subset of the jobs assigned to that server. It is very common to have servers play the roles of both file server and print server.

As a print server, Windows 2000 Server can support Windows, Macintosh, NetWare, and UNIX clients. Although there is a restriction of 10 connections on the number of concurrent connections when you use Windows 2000 Professional (or Windows NT Workstation 4.0), Windows 2000 Server does not have this limit and can support many more clients.

Two critical components required to support network printing are installed memory and hard disk space. Both are required to service documents: memory is required to process documents, and hard disk space is required by Windows 2000 Server both as a swap or paging file and for storing print jobs on disk in the print queue that are awaiting printing. As documents are printed, the temporary files written to disk are deleted from disk. When you consider that a high-color photograph letter page size might run in the 20MB–60MB size range, the demand placed on the server by that type of printing is considerable.

19

To maximize the utilization of your network printing resources, you might need to do some up-front planning. You might need to design your domain, the groups it contains, the users in each group, and the location and distribution of printers and print servers so that adequate print resources are available. The location of print devices might also be an issue in your enterprise.

The easiest and recommended way to add a printer to Windows 2000 Server is to use the Add Printer Wizard. The Add Printer Wizard, which has been a staple in Windows-based systems since Windows 95, enables you to add both local printers and network printers, assign a port, install a printer driver, and assign a printer name. The description of the wizard is the subject of the rest of this section.

In this example, we will assume the JetDirect print server or UNIX LPD server is up and running.

To have a Windows 2000 Server print to an LPD server

1. Log on to your network as an administrator.

2. Select the Add Printer command from the Printers folder on the Start menu to start the Printer Wizard, and then click the Next button.

3. On the Local or Network Printer page of the Add Printer Wizard, click the Local Printer radio button (the default) and uncheck the Automatically Detect My Printer check box. Click the Next button.

> Even though the device you are connecting to is a network printer device over TCP/IP, you select Local Printer because this computer is acting as the local spooler.

4. In the Select Printer Port step of the wizard, click the Create a New Port radio button, use the drop-down dialog to select an LPR port, and then click the Next button. A *port* is a communication channel between your server and your printer. Figure 19.5 shows the standard (default) LPT1 port selected in the Select Printer Port step of the wizard.

5. The Add LPR compatible printer dialog box appears, as shown in Figure 19.6. Enter the TCP/IP address of the LPD server as well as a reference name and click OK.

You can create an LPR compatible printer even if you do not have a TCP/IP print device. Enter any IP address and name in step 5, let it time out, confirm it by clicking the OK button at the error message, but DO NOT print a test page.

FIGURE 19.5

Choose to create an LPR port between you and your TCP/IP print device.

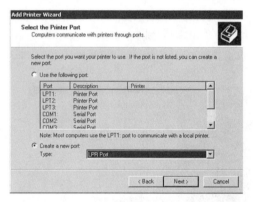

FIGURE 19.6

Enter the TCP/IP address of the LPD server device as well as a reference name.

6. You are taken to the Add Printer Wizard's printer driver selection screen. Select the manufacturer and the printer from the two lists, or click the Have Disk button to install a printer driver that the manufacturer provides; click the Next button.

7. In the Name Your Printer step of the wizard, enter a printer name of not more than 31 characters that your users will recognize. Click the appropriate radio button for the default printer option, and then click the Next button.

   Some applications can't recognize more than 31 characters. The name you use will show up in the Active Directory.

8. In the Printer Sharing step that next appears, enter the name of the printer share in the Share as text box. Or, click the Do Not Share This Printer radio button if you do not want to share the printer between network users, and then click the Next button.

19

9. The Add Printer Wizard then posts the Location and Comment step where you can enter information about the printer that shows up in the Active Directory. Enter appropriate information in the two text boxes, and then click the Next button.

10. On the Print Test Page step, click the Yes radio button (the default, and recommended) to test your printer, and then click the Next button.

11. In the Completing the Add Printer step, shown in Figure 19.7, the wizard summarizes the options you chose; click Finish to create the printer.

Or, click the Back button(s) to change any option you selected earlier.

FIGURE 19.7

In the Completing the Add Printer Wizard step, you are shown the options you selected before the printer is created.

The wizard enables you to define a default printer. However, if you want to change that assignment, right-click the desired printer and select the Default Printer command. The printer icon will show a check mark next to it. The default printer is the one that automatically shows up in the Print dialog box.

A printer icon in the Printers folder offers you some helpful commands on the context menu. The commands do the following:

- Open—Select this to open the Printers print queue.
- Set as Default Printer—This option enables you to reassign the current default printer.
- Printing Preferences—Each user can determine a preferred layout, paper, and print quality.
- Pause Printing—This command pauses printing from the queue, but leaves all jobs intact. Typically, the current page completes printing in your printer.
- Cancel All Documents—This command deletes all print jobs from the printer's print queue.
- Sharing—To change the way this printer is shared, select this command and make your changes in the Sharing tab of the printer's Properties dialog box.

- Use Printer Offline—This command makes the printer unavailable for clients, but still lets the server print to it.

- Create Shortcut—Puts a shortcut on your desktop for a printer, which you can move elsewhere. Windows 2000 supports drag-and-drop printing.

- Delete—This deletes the logical printer from your system.

- Rename—This command enables you to change the name of the logical printer.

- Properties—The Properties command opens the central dialog box that enables you to configure your printer. There are many advanced options for you to work with here that weren't specified in the Add Printer Wizard.

If you did not select the sharing option in the Add Printer Wizard, or if you want to modify the way in which a printer is shared, do the following:

1. Select the Printers command from the Settings folder on the Start menu.

2. Right-click the printer and select the Properties command.

   Alternatively, you can click the printer icon and select the Properties command from the File menu.

3. Click the Sharing tab, as shown in Figure 19.8.

FIGURE 19.8

The Sharing tab of the Printer Properties dialog box is where you set up shared print devices.

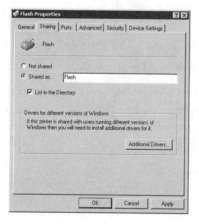

19

4. Click the Shared As radio button, and then enter the name of the printer share in the text box.

The name of the share appears in the My Network Places folder.

5. Click the List in the Directory check box if you want to publish the printer in the Active Directory. Doing so enables users to search for the printer using the For Printers command on the Search menu of the Start menu.

See Hour 10, "Active Directory Entities," for a discussion on searching in the Active Directory.

6. Click the Additional Drivers button to open the Additional Drivers dialog box (shown in Figure 19.9). Use this dialog to add drivers for computers other than Windows 2000 and for other hardware platforms, and to supply the Windows 2000 Server installation disk if required.

FIGURE **19.9**

The Additional Drivers dialog box enables you to install drivers for network clients.

These systems will download the driver when they connect to the server.

7. Click the OK button to close the Properties dialog box and create the share.

A printer share shows an icon for a printer with an open hand below it. Note that your group policies may prevent a printer being published to the Active Directory or shared. Only shared printers may be published. When you find a printer using the Find Printers Search command, you can highlight that printer, right-click it, and select Connect to print to that printer.

When a printer is shared, you need to set the permissions of the groups you want to access the printer. To set printer permissions, do the following:

To set the permissions for accessing a printer, do the following:

1. Select the Printers command from the Settings folder on the Start menu.

2. Right-click the printer and select the Properties command.

3. Click the Security tab, as shown in Figure 19.10.

4. To add a user or group, click the Add button, type a name in the Name text box, and click the OK button in the Select Users, Computers, or Groups dialog box.

5. To change or remove permission to access the printer share, click the name of the user and group, and then click the OK button to close the Select Users, Computers, or Groups dialog box.

FIGURE 19.10

The Security tab of the Printer Properties dialog box is where you determine who can access shared print devices.

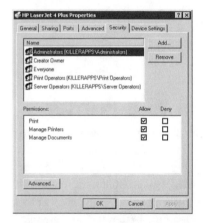

6. Click the appropriate check boxes in the Permissions box, and then click the OK button to set those new permissions.

Administrators, Print Operators, and Server Operators on a domain controller have Manage Printer permission. Everyone has Print permission, and a document owner has Manage Documents permission. Table 19.1 shows the different levels of printer permissions available to Print, Manage Documents, and Manage Printer. You can also enable and disable Web-based printing as a permission.

19

TABLE 19.1 Printer Permissions

Print Permissions	Print	Manage Documents	Manage Printer
Print documents	X	X	X
Pause, resume, restart, and cancel user's own documents	X	X	X
Connect to a printer	X	X	X
Control job settings for all documents		X	X
Pause, restart, and delete all documents		X	X
Share a printer			X
Change printer properties			X
Delete printers			X
Change printer permissions			X

When you create a logical printer, you own that printer. If you want to change ownership for a printer

1. Open the Security tab of the printer's Properties dialog box (as discussed earlier).

2. Click the Advanced button.

3. Click the Owner tab.

4. Click the account that you want to have ownership of, and then click the OK button twice.

Connecting Clients to a Printer

After you have created a printer share, the next step is to set up the client computers so that they can access that share. The procedure involved depends upon the particular client's operating system. For clients running recent versions of the Windows operating systems (Windows NT, 95, or 98), their computers automatically download the version of the driver that they need from the print server, provided that these drivers were loaded with the Additional Drivers dialog box. Different hardware platforms (microprocessors) require different drivers.

For older versions of the Windows operating system (3.1), MS-DOS, or for OS/2, you must manually install the printer driver on the client machine. You must also redirect the output of the LPT1 port of the client to the logical printer (\\PrintServerName\ Sharename) in the command syntax of that operating system. The command used for clients for Microsoft networks is:

```
Net use lptx: \\server_name\share_name
```

where x = 1, 2, or 3 for DOS and Windows 3.1, and higher for other operating systems.

Windows 2000 Server also supports Macintosh, NetWare, and UNIX clients. Each of these operating systems requires additional services be installed on the server. For Macintosh, you should install Services for Macintosh. For NetWare clients, the service is called File and Print Services for NetWare. For UNIX, the service is TCP/IP Printing or, alternatively, the Line Printing Daemon (LPD) Service. None of these three services are installed on your server as part of the default installation.

Any client using Windows 2000 Professional or Windows 2000 Server can connect to a printer using the TCP/IP protocol (an intranet). All the client needs to do is open a browser and enter the URL for that printer. If they have permission to access the printer, they will be able to print. For Web access, it is not necessary to use the Add Printer Wizard because Windows 2000 server will automatically send the printer driver to the client.

The syntax for the URL is `http://server_name/printers`, where the Web designer has placed a page showing the printers on the intranet, or `http://server_name/printer_share_name` for the specific printer.

Additionally, clients can connect to printers using examples shown in Hour 10 on the Active Directory. That hour discusses where attributes of printers (color, duplex, and so on) can be located.

Understanding the Print Queue and Print Jobs

A single print queue appears on every computer connected to a printer. Each connected user can see not only his own print job, but other people's print jobs as well. When an error occurs, the print queue can send a message to connected users. Processing for the print queue occurs on the server after the print job is sent from the client to the server.

To view a print job in the print queue, open the Printers folder and double-click the printer icon. You will see the name of the document, its print status, the owner, and the number of pages in the print job. From this dialog box, you can pause or cancel the print job, move a print job to another printer, as well as alter the printing order of the queue. To alter the print priority (the order in which documents are spooled in the queue), right-click the document in the queue and select the Properties command. Then alter the Priority slider on the General tab. The context menu of a queued document also supplies the restart, pause, resume, and cancel commands.

During printing, a print icon also appears in your system tray at the right side of your status bar. Double-click the printer icon there to access the printer queue window, as a shortcut.

Auditing a Printer

You can audit a printer's usage. This audit tells you who accessed the printer and at what time in a log entry. To turn auditing on, do the following:

1. Right-click the printer in the Printers folder and select the Properties command.
2. Click the Security tab, and then click the Advanced button.
3. In the Access Control Settings dialog box, click the Auditing tab, then the Add button, and select the group of users you want to audit from the Select Users, Computer, or Group dialog box. Then click the OK button to return to the Auditing Entry dialog box.
4. In the Auditing Entry dialog box (see Figure 19.11) you can set the events that you want to audit.
5. Click the OK button twice.

19

FIGURE 19.11

The Auditing Entry dialog box allows you to log successful and failed access events for a group to a printer.

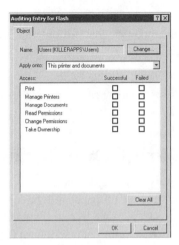

Print Pooling

In situations where you want to maximize an enterprise's printer resources, you can connect the same logical printer to multiple local or network printer devices. This configuration is called a *printer pool*, and it requires that you use the same kind of printers, or printers that use the same printer driver (typically the same print engine). When a logical printer prints to a printer pool, the first available printer port is used. You can also administer several print devices using the same logical printer.

To set up a printer pool, do the following:

1. Select the Printers command from the Settings folder on the Start menu.
2. Right-click the printer and select the Properties command.
3. Click the Ports tab and select the Enable Printer Pooling check box.
4. Click the Port check box for each of the printer devices you want the printer to print to.
5. Click the OK button to close the Properties dialog box and enable this feature.

Print Priorities

You can set the priorities of logical printers so that one printer will print in preference to another to a print device. You can create a high-priority printer that will always have its documents printed first. Setting priorities is useful when two or more printers use the same print device or port, and when you want to differentiate different groups of users. Each group can be assigned to a different priority printer.

To set a printer's priorities:

1. Select the Printers command from the Settings folder on the Start menu.
2. Right-click the printer and select the Properties command.
3. Click the Advanced tab.
4. In the Priority section move the spinner to set the desired priority; use 99 for highest priority and 1 for lowest.

Summary

You can print to a printer locally or over a network. You can also share a printer among clients on your network. By creating print servers, you can amortize and distribute the cost of this expensive resource.

You define logical printers that serve as an interface between your print server and a printing device. You have fine control over many aspects of the printing process, including security, print properties, performance, print queues, and more.

Q&A

Q How do I add a shared printer to the network?

A The easiest way to do this is to connect your printer to a server (a local printer) or connect the printer to a network hub through its network board (a network printer) and run the Add Printer Wizard. Select the Printers command from the Settings menu of the Start menu. Then double-click the Add a Printer icon. The wizard walks you through a basic configuration of a printer. For more configuration options, open the printer's Properties dialog box after you finish.

Q How can I control access to a shared printer?

A Windows 2000 offers you a rich security model for controlling a printer. You can set access and permissions by group and individuals using the Sharing tab of the printer's Properties dialog box. You can also audit access of that printer.

Q I've installed a printer, but not all of my clients can see it. What do I do?

A If you have installed additional drivers, recent Windows operating system clients will have the necessary device drivers downloaded to them. For other operating systems, you will need to manually install the drivers and redirect the port output to that printer.

19

Workshop

The following quiz tests for some of the concepts presented in the hour. The answers can be found in Appendix A, "Answers."

Quiz

1. What is a logical printer?
2. What advantages does a network printer offer you?
3. Where is the print queue stored?
4. What is the function of a printer driver?
5. How do you print to a printer with a browser from a client?
6. Where do you set up a printer share?
7. How are print commands transmitted over the Internet?
8. How do you change the priority with which a document gets printed in the print queue?
9. What is a port?
10. What is a printer pool?

Exercises

1. Add a printer to your server and assign access to that printer to a group of users. Log in as a client and connect to that server. Try logging in as a user in a group with no print privilege.
2. Set up auditing for a printer. After a period of time, open and examine the print log. Remember that the log file can be examined through the Security Log of the event viewer.
3. Create a Web page with a graphical representation of your enterprise's printers. Add links to each printer in a standard URL form that your users can use to connect to a printer.

PART IV

Managing Windows 2000 Server

Hour

HOUR **20**

Client Services, IntelliMirror, and ZAW

by Jeremy Moskowitz

At the heart of Windows 2000 Server is its ability to host clients. In this hour, you'll learn how to prepare your server so that different clients can attach to it.

IntelliMirror has received numerous mentions in the press—often shrouded in mystery as one of the most promising technologies for Windows 2000. In this hour, we'll separate what's fact from what's fiction. You'll explore the Zero Administrative for Windows initiative and harness some of its power to your advantage. You will learn how to have users' data files follow them around the network and be available when the network is unavailable. You will also learn how to load an entire Windows 2000 Professional machine complete with operating system and applications.

In this hour, you will learn to do the following:

- Connect clients to Windows 2000 Server
- Use the Windows Installer to publish and assign applications
- Configure offline folders
- Configure the Remote Installation Service (RIS)

Which Clients Can Connect to Windows 2000 Server?

You are already aware that Windows 2000 comes in many flavors, one of which is Windows 2000 Professional—the workstation product. Windows 2000 Professional isn't the only type of client that can connect to Windows 2000 Server. In this section, you'll see some of the clients you might connect to your Windows 2000 Network.

16-Bit MS-DOS and Windows Clients

Because Windows 2000 Server will continue to authenticate downlevel clients via the NTLM protocol (see the "Heterogeneous NT4/Windows 2000 Server Environments" section of Hour 7, "Advanced Planning for Domains, Domain Controllers, and the Active Directory"), using downlevel clients on your Windows 2000 Server is still a reality. There are two 16-bit MS-DOS and Windows clients that can utilize Windows 2000 Server.

The Microsoft Network client is small enough to fit on a bootable floppy, and is helpful for debugging network connectivity to a client, or for copying files on to a machine in a pinch. Microsoft Network clients can even automatically receive TCP/IP addresses via DHCP!

The Microsoft LANManager 2.2c for DOS client can also automatically receive TCP/IP addresses via DHCP. It also has some advanced features, such as bringing up a dialog box when messages are sent to the client.

32-Bit Clients

Since it came out with Windows NT Workstation 3.1, Microsoft has been pushing for administrators to install 32-bit clients on the desktop. Each of the 32-bit clients can connect and log on to Windows 2000 Server, although each has its quirks as to how it interacts.

Windows 95 and Windows 98 can make full use of the Active Directory, but these clients need a one-time, free upgrade that allows them to make use of the Active Directory and Kerberos authentication. To install the client, locate the upgrade pack in the Clients folder on the Windows 2000 CD-ROM. Both of these clients can make use of Dfs shares.

Windows NT 3.x and 4.x versions will continue to use NTLM for authentication. Windows NT 3.x cannot make use of Dfs shares. Windows NT 4.x versions can make use of Dfs shares without any additional client software.

Macintosh Clients

As noted in Hour 15, "Protocols and Network Fundamentals," Macintosh clients use a modified form of AppleTalk to connect to other machines on the network. In order to provide connectivity to Macintoshes, Microsoft Windows 2000 Server provides AppleTalk as an optional protocol to connect your Macs.

Before you go headlong into connecting your Macs, you must be sure that they meet certain requirements:

- Macintoshes must have System 6.07 or higher (including System 7).
- For Macintoshes with system 7.5 or earlier, the volume size must not be greater than 2GB.
- For Macintoshes with system 7.5 or later, the volume size must not be greater than 4GB.

The machine may not be a Macintosh XL or Macintosh 128.

In addition, for Windows 2000 Server, you'll need the following:

- An NTFS volume to set up directory space because Macintosh directory space can only be set up on NTFS volumes
- At least 2MB free disk space

To install Macintosh connectivity, multiple procedures are required. We must:

- Add the AppleTalk protocol
- Install the Macintosh File System
- Configure the Server Behavior
- Configure Macintosh Volumes
- Set Up Security on those Volumes
- Load the Client Software

20

Adding AppleTalk to Communicate with Macintoshes

In the "Implementing Alternative Protocols" section of Hour 15, you learned about alternative protocols. Alternative protocols allow you to connect foreign clients and servers such as Netware machines or Macintoshes. With this exercise, you can, if desired, implement the AppleTalk protocol which enables your Macintosh clients to communicate with the server.

To add the AppleTalk protocol:

1. Click Start, select Settings, and then open Control Panel.

2. Double-click Network and Dial-up Connections.

3. Right-click Local Area Connection and click Properties.

4. At the Local Area Connection Properties screen, click Install, Protocol, and then Add. Select AppleTalk Protocol and click OK.

Install the Macintosh File System on Your Windows 2000 Server

In Hour 3, "Installing Windows 2000 Server," you had the option of installing File Services for Macintosh. If you did not select File Services for Macintosh as an optional component, you can load it now.

To install the File Services for Macintosh:

1. Click Start, Settings, and then Control Panel. Double-click Add/Remove Programs. Click Add/Remove Windows Components.

2. Use the slider to scroll down and select Other Network File and Print Services. Click the Details button and select File Services for Macintosh. Click OK.

3. Click Next to finish loading the components.

Configure the Server Behavior for Macintoshes

You can specify many options for Macintosh clients. These options include a logon message for Macintosh machines and the choices of how passwords are passed between the client and server, how many sessions a Macintosh client can have, and which files associate with which programs.

To configure the server behavior for Macintoshes:

1. Click Start, Programs, Administrative Tools, and then Computer Management.

2. In Computer Management, open System Tools.

3. Right-click Shared Folders and select Configure File Server for Macintosh. The File Server for Macintosh Properties page appears.

You can now enter a logon message for Macintosh users, as well as set the authentication levels or maximum number of sessions, among other options.

Configure Macintosh Volumes

To create a Macintosh volume, you have to share a folder using the Create Shared Folders Wizard.

To create a Macintosh volume by using the Create Shared Folders Wizard:

1. Click Start, Programs, Administrative Tools, and then Computer Management.
2. In Computer Management, open System Tools.
3. In System Tools, expand Shared Folders.
4. Right-click Shares and select New File Share.
5. Enter in the path of the folder to share. You can choose to share the folders to Windows, Novell or Macintosh computers via the three checkboxes available to you. Click Next to finish the Wizard

Set Up Security on Macintosh Volumes

Now that your volume is set up, you can manage that volume. To manage a Macintosh volume:

1. Click Start, Programs, Administrative Tools, and then Computer Management.
2. In Computer Management, open System Tools.
3. In System Tools, open Shared Folders and click Shares.
4. Right-click the Macintosh volume (designated with a little computer and a share symbol) and select Properties. The volume Properties page appears.
5. Use the General tab to set an optional password on the volume and to allow or disallow guests. Use the Security tab to set granular permissions on the volume.

Load the Client Software on the Macintosh

By default, Windows 2000 has a Macintosh volume called the Microsoft UAM volume. The required client files are located in this volume. To install the client files on a Macintosh:

1. On a Macintosh client, open the Chooser and click Appleshare. Select the zone where you loaded File Services for Macintosh and select the file server.
2. On the desktop of the Macintosh, double-click the Microsoft UAM volume.
3. Run the Microsoft UAM Installer program.

ZAW and IntelliMirror

20

ZAW stands for Zero Administration for Windows. ZAW is an amalgamation of features integrated into Windows 2000 Server to support desktop clients with automated adminis-tration features. The intent of ZAW is to lower the total cost of ownership (TCO) on Windows 2000 networks by lowering the number of hands-on installations, deployments, and modifications that an administrator must make on desktop computers. ZAW describes a portfolio of technologies for server-based configuration of workstations and for application deployment and configuration.

Many of the ZAW technologies have grown up over the years. In fact, you've already set up several of the core ZAW components in Hour 14. You used profiles to enable users' desktops to roam with them. Additionally, you used policies to lock down certain aspects of the desktop so your users couldn't get into too much trouble. Profiles and policies are ZAW components.

Policies and profiles were available in previous versions of Windows NT Server. ZAW continues to add capabilities as part of the ongoing ZAW initiative. When new components to the initiative are available, they are integrated into the operating system. Windows 2000 Server has taken those previous abilities one step further and provided the following new abilities:

- Roaming applications—Applications can now follow the user from desktop to desktop as necessary. This functionality is provided via the "Windows Installer."
- Offline folders—Users' critical data directories can be synchronized with their desktops or laptops should they be disconnected from the network. The clients will continue to work as if the network were still available.
- Easy PC setup—PCs can be easily loaded from scratch, ready to go with minimal configuration required. This functionality is called Remote Installation Service or RIS.

To provide these great new features, Microsoft has introduced an underlying technology called IntelliMirror. IntelliMirror is the blanket term for the technology used when data or applications are stored centrally on the server and deployed to the desktop when needed. If a workstation crashes and all its files are lost, it is possible to use IntelliMirror to reestablish the entire working environment and data files for a user on that workstation or another workstation. Whereas the technologies you deployed in Hour 14 were under the auspices of ZAW, the technologies you deploy in this hour are under the ZAW and IntelliMirror umbrella.

Windows Installer

Windows Installer provides administrators with the ability to assign applications to certain users or computers based on OU membership. Administrators set up this ability via the already familiar group policy settings that were described in Hour 14: "Policies and Profiles."

It is highly recommended that you learn the skills in Hour 14 before continuing with this hour. These sections build on the skills already mastered in that hour. It is assumed that you already understand the concepts presented and can perform the tasks required.

Windows Installer can only set up applications that provide .MSI files. .MSI files are basically a database of how to install the application under certain conditions. Although some newer applications come with .MSI files, many legacy applications do not. A developer can author .MSI files for existing packages via third-party tools. Additionally, .MSI files can be coded such that if certain files become damaged or missing on the client machine, Windows Installer will automatically repair the installation.

> Windows 2000 Server ships with WinInstall LE which can assist you in creating basic .MSI files. Additionally, third party tools such as InstallShield can create .MSI files. Visit http://www.installshield.com/pro2000/comparison.asp for more details.

Before you can begin to use the Windows Installer to assign applications, there are several prerequisites:

- You must put similar users or computers into OUs. See Hour 10, "Active Directory Entities," for information on how to do this.

- You must share a directory or Dfs point to house the source of the application. See Hour 13, "Shares and Dfs," to create a sharepoint.

- You must copy the .MSI file to the sharepoint and make it readable for your users.

- You must create a new policy template for the OU. See Hour 14 for information on creating templates.

In the following example, you want the suite of Windows 2000 Administrative tools to be available to all administrators whenever and wherever they log in.

For this example, assume the following four steps have been performed:

- An AdminOU organization unit was created, and every administrator was moved into the AdminOU group.

- A new share named \\W2KSERVER1\MSIFILES was created and shared as read-only to administrators.

- D:\WINNT\SYSTEM32\ADMINPAK.MSI was copied to \\W2KSERVER1\MSI-FILES.

- An AdminOU_GPO template was created for the AdminOU OU created.

Publishing a Package to Your AdminOU OU

Next, you want to use a portion of the Group Policy template to provide a program to your AdminOU OU. In Figure 20.1, you can see that there are two places to publish

20

packages—one for computers contained in the OU and one for users contained in the OU. Because you want the package to follow the administrators wherever they log in (not from specific machines), use the setting found in User Configuration.

FIGURE 20.1

You can publish packages to either the computers or users in the GPO. You cannot, however, assign packages to computers (only publish.)

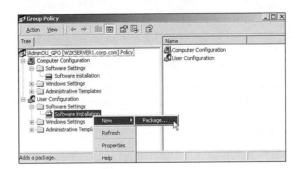

To set up a Windows Installer package:

1. When the Group Policy template editor is editing a policy, drill down to the Software Installation setting desired, as shown in Figure 20.1. Right-click the Software Installation setting and select the Package command from the New menu.

2. The Open dialog box appears. Select an .MSI file. In this case, type in
    \\W2KSERVER1\ MSIFILES\ADMINPAK.MSI and click Open.

> Do not select the adminpak.MSI file in the \WINNT\SYSTEM32 directory.
> Users can only install .MSI files from sharepoints. Use the ADMINPAK.MSI
> you copied to \\W2KSERVER1\MSIFILES.

3. The Deploy Software dialog box appears. If you want to force the package to everyone in the OU, choose Assigned. If you want to make it available in the Control Panel's Add/Remove Programs applet, choose Published. For advanced properties, click on the Advanced Published or Assigned button. For this example, keep the default as Published. Click OK.

> When you Assign packages, the icons appear on the Start Menu. The applications are downloaded from the server on first use. When you Publish packages, the users have the ability to install them from the Add/Remove Programs applet in the Control Panel.

4. After a long wait, Windows 2000 Administrative Tools should appear as a published application, as shown in Figure 20.2.

FIGURE 20.2

*The Windows 2000
Administrative Tools'
.MSI file is now
published in the
AdminOU_GPO.*

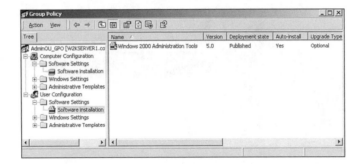

5. Close the Group Policy editor.

Testing the .MSIPackage

Now that you've created your package, you want to make sure it works. Only members
of the AdminOU will be granted the ability to install the package.

> You may have to manually refresh policies for them to take effect immedi-
> ately. In the Run line, type `secedit /refreshpolicy USER_POLICY` or `secedit
> /refreshpolicy MACHINE_POLICY`, as desired. Be sure there is an underscore
> between the word USER or MACHINE and the word POLICY.

To test a Windows Installer package:

1. From any workstation or server in the domain, log on as an Administrator. (Make
sure the account has been placed in the AdminOU OU.) In this case, you can log
on to martinspc.

2. Click Start, Settings, and then Control Panel. Double-click the Add/Remove
Programs applet. The Add/Remove Programs dialog box appears. Click the Add
New Programs button on the left side.

3. In the Add Programs from Your Network section, notice the Windows 2000
Administration Tools application you just published (see Figure 20.3). You can
install it on this machine by clicking the Add button next to the application.

4. The Windows Installer runs, and the application downloads from the installation
point (\\W2kSERVER1\msifiles). The application runs according to how it was
packaged. In this case, a wizard is invoked to set up the Administrative Tools.

20

FIGURE 20.3

Published .MSI files can be loaded from Control Panel's Add/Remove Programs applet.

You may continue to run through the wizard to install the Administrative Tools on martinspc.

Offline Folders

Here's a common dilemma: You instruct your users to keep their files on the server for backup purposes, but you want to enable them to use their files while they are on the road. And as soon as you copy a file from the server to a laptop (or workstation), your users have to remember which file is newer.

What you need is one common place where users can store their files and have them available on *or* off the network.

Enter ZAW's Policies and IntelliMirror's offline folders.

In other books and in the press, you may see references to "Change and Configuration Management" when ZAW is discussed. They are synonymous.

User Data Directory Setup

In Hour 14, you learned that when users save their data to their My Documents folder, the changed files are automatically copied back up to their roaming profile. You can modify this behavior somewhat, and change the location where the files are stored on the server. You might want to do this to centralize the subdirectories of all the users' data so that backing up and restoring is easier. You can create one setting, by using group policies, which can redirect the user's My Documents settings to any shared directory you like.

Additionally, you can use the new offline folder settings to guarantee that users always have a copy of their data.

To create and share a directory to store users' data:

1. Log on as Administrator to W2kSERVER1.

2. From the desktop, double-click My Computer. Double-click the drive you wish to use. In this example D:\.

3. Find a place to create a users directory. In this example, use D:\DATA. Right-click in the free space of the D:\ drive and select the New, Folder command.

4. Type in Data for the folder name.

5. Right-click the newly created Data directory, and select the Sharing command.

6. Click Share This Folder, keep the rest of the defaults, and click OK. The folder will be shared as \\W2kSERVER1\data.

Redirecting Users' Settings

Now that you have a shared directory for your users' data, you should determine which users will be redirected to the \\W2KSERVER\DATA share. You can choose any level of group policy—site, domain, or OU. For ease of learning, you will redirect all users in the corp.com domain to a \\W2KSERVER\DATA\%username% directory, where %username% will be an automatically created directory of each user's username.

> For directions on how to edit the default domain policy, see Hour 14.

To redirect users' My Documents settings:

1. Edit the Default Domain Policy settings. The group policy for the domain appears. Drill down to Folder Redirection by clicking on User Configuration, Windows Settings, and then Folder Redirection.

2. Right-click My Documents and select Properties. The My Documents Properties dialog box appears. Use the Setting pull-down list box and select Basic – Redirect Everyone's Folder to the Same Location. Type \\W2kSERVER1\data\%username% in the Target Folder Location text box, as shown in Figure 20.4. Click OK.

20

FIGURE 20.4

Enter the
\\SERVERNAME
SHARENAME
%USERNAME%
to redirect the My
Documents directory.

The %username% will automatically be evaluated and a new directory will be created for each user as necessary.

3. By default, users have exclusive NTFS permissions to their directories, and the contents of their My Documents folders are automatically moved to the new directory. You can change this behavior, if desired, by clicking on the Settings tab.

At the group policy screen, you can tweak the advanced offline folder settings as found in the User Configuration\Administrative Templates\Network\ Offline Files directory. (Do not do this now.)

4. Close the Group Policy screen.

Turn On Client-Side Caching

Now that the users' My Documents directories are centralized, you can instruct users to turn on this great new feature. In this example, Martin will log on to his PC, and turn on the client-side caching.

To turn on client-side caching:

1. If you're already logged on as Administrator on martinspc, log off now and log in again as mwier.

2. Right-click My Documents and click Make Available Offline as shown in Figure 20.5.

By default, offline folders are enabled for Windows 2000 Professional Workstations. To enable it for servers, you'll need to go to My Computer, Tools, Folder Options, and use the Offline Folders tab.

FIGURE 20.5

Turn on caching by right-clicking the My Documents folder and clicking Make Available Offline.

3. The Confirm Offline Subfolders dialog box appears. You can select either this folder or this folder and all subfolders and click OK. The Synchronization Wizard will synchronize the files then disappear.

4. The Confirm Offline Subfolders dialog box appears. Keep the default to propagate to all subfolders and click the OK button.

Ongoing synchronization will occur without any further interaction. Users may, however, adjust their synchronization settings from their Windows 2000 Professional workstations by selecting the Synchronize icon off the Accessories menu.

 An administrator can also force a client to automatically synchronize with specific shares. Once a folder is shared, click the caching button, and choose a setting in the setting drop-down box.

20

Rapid Client Deployment Methods

There has been much hoopla in recent years regarding the use of products such as Norton's Ghost, which rolls out multiple desktops in a hurry, all with similar configurations, a process called *disk cloning*.

Without products like Ghost, a system administrator would have to load the operating system on the machine by hand (or by scripted installation), and then hand-load each application in turn, and fine tune each one for the user. When hundreds or thousands of desktops have to be deployed, this quickly becomes an impossible task.

Microsoft has stated that deploying Windows NT (and Windows 95) using these rapid deployment methods is unsupported. System administrators have cried foul because there really was no way to quickly deploy similar desktops—until now.

These two sections explore two new workstation deployment methods: RIS and SYSPREP.

Remote Installation Service

Windows 2000 has introduced the Remote Installation Service, or RIS. Its goal is to provide the administrator with the ability to roll out multiple desktop configurations in a short amount of time. Simply prepare the server, boot from a floppy, and away the installation goes. After you create your first base installation, you can customize it with commercial or home-grown apps, and save that configuration to the server as well.

After the server is prepared with your desktop image, use your computer's network card (or special bootable floppy disk) to find the server and download the image.

To perform this magic, you'll have to make sure your network has a DHCP server to dish out temporary TCP/IP addresses and a DNS server to help clients find Active Directory servers. Additionally, you'll need to set up a server to be your RIS server. Although you can run all of these services on one machine, in practice you probably wouldn't want to, due to the heavy processor and disk load the RIS server will have to shoulder. For the sake of this example, however, you'll be using your trusty W2kSERVER1 as the DNS, DHCP, and RIS server.

Client Connections to RIS Servers

The newest PCI network cards have an additional feature their older cousins did not have: the PXE Boot ROM architecture. PXE is a new feature that, when fitted with the appropriate ROM (or boot disk), can enable the network card to connect to a server and obey commands.

A client can only connect to RIS servers in one of two ways:

- PXE Boot ROM—If your network card supports the PXE Boot ROM architecture, you can boot without any floppies, connect to the network, and start your installation.
- PXE Boot ROM Emulator floppy—Windows 2000 Server can help create a floppy that can fool your network card into thinking it has a PXE Boot ROM.

Only a handful of PCI network cards support PXE Boot ROMs or PCE Boot ROM Emulation, so be careful before you order your next batch of Ethernet cards. Some of the most popular PCI cards support PXE, but that's about it. Check with your network card manufacturer for PXE compatibility.

> You can get a definitive list of network cards that support the PXE
> Architecture by clicking the Adapter List button in the RBFG.EXE application
> (see the section "To Create a Remote Boot Disk " later in this hour).

As an administrator, you must decide which is more important to you: more-hands off administration or tighter security. RIS can respond to two types of clients: any PXE Boot client systems or only PXE Boot client systems that are *prestaged*.

Prestaged systems are also called managed PCs. A *managed PC* is one that has its GUIDs manually entered into Active Directory Users and Computers when New, Computer is selected, as performed in Hour 9: "Users, Groups, and Machine Accounts on Domain Controllers." (A GUID, or Globally Universal Identification, is a guaranteed unique identifier for a specific PC. The GUID is usually provided by your PC manufacturer, or, in some cases, listed in the BIOS.) After the computer name is entered, you are given the option to designate the computer as managed. For the utmost security using RIS, you can use the managed computer option to guarantee that a rogue Windows 2000 Professional machine can never spring up on your network spawned from your RIS server.

Setting Up RIS

RIS is a powerful service and has many customization options to assist in your rollout plans. In this section, we'll discuss how to set up some of the basic RIS options to get you off to a quick start.

Back in Hour 3, you had the option of installing RIS as an optional component. To fully activate it, you must now finish its setup.

> If you did not select RIS as an optional component, you can load it now by
> clicking Start, Settings, and then Control Panel. Double-click Add/Remove
> Programs. Click Add/Remove Windows Components. Use the slider to scroll
> down and select the Remote Installation Services check box. Click Next then
> click OK.

20

To install RIS:

1. Click Start, Settings, and then Control Panel. Double-click the Add/Remove Programs applet.

   The Add/Remove Programs dialog box appears.

2. Click the Add/Remove Windows Components button and in the Set up Services section, notice the Configure Remote Installation Services heading. You can finish installation on this machine by clicking the Configure button next to the service.

   The Remote Installation Setup Services Setup Wizard appears.

3. Click Next, and then the Remove Installation Folder Location screen appears.

4. Choose a directory on an NTFS volume that is not the system drive. Because W2KSERVER1's system is on D, you may choose R:\RemoteInstall, and then click the Next button.

   The Initial Settings screen appears. The RIS server must be turned on to accept client connections.

5. Click the Respond to Client Computers Requesting Service check box. For this example, do not choose Do Not Respond to Unknown Client Computers. Click Next.

6. The Initial Source Files Location screen appears. Type the path of the Windows 2000 Professional CD's i386 directory in the Path box. In this case, the directory is in F:\I386. Click Next.

7. The Windows Installation Image Folder Name screen appears. Enter the name of the directory to create on the server. Keep the defaults as win2000.pro, if desired. Click Next.

8. The Friendly Description and Help Text screen appears. Change these if you want to give special instructions to the people installing the workstations.

9. The Review Settings screen appears. Make sure the values are what you want and click Finish.

10. The Remote Services Setup Installation Wizard continues, as shown in Figure 20.6. It will take a while to copy all the files and create the initial directory. When the installation is finished, the Cancel button will turn into Done. Click Done.

Managing RIS

Now that you've set up RIS, you'll need to know how to manage the new service. Management of RIS is found inside Active Directory Users and Computers.

To manage RIS:

1. Open Active Directory Users and Computers by clicking Start, Programs, Administrative Tools, and then selecting Active Directory Users and Computers.

2. Drill down until you locate the server on which you loaded RIS and double-click it to see the server's properties. Click the Remote Install tab on the Properties screen to see some of the Remote Installation properties, as shown in Figure 20.7.

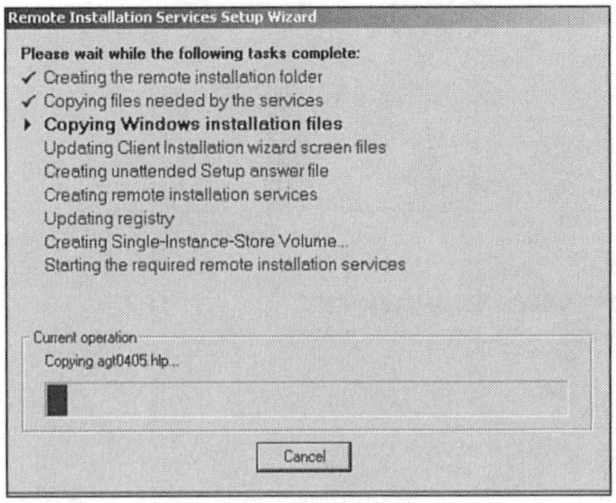

FIGURE 20.6

Windows 2000 Server loads all the Windows 2000 Professional files.

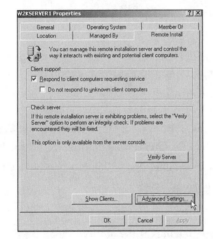

FIGURE 20.7

Use the Remote Installation tab to manage RIS

After RIS is installed, a Remote Install tab appears in the server properties dialog. Click the Advanced Settings button to see additional settings. The W2KSERVER1-Remote-Installation-Services Properties screen appears. as shown in Figure 20.8.

4. You can specify how client computers will be named. Use the drop-down box to select NP plus MAC. This will create computer names such as NP00502213323.

5. You can specify where computer accounts will be created. Use the Browse button to select the Computers directory. Click OK to close the Advanced Properties screen.

6. Click OK to close the Server Properties screen.

Creating a Remote Boot Disk

You're almost ready to start rolling out your clients. You will need a boot disk that emulates the PXE boot ROM if your network card does not have a PXE ROM.

20

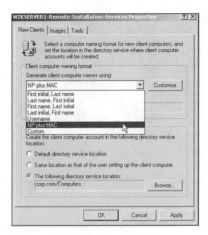

To create a remote boot disk:

1. Run the RBFG.EXE program from the \Admin\i386 directory where you installed
   the RIS service. Click Start, Run, and type `R:\RemoteInstall\Admin\i386\rbfg`
   in the Open dialog box.

2. The Windows 2000 Remote Boot Disk Generator appears. Put a blank floppy in
   the floppy drive and click the Create Disk button to start the boot disk generation.

3. When prompted to create another disk, click No, and click Close to close the
   Windows 2000 Remote Boot Disk Generator.

Installing a Client

One of RIS's most compelling features is the ability to load the client on vastly different
hardware. Because the entire operating system is actually loaded on the machine, the
Plug and Play subsystem can evaluate the differences in real-time.

With boot disk in hand, you're ready to install your first client.

> This procedure will completely erase the client computer's first hard drive, so
> use RIS with caution.

To install a client:

1. Insert the floppy disk into the client computer and turn on the machine.

2. The boot floppy will query for the nearest DHCP server and get an address. When
   prompted, immediately press F12 to start the DOS-based Client Setup Wizard.

3. When the first information screen appears, press Enter to continue.

4. The Client Installation Wizard Logon screen appears. Enter a valid username, password, and domain. In this case, you can enter the username and password of the administrator of the corp domain. Press Enter to continue.

5. At the Client Installation Wizard Caution screen, read the text explaining that all data on the hard drive will be deleted. Agree by pressing Enter.

6. At the Client Installation Wizard Information screen, verify the information is correct and press Enter. This is your last chance to reset the machine to abort the installation.

7. The deep-blue Windows 2000 installation screen will appear, load some necessary files into RAM, automatically format the hard drive, and start the installation.

8. At this point, take the floppy out of the drive and take a coffee break. It will be a while before you can get to the next step. If the floppy is out of the drive, the machine will automatically reboot, and then start and finish the graphical part of the installation.

If all goes well, the computer will be left at a logon prompt waiting for the user to log on for the first time. This type of setup, in conjunction with the power of IntelliMirror's Offline Folders and the Windows Installer (see earlier discussions), can deliver an operating system, the users' data files, and all the applications users need for their work.

There will be no Administrator password on the newly RIPrep'ed machine. You can gain finite control over many aspects of an unattended installation, including Administrator password via tools in the Resource Kit. See the resource kit documentation as well as Microsoft Article Q216300 for more information.

The Remote Installation Prep Tool (RIPrep)

Earlier, we detailed how the Windows Installer can be used to assign applications to users or PCs. If desired, you may alternatively choose to stock a machine full of applications and settings, then use RIS in your machine deployment.

To do this, Windows 2000 Server also comes with the Remote Installation Prep Tool or RIPREP. After you load a Windows 2000 Professional machine full of client software just the way you like it, you can simply run RIPREP and create another image on the server. You can load any applications you like, such as Microsoft Office, Boutell.com's Morning Paper, or anything else that you want to preload on an image. The only caveat is that you must load the software on a machine that you created with the RIS process. Since you just used RIS process to create your first workstation, you're ready to continue.

20

In this example, you will create a special image for the Sales group, which automatically has Microsoft Office and Boutell.com's Morning Paper loaded.

To create additional RIS images:

1. Create your first client as detailed in the preceding exercise.

2. Log on to the client with the local Administrator account, and load the software desired.

Since you're logged in as the local Administrator, the configuration changes, such as icons, only affect the Administrator account. In order for the changed to take affect for every user you'll need to copy the Administrator's profile to the Default User's profile.

3. Right click My Computer and select Properties. Click the User Profiles tab, select the Administrator profile, then click the Copy To button. In the Copy Profile To dialog box, enter the path for the Default User folder, usually c:\Documents and Settings\Default User. Click the Change button, and select the Everyone group to be able to use the profile. Click OK to close the Copy To dialog box, and OK again to close the System Properties dialog box.

4. Run RIPREP from the RIS server. Do this by clicking Start, Run, and then typing \\w2kserver1\remoteinstall\admin\i386\riprep in the shared RIS directory. The RIPREP Wizard starts. Click Next.

5. The Server Name screen appears. By default, the server you used to create this image appears in the Server Name box. Leave the defaults and click Next.

6. The Folder Name screen appears. You can give a somewhat descriptive name for how this image will be used. In this case, target it for the Sales group. Type in the name desired and click Next.

7. The Friendly Description and Help Text screen appears, as shown in Figure 20.9. You can elaborate on what this machine has loaded and click Next.

8. The Programs or Services Are Running screen appears next. You should close all running programs and stop the running services to get the cleanest image possible. Stop the running services and click Next.

To stop services, load the MMC by clicking Start, Run, and typing MMC. Use the Add/Remove Snap-in selection to add the Services snap-in, find the service, and stop it.

9. The Review Settings screen appears. Verify that the information is correct and click Next. One additional information screen appears, stating that this process can be repeated if desired. Click Next to continue.

FIGURE 20.9

When the PXE Boot disk is used, this is the information the people installing the worksta- tion will see to choose from.

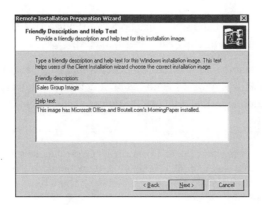

The modified image is loaded on the server (see Figure 20.10). A unique mechanism called Single Instance Store, or SIS, prevents multiple copies of the same system files from eating up your disk space. Each time you create new images, only one copy of each system file will be saved.

FIGURE 20.10

When you run RIPREP.EXE from the client, the changes are sent to the RIS server.

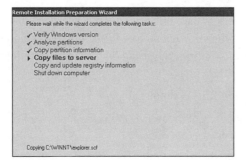

The next time your boot disk is used to load client images, a new menu selection will be available, asking which image is to be loaded.

The System Prep Tool (SYSPREP)

RIS and RIPrep work great to replicate machines' OS and applications if you have a net- work card which supports the PXE architecture. If however, you cannot or don't want to use RIPrep, you can use the System Prep Tool, or SYSPREP.

Deploying machines using SYSPREP may be faster than using RIS and RIPrep, although there is a price to pay: the target hardware must be identical or nearly identical. For instance, you can usually use SYSPREP to "get away" with duplicating a specific make with different models (i.e.: Dell Dimension XPS T 450 Mhz and Dell Dimension XPS T 600 Mhz) but not between a Dell Dimension XPS T 450 Mhz and an IBM PC 300PL

20

300 Mhz). Similarly, you can usually use SYSPREP when small changes between like machines is present, such as a net card or sound card.

Do note, however, that there are three components that may never be different when using the SYSPREP deployment method: a boot device (i.e: IDE vs. SCSI), the HAL (hardware abstraction layer), and the ACPI (power management) BIOS.

> Rumors are that the Microsoft SYSPREP product development team is working on a way to enable SYSPREP to work between dissimilar boot devices (i.e.: IDE vs. SCSI.) This functionality isn't there today, but stay tuned for more information.

SYSPREP does not work in the same fashion as RIS. Because RIS installations actually load the operating system and evaluates the platform and hardware as the installation is occurring, any type of hardware can be used (i.e.: The same RIS image may be used on a Dell Latitude or a Compaq Proliant.)

SYSPREP cannot do this, rather, the installation is "blasted" onto the hard drive, with whatever settings the original machine has. While it's true Windows 2000 has better Plug and Play facilities than Windows NT, using SYSPREP is only supported by Microsoft on like hardware.

The theory behind SYSPREP is simple:

- Install and configure a Windows 2000 Professional workstation chock full of the pre-configured software desired.
- Run SYSPREP on the workstation. SYSPREP will prepare the hard drive for duplication and then automatically instruct the computer to shut down.
- Use your favorite 3rd party disk-duplicator software or hardware product, such as Ghost, ImageCast, DriveImage Professional or ImageMASSter to replicate the computer to target machines.
- When the target machine starts for the first time, unique information will be generated for that machine.

A simple guideline for SYSPREP is presented below. For detailed configuration customization, be sure to read the information in the Windows 2000 resource kit.

> You cannot run SYSPREP on machines that are members of domains. To remove a workstation from a domain, refer to chapter 9, "Users, Groups, and Machine Accounts on Domain Controllers."

To prepare a workstation for duplication with SYSPREP:

1. Install a Windows 2000 Professional workstation using RIS, the CD, over the network, or otherwise. Configure the desired software on the workstation.

2. Create a directory on the workstation called c:\sysprep.

3. Use Explorer to enter the Windows 2000 Professional CD's \support\tools\deploy.cab folder. Copy SYSPREP.exe and Setupcl.exe to the workstation's c:\sysprep folder.

4. Locate and run SYSPREP from the c:\sysprep directory. SYSPREP will modify the workstation then automatically shut it down. Turn off the power to the system.

5. Follow the directions of your disk-duplication hardware or software to duplicate this system to other systems. For this example, don't do this now. Pretend that you've just duplicated this machine by turning on the machine and starting Windows 2000 Professional. When you do this, you will see what other machines will look like once they are restarted after duplication.

6. When the machine first starts up after being duplicated, you'll have several screens of data to enter to customize the machine including agreeing to the license agreements, Regional Settings, Name Personalization, Computer Name, Administrative password, and Time and Date settings.

> As stated, you can generate a completely automated SYSPREP deployment by inspecting and implementing the directives in the resource kit documentation.

Summary

Windows 2000 Server can service DOS, Windows, Windows 9x, Windows NT, Windows 2000 Professional, and Macintosh client computers.

Use Windows Installer to either publish or assign programs targeted for specific machines or users contained in OUs. Use ZAW's policies and IntelliMirror's offline folders and Windows Installer to have users data and applications follow them.

Use the Remote Installation Service (RIS) to roll out multiple desktops without the need for third-party imaging products. Use RIPREP to create customized images after prepping a Windows 2000 Professional machine (created via RIS) with additional programs.

Use SYSPREP to rollout multiple desktops alongside third-party imaging products. Use SYSPREP to create customized images of similar hardware once the desired software is loaded.

20

Workshop

The workshop provides a quiz and exercises to help reinforce your learning. Even if you feel you know the material, you will still gain from working these exercises.

Quiz

1. Which 16-bit clients can connect to Windows 2000 Server?

2. What 32-bit clients can connect to Windows 2000 Server?

3. What protocol must be loaded for Macintosh connectivity?

4. What types of files can Windows Installer load on client machines?

5. What are offline folders?

6. What additional services must be available before RIS will function?

7. What kind of boot ROM must the network card have or be able to emulate in order to support RIS?

8. What program do you use to create a boot disk?

9. What program do you use to load additional client images on to the RIS machine?

10. What program is used to load the changes from a client machine back to the server?

Exercises

1. Test offline folders by logging into a client, saving files to the server, and removing the network cable.

2. Load additional software on your RIS client. Use RIPREP.EXE to load additional client images.

3. Explore the Windows 2000 Resource Kit for additional automated setup options using RIS and SYSPREP.

Hour **21**

Performance Monitoring and Diagnostics

by Barrie Sosinsky

Windows 2000 Server offers you several tools to monitor the performance of your server and network. You can perform diagnostics to locate problems when they arise and to optimize your system. Built into the operating system is a set of events and performance counters that enable you to measure the state of your system and to keep an historical record of its performance.

The following topics are covered:

- How events are monitored by the Windows 2000 operating system
- Using the Event Viewer to check for entries in the log files
- What the Application, Security, and System logs contain, and how to manage them
- How to measure and log the performance of your system using the Performance Monitor
- Using the Performance Logs and Alerts service to create a historical record of performance

- How to use the Network Monitor to understand network performance
- How to create an alert based on a condition

About the Windows Event Model

Windows has a very sophisticated event model. The Event Log service is automatically started when you boot your server.

In fact, the entire operating system is based on the principle that it is reactive to events such as mouse clicks, mouse moves, keystrokes, and other actions. When your computer boots up, hundreds of events are fired off, and each of these is monitored by your system. Some events are recorded to indicate that they were successful, but many ordinary events aren't. Unsuccessful events are typically logged by your system. Events can be related to the operating system, hardware and peripheral devices, device drivers, and applications. User access to resources is monitored in the Security log, and provided you choose to monitor those events, they are also recorded. When you view, open, create, delete, and modify files, folders, and other objects, a system administrator can choose to log those events. This type of operating system is sometimes called a journaling operating system, referring to the log entries that are kept for an historical record.

Error messages indicate a failure of one component in your system, or possibly a setting or application error. These problems can arise from any variety of faults, including hardware malfunctions, disconnected network cables, a newly installed application, or some other error condition. As with all troubleshooting, the best way to find the cause is to isolate individual variables one at a time and work with them.

Using the Event Viewer and the Event Logs

The Event Viewer enables you to view the contents of one of Windows 2000 Server's three built-in logs:

- Application log—An application can post an error message or a condition message, based on an event that the creator of the application programs it to post.
- Security log—The security in the Windows 2000 system records events when resources on the server or network are accessed and used. Logons, access to shared resources, printer usage, and other items are recorded in the Security log. The Security log is turned off by default, and must be turned on by an administrator using the Group Policy console.
- System log—A large number of events are recorded by Windows 2000 Server to the System log.

There might be additional logs when optional components are installed, such as DNS or FTS.

Users can view both the Application log and the System log. Only administrators can view the Security log.

To view an event in the Event Log service, do the following:

1. Select the Computer Management command from the Administrative subfolder in the Programs folder on the Start menu.

2. Double-click the System Tools entry in the Computer Management console (Local) in the left pane.

3. Double-click the Event Viewer in the detail panel of the Computer Management console on the right.

    Figure 21.1 shows you Event Viewer opened to view the various logs.

FIGURE 21.1

The Event Viewer enables you to see various system, application, and security events and to check for successful and failed operations.

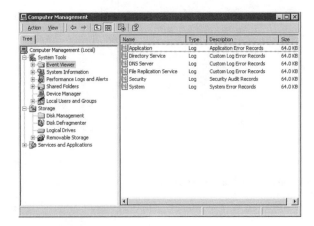

4. Double-click the log you want to view.

    The System log is shown in Figure 21.2.

5. To view the detail of an event, double-click that event in the detail pane on the right side of the console, or select Properties from the Action menu.

    Figure 21.3 shows you the details of an event. You can view the event properties as either binary data (DWORD) or as characters on the Record Data tab by clicking the Bytes radio button. This information is useful to programmers. The description field supports hyperlinks to more detailed information.

21

FIGURE 21.2

The System log (shown in the Event Viewer) offers you information about your system's operation.

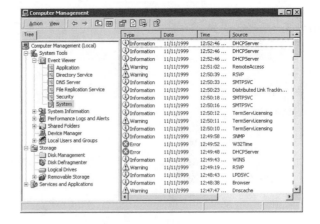

FIGURE 21.3

An error event that occurs when a network cable is disconnected.

6. Click the OK button to remove the event from view.

To use the Computer Management console to view events on remote computers

1. Select the Run command from the Start menu.

2. Type mmc in the Run dialog box, and then click the OK button.

3. Select the Add/Remove Snap-in command from the Console menu, or press the Ctrl+M keystroke.

4. Click the Add button on the Standalone tab.

5. Click Event Viewer in the Add Standalone Snap-in dialog box, and then click the Add button.

6. Click another computer in the Select Computer dialog box, and then enter the path to that computer in the syntax *domainname**computername*.

7. Click the Finish button, click the Close button twice, and then click the OK button.

Not all servers or workstations will have the MMC installed, or the MMC might be running in User mode and cannot be modified on your machine.

What you see in the Event Log service not only changes over time, but you can modify this view by using the commands on the View menu. From this menu, you can select the columns you want to see, filter events based on criteria you select, sort by date, and find events. For example, in your view, you can click a column heading to sort by that event property.

As you view the Event logs, the display might get out-of-date. This is particularly true in situations in which many events are being recorded. The Windows operating system records many events! To refresh the view, select the Refresh command from the Action menu with the log open. Archived logs can be viewed, but not refreshed.

Finding and Filtering Events

To search for a specific event in the log, do the following:

1. With the Event Log service open, select the Find command on the View menu.

   The Find dialog box appears, as shown in Figure 21.4.

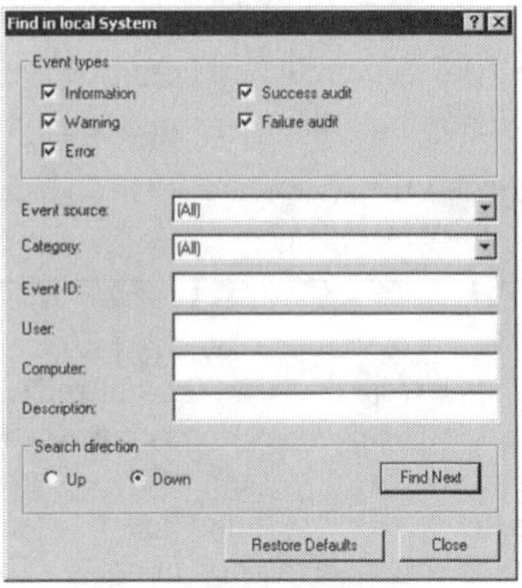

FIGURE 21.4

The Find dialog box is where you search for specific events.

2. Select the types of events to search for in the check boxes at the top of the dialog box.
3. Enter the criteria of the search into any of the following list boxes: Source, Category, Event ID, Computer, User, and Description.
4. Click the Find Next button to move to the first occurrence, either up or down.
5. Click the Close button when you are finished.

To filter the events you see in the Event Viewer:

1. With the Event Log service open, select the log you want to filter.
2. Select the Filter command from the View menu.

   The Filter dialog box appears, as shown in Figure 21.5.

21

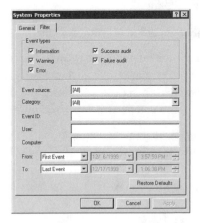

FIGURE 21.5

The Filter tab of the Log Properties dialog box.

3. In the From and To list boxes and spinners, select the range of dates and times for events you want to see.

4. Select the types of events to filter in the check boxes in the middle of the dialog box.

5. Enter the criteria of the search into any of the following list boxes: Source, Category, Event ID, Computer, User, and Description.

   The Filter dialog box properties have much in common with the properties that you can search for in the Find dialog box discussed previously.

6. Click the OK button to return to the Event Viewer with your events shown.

You can clear an Event log so that you see only future events by selecting the Clear all Events command from the Action menu. You will be prompted to save the log as an archive *.EVT file before proceeding. As the Event logs fill up to the maximum allowed size, the oldest events are discarded (last in, last out) if you deselect the Do Not Overwrite Events (Clear Log Manually) option in the Properties dialog box. If you leave this option on, Windows 2000 posts a message box that the log is full when the maximum size is achieved, and you must use the Clear All Events command on the Action menu to flush the log contents.

If you use the Do Not Overwrite Events (Clear Log Manually) option, Windows 2000 will stop when your log is full. You must use the Registry Editor to reset the HKEY_LOCAL_MACHINE\SYSTEM hive's \CurrentControlSet\ Control\Lsa key to CrashOnAuditFail, REG_DWORD, value =1, and then reboot your system.

After you filter your view of the log, you might want to return to the default view of logged events. To do this, you click the General tab of the Log Properties dialog box. Figure 21.6 shows the General tab for the System log. Click the Default button to return to the default view. On this tab, you can also set the log size and what happens to events as they age or the log fills up.

FIGURE 21.6

*On the General tab of
the Log Properties dia-
log box, you can set
the size of an Event log
and its behavior when
it fills up.*

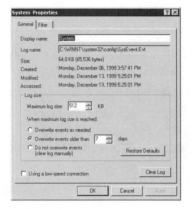

Working with Log Archives

To save the events in a log that you can view later, create an archive file:

1. Open the Event Viewer in the Computer Management console, and select the log
   you want to archive.

2. Select the Save Log File As command on the Action menu.

3. Select the place in the file system you want the log to be stored.

4. Enter the name of the archive in the File Name text box.

5. In the Save As Type list box select Event Log (*.EVT), Text (*.TXT), or CSV
   (comma delimited) (*.CSV).

   An EVT file saves binary and DWORD data, the other two formats save only
   descriptions.

6. Click the Save button.

You can open a saved archive from the console by first opening the Event Viewer and then
selecting the Open Log File on the Action menu. You will be prompted to locate the log file
using the standard system Open file dialog box. Select the file and click the Open button.

Working with the Security Log

Whereas the System log will always contain entries because many things are turned on
by default by the Windows 2000 operating system, that is not the case for the Security
log. You must manually turn on security logging. To perform the following procedure,
you must have administrative privileges.

To turn on security logging, do the following:

1. Select the Run command from the Start menu.

2. Enter mmc /a and then click the OK button.

   Note that the space between the mmc and /a is necessary.

21

3. On the Console menu, select Add/Remove Snap-in, and then click the Add button.

4. In the Snap-in list, select the Group Policy object, and then click Add.

5. In the Select Group Policy Object Wizard that appears, keep the default as Local Computer, and then click the Finish button.

6. Click the Close button followed by the OK button to return to the MMC console.

7. Click the Audit Policy setting in the console, as shown in Figure 21.7.

FIGURE 21.7

The Audit Policy setting for the Security log enables you to control what events are logged in the Security log. You must turn on this feature for it to operate on your system.

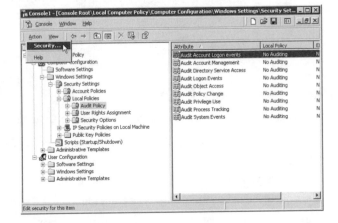

8. In the detail pane, select the event you want to audit.

9. Select the Security command from the Action menu, as shown in Figure 21.7.

10. In the Audit Account Logon Events dialog box, click the events you wish to audit.

11. Click the OK button and continue to enable the events you want to audit in the Security log.

You will probably want to audit the security of the Domain Controller. To do this, you must open the Active Directory Users and Computers console, select the Domain Controller from the list, and select the Properties command from the Action menu. In the Group Policy window, click Audit Policy, and then in the details pane, select the attribute you want to modify. Use the Security command on the Action menu to modify that attribute, exactly as in the preceding procedure.

The same procedure can be used to monitor auditing of files and folders in the Security log. You add a group audit policy for a local machine under the Windows Settings for Audit Object Access, and then use the Security command to set the local policy. After you have enabled files and folders auditing, you can specify which files and folders are audited in the Windows Explorer on an NTFS volume.

To enable file or folder auditing:

1. Open the Windows Explorer.

2. Right-click the file or folder to audit and then select the Properties command.

3. Click the Security tab, and then click the Advanced button.

4. Click the Audit tab; click Add, and in the Select User, Computer, or Group dialog box, select the name of the user or group you want to audit, and then click the OK button.

5. In the Auditing Entry dialog box (shown in Figure 21.8), click the events you want to audit in the Security log.

FIGURE 21.8

The Auditing Entry dialog box for a file or folder enables you to control specific actions that are audited by a user or group.

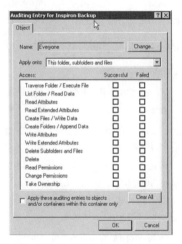

6. Click OK and close all the dialog boxes back to the Windows Explorer.

About Windows Counters

Built into the Windows 2000 operating system is a set of counters of regular events that determines the performance of your system. A counter is often similar to a heartbeat where a signal is generated and sent to a device. Some aspect of the signal is then measured: how long it took for the signal to be recognized, how long it took for the signal to be processed, or how long it took for the signal to be returned. Some counters are always turned on, such as those measuring CPU performance. However, some counters, such as disk measurement counters, require that you add and enable them. The data derived from counters is often referred to as a *performance object*.

21

Counters are supported by different parts of the Windows operating system. The Performance snap-in monitors data from the Windows Management Instrumentation (WMI) interface, which manages hardware and application support. The Performance Helper DLL is the library that interprets WMI output for the Performance snap-in. Other DLLs in the operating system offer counters that measure memory, disk, processor, network cards, and monitor protocols.

When you install a new program or service, that program will often install its own particular performance counters. For example, WINS and SQL Server each add performance counters that help an administrator understand how those programs are running, or help the administrator optimize their performance. When you turn on disk counters, you can measure I/O to disk in bytes per second. You can also measure the performance of your page or swap file to determine how efficiently memory is being used.

The list of commonly used counter objects includes the following:

- Cache—Measure Cache\Data Map Hits%.
- LogicalDisk—For bottlenecks, measure the Logical Disk\Avg. Disk Queue Length. For usage, measure LogicalDisk\% Free Space and Logical Disk\%Disk Time.
- Memory—For bottlenecks or leakage, monitor Memory\Pages/sec, Memory\Pages Reads/sec, Memory\Transition Faults/sec, Memory\Pool Paged Bytes, and Memory\Pooled Nonpaged Bytes. For usage, monitor Memory\Available Bytes and Memory\Cache Bytes. Also related to memory usage are Paging File\%Usage object (all instances), Cache\Data Map Hits%, Server\Pool Paged Bytes, and Server\Pool Nonpaged Bytes.
- Network—For usage, measure Network Segment\%Net Utilization. For throughput, measure the various protocol transmission counters, Network Interface\Packets/sec, Server\Bytes Total/sec, Server/Bytes Sent/sec, and Server\Bytes Received/sec. You might also want to use the Network Monitor here for observations.

 Not all counters are installed on your system, and many counters are not turned on so that they don't create a performance drag on your system. For example, if you want to measure disk performance, you must manually turn on disk counters.

- Paging File—Measure Server\Pool Paged Bytes and Server\Pool Nonpaged Bytes.
- PhysicalDisk—For bottlenecks, measure Disk\Avg. Disk Queue Length (all instances of the physical disk). For usage, monitor Physical Disk\Disk Reads/Sec and Physical Disk\Disk Writes/sec.

- Process—This counter tracks the progress and number of processes running in memory. You can also see the processes running in the Task Manager.
- Processor—For usage, measure Processor\%Processor Time (all instances). For bottlenecks, measure System\Processor Queue Length (all instances), Processor\Interrupts/sec, and System: Context switches/sec.
- Server—The server counters measures server loading.
- System—This counter measures system resources.
- Thread —Processes spawn threads of execution, and this counter tracks the number and progress of threads, which also show the load on your system's CPU from a task standpoint.

For some instructions on using these counters to monitor and troubleshoot specific problems, see the section "Solving Performance Problems" in the online help system. Among the topics discussed are processor, disk, network, Directory Services, QoS ACS, DHCP, browser service, Internet Authentication, DTC, Index service, SMTP service, Internet Information Service, IMDB service, Phone Book service, WINS, fax service, telephony counters, and other activities. A fuller discussion of this topic is also found in the Windows 2000 Resource Kit and in the Windows Knowledge Base. The Knowledge Base is available through the MSDN, and articles can also be found at the Microsoft Web site by entering a problem in the Search text box.

Some of these counters, such as Processor, are single instanced for a single-processor computer, but are multi-instanced when you are working with a multi-processor machine. Instances in which a single counter measures multiple instances, such as a LogicalDisk object measuring the performance of multiple disks or partitions, you can spawn child instances of the counter from the parent instance of the counter. Each instance is separately named or labeled. The definition of the instance and its description as an address using the following syntax

```
Computer_name\Object_name(Instance_name#Index_Name)\Counter_name
```

are called the *counter path*.

When you want to monitor a network or server service, here are some examples of the performance objects you should examine:

- Browser, Workstation, and Server services: Browser, Redirector, and Server objects
- Connection Point service: PBServer Monitor Object
- Directory service: NTDS object

21

- Index and Search features: Indexing Service, Indexing Service Filter, and HTTP Indexing Service objects

- NetBEUI: NetBEUI and NetBEUI resource objects

- Print server: Print Queue object

- QoS ACS (a service that provides a guaranteed network connection): ACS/RSVP Service and Interface objects

- WINS: WINS objects

The Performance Monitor provides an explanation of each counter when you click the Explain button in the Add Counters dialog box.

The Performance Monitor and Performance Logs and Alerts can monitor network computers using remote connections. Both use the Winlogon process to manage user logons and logoffs to these network computers. The Messaging service in Windows is used to give alert notification when these tools are programmed to do so.

Using the Performance Monitor to Measure System and Network Performance

The Performance Monitor is one of the most interesting and useful diagnostic tools in your Windows 2000 arsenal. It allows you to monitor your system in a large number of ways to better understand the capabilities and limitations of your system, as well as to troubleshoot problems. The Performance Monitor is one tool that rewards you for the time you spend with it. With the Performance Monitor (often referred to as *PerfMon*), you can do the following things:

- Measure your server's current workload and analyze device utilization

- Observe changes in a workload as different activities, such as an application's execution in progress

- Monitor the effect of changing your computer's configuration

- Troubleshoot your system by modifying different parameters

- Optimize your system's performance

You can use graphs to monitor current performance or store logs to get an historical record and trends. Logging is also a good way to monitor multiple systems concurrently. When you set up logging, keep the interval long enough so that it doesn't affect network performance. A good place to start is to log settings and conditions every 15 minutes for historical records. Shorter intervals might generate very large log files, and will increase network traffic if you are monitoring a large number of objects and counters. After you determine the proper operation of your system and record it, that information is your system's baseline against which all other activity may be compared.

Microsoft publishes a chart of acceptable values for counters to which you might want to adhere. For example, Microsoft recommends that you utilize no more than 90% of your logical disk, keep processor utilization under 85%, and keep a multiple processor System\Processor Queue Length of 2. To see this chart, go to "Determining acceptable values for counters" in the online help system.

Performance Monitor

Some of the really nice features about the Performance Monitor are that it displays information in a very graphical form, and that you can log the performance counters it measures to log files. You can output data to a printable graph, a histogram, a report, or to an HTML page. You often see graphs from Performance Monitor appear in many articles in the trade press when systems are tested. You can also set thresholds above or below which messages are sent to users to alert them that a condition exists. By saving a monitoring configuration in the Microsoft Management Console, you can return to a performance-monitoring situation or share that configuration with others.

You have seen information about processes that run on your computer in the Task Manager window, as described in "The Task Manager" section of Hour 4, "Using the Windows 2000 Interface." Task Manager provides a snapshot of the applications and processes that are run and a summary of processor and memory usage. In contrast, Performance Monitor can measure these parameters as they are happening in real time or view them from a performance log.

To view a counter in the Performance Monitor, do the following:

1. Select the Performance command from the Administrative Tools folder on the Programs menu of the Start menu.

2. In the Performance Monitor details section, click the + (Add) button on the toolbar.

   The Add Counters dialog box appears (as shown in Figure 21.9); when you click the Explain button, the text window below it will appear.

3. Select the computer you want to monitor by selecting either the Use Local Computer Counters option button or the Select Counters from Computer option button (and naming that computer).

4. In the Performance Object, click the object you want to monitor (CPU, memory, and so on).

5. In the Performance Counter, click the counter(s) you want to add, and then click the Add button to complete the addition.

21

FIGURE 21.9

*In the Add Counters
dialog box, you select
what the Performance
Monitor monitors.
Click the Explain but-
ton to view the
description of the
counter in the window
below.*

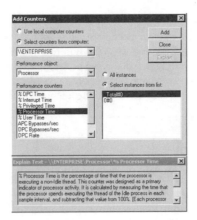

6. If you want to monitor all instances of a counter, click All Instances, or click Select
   Instances from List for selected instances.

   Use the Shift key to scroll and select multiple instances, or the Ctrl key to select
   multiple, nonconsecutive instances.

7. Click the Close button to return to the Performance Monitor and begin tracing the
   performance.

Figure 21.10 shows the Performance Monitor tracing the activity of the CPU.

To delete a counter, select that counter in the bottom pane and press the Delete key.

If you want to view logged data, do the following:

1. Open the Performance Monitor.

2. Right-click the data pane and select the Properties command from the context
   menu.

3. Click the Source tab, and then click the Log File radio button.

4. Click the Browse button and locate the log file of interest.

5. Click the OK button.

The System Monitor Properties dialog box is where you alter many other aspects of the
Performance Monitor's appearance. On the General tab, you can change the type of display (graph, histogram, or report), alter its appearance and values, as well as update the
time. You can also show or hide the legend, value bar, and toolbar by using those check
boxes. On the Data tab, you can add and delete counters from the display. If you have
many counters running in the Performance Monitor, you will also want to change the
color, line width, and styles of the lines on the Data tab. The Graph tab enables you to
label the axis and to set the range or scale of the Y axis so that it is easier to view the
traces. The Colors and Fonts tabs also help you modify the appearance of the display.

FIGURE 21.10

The Performance Monitor is shown tracing CPU performance. The large gray line (red on your monitor) on the left is the current location of the trace.

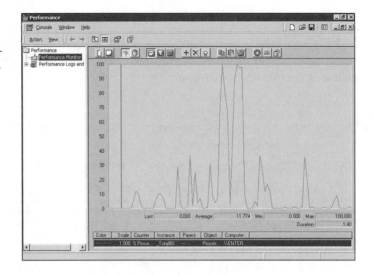

The Performance Monitor can monitor a wide variety of data. Broadly speaking, you can monitor performance objects, performance counters, and object instances. Objects can provide a view into memory usage, application performance, system services, and other processes running on your computer. You can monitor data from your local computer and from other computers over the network to which you have administrative privileges. Data you collect can be in real time or accessed from a Counter log. Performance Monitor allows you to collect data either manually or automatically, stopping and starting your observations as required.

Use Performance Monitor to analyze capacity for your network and to upgrade components when required. You can compare logged data with current data to observe changes.

Generally speaking, because you can monitor both locally and remotely using the Performance Monitor, it is a good idea to consider the impact of such monitoring activity on both the local computer and on the network. Although it is simpler to collect information at a central console, you might want to split up the monitoring into local instances to avoid unnecessary network traffic.

Performance Logs and Alerts

Starting with Windows 2000, the Performance Logs and Alerts service was added that enables you to either view the data as it is collected, or view it later. Information about your local computer or other computers on the network can be collected by this service.

21

Counter data can be viewed in a variety of programs in real time, or it can be exported in standard file formats to be used in other programs at a later date. Performance Logs and Alerts is another way that you can view system and network performance, and it is independent of the Performance Monitor.

To create a counter log:

1. Select the Performance command from the Administrative Tools folder on the Programs menu of the Start menu.

2. Double click Performance Logs and Alerts in the left pane.

3. Click Counter Logs in the tree panel on the left side.

   Any counter logs will appear in the detail pane on the right. A green light indicates a running log, whereas a red light is a stopped log.

4. Right-click the details pane and select the New Log Settings command from the New command from the context menu.

5. Enter a name in the Create New Log Settings dialog box, and then click the OK button.

   The My Log dialog box appears.

6. On the General tab, click the Add button to add the counters of interest to your log file.

7. Click the Files tab to set the file size, type, location, and other attributes, as shown in Figure 21.11.

FIGURE 21.11

The Log Files tab of the My Log dialog box is where you set file attributes for your log.

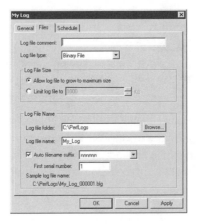

8. Click the Schedule tab to set the start and the stop times for data collection.

9. Click the OK button to save your settings.

To start your log, right-click the log in the detail pane and select the Start command. Use the Stop command from this same menu to stop collecting data. Windows ships with a Systems Overview log that you can use as an example for your work. The Start and Stop commands are also on the All Tasks from the context menu you see when you right click on the log.

You can save your log file in any of the following formats:

- Comma Separated Values (*.CSV), a text file read by databases, spreadsheets, and word processors.
- Tab Separated Values (*.TSV), a text file read by databases, spreadsheets, and word processors.
- Binary file (*.BLG for binary log), a sequential file that saves multiple instances.
- Binary Circular file (also *.BLG), which records a file of a certain size, overwriting previous entries.
- Circular Trace file (*.ETL), which records data continuously to the same file, over-writing previous data.
- Sequential Trace file (*.ETL), which also records a sequential trace log file until the maximum size of the log is reached. Then a new file is started.

Performance Logs and Alerts shares many of the same attributes as the Performance Monitor. It measures performance objects, performance counters, and object instances. You can set up automatic or manual sampling and schedule logging. You can also create trace logs to record data about a specific kind of activity. A trace log takes a snapshot of a condition at an interval you determine.

Using the Network Monitor

The Network Monitor allows an administrator to view and correct problems on your net-work. You might need to go to the Add/Remove Windows Components applet in the Control Panel to install the Network Monitor, if it isn't already on your server. You might also need to go to the Network and Dial-Up Connections folder on the Settings submenu of the Start menu to install a Network Monitor driver. To do either of these procedures, look in the online help system under the topics "Install Network Monitor" and "Install the Network Monitor Driver." Network Monitor uses a network driver interface specifica-tion (NDIS) driver to copy all frames it detects into its capture buffer. This driver can work with and be bound to your server's network adapter.

To understand network activity, you need to "listen" to your network using the Network Monitor by capturing a few frames or examining the packets those frames contain. Frames may be broadcast or multicast; the difference being that with a broadcast frame there is one intended destination, whereas with a multicast frame, additional com-puters may receive the data. A directed frame has a host sender and a specific recipient.

21

A broadcast frame must be examined by each host to determine if it was intended for that computer.

This will tell you information about the level of usage of your network, the types of packets being transmitted, by whom and to whom those packets are being transmitted, network-related hardware and software problems, and many other things. The Network Monitor that comes with Microsoft Systems Management Server (SMS) is a more complete version of this product.

To capture (or copy) network frames:

1. Select the Network Monitor command from the Administrative Tools submenu on the Program menu of the Start menu.

2. You are prompted to select a default network, or else the Network Monitor selects your current LAN for you; click the OK button at the default local network screen, then click the OK button at the network introduction message screen.

3. Select the Start command from the Capture menu, or press the F10 key.

   Figure 21.12 shows the Network Monitor with some frames captured. The top-left pane shows network throughput and utilization, the middle-left pane shows network addresses, and the bottom pane shows the frames that were detected. Additionally, the right pane shows overall statistics.

FIGURE 21.12

The Network Monitor enables you to listen in to your network and view network utilization.

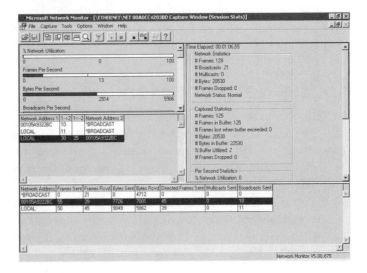

4. When you are done, select the Exit command from the File menu.

5. Network Monitor asks whether you want to save the captured frames; click Yes to do so, or No to discard the data.

You can capture all frames, or just the frames that a filter you create allows. Using filters helps simplify the analysis of your network monitoring. You can also create display filters to output only specific kinds of data for analysis.

You can also use the Network Monitor to respond to frames that it receives. For example, you can specify a trigger event that will launch a program (executable file) when it is detected. In order to protect network traffic, the Network Monitor will capture only frames sent to and from the local computer, as well as overall network statistics. That makes it impossible to eavesdrop on communications meant for others. There is also a facility to detect other instances of the Network Monitor on the network in the program.

The Network Monitor comes with its own online help system that describes its use. Select the Help Topics command to view this information. Among the topics covered in the help system are

- Configuring Network Monitor
- Capturing network data
- Interpreting results of captured data

You can do a wide range of network diagnostics using the Network Monitor, but it is a fairly simple tool compared to some of the third-party utilities on the market today. The Network Monitor is most useful in determining network utilization and which computer is generating large amounts of network traffic (the largest broadcaster), as well as which computer is the recipient of large amounts of network traffic. You can look at individual network frames, but the capabilities of this tool in that area are limited.

How to Monitor Services

Many Windows 2000 services install their own counters when you install those services, and activate those counters when you turn on the services. The following services can be monitored in this way: Browser Service, DHCP Service, Directory Service, Fax Service, IMDB Service, Indexing Service, Internet Authentication Services, Internet Information Service, Monitoring WINS Service, Phone Book Service, QoS Service, SMTP Service, Telephony Service, and WINS Service. The counters for each of these services are described in more detail in the online help system.

How to Create Alerts

You can set the Performance Monitor or Performance Logs and Alerts so that an alert is created when a certain minimum or maximum threshold is reached. The following exercise shows you how.

21

To create an alert, do the following:

1. Open the Performance Monitor as before.

2. Double click on Performance Logs and Alerts in the tree pane on the left.

3. Click Alerts.

   Existing alerts will appear in the detail pane with a green icon if they are active and a red icon if they are stopped.

4. Right-click the detail pane and select the Create New Alert Settings command on the context menu.

   The Create Alert Settings From command enables you to create an alert from an HTML page.

5. In the Create New Alert Setting dialog box, enter a name for the alert, and then click the OK button.

6. On the General properties tab, enter a comment for the alert, and then add the counters to be measured, the alert thresholds, and the sampling interval.

7. Click the Action tab to set up an action based on the alert; launch a log entry, a network message, or an executable file, as shown in Figure 21.13.

FIGURE 21.13

On the Action tab of the New Alert Properties dialog box, you set the result of the alert.

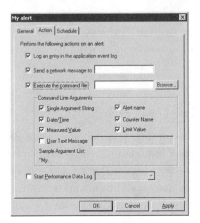

8. Click the Schedule tab to start and stop the log.

9. Click the OK button to return to the Performance Monitor and create the alert.

Summary

Windows 2000 gives you a rich set of tools to monitor the condition of your system, other computers on your network, and the network itself. By using counters built into the operating system and measuring events that are either turned on by default or that you can enable yourself, you can troubleshoot many problems that might arise.

In this hour, three main tools were described. The Event Viewer enables you to view a record of successful and failed events that your system posts. There are three log files you can open with the Event Viewer to determine your system's performance: the Application, Security, and System logs. The Performance Monitor enables you to measure counters that determine the performance of a whole host of parameters. You can use this tool to get a baseline of your system to compare with when problems arise. You can also use PerfMon to optimize your system and to do capacity planning. The third tool described was the Network Monitor. This tool enables you to view network traffic and utilization and other information of your computer and other computers across the network wire.

Workshop

The workshop provides a quiz and exercises to help reinforce your learning. Even if you feel you know the material, you will still gain from working these exercises.

Quiz

1. How do I open the System log to see why my computer is malfunctioning?
2. Why don't I see any events in the Security log?
3. What happens when a log reaches its maximum size?
4. What is the difference between a counter and a performance object?
5. What counter(s) should I use to view processor usage?
6. What is a baseline and why would I want to have one?
7. What is a performance log?
8. Why do I need a network monitor driver?
9. How do I create an alert based on a condition?
10. Why do system administrators get paid the big bucks?

Exercises

1. In a multiprocessor system, set up processor utilization counters for each processor in the system and view the performance as your run different applications.
2. If you have a RAID system, measure performance for each physical and logical disk.
3. Set up an alert when your disk usage goes above 85%.

21

HOUR **22**

Programming Tools

by Barrie Sosinsky

Windows continues support for the command-line interface that began in MS-DOS. The Command Prompt applet supports many MS-DOS commands, batch files, and commands of individual applications, such as Windows Terminal Services. Microsoft added the Windows Scripting Host (WSH) in Windows 98 and upgraded it in Windows 2000. The Windows Scripting Host is a shell and management tool that enables you to call and run programs to administer many elements of the operating system. This powerful feature enables you to change many fundamental networking properties, such as the Active Directory, and it is the key to many advanced capabilities of the operating system.

The following topics are covered in this hour:

- How to open the Command Prompt applet and modify its window
- Some of the commands and batch files supported by the Command Prompt
- The Windows Management Interface and its support for programmed control of devices

- The Windows Scripting Host's support for programs written in high-level languages
- How the Windows Scripting Host works, and how to control aspects of the Active Directory with it
- Writing logon and logoff scripts with the WSH
- Controlling environmental variables with the WSH

Using the Command Line

Windows 2000 retains the Command Prompt applet found in Windows NT 4.0, Windows 98, and other versions of the Windows operating system. This Control Panel applet contains a 32-bit program that duplicates many of the commands found in MS-DOS. As an administrator, you will often find yourself opening a command prompt to run an Internet or TCP/IP utility, such as PING, to modify an environmental variable, or to perform some other function, such as to create and run a batch file, to perform interprocess communication, and to provide redirection between applications and subsystems. This brief section and the section that follows introduce some of the things you might want to do at the command prompt.

You open the Command Prompt by choosing the Command Prompt command from the Accessories folder on the Programs submenu of the Start menu. You quit the Command Prompt by entering EXIT at the prompt and pressing the Enter key; by selecting the Close command on the System menu; by double-clicking the System menu box; or by clicking the Close box on the window title bar. Figure 22.1 shows the Command Prompt window with a command's help shown.

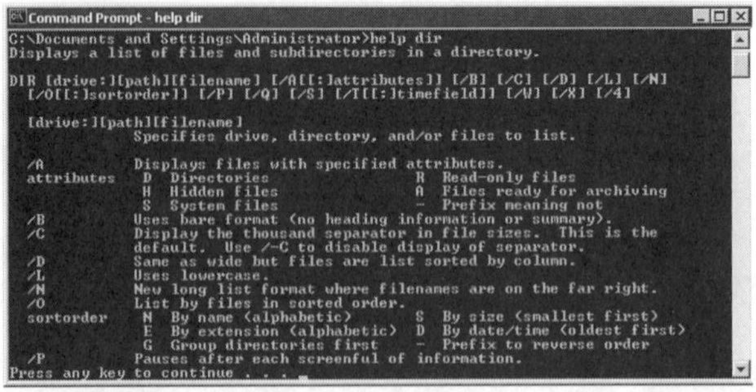

FIGURE 22.1

The Command Prompt window with displayed help syntax.

The Command Prompt usually opens by default on x86 systems in a window, and you can switch between a window and full screen by using the Alt+Enter keystroke. (Alt+Enter is not to be confused with Alt+Tab, the "Cool Switch," that switches sequentially between open applications on Windows.) On RISC systems, the Command Prompt is usually full screen.

You can modify the properties of the Command Prompt window through the Command Prompt Control Panel applet, or by selecting the Properties command from the System menu on the Command Prompt window. Obvious things such as fonts, font size, layout, and color can be changed. You can also change the Command History buffer, put the editing into insert or overstrike mode, and change other features.

Getting Help at the Command Prompt

To get Command Prompt help, type the following at the prompt:

help—A brief list of commands is displayed.

commandname/?—A specific command instruction is displayed.

net help—A brief list of network commands is displayed.

net help *commandname*—Help for a specific command is listed.

net *commandname* /?—The syntax for the network command is shown.

net helpmsg *message#*—An explanation of a numbered network help message is shown.

A Command List

The following commands are among those offered in the Windows 2000 operating system:

AT—A timed command using the Scheduler service.

ATTRIB—Displays file attributes.

CACLS—Displays or modifies the access control lists (ACLs) of files.

CHDIR (CD)—Changes directories.

CHKDSK—Runs CheckDisk to correct disk problems.

CLS—Clears the screen.

COMP—Compares the contents of two files on a byte-by-byte basis. Use DISKCOMP to compare two floppy disks. Use FC to compare two files and list the differences between them.

COMPACT—Displays and changes the compression of files and directories on an NTFS volume.

CONVERT—Converts FAT to NTFS.

COPY—This command copies files to another location. Use DISKCOPY to copy the files on one floppy disk to another.

DATE and TIME—Display the system date and time, and offer you the chance to change them.

DEL (ERASE)—Deletes files.

DIR—Displays the current directory.

EXIT—Closes the Command Prompt window and ends a CMD.EXE session.

EXPAND—Expands a compressed file, such as those on distribution disks.

FIND—Searches for a string within a file or files. Use FINDSTR to search for text using liberal text or regular expressions.

FORMAT—Formats disks and drives. Its many switches enable you to have fine control over the file systems created.

LABEL—Creates or modifies a disk label.

MKDIR (MD)—Creates or makes a directory.

MODE—Configures system devices such as printers, Command Prompt windows, keyboards, serial devices, and communication devices, and modifies their properties.

MORE—The MORE command stops screen output when you fill the screen and displays another screen full when the Enter key is pressed.

RENAME (REN)—Renames files.

RMDIR (RD)—Deletes a directory.

START—Starts an application or command in another window.

SUBST—Substitutes a path with a drive letter.

XCOPY—Copies files and directories, and when the E and S switches are used this command will also copy all subdirectories that are not empty. Use the Help system for detailed information about options, switches, and syntax.

Batch Files

You can create text files that can be run from the Command Prompt window by using the preceding list of commands. Create the files and give them the extension of BAT or COM for batch or command files, respectively. Batch files also offer additional commands, such as GOTO, for conditional branching and logic. Running a batch file is similar to executing commands one at a time automatically from the Command Prompt. Other batch commands enable you to run other batch files inside a batch file, input data, send data to the console (screen), and call other batch files.

You start a batch file by entering its name and path at the command prompt. To pause an executing batch file, use the Ctrl+S keystroke or the Pause button. To cancel a running batch file, press the Ctrl+Break keystroke or the Ctrl+C keystroke. Sometimes you will find that the ESC key will also end command execution.

You can create batch files using most of the commands that were supported in MS-DOS.

Windows Terminal Commands

> Many programs have their own command-line support. For example, you can administer many databases, such as SQL Server, by using the command line. Check the online help for an application to see what command-line support is offered.

WTS supports a command-line interface. If you go to the Command Prompt window and type in the commands shown in Table 22.1, you can alter the behavior of WTS. Consult online help (see the "Terminal Server Command Reference" section) for the additional options offered by these commands.

TABLE 22.1   Console Commands

Command	Purpose
CHANGE LOGON	Turn on and off logons to WTS
CHANGE PORT	Modify COM port mappings for MS-DOS programs
CHANGE USER	Modify .INI file mappings for current user
CPROFILE	Remove user file associations from the user's profile
DBGTRACE	Turn on and off debug tracing
FLATTEMP	Enable or disable flat temporary directories
LOGOFF	Terminate a client session
MSG	Send a message to a client
PERUSER	Enable or disable per-user file associations
QUERY OBJECT	Display the objects in a namespace
QUERY PROCESS	Display information about processes
QUERY SESSION	Display information about sessions
QUERY TERMSERVER	Show the terminal services active on a network
QUERY USER	Display a list of users logged on to the system
RESET	Reset settings

continues

TABLE 22.1 continued

Command	Purpose
RESET SESSION	Reset a session
SHADOW	Monitor a user session
TSCON	Connect to an existing session
TSDISCON	Disconnect a client from a current session
TSKILL	Terminate a process
TSPROF	Copy user configuration and change the profile path
TSSHUTDN	Shut down a Terminal Services server

About the Windows Scripting Host

Starting with the introduction of Windows 98 and continuing in the Windows 2000 operating system, Microsoft has quietly introduced a scripting framework, called the Windows Scripting Host, that enables an administrator to automate many tasks using the language of his or her choice. Although the WSH has received little trade press exposure, it is actually one of the most significant system management tools in an administrator's arsenal. WSH 1.0 shipped with Windows 98. WSH 2.0 is installed with Windows 2000, and the software is available for download from the Microsoft Web site for the Windows 95, Windows NT 4.0, and Windows 98 operating systems.

The WSH will be used mostly to build administrative scripts. As such, Microsoft sees the WSH as a long-term replacement for the batch files that have been used for many years with MS-DOS. The WSH is not a language, but is instead a framework that allows a script to call a language interpreter and pass instructions and parameters to it. The language, be it VBScript (Microsoft Visual Basic Scripting Edition), JavaScript, or Microsoft JScript, will then interpret the script and compile the program for execution. Microsoft intends to work with developers to see that other popular languages, such as Perl and REXX, have interpreters written for the WSH. When a script is executing, it is the role of the WSH to manage the necessary windowing, supply input and output files, and perform other high-level system functions that let the programs operate. You can think of the WSH as a kind of programming framework.

The WSH is also part of the Microsoft management infrastructure that also includes the Windows Management Instrumentation (WMI) specification. The WMI is a device-management specification. A device driver written to the WMI specification on a Windows system supports the WMI interface and lets the driver interact with other system services. A WMI driver can record performance counters, measure error statistics, and record device failure alerts. Applications designed to interact with the WMI can report on this information.

Additionally, applications that conform to the WMI standard have control over device characteristics and can change low-level device settings. An WMI application could change an interrupt or memory setting on a board without a jumper being physically changed. Furthermore, WMI applications can be accessed over TCP/IP and can appear as applets within a browser on a console elsewhere on the network.

The WMI operates as a layer in the kernel mode, communicating directly with Windows device drivers built to the Windows Driver Model (WDM) specification. As such, it gathers information from the drivers that applications can display. The WMI is a Windows-specific technology that currently runs only on Windows 98 and Windows 2000. The WSH is a set of user-mode routines to manage scripts that can automate administrative actions that work through the WMI. The WDM drivers support the WMI standard, but vendors writing the driver must add support for WMI features into the driver to take advantage of the WMI. The WMI also supports other device driver standards, such as the NDIS (Network Driver Interface Specification) network adapter drivers and SCSI drivers.

Drivers written to avail themselves of WMI services use a Managed Object Format (MOF) file to store device information. An MOF enables you to store errors, performance, and other data as attributes for entities. MOFs are used by Windows 2000 to store information about a variety of common devices. Developers and vendors can also extend MOF definitions to add attributes and capabilities.

Using Scripts

The WSH is COM-aware and is a controller for the ActiveX scripting engine. In that regard, it is similar to Internet Explorer, but with much lower memory requirements. The WSH is useful for both interactive and noninteractive scripting.

The WSH enables you to write scripts as text files that can be interpreted by languages to run on 32-bit Windows systems. The interpreter doesn't actually compile the script into machine-readable commands until the script is executed. That makes this system slower than typical binary programs, but it is significantly easier to work with, modify, and maintain. You write the script in the language you want to program in (such as VBScript), and then you call the script from a command prompt with a command such as the following:

```
cscript //[host parameters] myscript.vbs /[script parameter]
```

In this command, CSCRIPT (CSCRIPT.EXE) starts the command-line version of the WSH, passing it the name of the program you want to run. You can pass along a set of host parameters. For example, the T:60 parameter tells the WSH to terminate the program if there is one minute of inactivity. In the sample command, the // portion passes parameters to the WSH, whereas the / portion passes parameters to the script itself.

The following is a list of host parameters you can pass to the CSCRIPT engine:

//B—Run in batch mode without alerts, errors, or user input.

//H:cscript or //H:wscript—Set the command-line or Windows version of WSH as the default.

//I—Run in the interactive mode with alerts and errors displayed, and with input prompts shown.

//Logo—Display the banner at run time. Use //Nologo to suppress the banner.

//S—Save the current command-prompt options for a particular user.

//T:nnnn—End the script after inactivity of nnnn seconds (up to 32,767 seconds). Without this setting, the script will execute without limit until you terminate it or it ends. Typically, scripts are passed this parameter.

//?—Show command usage.

When you create a script file for use in the graphical mode, you must register the extension of that file with the Windows-based scripting host (WSCRIPT.EXE). When you double-click an unassociated file, you are given the chance to create an association in the Open With dialog box. After association, all files of that extension will open and run automatically in the WSH.

To set global properties for the Windows-based scripting host, locate the WSCRIPT.EXE file using the Windows Explorer (it's in the d:\winnt\system32 directory), right-click WSCRIPT.EXE, and select the Properties command. You can also set properties for individual script files in this manner. Properties for scripts are saved in a .WSH file, which is a text file that looks like an .INI file. In many ways, a .WSH file is like the old .PIF files that were used for running 16-bit applications in Windows NT 3.51 and Windows 3.1. You can run a script by double-clicking the .WSH file in Windows Explorer, or by passing the script name as an argument to CSCRIPT.EXE or WSCRIPT.EXE in the Run dialog box.

 The Windows Scripting Host is part of Windows 2000 and Windows 98. You can add the WSH to Windows 95 OSR2 as well as to Windows 4.0.

The WSH also has a version (WSCRIPT.EXE) that will run a script as a file in the Windows interface. When you create a script file, you can either double-click the file icon to launch the script and run the program, or you can enter the script file and its path in the Run dialog box opened from the Start menu. The WSH will then send the script to the language interpreter, pass along any required files, and open any required windows on your screen where the script interpreter can display the results.

22

The WSH provides a much richer programming model than writing batch files. By using the WSH, you have access to the WSH object model, which is similar to the object models you would use in Visual Basic or JScript. Every script can access WSCRIPT objects, including all their methods and properties. This enables you to use standard methods to invoke things such as OLE automation object. You can, for example, command components of Microsoft Office or any other application that is a registered automation server, to provide services to your script.

Among the tasks you might want to use the WSH for are

- Logon and logoff scripts
- Turning on and off computer and network devices such as printers
- System administration
- Installing software
- Backing up or optimizing hard drives
- Writing macros or batch files
- Sending email to users when a condition is met

> There are Windows Scripting Host sample scripts on the Microsoft Web site that you can download and run.

Even more interestingly from a Windows 2000 administrator's viewpoint, the WSH enables you to command services from the Active Directory by using the ADSI (Active Directory Services Interface). All the information in the Active Directory is available to your script, and it can be modified by a script. This feature enables you to automate the control over users and groups, machines, and other properties of your network.

For example, imagine a situation in which you want to deploy a large number of new computers on your network and create machine accounts in the Active Directory. You could do it by opening up the Active Directory Users and Computers administrative tool and by adding the computers one at a time using the MMC. For a few computers, that would be fine. For tens—or hundreds—of computers, that would be tedious. As an alternative, you could automate the procedure using the WSH.

Because you have the ability to manage the Active Directory properties, you can create a script that accesses the data stored in an Excel spreadsheet, an Access database, or even a simple data file, parses that data, and then registers the data in the Active Directory. Your data could contain fields for the Directory Services (DS) root, machine name, machine description, and other properties of the computers you want to register.

Logon Scripts

Logon scripts are a particularly valuable application of the Windows Scripting Host. You can create a script that establishes network connections (but not to create new connections), sets an environmental parameter (such as the search path, TEMP directory, and so on), and launches a program at startup. Creation of logon scripts is optional, but it is worth exploring for an administrator with some basic programming skills.

To create a logon script, create a text file in your text editor for each user type or group of users, and then use the User Properties page to assign the script to multiple users, domains, and organizational units. Among the parameters you can pass in this logon script are the following:

%HOMEDRIVE%—The user's drive containing his or her home directory

%HOMEPATH%—The user's home directory path

%OS%—The user's operating system

%PROCESSOR_ARCHITECTURE%—The user's processor type

%PROCESSOR_LEVEL%—The user's processor level or speed

%USERDOMAIN%—The user's domain name

%USERNAME%—The user's name

You assign logon scripts to a user account or group account by entering the path to the script file in the Directory Service Manager User Properties page. You can also assign logon and logoff scripts, as well as machine startup and shutdown scripts, as a policy in the Group Policy editor. Paths can be absolute or relative to the logon script path.

Logon scripts are something that you will probably want to replicate across the network so that if the domain controller fails, additional copies on other domain controllers can be used. Every primary and backup domain controller should have replicated logon scripts for users. You can use the Replicator Service to create identical copies of the directory tree on other computers. The master copy is maintained on the Export server and replicated to the Import servers using this service.

To set the logon script path for each server in a domain, use the Server Manager or the Server option in each server's Control Panel, and enter the local path to user logon for the replicated scripts.

Managing Environmental Variables

You might also want to control various environmental variables as part of your startup script. Among the variables you might want to change are the search path (PATH), the TEMP directory, and memory usage. To view a system's current environmental settings, open the System applet of the Control Panel and click the Environmental Variables tab.

22

System environmental settings are machine specific and not user specific. No matter who logs on, these environmental settings are specified at startup. User environmental settings change for the particular user. You can set user environmental settings in logon scripts.

Summary

In this hour, you were briefly introduced to batch files and to the commands supported by the Command Prompt. The commands that Windows Terminal Server offers you were described as an example of how that service can be controlled with commands at the command line.

The main part of this hour was the discussion of the Windows Scripting Host and the Windows Management Interface. The WMI offers low-level device driver support for control of various real and virtual devices through an API. The Windows Scripting Host is a framework and management tool for calling programs in VBScript, JScript, and other high-level programming languages that enable you to modify the Windows 2000 interface, network properties, and the properties of the Active Directory by using the ADSI. The WSH manages the windows and other interface features needed to support these programs.

Workshop

The workshop provides a quiz and exercises to help reinforce your learning. Even if you feel you know the material, you will still gain from working these exercises.

Quiz

1. What is the file that controls the Command Prompt applet?
2. How do I switch between windowed and full-screen sessions of the Command Prompt applet?
3. What is a batch file?
4. What command do I use from the Command Prompt window to modify .INI file mappings for a current user in WTS?
5. What operating systems support the Windows Scripting Host 2.0?
6. What programming languages does the WSH support?
7. What is the Windows Management Interface?
8. What are the versions of the WSH?
9. How does the WSH modify domain properties?
10. Why would I use a logon script?

Exercises

1. Get a listing of the various commands supported by the Command Prompt applet and try to use them.

2. Create a simple batch file that copies a directory and all of its subdirectories and then deletes the original directory.

3. Log on to the Microsoft Web site and download some of the examples of script used with the WSH. Try some of those examples.

Hour **23**

Security Services

by Barrie Sosinsky

Some of the most important aspects of network computing are the establishment of security services, authentication mechanisms, and limits of data access. In previous hours, you were introduced to the assignment of access rights and privileges to users and groups, as well as methods for managing password authentication in domains. The security requirement of WAN internetworking technology requires a whole new level of security concerns. New secure Internet protocols are now supported.

Windows 2000 Server adds a security system based upon certificates using the Kerberos version 5 authentication protocol that identifies the user and provides access to services. This certificate service is built into the Active Directory. Software is added to the operating system to provide support for a certificate authority, which is a server service that can be set up on your network. A certificate server can be based upon an outside authority or can be set up on your internal network. In addition to certificates, Windows 2000 Server adds security features in hardware, such as the Encrypting File System (EFS) and smart card support. Many of these new features are described in this hour.

The following topics are covered:

- How public and private keys are used to provide secure data transfer between users and systems
- What a certificate is, and how to set up a certificate server
- What types of hardware security devices you can add to Windows 2000 Server
- How to use the Encrypting File System to secure files and folders on an NTFS volume
- The benefits offered by using the IPSec protocol, and how that protocol functions

How Key Pairs Work

The principles used to establish your network identification in a transaction aren't much different than what you would use in a store—it's just a lot more secure. When you purchase an item in a store, you march up to the counter with your items and offer money to the clerk. Money is a secure transaction (in theory) because currency carries identification issued by the government that can be recognized. Real money is déclassé entering the new millennium, so perhaps you offer a check. In that case, the clerk will likely ask you for a driver's license, which also is certified by a government agency. So, let's say you decide to present a credit card. In that case, the transaction is sent to the credit card agency, the account is validated, and your signature is matched to the signature on the credit card. Often, you are also asked to present a driver's license to cross-check the credit card signature.

What's common to all these mechanisms is that a standards organization provides a credential that tells the store that you are using a valid method of payment, and in some of these cases (not with checks), that money exists to assure the store owners that they will be paid. Additionally, in all cases other than direct monetary payment, you provide credentials in the form of a signature and photo match to verify that you are who you say you are and that these payment vehicles belong to you.

In a Windows 2000 network, a user can log on to any computer in the system; an IP address is not a validation of a user's identity. Therefore, your login must be your validation in a distributed networking system. Windows NT did a good job of validating usernames and passwords at login, encrypting this information, and passing along the access information to other servers.

Consider a situation in which authentication is passed along from one server to another. Not only does a distributed networking system require that the user be authenticated, but also it is equally important that servers require authentication from one another. Therefore, both the server and the user must be able to prove their identities. In a situation in which a server isn't identified, it's possible for that server to impersonate another server. That couldn't be the case in a tightly controlled network environment because two servers can't share the same names or IP addresses. But in an Internet environment, you don't have control over server names, and this risk is much greater.

The method used to identify resources on a network is based on a set of key pairs. In a key pair, a public key is transmitted to others and a private key is closely held. Authentication requires that the two keys be used together. Any information sent by using data encrypted with a public key can be decrypted only by using the private key. If you have only one of these keys, the encryption process is a one-way street.

Following along in our analogy of the store sale, key pairs require that someone authenticates that a key is both valid and that it belongs to a particular individual or enterprise. That organization is called a *Certificate Authority* (CA). A CA stores the public key and keeps a listing of the certificates that have been issued. In a secure transaction, key pairs are used to verify the identification of the server, and the CA is used to identify the ownership or identity of the server. There are several CAs offering these services, but the best-known company in this small industry is Verisign. When you open the Microsoft Management Console's Certificate snap-in in Windows 2000 Server, you will see several different commercial CAs that are trusted by default by this operating system.

23

Kerberos Authentication

Although key pairs and certificates provide a means for identifying servers and users to one another in a distributed networking architecture, after a user has been identified to the system there must be a method to allow that user to gain access to the networking resources to which that person is allowed access. In Windows NT Server, after the login was completed, additional access to network resources still required that a domain controller authenticate the user for additional access. This system of authentication increases network traffic, places additional burdens on domain controllers, and makes the network susceptible to failure when a domain controller becomes unavailable—as might often be the case in an Internet connection where the connection is transient in nature.

Windows 2000 introduces a new method for authentication based on the Kerberos protocol, which is part of the Active Directory. Kerberos is an Internet standard approved by the Internet Engineering Task Force in RFC 1510. When you install Active Directory, you also install the Kerberos Key Distribution Center (KDC) as a service. Any Windows 2000 system supports the Kerberos protocol, and its operation is handled transparently by the operating system. There are no settings for a system administrator to attend to.

Kerberos both authenticates a user and creates a session ticket. Continuing the previous analogy to purchasing items in a store, Kerberos asks you for identification when you walk into the store and issues you a ticket. You can show this ticket to the teller any number of times, or use the ticket to access other services in the store, and no additional identification is required. When you leave the store, your ticket expires.

In Windows 2000 network terms, any time you request access to a network resource, the ticket Kerberos creates for your session is passed along to the access control list for that resource.

A domain controller isn't required for the additional validation, allowing your domain controllers to attend to other services. Kerberos is an industry standard, so the same authentication server can validate both Windows 2000 clients and UNIX clients.

Applications can use the Security Support Provider Interface (SSPI) to utilize the security protocols built into Windows 2000. The API creates authenticated connections, hiding the specific method used to create the connection. An administrator can then choose one of the Security Support Providers (SSP) that ship with Windows 2000. For example, Windows NT 4.0 used the LAN Manager (NTLM) SSP. Windows 2000 Server uses the Microsoft Kerberos SSP, with other SSPs likely to ship at a later date. Use of SSPI in the future will be backward compatible with previous implementations.

Working with Certificates

Certificates are managed as a snap-in to the Microsoft Management Console. In the MMC, you manage keys and control which Certificate Authorities your enterprise will trust. Because private keys are managed as part of the Windows 2000 operating system, the CAs you specify as trusted are made available to the various services and applications that access Windows' security system. Although certificates have been used for a couple of years, Windows 2000 differs from previous operating systems in that it provides a centralized management tool and operating system support for the concept.

In the past, the use of certificates required that an application be specifically written to support this security mechanism. For example, although Microsoft Internet Explorer stored certificate information in the Registry, other applications used other mechanisms to manage certificates. Also, each application had to be managed independently, making the whole topic time-consuming and confusing.

When you create a CA, you must import its certificate to add it as a trusted CA in the Microsoft Management Console's Certificates snap-in. Importing the certificate enables trust for a single user. You use a group policy to apply the certificate to a group of users.

As described in Hour 14, "Profiles and Policies," you use policies to apply security settings to computers and users within OUs. Additionally, you may choose to use the Security Configuration Analysis MMC snap-in. This tool enables you to apply some ready-to-use security templates. Some included templates are for normal, medium, and high levels of security, but you can customize your own templates. The Security Configuration Analysis tool manages settings that were previously part of the User Manager, Event Viewer, Windows Explorer, and the Registry Editor. If you want to use this tool, you must manually add this snap-in to an MMC console (see the "The Microsoft Management Console" section of Hour 4, "Using the Windows 2000 Interface").

You can add a CA to the list of trusted CAs in the Certificate snap-in. You will also notice that several commercial CAs are included in the Certificate snap-in when you open the MMC. If there is a CA that you do not want to trust, you should remove that CA from the list. For a tightly specified network system without any outside access, the most secure system would remove all CAs from the list except for your own.

You can create your own Certificate Authority, and use that CA to validate security requests. Doing so allows you to work with key pairs on your network without having to pay the registration fee. Keep in mind that your CA will not be recognized outside your network. However, creating your own CA is a very secure system because you are in control of the users and computers on your network. You can assign certificates to users and services, and the result will be a secure and transparent security scheme that validates users for the services your network offers.

To install the Certificate Services, you choose that option during your initial server installation. If Certificate Services aren't installed on your system, use the Add/Remove Programs Control Panel applet's Windows Components tab to install this service at a later date. The Windows Components Wizard walks you through a number of steps in which you select what level of CA services you wish to install. In Figure 23.1, you see the Certification Authority Type Selection step. The four choices you can select from are

- Enterprise Root CA—When you are using Active Directory and this is your first CA, select this option. The Enterprise Root CA must be the first CA that you install if you are installing it among other CAs.

- Enterprise Subordinate CA—Select this option when you are using Active Directory, but an enterprise root CA already exists.

- Stand-alone Root CA—Select this option when you are not using the Active Directory and this is your first CA.

- Stand-alone subordinate CA—This option should be selected if you are not using the Active Directory and you already have a stand-alone root CA assigned.

After you select the CA type, you will be prompted to enter the information identifying the certificate server, as shown in Figure 23.2. This information is added to every certificate created, and is the way that interested parties can contact you to verify the authenticity of any certificate called into question.

The third important step in the wizard prompts you for the location of the log files that the CA writes. You should store these files on an NTFS file system on a Windows 2000 Server if at all possible. This is the most secure file system that Windows offers you. Figure 23.3 shows you the log location step of the wizard.

After you have installed Certificate Services, you next must manage those services in the Certification Authority MMC snap-in. You do not need to reboot the computer to access the Certificate Services.

FIGURE 23.1

The Certification Authority Type Selection step of the Windows Component Wizard is where you select the level of CA services that your server provides.

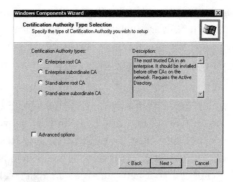

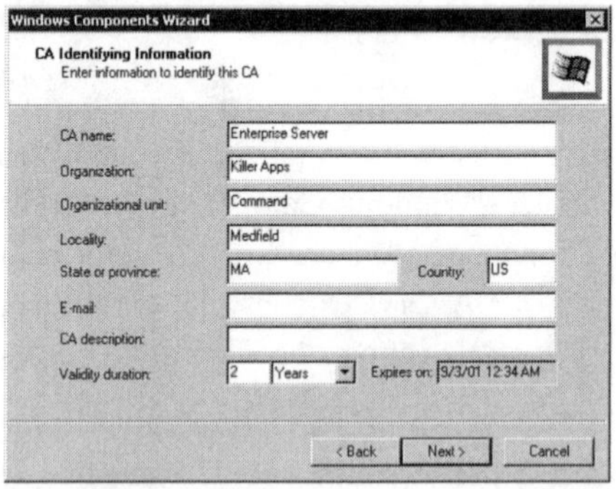

FIGURE 23.2

Enter information about your CA into this step of the Windows Components Wizard.

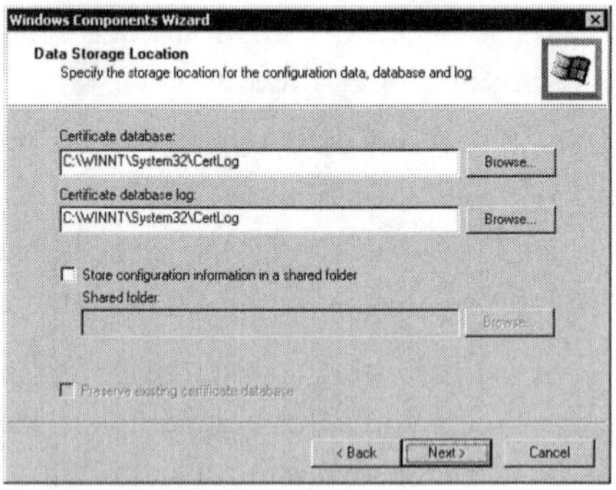

FIGURE 23.3

This step of the wizard enables you to select the location of the log files of your newly created CA.

You open the Certification Authority by selecting that command from the Administrative Tools folder on the Programs folder of the Start menu. Figure 23.4 shows the Certification Authority snap-in. In this snap-in, you can view all certificates, revoke, request, and reject certificates.

FIGURE 23.4

Use the Certification Authority MMC snap-in to manage certificates in your enterprise.

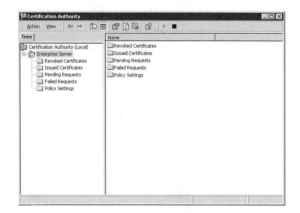

23

Hardware Security

Windows 2000 also supports hardware devices that provide for secure login to the system. In a network without hardware security, any person who gets access to a username and password can log in to the network. If that password is at the administrator level, that person has full control over the security of the domain.

To further protect computers from unauthorized entry, many enterprises are installing device access hardware, typically as serial devices. These devices can take many forms, but the most common form is a smart card that contains the user identification on it and an embedded processor so that it can be reprogrammed. Without the smart card, login doesn't proceed further. With a smart card, the user is required to enter a personal ID number or PIN that allows the login to start. Then the user logs in and is authenticated by Windows 2000 using the Kerberos authentication system. Now an additional layer of protection exists because not only does the "logee" need a username and password, but he or she also needs physical possession of the smart card and knowledge of the PIN. It's unlikely that someone could get that information without the intervention of the owner of the smart card.

Not all smart cards work in this manner. Some smart cards log the user into the system after the PIN is entered into the system. Even with this lower form of security in place, the system is still superior to the standard Windows 2000 logon. No longer is the password required or transmitted, the physical card must be carried, and the person logging into the system still needs to know the PIN.

Other systems in use are magnetic strip card readers of the type used to read credit cards. These devices can read a card that contains user identification and a private key, which is typically more information than a smart card contains. The system is more expensive than smart card readers and requires every computer to have a magnetic strip card reader.

In the near future, we are going to see low-cost hardware security devices based on fin-gerprints and eye retina patterns. At a recent Intel networking conference, a fingerprint device was shown integrated into a Compaq workstation. Windows 2000 makes it easy for developers to access operating system authentication methods.

The Encrypting File System

Windows 2000 offers you additional protection for encrypting files and folders on an NTFS partition by using the Encrypting File System (EFS). When you are in Windows 2000, you have access only to volumes you are allowed to access. The problem with unencrypted file systems is that if you can boot a remote volume over the network, or start up a server using another operating system (such as DOS or a Windows 98 startup disk), you can read the contents of a disk. The access restrictions contained in the access control lists no longer apply to the files contained on a disk.

With the EFS, the files and folders you specify on a disk are encrypted using a public/private key pair scheme. Any user wanting to access a file must be able to provide the private key to decrypt the file. EFS provides a secondary file security scheme within Windows 2000. When you encrypt a volume, be aware that you will suffer some performance degradation.

To encrypt a file or folder:

1. Open the Windows 2000 Explorer, right-click the file or folder you want to encrypt and select the Properties command.
2. On the General tab of the Properties dialog box, click the Advanced button.
3. In the Advanced Attributes dialog box shown in Figure 23.5, click on the Encrypt Contents to Secure Data check box.
4. Close the two dialog boxes open on your screen.

FIGURE 23.5

To encrypt files or folders in EFS, select that attribute in the Advanced Attributes dialog box from the Windows 2000 Explorer.

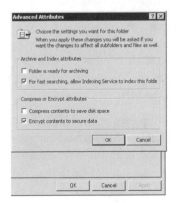

Secure Internet Protocols

Another security improvement added in Windows 2000 is the IPSec protocol. This is an Internet standard based on the work of the Internet Engineering Task Force (IETF); as such, it is a cross-platform transfer protocol that adds a security scheme to TCP/IP packets. By using IPSec, a Windows 2000 system can communicate over the Web with other Windows systems, UNIX servers, and any other computers and browsers using that standard. IPSec is predicted to become one of the primary protocols used to create Virtual Private Networks (VPNs) over the next couple years. IPSec is built into Windows 2000, and it offers automatic operating system–level support authentication of clients and servers, secure data transmission on a TCP/IP network (and over the Internet), and IP application support.

IPSec uses the Encapsulating Security Payload (ESP) standard to validate and encrypt IPSec data transmission. The standard encrypts data transmitted using high-level protocols, such as TCP/IP, at a low level (network or transport layer) of the network transmission scheme. By using ESP, it is possible to use a Telnet session to view data and have that data transmitted securely through tunneling using the IPSec protocol. ESP works by inserting an ESP header between the IP header and the TCP header and by encrypting all of the data contained within it. ESP also can obscure the IP address of the packets so that the destination of the packets cannot be read during transmission. This prevents capturing the data and retransmitting new data to the intended destination address.

Other secure IP transmission systems are being designed at the IETF, including one that provides for an IP Authentication Header(AH). With AH, a client and server can validate each other prior to data exchange, and thus qualify the communication traffic.

Windows 2000 is at the forefront of adding new secure transmission protocols to Windows 2000 as they are developed and ratified. In many instances, Microsoft is a key participant in the committees assigning and ratifying these new standards.

Summary

Windows 2000 Server adds a number of new security services to enhance network computing both locally and over the Internet. By using certificate servers and a public/private key cryptography scheme, users and servers can identify themselves to one another. After the user is logged in to the network system, Windows 2000 authenticates the user and provides a session ticket that allows user access to network resources without the intervention of a domain server. This hour described how to install a certificate server and work with certificates to provide this type of security. With a key pair scheme, one key encrypts and the other decrypts data, requiring the user to have possession of both keys.

23

In addition to software support, Windows 2000 adds APIs that support hardware security devices. The uses of smart cards, magnetic card readers, and more advanced devices based on fingerprint and eye retina patterns were briefly described. These systems will become more available and cheaper over the next two years.

Public/private keys are also used in the Encrypting File System (EFS). The Windows 2000 NTFS file system supports encryption of files and folders on an individual basis. EFS is part of the Zero Administration for Windows (ZAW) initiative.

Finally, Windows 2000 Server adds secure Internet protocols, such as IPSec, to its communication services. By using IPSec, it is possible to create secure encrypted communications between systems. IPSec will likely be used to create low-cost VPNs using the Internet as a transport medium.

Workshop

The workshop provides a quiz and exercises to help reinforce your learning. Even if you feel you know the material, you will still gain from working these exercises.

Quiz

1. What is a key pair?
2. How are users and system validated in Windows 2000?
3. Who issues a certificate?
4. What is the purpose of Kerberos authentication?
5. How do I install a Certificate Server?
6. Where do I manage Certificates?
7. What is the purpose of a stand-alone root CA?
8. What form of access does a smart card require?
9. How do you encrypt a file or folder using the EFS?
10. Why is IPSec important?

Exercises

1. Create a Certificate Authority on your server and assign certificates to users on your network.
2. Use a security template to propagate certificates to a group of users.

HOUR 24

Internet Information Server

by Robert Mullen

Microsoft's Internet Information Server (IIS) 5 is an upgrade from the Windows NT 4 Option Pack. This Windows 2000 component offers more power and flexibility than previous versions of IIS.

Windows 2000 Internet Information Server (also known as version 5) provides you with everything needed to set up and manage services for Intranet, Extranet, or Internet Web sites. This version of IIS also provides easier set up and management of multiple Web sites and user applications. IIS supports more robust delivery of ASP-based (Active-Server-Pages–based) applications. Expect this version of IIS to be easier to configure and more usable than previous versions.

This hour introduces you to the methods you need to quickly set up and operate Internet Information Server version 5.

In this hour, you will learn how to

- Install and upgrade Internet Information Server components
- Configure IIS and Web sites by using the Internet Services Manager

- Specify the home directory for your server
- Create Web sites
- Install and work with FrontPage extensions
- Manage user access with IP and domain filtering
- Redirect users to other Web sites
- Enable and manage authentication
- Enable and manage logging
- Tune for performance

How to Install or Upgrade IIS Components

Internet Information Server is installed by default only if you are upgrading from a previous version. You can reinstall IIS or optionally install only individual components of IIS. In this section, you will learn how to install and upgrade IIS and to install individual IIS components that support extended functionality.

> IIS will utilize existing IIS settings and configuration information when performing an upgrade. If you are upgrading to Windows Server 2000 and IIS from another Web server software product, it is best to perform a backup of existing server logs and other Web server–related files before upgrading to Windows Server 2000 or IIS.

You can install or upgrade Internet Information Server (and its components) by doing the following:

1. Insert the Microsoft Server 2000 disc into the CD-ROM drive. The Windows 2000 CD Wizard should be displayed in a matter of moments.

2. IIS is an add-on component for Windows Server 2000. Select Install Add-On Components on the menu. The Windows Component Wizard dialog will be displayed.

3. Click the Internet Information Server (IIS) item to select available IIS components, as shown in Figure 24.1.

4. Click the Details button to select IIS components for installation or upgrade. Windows Server 2000 indicates components already installed with a checked box. Review the list of available IIS components and select the ones you want installed.

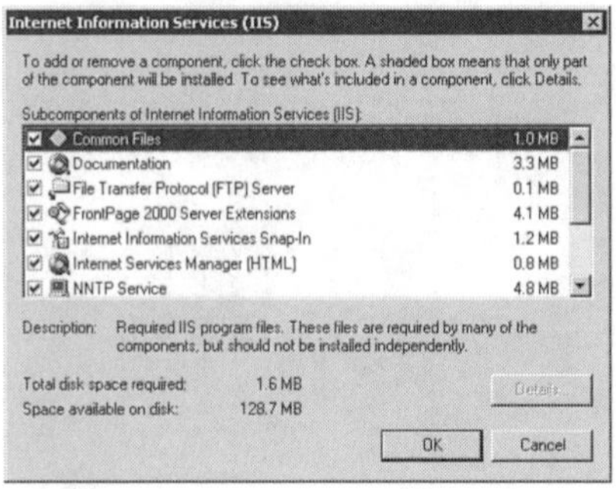

FIGURE 24.1

A view of the list of installable IIS components.

Here is a list of available IIS components and their uses:

- Common Files—Files used by both IIS and other software.
- Documentation—HMTL help to support your use of IIS.
- File Transfer Protocol (FTP) Server—Useful if you want others to move files to specific folders using FTP. Non-FrontPage Web editors will use FTP to work with their Web content.
- FrontPage 2000 Server Extensions—Required to leverage extended FrontPage 2000 features.
- Internet Information Services Snap-in—Installed via the Microsoft Management Console.
- Internet Services Manager (HTML)—Allows you to manage IIS remotely—but by using a browser rather than the IIS Snap-in.
- NNTP Services—Enables you to set up newsrooms.
- SMTP Services—Enables mail and messaging services.
- Visual InterDev RAD Remote Deployment Support—Allows Visual InterDev users to access Web sites without requiring file-level access. Not recommended for production servers.
- World Wide Web Server—Supports the HTTP protocol that enables you to serve Web sites.

You should restart your server after the installation or upgrade is complete.

How to Use the Internet Services Manager

The Internet Services Manager is a simple way to manage the properties of IIS and Web sites hosted by Internet Information Server 5. You can work with the properties of the IIS default sites for each service, including default HTTP (Web), NNTP (news), SMTP (mail), and FTP (File Transfer Protocol). Base settings exist for each IIS 5 component service you have installed. Figure 24.2 shows you an example of a typical list of Web sites and folders.

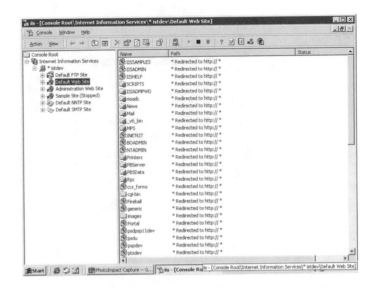

Figure 24.2

A view of the default installation of the Internet Services Manager.

You can work with the properties of individual Web sites and IIS components by doing the following:

1. Click the Start menu, and then select Internet Services Manager from the Administrative Tools menu.

2. Expand the directory structure in the left pane until the list of installed components is displayed.

3. Select any component or Web site (for example, the Administration Web Site) item.

4. Select Properties from the context menu to view the specific properties for the selection you have made. Note that properties sheets vary with the component or Web site selected.

The IIS Internet Services Manager is the pulse of IIS, providing you with easy access to properties for Web sites and the IIS components you have installed. Read other sections of this hour to learn how to use the Internet Services Manager to perform specific tasks that are part of the everyday management of Web sites hosted by Internet Information Server 5.

How to Specify the Home Directory for Your Server

By default, IIS 5 creates a default Web site for your server in the INetpub/wwwroot folder of the boot drive of your server computer. IIS assigns the name Default Web Site to this default or home Web site. The default Web site serves Web pages from the INetpub/wwwroot (also known as *document root*) folder if the viewer fails to specify any other site hosted by IIS.

If you are operating an intranet, you can use the default Web site or home directory to represent an entire organization with other suborganization sites located below the home directory on the folder tree. Internet service providers can also use the home directory to host Web pages that represent the ISP organization with other customer Web sites that are supported lower on the directory structure.

You can assign any Web site the role of home directory for the server by doing the following:

1. Click the Start menu, and then select Internet Services Manager from the Administrative Tools menu.

2. Expand the directory structure in the left pane until the Default Web Site folder is displayed.

3. Select Properties from the context menu to open the properties sheet for the default Web site.

4. Click the Home Directory tab to view the home directory settings.

   You can assign one of three kinds of resources as your home directory:

   - Select a Directory on This Computer to Assign a Folder on the Same Computer with IIS 5—This is the default property and the most commonly used setting. Click this option button and specify the local path.

   - Select a Share Located on Another Computer to Assign a Directory on Another Computer on Your Network—Use this setting to send a user to a folder on a networked central server managing a farm of IIS servers. Click this option button, and then specify the network directory.

   - Select a Redirection to a URL to Assign a Virtual Home Directory to Another Web Site Hosted by Any Web Server Able to Display Documents—Use this setting to send viewers to another server or site automatically. Click this option button, and then specify the URL.

5. Click the Apply button to invoke your changes, and then click the OK button to save your changes and close the properties sheet.

How to Create Web Sites

IIS administrators are typically expected to create new Web sites for those who want to populate them with content. The process of creating a new Web site requires you to use the Internet Services Manager.

You can create a Web site by doing the following:

1. Click the Start menu, and then select Internet Services Manager from the Administrative Tools menu.

2. Expand the directory structure in the left pane until the Default Web Site folder is displayed.

3. Select the Default Web Site folder.

4. Select New, Site from the context menu to run the Web Site Creation Wizard.

5. Click the Next button and enter a description for the new site.

6. Click the Next button to work with port and IP settings:

    - Leave the All Assigned property set unless you want to specify a single IP address to use.

    - Leave the default TCP port property in place unless you want to specify another specific port.

    - Leave the default Host Header property blank unless you want to specify the URL location of a standardized header used by the host.

    - Leave the default SSL Port value blank unless you have first enabled Secure Sockets Layer support and you want to assign another port for this service.

7. Click the Next button to assign the folder location to serve as the document root for the new Web site. All other folders for this site must reside below the doc root.

8. Click the Next button to assign access permissions to the new Web site:

    - Select the Read option to allow users to view standard Web content. This option is selected by default.

    - Select the Run Scripts option to enable server-side scripting to run. This option is selected by default.

    - Select the Execute option to allow CGI and Java applets to run. This option is not selected because security can be reduced somewhat.

    - Select the Write option to allow users to modify the contents of files by default. This option is not selected by default.

    - Select the Browse option if you want users to be able to display browsable folder trees that represent site content. This option is not selected by default because it can provide user access to folders and files not intended to be viewed with a browser.

9. Click Next, and then Finish to complete the creation of the Web site. Note that new Web sites are preconfigured for Microsoft FrontPage by default and will display hidden folders useful only to FrontPage.

How to Install and Use the FrontPage Extensions

The Microsoft FrontPage extensions are essentially a component that offers expanded functionality to content editors using Microsoft FrontPage 2000. The MS FrontPage 2000 server extensions are backward compatible with all previous versions of FrontPage.

The FrontPage server extensions are not installed by IIS 5 by default. In this section, you will learn how to install the FrontPage 2000 server extensions.

You can install and manage FrontPage 2000 server extensions by doing the following:

1. Insert the Microsoft Server 2000 disc into the CD-ROM drive. The Windows 2000 CD Wizard should be displayed in a few seconds.

2. Select Install Add-On Components on the menu. The Windows Component Wizard dialog will be displayed.

3. Click the Internet Information Server (IIS), and then click the Details button to view a list of IIS components for installation or upgrade.

4. Select the FrontPage 2000 Server Extensions check box, and then click the OK button to close the dialog box.

5. Click the Next button to proceed to the end of the installation process.

24

Windows Server 2000 might shut down Internet services during the installation of some components such as the FrontPage 2000 extensions. Remember that your users might temporarily lose access to Web site content until the server has the chance to automatically restart IIS again.

How to Manage User Access with IP and Domain Filtering

You can limit who can access Web sites by directing IIS 5 to restrict open access to content or by granting limited access to restricted content based on the IP filter reported by the user's browser. This process is called *IP filtering*.

You must decide whether you want to allow all to access by default and to limit access to browsers reporting specific IP addresses or domain names; or if you want to allow none to access by default and to grant access to browsers reporting specified IP addresses or domain names.

You can use IP filtering to assign or limit access by doing the following:

1. Click the Start menu, and then select Internet Services Manager from the Administrative Tools menu.

2. Using the Internet Services Manager, expand the directory structure in the left pane, and then select the Web site you want to filter.

3. Select Properties from the context menu to open the properties sheet for the selected Web site, and then select the Directory Security property sheet.

4. Click the Edit button to change the IP address and domain name restrictions.

5. Select the Granted Access option if you want to grant access to all users except those with specific IP addresses or domain names. Or, select the Denied Access option if you want to grant access only to users with specific IP addresses or domain names.

6. Click the Add button, and then specify the criteria for either access or denial of services.

   • Select the Single Computer option to allow or deny access to a specific user based on the specified IP address. Enter the IP address and click the OK button to close the dialog box.

   • Select the Group of Computers option to allow or deny access to a specific group of users based on the specified network ID and subnet mask, and then click the OK button to close the dialog box.

   • Select the Domain Name option to allow or deny access to a group of users based on the domain name specified by the users' browsers, and then click the OK button to close the dialog box. Figure 24.3 illustrates how you can set all users to have access except those accessing from within a Microsoft network.

FIGURE 24.3

A domain name has been selected at random to illustrate how all users from a single domain can be filtered for access or denial.

How to Redirect Users to Other Web Sites

System administrators might need to cause a user to be redirected to another Web site. Redirection is commonly used to move a Web site to another server. This technique can also be used to take a site offline temporarily for redesign or other purposes.

Redirection is an event that forwards a user to another specific site without any interaction on the part of the user. Redirection can be accomplished instantly by the server alone, and optionally in conjunction with a Web page that displays a message to the user before requiring the user to click to be forwarded, or to forward the user when a period of time has elapsed.

Redirect users by doing the following:

1. Click the Start menu, and then select Internet Services Manager from the Administrative Tools menu.

2. Expand the directory structure in the left pane, and then select the Web site you want to redirect users from.

3. Select Properties from the context menu to open the properties sheet for the selected Web site.

4. Click the Home Directory tab to view the home directory settings.

5. Select the Redirection to a URL option to assign the Web site where you want users to be redirected to.

6. Click the Apply button to invoke your changes, and then click the OK button to save your changes and close the properties sheet.

How to Enable and Manage Authentication

Authentication requires users to qualify themselves before they can access content. You can specify how you want to allow users to access content. The process of qualifying user access is called *authentication*.

Configure IIS to authenticate users by doing the following:

1. Click the Start menu, and then select Internet Services Manager from the Administrative Tools menu.

2. Expand the directory structure in the left pane, and then select the Web site where users should be authenticated.

3. Select Properties from the context menu to open the properties sheet for the selected Web site.

4. Click the Directory Security tab and select an authentication method:

   - Anonymous—Enables any user to access content by opening a guest account when he or she accesses, but subjects that access to Windows 2000 Server settings that restrict guest access to files and folders. You can also assign anonymous access to users who report specific accounts.

   - Basic—Directs all uses to enter a username and password. This setting can also require a user to enter a specific username, password, and domain name. This authentication information is sent in clear text.

   - Digest—Requires the user to have Internet Explorer version 5 and a Windows 2000 domain server in order to authenticate using this method. All other accesses are denied. This option causes IIS to perform a basic "hash" process in which the information passed between user and IIS 5 is not in clear text, making it harder to read.

   - Integrated Windows—Encrypts authentication information passed between browser and server during the authentication process. Requires Internet Explorer 2 or higher. Figure 24.4 shows you how to select the most secure setting to use.

24

FIGURE 24.4

This dialog sets the authentication level for the selected site.

How to Enable and Manage Logging

You can enable the active logging feature of IIS in order to create log files that store information about IIS activity. You can then analyze those logs to determine access frequency for users, activity in specific areas of Web sites, and so on.

Remember that logging is server intensive, and that the most active logging to specific databases on a slower, remote network share can seriously impair IIS performance under heavy load scenarios.

Enable and tailor IIS logging by doing the following:

1. Click the Start menu, and then select Internet Services Manager from the Administrative Tools menu.

2. Expand the directory structure in the left pane, and then select any Web site where IIS activity is important to you.

3. Select Properties from the context menu to open the properties sheet for the selected Web site.

4. Click the Web Site tab to open the Web site properties sheet.

5. Select the Enable Logging option.

6. Choose an Active Log format from the three options presented:

   - W3C Extended Log File Format—This most comprehensive format is primarily ASCII text, but when selected, can be further tailored. Clicking the Properties button enables you to specify how often you want log files to be overwritten with new ones and the kind of information you want to be logged.

   - NCSA Common Log File Format—Offers the same feature set as W3C Extended Log File Format without the capability to select the names of many of the logged fields.

   - ODBC logging—Prompts you to provide the name of the ODBC DSN, the table name, username, and password needed in order to log in to a specific database.

7. Click the Apply button to invoke your changes, and then click the OK button to save your changes and close the properties sheet.

How to Tune for Performance

One of the more robust feature additions to IIS 5 is this Web server's ability to throttle user demand on the server.

Enable and tailor IIS performance by doing the following:

1. Click the Start menu, and then select Internet Services Manager from the Administrative Tools menu.

2. Expand the directory structure in the left pane, and then select any Web site where IIS activity is important to you.

3. Select Properties from the context menu to open the properties sheet for the selected Web site.

4. Click the Performance tab to open the properties sheet.

5. Tailor any of the three throttling options presented on this property sheet:

   - User/Count Throttling—Specify how much memory is to be allocated to an expected number of users visiting a Web site daily. Estimating this amount can be tricky at best. If you are running low on memory on a consistent basis, use this throttling method to keep waste at a minimum. The default is set to less than 100K.

   - Bandwidth Throttling—Limit the amount of activity that can occur at a specific Web site. High-demand sites take more bandwidth from other sites unless you set some limitations. This method is called *bandwidth throttling*. Use this method to throttle activity when you cannot scale your server to handle extra-heavy loads directed at more popular, specific sites. ISPs often use this approach to provide more bandwidth to e-commerce sites where unbridled load conditions translate directly into reduced revenues for the site. This method is also used to level the load on a busy intranet with identifiable bandwidth constraints. The default amount of bandwidth is set to 1KB of information per second.

   - Process Throttling—Restrict the amount of CPU intensity allowed to occur at a specific site. Some activities are very CPU intensive. I/O activity and application-based activity are among the greatest loads on a production Web server. Limit the amount of allocated CPU activity to 10% of the total demand when server performance degrades unacceptably due to excessive demand on CPU time, if the CPU cannot readily be upgraded or scaled.

6. Click the Apply button to invoke your changes, and then click the OK button to save your changes and close the properties sheet.

24

Summary

Windows 2000 comes with Internet Information Server 5, a major upgrade from IIS 4. IIS 5 is now more fully integrated into the server software, providing more robust service than a layered Web server could provide running as an NT service alone. For more detailed information on this product, read Macmillan's publications *Special Edition Using Microsoft Internet Information Server* and *Microsoft Internet Information Server Unleashed*.

Workshop

The workshop provides a quiz and exercises to help reinforce your learning. Even if you feel you know the material, you will still gain from working these exercises.

Quiz

1. True or false: IIS 5 will host only one large Web site.
2. True or false: To fully enable MAPI features in Web applications, another server other than the IIS 5 SMTP server is required.
3. True or false: Gopher is still supported by Internet Information Server 5.
4. FrontPage does not seem to respond, but sites are being served. Why can't FrontPage save a page?
5. What is bandwidth throttling?
6. What is CPU throttling?
7. What do I do about server extensions if the FrontPage 98 users I support are not willing or able to upgrade to FrontPage 2000?

Exercises

1. Create a new Web site. Delete the site.
2. Create a new site and redirect users to it.

PART V
Appendixes

Hour

APPENDIX A

Answers

Hour 1

1. What was the number one concern and desired feature of administrators for Windows 2000?

   Stability.

2. What is the Windows Driver Model?

   The WDM is a unified driver model that allows a common driver to be written for Windows 98 and Windows 2000, and to be compiled for each operating system.

3. When did the Microsoft Management Console first appear?

   The MMC first appears in the Windows NT Option pack with IIS as a snap-in.

4. What is the Zero Administration for Windows initiative?

   ZAW is a portfolio of features that allow for easier management and deployment of software meant to lower the total cost of ownership of Windows.

5. What is the Distributed File System?

Dfs enables you to create shares to store files and programs replicated throughout the network.

6. What is the Windows Management Instrumentation standard?

WMI is a standard by which computers running different operating systems may be managed over the Internet using a browser.

7. What is mixed-mode domain operation?

Mixed mode is a domain with both Windows 2000 Servers and Windows NT Server 4.0 Domain Controllers. In mixed mode, not all the features of the Active Directory are enabled.

8. What major security model does Windows 2000 add?

Kerberos 5, a system that issues session tickets to users.

9. How many processors in an SMP system do Advanced Server and Datacenter Server support?

Advanced Server supports up to eight processors (an 8-way). Datacenter Server supports from 16–32 processors.

10. What group of people is Windows 2000 Server meant for?

Windows 2000 Server is a departmental or small enterprise workgroup deployment meant for medium-size application deployments (<500 users), Web servers, workgroups, and branch offices.

Hour 2

1. What part of the operating system needs to be changed to support different processor types?

The Hardware Abstraction Layer, or HAL, needs to be recompiled.

2. What is the Windows 2000 Executive?

This is a service layer that allows the kernel mode to communicate with modules in the user mode and vice versa.

3. What does SMP mean?

Symmetric multiprocessing used by Windows 2000 is a scheme by which multiple CPUs process threads from all executing processes.

4. What is dynamic process leveling?

The operating system has the capability to raise or lower the tendency of a thread to be executed based on current system conditions.

5. How much memory can a 32-bit operating system address?

   4GB. The first 2GB are reserved for kernel mode processes, and the second 2GB can service both user mode and kernel mode.

6. What module is responsible for paging?

   The Virtual Memory Manager.

7. What does POST stand for?

   The Power-On Self Test routine built into BIOS that checks and inventories various hardware components, such as memory.

8. What is the last known good configuration and how do you access it?

   This is the configuration saved to the Registry when you last were able to successfully log on to your system. Press the Spacebar during the menu to show the various operating systems at startup, and then press the L key.

9. What files do I need on an emergency boot floppy to start up Windows 2000 Server?

   For Intel X86 systems, those files are NTLDR, NTDETECT.COM, NTBOOTDD.SYS (for SCSI controllers lacking a SCSI BIOS), and BOOT.INI. For Alpha systems: OSLOADER.EXE, HAL.DLL, and the various *.PAL files.

10. What operating system has the largest beta program in history?

    Windows 2000 shipped 500,000 copies of beta 3, which was probably the largest beta program to date. Many people, however, consider the shipped version of Windows 3.0 to be the largest beta program for an operating system.

Hour 3

1. What operating systems can Setup perform a full upgrade over instead of a clean install?

   Windows NT Server 3.51, Windows NT Server 4.0, and Windows NT Server 4.0 Terminal Server Edition.

2. What is the HCL?

   The HCL, or Hardware Compatibility List, is a listing of all hardware that has been checked and listed by Microsoft as being compatible with a specific operating system.

3. What are the floppy disks that come with Windows 2000 Server for?

   You can use them to initiate a clean installation on a system. They copy a small part of the operating system to your hard drive and let the computer reboot into that operating system to proceed with the installation.

A

4. What choices do I have for a file system during Setup?

   The installation partition for Windows 2000 Server can be FAT, FAT32, or NTFS. For dual boot, use FAT. To make 2000 Server a domain controller, use NTFS.

5. I've installed DHCP during installation, but for some reason it doesn't seem to work. What's wrong?

   DHCP must be turned on after the operating system is completely installed.

6. During installation I can't seem to find the domain, although I know it exists and my network connections are good. What could explain that?

   Setup defaults to using DHCP for TPC/IP network addressing. If you get to the step in Setup on network services and let Windows automatically install the options for you, it will not get a network address if you aren't using DHCP on the network. In that case, use the Custom install option and set a static IP address that you know will work.

7. What is saved during an upgrade?

   Users and groups (for a domain controller), rights and permissions, settings, applications, and files.

8. What is the actual program file that I use for Setup?

   Use WINNT.EXE for Windows 3.1 or MS-DOS installations, or use WINNT32.EXE for Windows 98 or NT installations.

9. How do I install Windows Terminal Services?

   This is one of the networking services options during setup. You must turn on the service after installation.

10. What are the licensing requirements for Windows 2000 Server?

    You will need a server license and client access licenses. You will also need to choose between a Per Server or a Per Seat licensing model.

Hour 4

1. What is the default location for the storing of documents?

   ```
   <root drive>\documents and settings\%username%
   ```

2. How do you kill a process or a program?

   Hit Control+Alt+Delete, click the Task Manager, locate the Application or Process and click End Task or End Process.

3. Where should users store their documents?

In the My Documents directory. We'll see later how to use this to our advantage.

4. Who makes MMC snap-ins?

Microsoft and third-party vendors make snap-ins.

5. Why would you want to create customized MMC consoles?

To send them to specific types of workers, such as help desk personnel.

Hour 5

1. How can you start a Control Panel entry without entering the Control Panel?

On the Run line, type `control <applet>.cpl` where *applet* is the name of the corresponding applet, such as `joy` for joystick.

2. How can you be sure your hardware will work with Windows 2000?

Check the HCL at `http://www.microsoft.com/hwtest/hcl`.

3. What is the best video card for Windows 2000 Server?

The less you spend, the better. Make sure the card is on the HCL list and uses the Microsoft VGA or SVGA drivers.

4. What screen saver should you run on a Windows 2000 server?

Avoid the OpenGL screen savers due to their processor usage.

5. What additional precautions should be taken to protect your Windows 2000 server?

Password protect the console and physically isolate it from other machines.

6. How can you determine how much RAM is installed on a machine?

Use the General tab located in the System applet in the Control Panel.

7. Which feature of Windows 2000 prevents bogus hardware drivers from bringing down your machines?

Driver signing.

8. If a device is conflicting, which values should you check?

IRQ, DMA, and I/O settings.

9. How should you create your server's virtual memory paging file?

Ideally, it is best to spread the file over multiple disks.

10. Which applet helps you run batch files during off-hours?

The Scheduled Tasks applet lets you run any executable process any time of the day or night.

A

Hour 6

1. What type of machine is required to form a domain?

   A Windows NT PDC or Windows 2000 domain controller.

2. What is the difference between a tree and a forest?

   A tree is a hierarchy of linked domains in the same namespace. A forest is two or more trees where the roots of the trees (top) trust each other.

3. Name two non-Microsoft directory services.

   Novell Directory Services and Banyan StreetTalk.

4. What are some attributes that may be added to the Active Directory schema?

   You can create custom attributes to store information such as a user's Social Security number or photograph in the Active Directory.

5. What is a trust? What is a transitive trust?

   A trust is when two domains trust each other. This allows one domain to assign rights to another domain's users or groups. A transitive trust allows trusting rights to flow through the trust links, without a direct trust relationship required.

6. What is a root domain.

   The top level of a domain.

7. What is a parent domain? A child domain?

   A parent domain is the level of a domain above, whereas a child domain is the level below.

8. How do you promote a standalone server to a domain controller?

   Run the dcpromo program from the command line.

9. What Internet service must be running for the Active Directory to function properly?

   The Domain Naming Service or DNS.

10. What is the difference between NT domains and Windows 2000 Server domains?

    NT domains do not support fully qualified names used on the Internet with DNS as a domain name. Additionally, Windows NT domains do not support transitive trusts.

Hour 7

1. What happens when the Active Directory is changed from Mixed mode and Native mode?

   Full transitive trusts take over, Kerberos authentication comes alive, universal groups are available, and multiple-level nested groups are activated.

2. In what order do you upgrade domains?

Upgrade the top of the Active Directory tree first, and then work down.

3. In what order do you upgrade Domain Controllers?

Update the PDC first, and then upgrade each BDC in the domain.

4. What does the global catalog server do? Why would you want to place it close to users?

The global catalog keeps an index of the most searched-on information. You want it close to users because this is the first point of contact when users search the Active Directory.

5. What is a site?

A location with fast connectivity, at least as fast as 10 megabits per second.

6. What is a site link?

A site link joins two sites together. Site links should more or less shadow your WAN structure.

7. How many global catalog servers should you have per site?

At least one.

8. When should you create domains?

Create domains when you have a language barrier in the organization, approach a large number of users, or want a single administrator to have 100% autonomous control.

9. When should you create OUs?

Create OUs when your users bounce from division to division. Also create OUs if you're collapsing a Windows NT resource domain.

10. Whom do you contact to get on the Internet?

The InterNIC at `www.internic.net`.

Hour 8

1. What are the three modes Windows 2000 Server can be in?

Standalone, member server, or Domain Controller.

2. Which type(s) can participate in the domain?

Member server and Domain Controllers participate in the domain.

3. Which type(s) has a local accounts database?

Standalone and member servers have a local accounts database.

4. Which type(s) can assign security to objects in the domain?

   Member servers and Domain Controllers can assign security to domain objects.

5. What are the two built-in user accounts?

   Administrator and Guest.

6. What are some of the built-in local groups?

   Backup Operators and Power Users.

7. Which built-in local groups should you avoid placing users in?

   Replicator and Guests.

8. What can you do to signify an account is a temporary account?

   One option is to put a t- in front of the account, as in t-tempaccount.

9. What can you do to turn off an account at a moment's notice?

   Click the Disable Account check box.

10. A user quits at your organization. Should you delete his account? Why or why not?

    Don't delete the account; rather, just disable the account, and then rename it when the person is replaced. After an account it deleted, the associated SID is deleted as well.

Hour 9

1. How do you create local users on Domain Controllers?

   Use the Active Directory Users and Groups applet.

2. What is a friendly name?

   A friendly name is a logon name that takes the form of username@domain.com.

3. What is a downlevel client?

   A downlevel client is one that sees your domain (domainname.com) as "domainname" only. Typically, these are Windows 95, Win16, or DOS clients.

4. How do you restrict what machine a user can log on from?

   Entering machine names in the Username - Logon Workstations dialog box restricts the users to logging in only on the machines specified.

5. What are some of the domain local built-in groups?

   Administrators, Print Operators, and Server Operators.

6. What are some of the domain global built-in local groups?

   Domain Administrators, Domain Users, and Guests.

7. What are the two types of groups?

Security and Distribution.

8. What are the three scopes of groups?

Domain Local, Domain Global, and Universal.

9. When do you use a local group, global group, and universal group?

Use local groups to assign security to resources. Use global groups to lump like users together. Use universal groups to assign security to resources such that they are accessible outside the domain.

10. How do you change from Native to Mixed mode?

In the Active Directory Users and Computers console, right-click on the computer name and select the Change Mode command.

Hour 10

1. What are some of the OU models you can use to shape your domain?

Business Division, geographic, and administrative are just three.

2. What types of resources are automatically published in the Active Directory?

Users and printers created on Windows 2000 servers are automatically published in the Active Directory.

3. What types of resources are not automatically published in the Active Directory?

Printers and shares from downlevel machines are not automatically published in the Active Directory.

4. How do you create a security group from an OU?

First, create the group. Then select the OU and choose Add Members to Group.

5. What are some of the types of powers that may be delegated?

The abilities to create users and to change passwords may be delegated.

6. How can you search for a partial string in a name in the Active Directory?

Enter only that partial string.

7. How can you drag and drop users to move them from one OU to another?

You cannot drag and drop users from one OU to another. They can, however, be moved via an Explorer-like interface.

8. What kind of printer attributes are automatically published?

The Color and Duplex attributes are some automatically published attributes.

A

9. What additional information sources can be searched besides the Active Directory?

Yahoo!, Bigfoot, and WhoWhere are additional information sources that can be searched.

10. What is the best OU model?

The model that most closely resembles your business.

Hour 11

1. True or false: A basic disk is incapable of containing more than one partition.

False.

2. True or false: Windows 2000 Server allows up to 32 disks to be managed in a spanned volume.

True.

3. True or false: After you convert a basic disk to a dynamic disk, you cannot go back.

False. You can go back, but you need to save your previous configuration to do so.

4. True or false: Mirroring is a fault-tolerant solution.

Partly true. If one part of a mirror fails, you can use the other part of the mirror. However, if corrupt data is written to one disk, it is written to both.

5. True or false: Spanned volumes is a good solution when you want to create a larger volume from different areas of unallocated or free space.

True.

6. True or false: When a disk in a RAID-5 volume goes bad, the entire volume is lost.

False. RAID-5 or striping with parity enables you to substitute for a bad disk or volume and regenerate the disk.

7. True or false: Disks used on one Windows 2000 Server cannot be used on another.

False. Foreign disks can be moved to another server and be imported. The volumes that were on those disks will be recognized.

8. True or false: Any volume on Windows 2000 Server can be seen across the network by a Windows 98 client.

False. NTFS volumes are invisible to Windows 98 clients. FAT and FAT32 volumes should be visible.

9. True or false: A disk defragmenter will dramatically improve your server's performance.

False. Typically, improvements are more modest in a multiuser environment, in the 7% to 10% range.

10. True or false: You can use a boot volume in a spanned set, and even extend a boot volume with unallocated space.

Both false. Boot volumes may not participate in a multidisk volume, and cannot be extended.

Hour 12

1. What is inheritance?

Inheritance is the general term for when permissions or properties flow from folders to subfolders.

2. When would you need to take ownership of a file?

When someone has exclusive access to read or write a file and he or she is not available.

3. What are the basic NTFS permissions for folders?

Full Control, Modify, Read & Execute, List Folder Contents, Read, and Write.

4. What are the basic NTFS permissions for files?

Full Control, Modify, Read & Execute, Read, and Write.

5. Why would you want to compress folders or files?

Compressing folders or files saves space and sometimes shortens read times.

6. How are NTFS group permissions figured?

Add all group membership privileges together (read, write, and so on). Deny access only when a Deny right is encountered.

7. You move a file with read-only permissions from one directory to another directory on a different volume. Does it keep its permissions? Why or why not?

The file loses its permissions. When you move files between volumes, it is as if you copied the file.

8. You copy a file with read-only permissions from one directory to another directory on the same volume. Does it keep its permissions? Why or why not?

When you copy a file, it always loses its permissions, regardless of what volume it's being moved to.

9. Which takes precedence: file permissions or folder permissions?

Explicit file permissions always take precedence.

10. Which takes precedence: file attributes or folder attributes?

Explicit file attributes always take precedence.

A

Hour 13

1. What types of users can create shares on a Windows 2000 Domain Controller?

   Administrators or Server Operators can create shares on Windows 2000 Domain Controllers.

2. How do you create a hidden share?

   Add the $ character to the end of the share name.

3. What share is automatically created at the root of a drive?

   C$, D$, and so on for each installed drive.

4. What share is automatically created at the installation point of Windows 2000?

   Admin$ is automatically created at the %systemroot% installation point, usually c:\winnt.

5. What are the possible permissions for shares?

   Full Control, Change, and Read.

6. How are group permissions figured on shares?

   All group membership privileges are added together (Read, Write, and so on). Deny access only when Deny is encountered.

7. What is a UNC name?

   Universal Naming Convention shares take the form of \\MACHINE\SHARENAME\DIRECTORY\SUBDIRECTORY.

8. Where are standalone Dfs roots hosted?

   Standalone Dfs roots are hosted on one server.

9. Where are fault-tolerant roots stored?

   Fault-tolerant roots are stored over multiple Domain Controllers in a domain.

10. When would you use a standalone Dfs root rather than a fault-tolerant root?

    Use a standalone root to centralize shares in one place. Use a fault-tolerant root to prevent data loss and downtime.

Hour 14

1. What are profiles?

   Profiles are collections of settings, such as desktop settings and saved network connections.

2. Where are local directories stored?

   Local directories are stored in the root of where Windows 2000 was installed. For instance, d:\ and then in Documents and Settings\<userid>.

3. Where are roaming profiles stored?

   Any shared directory on any server.

4. How do you convert a roaming profile to a mandatory one?

   Rename ntuser.dat to ntuser.man.

5. In what order are policies applied?

   Site, domain, and then each nested OU.

6. What are the two major groupings of policies?

   Computer configuration and user configuration.

7. How do you set up policies that don't affect a nested OU?

   Block the inheritance of the policy.

8. How do you manually refresh the policies?

   Run `secedit /refreshpolicy USER_POLICY` or `secedit /refreshpolicy COMPUTER_POLICY`.

9. What are some computer configuration policy settings?

   Audit settings and the Task Scheduler settings are found under computer configuration.

10. What are some user configuration policy settings?

    The Control Panel and the desktop are found under user configuration.

Hour 15

1. What must be common between two computers before communication happens?

   Computers need a common protocol to communicate. Additionally, if the protocol is NWLink, the same frame type must be used.

2. What are the four major protocol layers?

   Physical, Internet, transport, and application.

3. Which protocols may be used in a routed environment?

   Either TCP/IP or NWLink may be used.

4. When would you use DLC?

   Use DLC to connect to HP-JetDirect print servers.

5. What is the loopback address?

   127.0.0.1. It represents "this computer."

6. How can you determine if your TCP/IP protocol stack is alive?

   Try pinging the loopback address and your own IP address.

7. How can you figure out the subnet shorthand?

   Count the number of unmasked bits subtracted from 32.

8. Which command will easily show your IP address?

   `ipconfig`.

9. Which utility moves files from one machine to another?

   `ftp`.

10. Which utility enables you to test for connectivity?

    Both `ping` and `tracert` test for connectivity.

11. Why would you make a custom subnet mask?

    You would make a custom subnet mask to maximize the number of hosts or subnets in a range.

Hour 16

1. In DNS, what are some top-level DNS domains?

   .edu, .com, and .gov are some top-level domains.

2. What is the root domain?

   "." (dot) is the root or top-level domain. It comes before .gov, .com, .edu, and so on.

3. What version of BIND must be used to integrate with Microsoft DNS server?

   Non-Microsoft DNS servers must be running BIND higher than 4.xx.

4. What does a forward lookup query do?

   A forward lookup query translates host names to TCP/IP addresses.

5. What does a reverse lookup query do?

   A reverse lookup query translates TCP/IP addresses to host names.

6. What does WINS resolve?

   WINS resolves NetBIOS names to TCP/IP addresses.

7. How can you make WINS fault-tolerant?

   Set up a replication partner.

8. What networking component can you use to assign TCP/IP addresses, DNS server addresses, and WINS addresses?

   Use DHCP to configure the clients to receive this information.

9. Why would you want to exclude IP addresses in a DHCP scope?

   You don't want the same address assigned to two or more machines.

10. What feature allows automatic updates of DHCP information into the DNS database?

DDNS or Dynamic DNS.

Hour 17

1. What is Dial-up Networking?

DUN, as it called, is the process of connecting one computer or network device to another by using standard telephone lines such as analog modems or ISDN circuits.

2. What are some reasons I would want to use DUN?

Users at branch offices can connect to the home office via DUN and a standard analog modem to get email, have online conferences, and print documents remotely. DUN can also be used to connect a remote branch office network to the home office network by using communications such as ISDN.

3. When DUN is used to connect different office networks, can I make the communications path a secure link?

Yes, Microsoft Windows 2000 has several means to secure dial-up sessions, including using Point-to-Point Tunneling Protocol as well as Layer 2 Tunneling Protocol.

4. Are these means of security absolute, or are there other security issues to be aware of?

No security system standing alone is perfectly secure. Even the most secure operating system benefits from a second protection system, such as a firewall. For servers that need this kind of security, administrators should do a risk analysis to determine the desired level of security.

5. What is Routing and Remote Access Server?

RRAS, as it is called, is a Microsoft Windows 2000 feature that enables routing of different network segments much like a hardware-based router (such as Cisco Systems), but without the need to know the internal workings of such a router. RRAS also has an additional function in that it serves as a Remote Access Server for aggregation of dial-up clients or other networks.

6. Can I use RRAS as an enterprise router?

The volume of traffic that RRAS can handle is dependent on the power of the server, the type of network adapters, and what other server processes are being used on the RRAS machine. Generally speaking, any server faster than a Pentium-II 400MHz server with 192MB or more of installed memory should be able to handle four segments of fewer than 50 users on each segment of 10Mbps speed. Using 100Mbps Fast Ethernet places heavier demands upon the server.

A

7. Can I use multiple Microsoft Windows 2000 Servers as additional routers?

   You can use as many RRAS machines as routers that you may need on the network. RRAS creates and manages routes statically or dynamically, just like hardware routers. However, RRAS supports only Open Shortest Path First (OSPF) and Routing Information Protocol v1 or v2 (RIP). If there are existing hardware routers using any other protocol, those routers must run either OSPF or RIP to be compatible with RRAS systems.

8. How can I use Dial-up Networking and RRAS in combination to join disparate networks?

   Microsoft Windows 2000 supports various adapters for dialup technologies; among these are ISDN and 56Kbps modems. With several adapters or modems installed, Microsoft Windows 2000 and RRAS can receive calls from remote networks at speeds up to 128Kbps over a Point-to-Point Tunneling Protocol link to join TCP/IP sessions. You can do the same thing with Novell NetWare IPX/SPX networks using Layer 2 Tunneling Protocol.

9. What is Microsoft Windows 2000 telephony?

   It is the process of using standard telephone lines or ISDN to create voice, video, and streaming media communications sessions. TAPI, as it is called, is in its third version and provides high-end support for various media sessions such as video conferencing, netmeetings, and distance learning.

10. Do I need specialized equipment or devices to use TAPI?

   TAPI requires a programming approach to create and implement the software that connects these TAPI devices together. Microsoft Windows 2000 lays the groundwork, and programmers plug in the component parts to finish it off so it runs over standard telephone circuits or ISDN.

Hour 18

1. How do I install WTS?

   Installation can be done during a standard install or by adding the component later on from the Add/Remove Programs applet in the Control Panel.

2. What do I need to do to install a Windows-based terminal?

   Nothing, just turn it on. It self-discovers WTS servers.

3. How many users can a WTS server support?

   That depends upon the speed of the server and the amount of installed RAM.

4. Where do I go to see who is connected to a WTS?

   The Terminal Services Manager applet gives you this information.

5. What kinds of licenses do I need?

   WTS requires both server licenses and client licenses. If you use the Internet connector, there is a licensing scheme for that based on your server. Use the Terminal Services Licensing applet to manage this.

6. Can I use a Macintosh to connect to WTS?

   No. But you can add MetaFrame to WTS and connect to Mac and to UNIX clients.

7. Why aren't roaming profiles recommended?

   Roaming profiles enable users to log on to WTS twice (or more). When the second session ends, it overwrites the changes in the profile that the first session created.

8. What is the minimum wire speed WTS supports?

   WTS will work well with clients connected with a 28.8Kbps dial-up connection.

9. Why does WTS work with modem speed dial-up connections?

   Very little data is being transferred over the wire. On the client end only keystrokes and mouse moves are sent to the server. On the server side only a screen buffer is transmitted, and after that only changes in the screen buffer.

10. What is shadowing?

   Shadowing is the ability to view and control a client's sessions. Shadowing enables you to use WTS for training, help desk, and teaching purposes.

A

Hour 19

1. What is a logical printer?

   A logical printer is a software interface between a print server and a printing device.

2. What advantages does a network printer offer you?

   You can share and manage printing resources.

3. Where is the print queue stored?

   The print queue is stored on the server in a location that you can specify. A client will maintain its own print queue should a printer be unavailable.

4. What is the function of a printer driver?

   It translates a print job into print commands that a printing device can understand.

5. How do you print to a printer with a browser from a client?

   Enter the URL for the printer into your browser's address box.

6. Where do you set up a printer share?

   On the Sharing tab of a printer's Properties dialog box.

7. How are print commands transmitted over the Internet?

   Using the IPP protocol embedded in an HTTP stream.

8. How do you change the priority with which a document gets printed in the print queue?

   Right-click the document in the queue, select Properties, and change the Priority slider on the Advanced tab.

9. What is a port?

   A port is a channel of communication between a server and a print device: LPT, COM, USB, and infrared are examples of ports. You can also assign protocols to ports to support different operating systems.

10. What is a printer pool?

    A set of identical printers that a single logical printer prints to. The logical printer sends a print job to the first available printer.

Hour 20

1. Which 16-bit clients can connect to Windows 2000 Server?

   DOS clients such as the LANManager 2.2c and Microsoft Network Client can connect, as well as Windows for Workgroups.

2. What 32-bit clients can connect to Windows 2000 Server?

   Windows 95, Windows 98, and Windows NT 3.5 and higher.

3. What protocol must be loaded for Macintosh connectivity?

   AppleTalk.

4. What types of files can Windows Installer load on client machines?

   Windows Installer can assign or publish only. MSI files.

5. What are offline folders?

   Offline folders enable users to use their data even when the network is unavailable.

6. What additional services must be available before RIS will function?

   A DHCP server must be available to dish out addresses and DNS must be available to allow the client to find our RIS server.

7. What kind of boot ROM must the network card have or be able to emulate in order to support RIS?

   A network card must have or emulate the PXE architecture.

8. What program do you use to create a boot disk?

Use the RBFG.EXE program, located in the \admin\i386 directory of the directory where you installed the RIS service.

9. What program do you use to load additional client images on to the RIS machine?

Use the RIPREP.EXE program located in the \admin\i386 directory of the directory where you installed the RIS service.

10. What program is used to load the changes from a client machine back to the server?

RIPREP.EXE.

Hour 21

1. How do I open the System log to see why my computer is malfunctioning?

Open the Event Viewer and double-click the System log in the tree pane on the left.

2. Why don't I see any events in the Security log?

You must turn on security logging as a policy and enable the specific security items you want to audit.

3. What happens when a log reaches its maximum size?

You control this behavior as a property of the log. You can overwrite the data, start a new log, or if it is the System log, you can stop your system.

4. What is the difference between a counter and a performance object?

A counter is a process that is monitored by your system. A performance object is some part of your system that has counters associated with it.

5. What counter(s) should I use to view processor usage?

Use the Processor\%Processor Time counter.

6. What is a baseline and why would I want to have one?

A baseline is the measure of your system performance using PerfMon when your system is operating correctly. You can use this as a guide to finding and correcting future problems.

7. What is a performance log?

A performance log is a log file in a standard file format that you can open in a spreadsheet or database. It is associated with the Performance Logs and Alerts service.

8. Why do I need a network monitor driver?

This driver lets the Network Monitor listen to the network traffic on a specific network adapter.

A

9. How do I create an alert based on a condition?

Click Alerts in the Performance Logs and Alerts console, and then right-click the detail pane and select the Create New Alert command. Fill in the New Alert Properties dialog box. Voilá.

10. Why do system administrators get paid the big bucks?

They get the big money because they read books like this, and they know how to use the tools you've just learned about.

Hour 22

1. What is the file that controls the Command Prompt applet?

CMD.EXE.

2. How do I switch between windowed and full-screen sessions of the Command Prompt applet?

Press the Alt+Enter keystroke.

3. What is a batch file?

A batch file is a text file with MS-DOS commands that can be run as a single command from the Command Prompt window.

4. What command do I use from the Command Prompt window to modify .INI file mappings for a current user in WTS?

CHANGE USER.

5. What operating systems support the Windows Scripting Host 2.0?

Windows 2000 was the first operating system that supported the Windows Scripting Host 2.0; Windows 98 SE was the second. Versions of the WSH will be available for download for Windows 98, Windows NT Server and Workstation, and Windows 95 from the Microsoft Web site over time.

6. What programming languages does the WSH support?

VBScript, Microsoft JScript, and JavaScript.

7. What is the Windows Management Interface?

The WMI is a specification for device drivers that allows them to monitor device status and control device properties and operation. Programs written to interact with WMI device drivers have low-level device access, and can display device properties in a browser on a management console over a TCP/IP network.

8. What are the versions of the WSH?

There are two versions. CSCRIPT runs programs from the Command Prompt window. WSCRIPT executes programs from the Run dialog box or by double-clicking the icon for the program file on the desktop or in the Windows Explorer.

9. How does the WSH modify domain properties?

The WSH can use the Active Directory Services Interface (ADSI) to modify the properties of the Active Directory and to add, modify, or delete users, machines, and other properties.

10. Why would I use a logon script?

Logon scripts can establish network connections, set an environmental parameter, and launch a program at startup.

Hour 23

1. What is a key pair?

A key pair is a set of two identifying strings that, when run through an algorithm, identifies a user or system. One key is public and sent with transmitted encrypted data. The other key is private and used to decrypt the data. Both keys are required for two-way communication.

2. How are users and systems validated in Windows 2000?

Windows uses a system based on certificates to validate users.

3. Who issues a certificate?

A trusted authority generally issues certificates. In some instances you might want to create your own Certificate Authority to provide this service locally on your network.

4. What is the purpose of Kerberos authentication?

This system provides a method for authenticating a user at login and providing an identifying session ticket to provide network access to secure resources.

5. How do I install a Certificate Server?

A certificate server is installed as part of the Windows 2000 installation routine. If you choose not to install it at that point, go to the Add/Remove Programs Control Panel applet and add it there after the fact.

6. Where do I manage Certificates?

When you install a Certificate Server you install a Certification Authority snap-in in the MMC. Select the Certification Authority command in the Administrative Tools folder to access this tool.

7. What is the purpose of a standalone root CA?

You use this type of CA when it is the first CA in a domain that isn't using the Active Directory.

A

8. What form of access does a smart card require?

Typically, a personal identification number, or PIN, must be entered.

9. How do you encrypt a file or folder using the EFS?

Select that file or folder in the Windows Explorer, open its Properties dialog box, and then open the Advanced Attributes dialog box. Click the Encrypt Contents to Secure Data check box in that dialog box.

10. Why is IPSec important?

With IPSec, you can create secure, encrypted transmissions across the Internet. This enables the construction of low-cost Virtual Private Networks (VPNs) that will allow secure tunnels to be created between organizations and system.

Hour 24

1. True or false: IIS 5 will host only one large Web site.
False.

2. True or false: To fully enable MAPI features in Web applications, another server other than the IIS 5 SMTP server is required.
False.

3. True or false: Gopher is still supported by Internet Information Server 5.
False. Gopher is not supported by either IIS 4 or IIS 5.

4. FrontPage does not seem to respond, but sites are being served. Why can't FrontPage save a page?

FrontPage Server Extensions can become overwhelmed. When FrontPage will not allow content editors to save their work but IIS 5 is clearly serving pages well, restart IIS 5 from the Component Services utility started from the Administrative Tools menu.

5. What is bandwidth throttling?

Bandwidth throttling controls how much data users can download or upload to IIS 5 and hosted Web sits.

6. What is CPU throttling?

CPU throttling limits the amount of demand on your server computer's central processing unit.

7. What do I do about server extensions if the FrontPage 98 users I support are not willing or able to upgrade to FrontPage 2000?

The FrontPage 2000 server extensions are fully backward compatible with previous versions of FrontPage except the Vermeer (pre-Microsoft) version of the FrontPage product.

APPENDIX B

Glossary

.MSI   Microsoft Installer files. Required file type to assign or publish programs via Windows Installer.

Access Control List   The permissions assigned to a resource that enable users to have access.

ACPI   The Advanced Configuration and Power Interface. A set of hardware routines that work with the operating system to save power.

Active Directory (AD)   A distributed database of enterprisewide information that lives on Windows 2000 Server Domain Controllers (DCs). Information in the AD includes usernames, printers, and administrator-controlled attributes. The ADSI is the Active Directory Services Interface, the functions that let programs work with Active Directory.

Active Server Pages (ASP)   A server-side scripting environment, usually performed with VBScript, which is a subset of the Visual Basic programming language.

Address Space   A set of possible addresses allowed for an operating system of a certain bit width. For Windows 2000 Server running in 32-bit space, there are 4GB of possible addresses.

Administrative Model   A way to design organization units such that each IT group is subordinate to the preceding IT group.

Alpha   A microprocessor developed by Digital Equipment Corporation that runs the Windows NT and Windows 2000 operating systems.

Applet   A mini-program run by a larger program. Control Panel has many applets. Also, a small program that can be downloaded from a Web server to execute on the client.

AppleTalk   Apple Computer protocol designed to easily connect computers together.

Application Log   An application can post an error message or a condition message, based on an event that the creator of the application programs, into the application log.

ASF   Advanced Streaming Format. This format is used by the Windows Media Player for streaming media presentations.

Authentication   A process by which a server qualifies access by a user. The authentication header is the part of IpSec that provides for authentication.

Auto Detection   The ability to automatically detect peripheral devices that is part of Windows Plug and Play capabilities.

Backup Domain Controller   An NT machine that houses a read-only copy of the SAM database.

Bandwidth Allocation Protocol   The part of the operating system that lets multiple lines be combined in a dial-up connection.

Bandwidth Throttling   Limiting the amount of information that can be served at one time.

Basic Disk   A basic disk is one that can contain either four primary partitions or three primary partitions and one extended partition. Partitions on a basic disk can participate in multidisk or multipartition groupings. You can convert a basic disk to a dynamic disk, and in doing so, convert partitions to volumes.

Boot Sequence   The startup process initiated in hardware and handed off to the operating system that loads your operating system and enables hardware devices.

Boot Volume (partition) or System Volume (partition)   The boot volume contains the files necessary to boot your server. The system volume contains the system files. Generally these two volumes are the same, but these is no requirement in Windows 2000 Server that they be so. When these files are on a dynamic disk, they are in a volume. When they are on a basic disk, they are on partitions.

Built-in Domain Local Groups   System groups that provide some elevated system privileges to the users and groups within.

Business Division Model   A way to design organization units such that each business unit is partitioned into a separate organization unit.

CALS (Client Access Licenses)   A connection license that allows a client computer (a desktop, workstation, or another server) to access a Windows 2000 Server.

Captured Data   Data that is copied to the Network Monitor.

Certificate Authority   CA is an organization that validates the identity of a person and organization by providing a key that is used to both authenticate and encrypt their communications.

Clean Install   An installation where Windows 2000 Server is installed to a fresh partition and into a new folder.

Clone Control Set   A copy of the hardware configuration of a computer after it boots up that is written to the Registry as a reference.

COM   The Component Object Model is a framework of programming methods and access to operating system services that can be used to build applications.

Common Gateway Interface (CGI)   A method of executing compiled scripts on a web server.

Computers Near Me   Shows the computers in the same workgroup or domain that you are in.

Counter   A measure of some aspect of your system's performance.

CPU   The central processing unit or microprocessor. The chip in the computer that does calculations and orchestrates activity.

Data Encryption   The scrambling of data so that it cannot be read or deciphered. The larger the number of bits that the algorithm uses to encrypt data, the harder the data is to decrypt, and the more secure it is. High encryption (128-bit for WTS) imposes a performance penalty.

Data Source Name (DSN)   A set of information specific to a database that allows IIS 5 or an application to access that database.

DDNS (Dynamic DNS)   Protocol that allows for automatic updates in the DNS database after DHCP addresses are assigned.

Default Subnet Mask   Mask for each of Class A, B, and C.

Defragmentation   The process by which files are written in pieces in various places on your disk so that it is slower to read and write to the disk.

Delegation   Granting control to a trusted user to perform limited administrative duties.

Despooled   The process by which data written to disk and referenced in the print queue is read back into memory and sent to the printer.

Device Driver   A device driver contains the routines that communicate with a hardware device, including both physical hardware devices and virtualized (running in software) devices.

Dfs   The Distributed File System is a part of the operating system that lets file shares be replicated across servers.

DHCP (Dynamic host configuration protocol)   Protocol that automatically assigns TCP/IP addresses as well as critical server information, such as WINS server address.

Dial-up Connection   A named connection with a set of properties for connecting to another computer using Windows 2000 Server.

Directory Services   An approach to operating systems management in which critical items are housed or referenced in a centralized manner.

Disk Quota   The set limit that a user's files can occupy on a disk.

Distribution Group   A group used expressly for email distribution lists.

DLC (Data Link Control)   A protocol originally designed for mainframe connectivity, now used in older HP-JetDirect print servers.

B

DMP (dump file)   A full memory dump of the current contents of RAM. Useful for Microsoft debugging purposes.

DNS (Domain Name Service)   Protocol that resolves host names to IP addresses.

DNS Zone   A partition in the DNS space.

Domain   A security boundary in which settings do not automatically spill over.

Domain Controller   One of the three modes of Windows 2000 Server. In this mode, the server physically houses some of the Active Directory and user accounts.

Domain Global Groups   A group used to group similar users together.

Domain Local Groups   A group used to assign privileges to resources.

Domain Name Service (DNS)   An Internet standard that converts easy-to-use names to IP addresses. To make the most of the Active Directory, DNS must be present in your environment.

Dotted-Decimal   Base 10 representation for underlying binary.

Downlevel Client   Any non–Windows 2000 client that cannot use "friendly" names to log on.

Drilling Down   The term for expanding folders or menu items to find an option somewhere down the tree.

Dual Boot   The ability to switch between two or more operating systems at startup.

Dynamic Disk   A disk that contains volumes, and one that can participate in multivolume storage schemes.

EFS   The Encrypting File System allows data to be encrypted on an NTFS volume.

EMA   Enterprise Memory Architecture allows Windows 2000 to access up to 64GB of RAM, provided the processor allows it.

Environmental Subsystem   An environmental subsystem is an emulator that lets a program run even when it is written for another operating system. The Win32 subsystem is a special environmental subsystem that runs 32-bit Windows programs, and there are also integral subsystems for security and networking routines.

EULA (End User Licensing Agreement)   The EULA describes the legal terms of your agreement with Microsoft for the use of the Windows 2000 operating system.

Event Viewer   A tool for viewing the Application, Security, and System logs.

Explorer   An interface into the computer's files. Explorer has two interface types: the Desktop view and the tree view.

FAQ   A frequently asked question.

FAT and FAT32   Two file systems based on the file allocation table. FAT supports MS-DOS and Win16 clients. FAT32 supports Win32 clients.

Fetching   The process of fetching is when your operating system recalls instructions and data that are required to complete an operation from the paging file.

Filter   A feature of IIS 5 and other Web servers that allows user requests to be limited in some way for the sake of authentication or performance.

Foreign Disk   A foreign disk is a disk from another server that is placed into your current server. You can import a foreign disk and use it in Windows 2000 Server.

Forest   Any two or more trees in which the roots trust each other.

Frame   A set of network packets communicated as a group.

Friendly Name   A logon name that takes the form of username@domain.com.

Geographic Model   A way to design organization units such that each object can be placed under an organization unit that represents a physical location.

Global Catalog Server   The GC server is a special type of Domain Controller that houses a partial replica of the objects in the forest.

Gopher   An older, rudimentary Internet protocol and program used to search and retrieve text over the Internet.

Graphics Device Interface or GDI   The set of programs that render graphics for display.

Group   A collection of users for security or distribution purposes.

Group Scope   Either Domain Local, Domain Global, or Universal. See below.

Group Type   Either Security or Distribution. See below.

GUID   Globally Unique Identifier—a hexadecimal number, taking the form of 8-4-4-4-12, that is unique in all the world. Usually assigned by hardware manufacturers.

Hardware Abstraction Layer   The layer of the Windows operating system that communicates directly with hardware, intercepting and interpreting commands for hardware from the rest of the operating system.

Hardware Compatibility List (HCL)   A list of devices known to be compatible with the Windows 2000 operating system.

HCL   Hardware compatibility list. A list of hardware guaranteed to work properly on Windows 2000.

Home Directory   A legacy method for the repository of user data files.

HSM   Hierarchical Storage Management enables you to write infrequently used data to tape and retrieve it when you need it.

HTML   The Hypertext Markup Language is a standard for page description used on the Internet.

HTTP   The Hypertext Transfer Protocol is the IETF Internet protocol for communications on the World Wide Web.

ICA   Citrix Independent Computing Architecture protocol is another wire protocol for connecting clients to WTS and MetaFrame. Because ICA is an older standard, it has broader industry support than RDP.

IIS   The Internet Information Server is a Web server from Microsoft that you can install with Windows 2000.

IntelliMirror   A set of technologies that puts redundant information on both the client and server for backup and mobile use.

B

IPX/SPX (Internetwork Packet Exchange/Sequenced Packet Exchange)   NetWare-based protocol ported to Windows NT and Windows 2000 as NWLink.

IPSec   Internet Protocol Security, a standard for virtual private networks.

ISP   An Internet Service Provider, a company that provides dial-in connectivity and Web hosting services.

Job Object   An object that the kernel uses to orchestrate multiprocessing.

Kernel   The part of the operating system that manages the CPU.

LAN   Local Area Network.

Layer 2 Tunneling Protocol   L2TP is a virtual private networking standard.

Local Group   A group that resides in a local security database.

Local Printer   A printer attached to the computer you are sitting at.

Local Profiles   Personalized configuration settings, including desktop settings. Local directories are stored in the root of where Windows 2000 was installed; that is, d:\ and then in Documents and Settings\<userid>.

Local Security Database   A simple database comprised of usernames, passwords, and membership.

Local   A term to describe the place where accounts are created.

Log File   Any file where logging records are stored.

Mandatory Profiles   A profile that will not maintain any saved attributes. Roaming profiles can be converted to mandatory profiles by renaming ntuser.dat to ntuser.man.

Member Server   One of the three modes of Windows 2000 Server. In this mode, the server participates in the domain, and has a local accounts database, but also can assign rights to objects based on information in the domain.

Membership   The act of belonging to a group.

MetaFrame   A product from Citrix that runs on top of WTS, and that provides client connections to Macintosh and UNIX, load balancing, and specialized application server support.

Microsoft Management Console   A shell in which snap-ins can be loaded to perform administrative functions.

Minifile   A set of system drivers loaded by NTLDR at startup that allow Windows 2000 to be loaded from the different types of file systems that the system partition can be formatted in: FAT, FAT32, and NTFS.

Mirrored Volume   A volume that has a twin with a synchronized data set.

Mixed Mode   An emulation mode of Windows 2000 Server Domain Controllers in which older-style NT authentication (NTLM) is supported.

Multiprocessing   Multiprocessing is the ability to run several processes concurrently on two or more processors.

Multitasking   Multitasking is the ability to have two or more programs or processes seem to run concurrently by time slicing a CPU work time.

Multithreading   Multithreading is the ability to execute and manage multiple threads (parts of processes) at the same time.

NAT   Native address translation is the process by which packets are transparently sent via proxy between an internal and external network address.

Native Mode   A mode of Windows 2000 Server in which the Active Directory is fully functional and no additional NT servers may be added to the structure.

NDIS   The network driver interface specification is a standard for creating Windows drivers.

Nest   To put groups in other groups.

Nesting   The general term for the placement of like items inside another item. Nesting can take place with folders or groups.

NetBEUI (Network Basic User Interface)   Microsoft-designed protocol for non-routable environments.

Network Monitor   A tool for listening to network traffic and determining various factors, such as who is sending and receiving network traffic, network utilization, and more.

Network Printer   A printer attached through a network interface card to the network. Typically, the printer has a network address.

NLM   Native Language Support enables an administrator to support different locations.

NTLM   (NT/LANManager authentication) A fairly basic challenge-response system in which the client sends an encrypted password over the network, and the server compares that encrypted password to the password in the SAM database.

Object   An entity in Windows 2000 Server that is involved in the security model.

OPSF   The Open Shortest Path Fast is a routing protocol.

Organization Unit (OU)   A logical grouping of objects for administrative purposes. When an organization unit is defined, its control may be delegated if desired.

OSI Model   Theoretical 7-layer model for protocol stacks.

Page Fault   An error condition resulting from a request for instructions at an address that isn't in physical RAM. The Virtual Memory Manager will then find the code in virtual memory and load it into physical memory.

Page File   A disk file that serves as an extension of physical RAM to which and from which instructions may be written to or read from.

Paging   The act of moving RAM contents temporarily into hard drive space and vice versa.

Partition   An area of your disk that is defined as a logical unit and that can be mapped as if it were a disk drive.

Pass-Through Authentication   Validation of access when cached (current) information is used to gain local access.

B

Per Seat Licensing Model   In this licensing model, each client requires a connection license to *each* server that it connects to.

Per Server Licensing Model   In this licensing model, each server requires a connection license for the largest number of concurrent clients that will connect to that server at any one time.

Performance Monitor (PerfMon)   A tool for measuring the various counters your system has.

Performance Object   A part of your system that has counters associated with it.

Plug and Play   The capability, enabled in BIOS and supported by the Windows operating system, to identify hardware devices and configure them automatically.

Policy   Collection of settings that is applied to a site, domain, or OU.

Port   A channel of communication between a print server and a printing device.

PPTP   The Point-to-Point Tunneling Protocol is a Windows virtual private networking communications standard.

Preboot   The part of your computer's startup sequence in which hardware is checked and configured, and when the Power On Self Text (POST) is performed.

Primary Domain Controller   An NT machine that houses a readable and writeable copy of the SAM database.

Print Device   The actual physical printer that outputs your print job to the medium of your choice.

Print Job   A document that is sent to the print queue to be printed.

Print Queue   A set of files awaiting printing. These files are stored in printer file formats on your print server's hard drive and recalled as required.

Print Server   A Windows 2000 Server that handles print jobs, services the queue, and manages both processing and communication of printing.

Print Spooler   A set of routines that handles sending a print job into the print queue and manages the print queue.

Printer   A logical printer is a software interface between a print server and a printing device. This is what the icon in the Printers folder represents.

Printer Driver   A set of routines for translating print communication between the printer and the printing device. They are printer- and operating system–specific.

Printer Share   A shared logical printer that clients over a network can access.

Private Addresses   Blocks of IP addresses guaranteed to not be routed to the Internet.

Process   A part of a program command that requires action or calculation.

Processor Accounting   A capability of the kernel to track how much time a CPU spends on a particular process. It is used by IIS virtual servers to monitor which processes are hogging the computer.

Program Manager   Old Windows 3.1 construct that held icons to launch programs. Replaced by the Start Menu in Windows 95 and 2000.

Protocol Stack   Layers of encapsulation to create and receive messages.

Protocol   The means by which computers communicate. Internet protocols include HTTP, FTP, and SMTP.

Protocol   An agreement on how to start, stop, and transmit data.

Publishing   The ability to make objects available in the Active Directory. Most Windows 2000 objects are published automatically. Windows NT and Windows 9x objects are not.

PXE (Preboot eXecution Environment)—Architecture supported by network hardware to allow the network card to talk without any operating system loaded.

QoS ACS   Quality of Service is a standard the allows an application to guarantee that a certain bandwidth and latency will be available to allow streaming media presentations to proceed and execute acceptably.

QoS ACS   The QoS Admission Control Server enables an administrator to control users and groups, and to set their allowed bandwidth.

Quantum   The amount of time that a thread is executed by the CPU before its context is saved and the CPU context switches to another thread of execution.

RAID (Redundant Array of Independent Disks)   Using multiple disks, you can configure volumes so that you get faster I/O, utilize storage capacity better, and provide fault tolerance.

RAID-5   A version of RAID that has three or more disks striped with parity information. If a disk in a RAID-5 volume fails, you can substitute another and have the volume regenerate itself.

RAM   Random Access Memory is the volatile memory chips used by a computer as a scratchpad to temporarily store data used in processing.

RDP   The Microsoft Remote Desktop Protocol enables you to connect Windows computers to WTS over a network or remote connection. The protocol is optimized for low bandwidth and for graphics display.

Real Mode   In real mode, an operating mode of the Intel x86 family of processors, only one program can execute at a single time. No more than 1MB of memory may be accessed in real mode.

Recycle Bin   A place for files to be captured after being deleted. Only protects files deleted in the Explorer interface.

Redirection   The process of accessing information different from that which would normally be the target or the source.

Remote Access Service (RAS)   Part of the Dial-Up Networking (DUN) component of Windows 2000 that enables you to connect via various devices to another computer over various transmission media and by using various protocols. RAS allows two-way access.

B

When a client connects to a RAS server, it can be a virtual node on the network and have access to the server only or the entire network.

Remote Storage   Storage contained on a server that you manage from a different Windows 2000 Server via the Disk Management console.

Resident   Staying dormant in the background, or silently performing a task, or waiting for input.

RIP   The Routing Information Protocol is an old standard routing protocol used by routers on a network.

RIS   Remote Installation Service—Allows for legitimate cloned machine rollouts.

Roaming Profiles   Profiles stored on any server that follow the user from machine to machine. User accounts must have their profile locations specified.

Routing and Remote Access Service (RRAS)   A form of RAS in which the server routes packets to and from specific computers on the network.

SAM (Security Accounts Manager) Database   A flat database of usernames, passwords, and other data for Windows NT. No additional fields can be added to the SAM.

Schema   The underlying structure of a database (that is, how the fields are constructed).

Script   A file containing instructions to be executed. Typically, scripts are high-level languages that must be first interpreted and then compiled.

Security Group   A group that makes a logical partition of users for security rights.

Security Log   This logs system events when resources on the server or network are accessed and used. Logons, access to shared resources, printer usage, and other items are recorded in the Security log. The Security log is turned off by default, and must be turned on by an administrator using the Group Policy console.

Setup   The program routine that installs the Windows 2000 operating system to your computer. To initiate an installation, you can run Setup from the command line and Setup will guide the installation through both its text and graphical phases.

Shadowing   The process by which an administrator views and controls the Windows Terminal Service session of a client.

Shortcuts   Pointers to applications or data files that make it convenient to place the actual files somewhere else.

SID (Security Identifier)   An underlying unique code that is assigned to a user (or computer) account.

Simple Mail Transfer Protocol (SMTP)   A protocol used specifically for sending messages from one computer to another on a TCP/IP network.

Simple Volume   A volume on a single disk mapped with a volume letter as if it were a disk drive.

SIS   A single instance store is a Windows 2000 service that eliminates duplicate files in IntelliMirror disk partitions.

Site Link   A site link is a representation of how the data flows between the sites. The representation should mirror your WAN structure.

Sites   A single physical location with high bandwidth connected by TCP/IP.

Spanned Volume   A spanned volume is one that uses disk space on two or more (up to 32) disks. Spanned volumes write data to the first disk first, fill that disk, and then fill the next disk, sequentially.

Spin Count   The number of times a process will try to use a shared resource, such as your CPU, before stopping and waiting.

Standalone Server   One of the three modes of Windows 2000 Server. In this mode, there is a local accounts database, and there is no participation in the domain.

Start Menu   The starting point for launching program files, getting help, and performing searches.

Striped Volume   A striped volume is one that uses disk space from two or more (up to 32) disks with information written across each disk equally in stripes. RAID-5 (which requires three or more disks) is striped with parity.

System Log   The System log records successful or failed operations of your system and peripheral devices..MSC: The file type of saved MMC consoles.

Systemroot   The location of the folder containing the system's startup files.

TAPI   The set of Windows Telephony functions that are accessed through the API, and that let Windows 2000 participate in telephone transactions.

Taskbar   The tract of land to the right of the Start Menu. Displays all currently running files and open folders, as well as showing all resident programs.

TCO   The Total Cost of Ownership is a measure of the cost to a company for the lifetime of implementing and managing a system.

Thread   A part of a process that can be executed atomically.

Tree   Any hierarchically linked domain with contiguous namespace.

Trust   A mechanism between two domains in which one domain has the ability to authenticate users from another domain.

Tunnel   An established communications pipe used in virtual private networking.

Unicode   Unicode is a standard that codifies the characters of the world's common languages.

Universal Group   A group used to assign privileges and resources, but can be viewed in the forest.

Upgrade Install   With an upgrade installation, Setup will attempt to preserve as many of your system's settings as possible. Upgrades of Windows NT 3.51, NT 4.0, and NT 4.0 Terminal Server are possible; upgrades of Windows NT Server 4.0 Enterprise Edition can be done only to Windows 2000 Advanced Server.

B

Virtual Memory   The system by which instructions are swapped out from RAM to disk and back again. Virtual memory extends the amount of a program that can be readily accessed for processing.

Virtual Memory   Hard drive space used when available RAM is used up.

Virtual Private Network (VPN)   A form of DUN using secure encrypted communications between two computers.

Volume   An area of a disk that is a logical drive, and one that can be extended, mirrored, striped, and spanned.

WAN   Wide Area Network.

Window Manager   The Window Manager is the kernel mode module responsible for managing the display of windows on your monitor.

Windows Executive   The Windows Executive is a service layer that allows the user mode and kernel mode to communicate with one another.

Windows Terminal Services   A Windows 2000 Server service that runs applications and processes on the server that a client computer can control and view onscreen.

Windows-Based Terminal   A WBT is monitor with a basic processor, network connection, and, often, a hard drive for local caching. Many WBTs run the Windows CE operating system.

WINNT32.EXE   The executable file or program that controls the graphical portion of Setup's installation routine. For Windows 3.1 or an MS-DOS system, you would use the WINNT.EXE program for this purpose.

WINS (Windows Internet Name Service)   Protocol that resolves NetBIOS names to IP addresses.

WINS Replication Partner   Another WINS server that shares registration data for fault-tolerant purposes.

Wire Protocol   The protocol by which a terminal connects to a Windows Terminal Service server.

Wizard   Software that guides the user through a setup one step at a time.

WMI   Windows Management Instrumentation. A hardware interface that provides information and control to the operating system.

WSH   The Windows Scripting Host is a part of the operating system that lets scripts execute in different programming languages.

World Wide Web Consortium (W3C)   A standards organization hosted by the Massachusetts Institute of Technology Laboratory for Computer Science (MIT/LCS) in North America, the Institute National de Recherche en Informatique et en Automatique (INRIA) in Europe, and by the Keio University Shonan Fujisawa Campus in Asia.

Zero Administration for Windows (ZAW)   An initiative by Microsoft to lower administration costs and Total Cost of Ownership. IntelliMirror, RIS, and other technologies are part of ZAW.

INDEX

M

X-Z

Other Related Titles

Sams Teach Yourself Microsoft Windows 2000 Server in 21 Days
Peter Davis & Barry Lewis
Sams
ISBN: 0-672-31703-6
$29.99

Microsoft Windows 2000 Server Unleashed
Rob Scrimger & Chris Miller
Sams
ISBN 0-672-31739-7
$49.99

Sams Teach Yourself Windows Networking in 24 Hours
Peter Kuo
Sams
ISBN 0-672-31475-4
$19.99

Programming Microsoft Windows 2000 Unleashed
Mickey Williams
Sams
ISBN 0-672-31486-X
$49.99

Sams Teach Yourself TCP/IP in 24 Hours
Joe Casad & Bob Willsey
Sams
ISBN 0-672-31248-4
$19.99

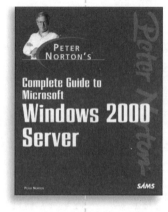

Peter Norton's Complete Guide to Microsoft Windows 2000 Server
Peter Norton & John Mueller
Sams
ISBN: 0-672-31777-X
$29.99

Microsoft Windows 2000 Professional Unleashed
Paul Cassel
Sams
ISBN: 0-672-31742-7
$49.99

SAMS
www.samspublishing.com

All prices are subject to change.